If anyone asked me which season I liked best, I'd tell them I like the time between the seasons. And if I wasn't allergic to pollen, I think I'd like it at least three times more.

–Tite Kubo

BLEACH is author Tite Kubo's second title. Kubo made his debut with *ZOMBIEPOWDER.*, a four-volume series for *WEEKLY SHONEN JUMP*. To date, *BLEACH* has been translated into numerous languages and has also inspired an animated TV series that began airing in the U.S. in 2006. Beginning its serialization in 2001, *BLEACH* is still a mainstay in the pages of *WEEKLY SHONEN JUMP*. In 2005, *BLEACH* was awarded the prestigious Shogakukan Manga Award in the *shonen* (boys) category.

BLEACH
Vol. 22: Conquistadores
The SHONEN JUMP Manga Edition

This volume contains material that was originally published in SHONEN JUMP
#60-62. Artwork in the magazine may have been altered slightly from what is
presented in this volume.

STORY AND ART BY
TITE KUBO

English Adaptation/Lance Caselman
Translation/Joe Yamazaki
Touch-Up Art & Lettering/Mark McMurray
Design/Sean Lee
Editor/Pancha Diaz

Editor in Chief, Books/Alvin Lu
Editor in Chief, Magazines/Marc Weidenbaum
VP, Publishing Licensing/Rika Inouye
VP, Sales & Product Marketing/Gonzalo Ferreyra
VP, Creative/Linda Espinosa
Publisher/Hyoe Narita

Printed in the U.S.A.

Published by VIZ Media, LLC
P.O. Box 77010
San Francisco, CA 94107

SHONEN JUMP Manga Edition
10 9 8 7 6 5 4
First printing, March 2008
Fourth printing, December 2008

PARENTAL ADVISORY
BLEACH is rated T for Teen and is recommended
for ages 13 and up. This volume contains
fantasy violence.
ratings.viz.com

www.viz.com

www.shonenjump.com

There is no meaning to our world.
There is no meaning to those of us living there.
We meaningless beings ponder the world,
Though the realization of meaninglessness
itself means nothing.

BLEACH22 CONQUISTADORES

STARS AND

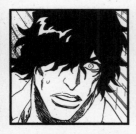

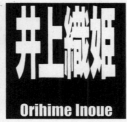

井上織姫

Orihime Inoue

Ichigo Kurosaki

黒崎一護

Chad Yasutora

茶渡泰虎

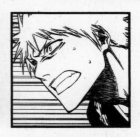

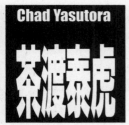

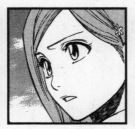

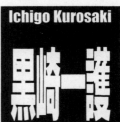

plot

After a fateful encounter with Soul Reaper Rukia Kuchiki, Ichigo becomes a Soul Reaper himself. So, when Rukia is arrested and sentenced to death, Ichigo travels to the Soul Society to rescue her, and in the process uncovers a fiendish plot. But the conspirators escape and Ichigo returns to the world of the living. Now a Deputy Soul Reaper, Ichigo spends his days fighting Hollows. But his life soon gets even more bizarre with the appearance of a new menace, the Arrancar, and the discovery that his own father is a Soul Reaper! And still more disturbing, Ichigo is confronted with the possibility that his own inner demon may be far more terrible than he ever imagined.

BLEACH ALL

ウルキオラ
Ulquiorra

平子真子
Shinji Hirako

Yammy

ヤミー

STORIES

BLEACH22

CONQUISTADORES

Contents

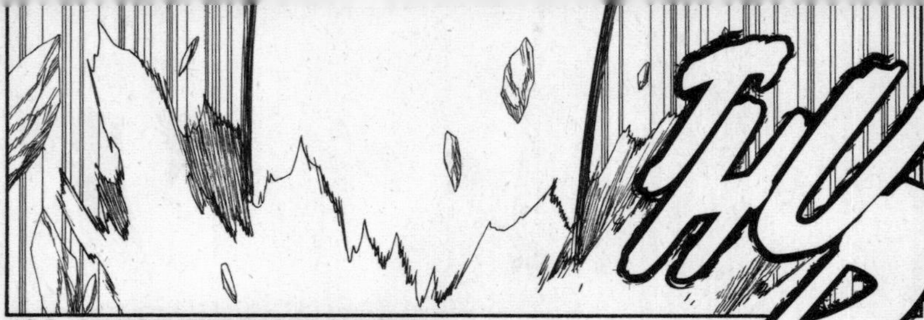
THUD

188. CRUSH THE WORLD DOWN

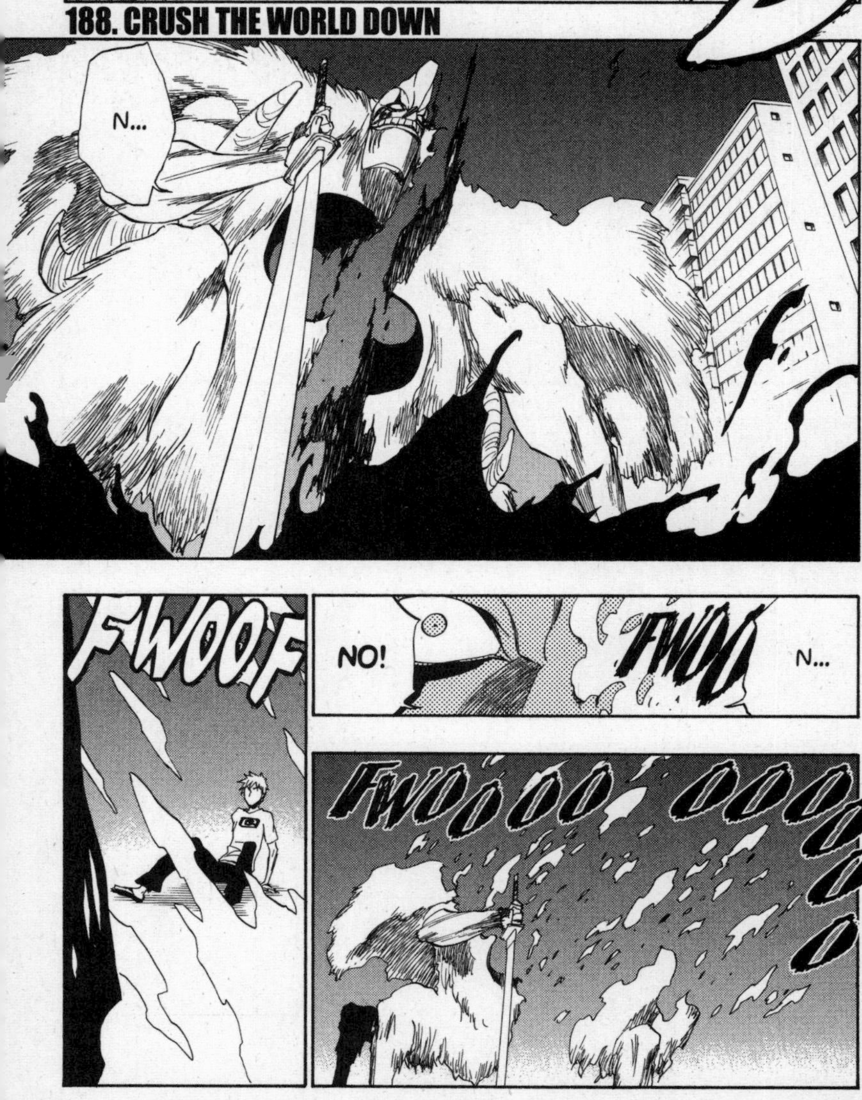
N...
N...
FWOO
NO!
FWOOOOOOOOOOOOO
FWOOF

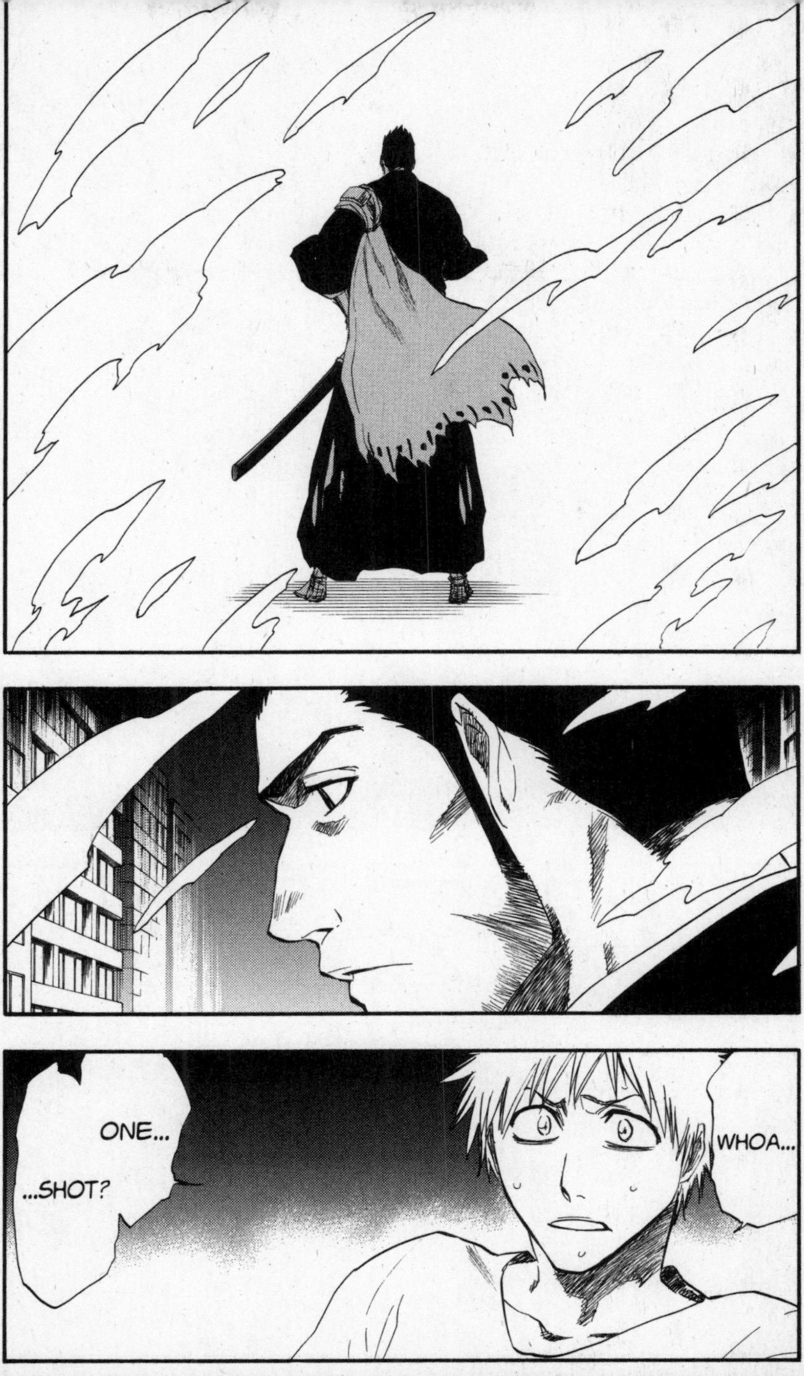
WHOA...
ONE... ...SHOT?

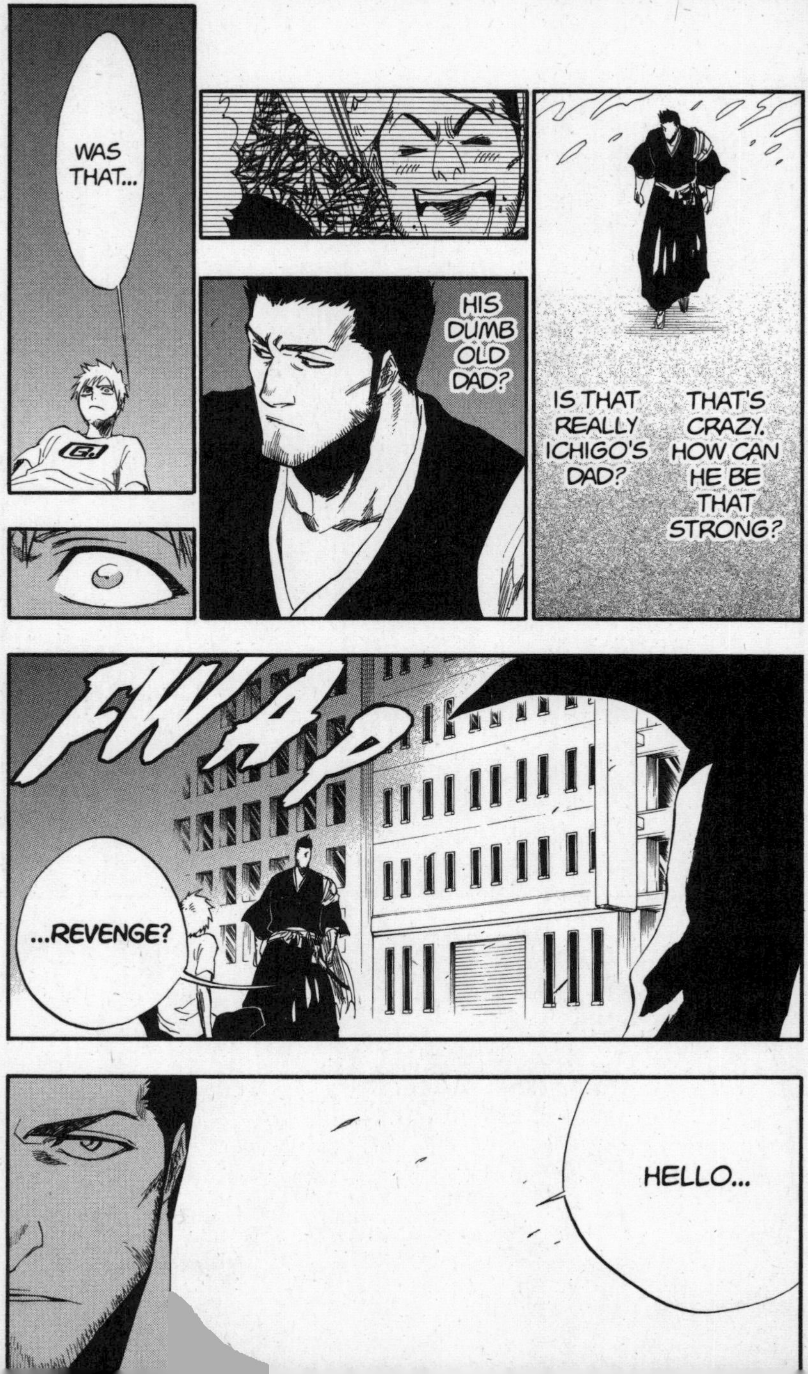
THAT'S CRAZY. HOW CAN HE BE THAT STRONG?
IS THAT REALLY ICHIGO'S DAD?
HIS DUMB OLD DAD?
WAS THAT...
FWAP
...REVENGE?
HELLO...

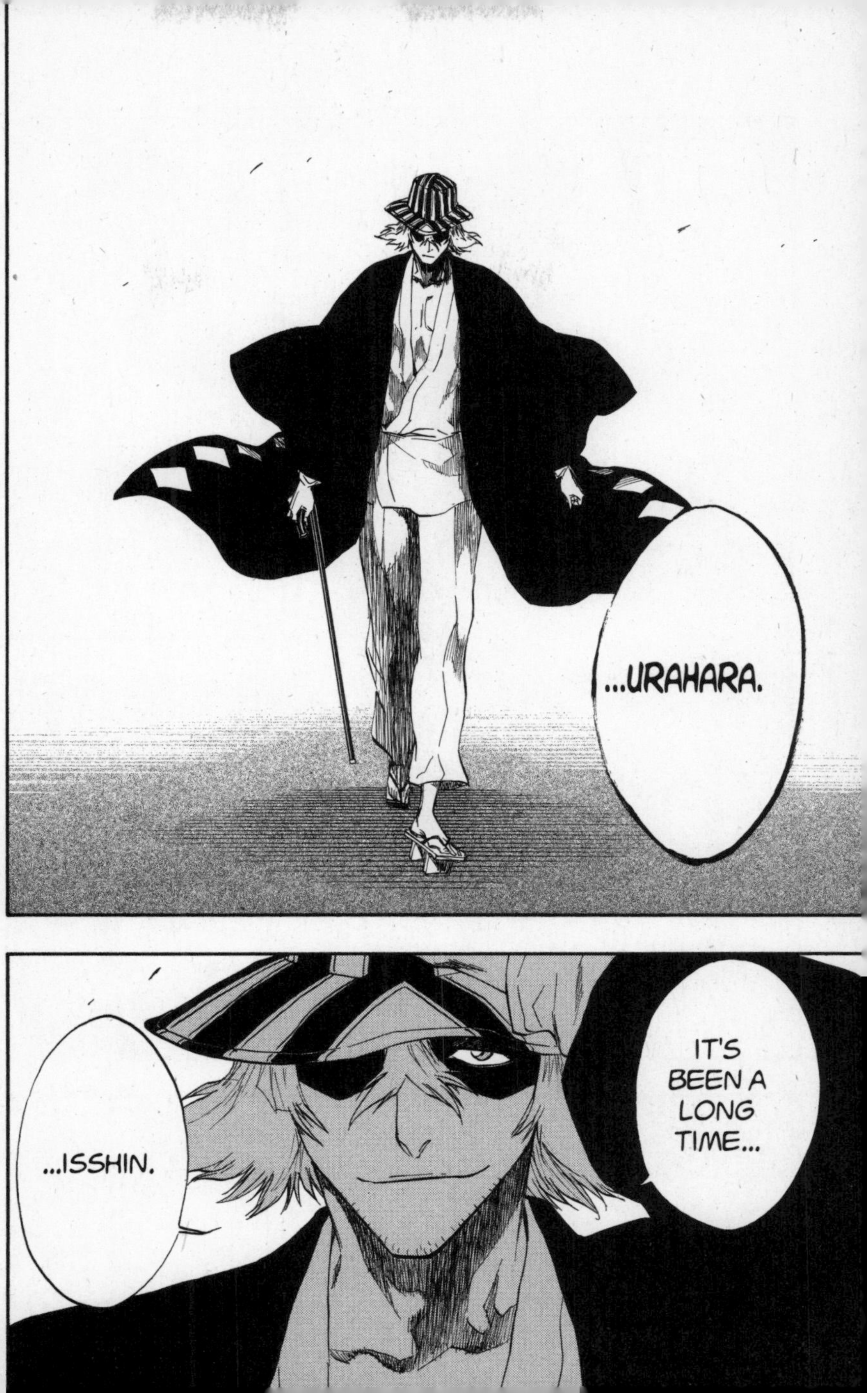
...URAHARA.
IT'S BEEN A LONG TIME...
...ISSHIN.

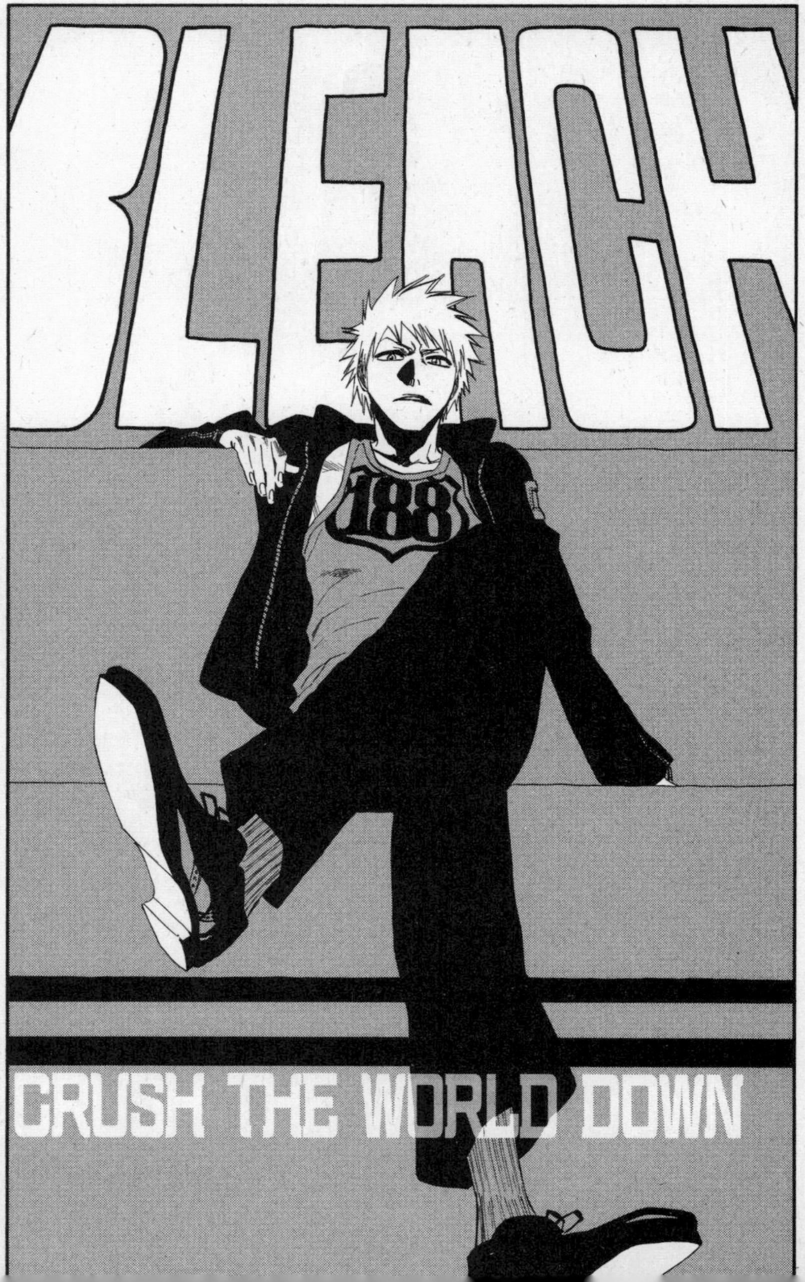
BLEACH
188
CRUSH THE WORLD DOWN

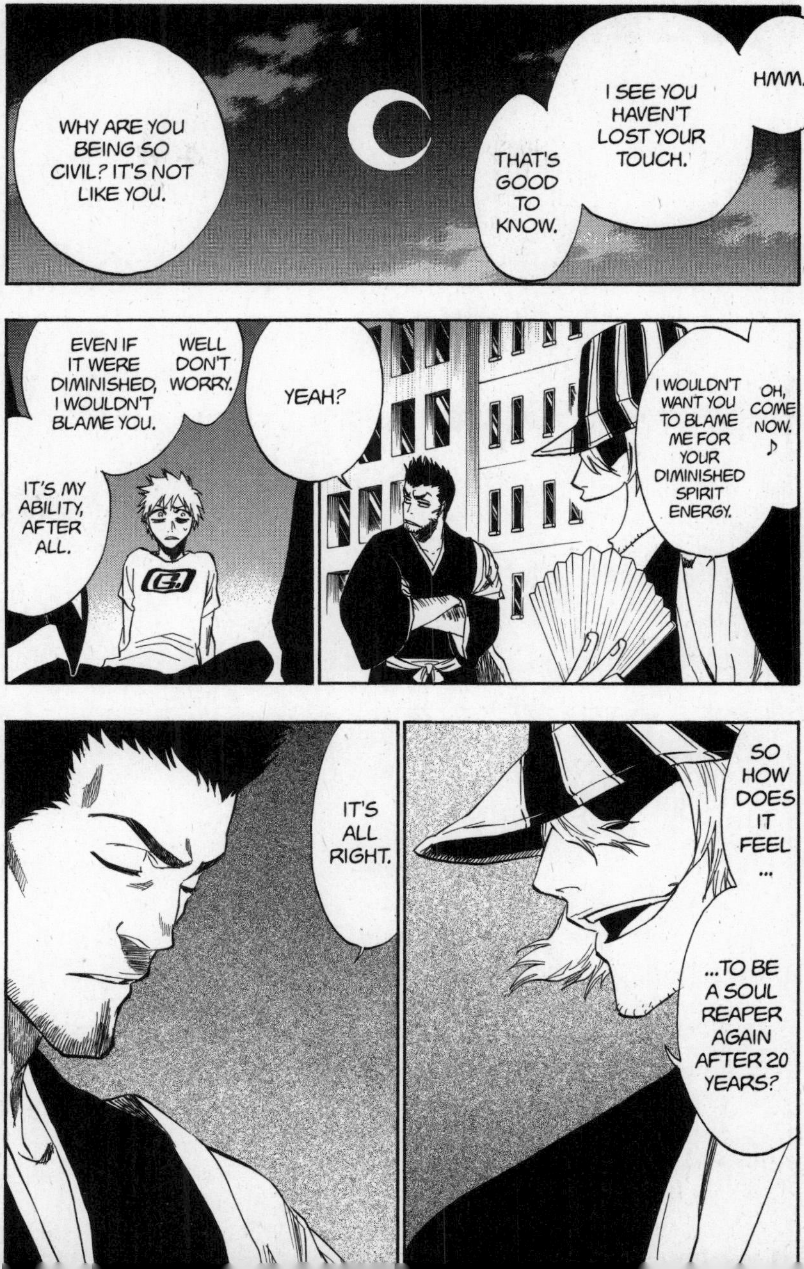
HMM...
I SEE YOU HAVEN'T LOST YOUR TOUCH.
THAT'S GOOD TO KNOW.
WHY ARE YOU BEING SO CIVIL? IT'S NOT LIKE YOU.
OH, COME NOW. ♪
I WOULDN'T WANT YOU TO BLAME ME FOR YOUR DIMINISHED SPIRIT ENERGY.
YEAH?
WELL DON'T WORRY.
EVEN IF IT WERE DIMINISHED, I WOULDN'T BLAME YOU.
IT'S MY ABILITY, AFTER ALL.
SO HOW DOES IT FEEL ...
...TO BE A SOUL REAPER AGAIN AFTER 20 YEARS?
IT'S ALL RIGHT.

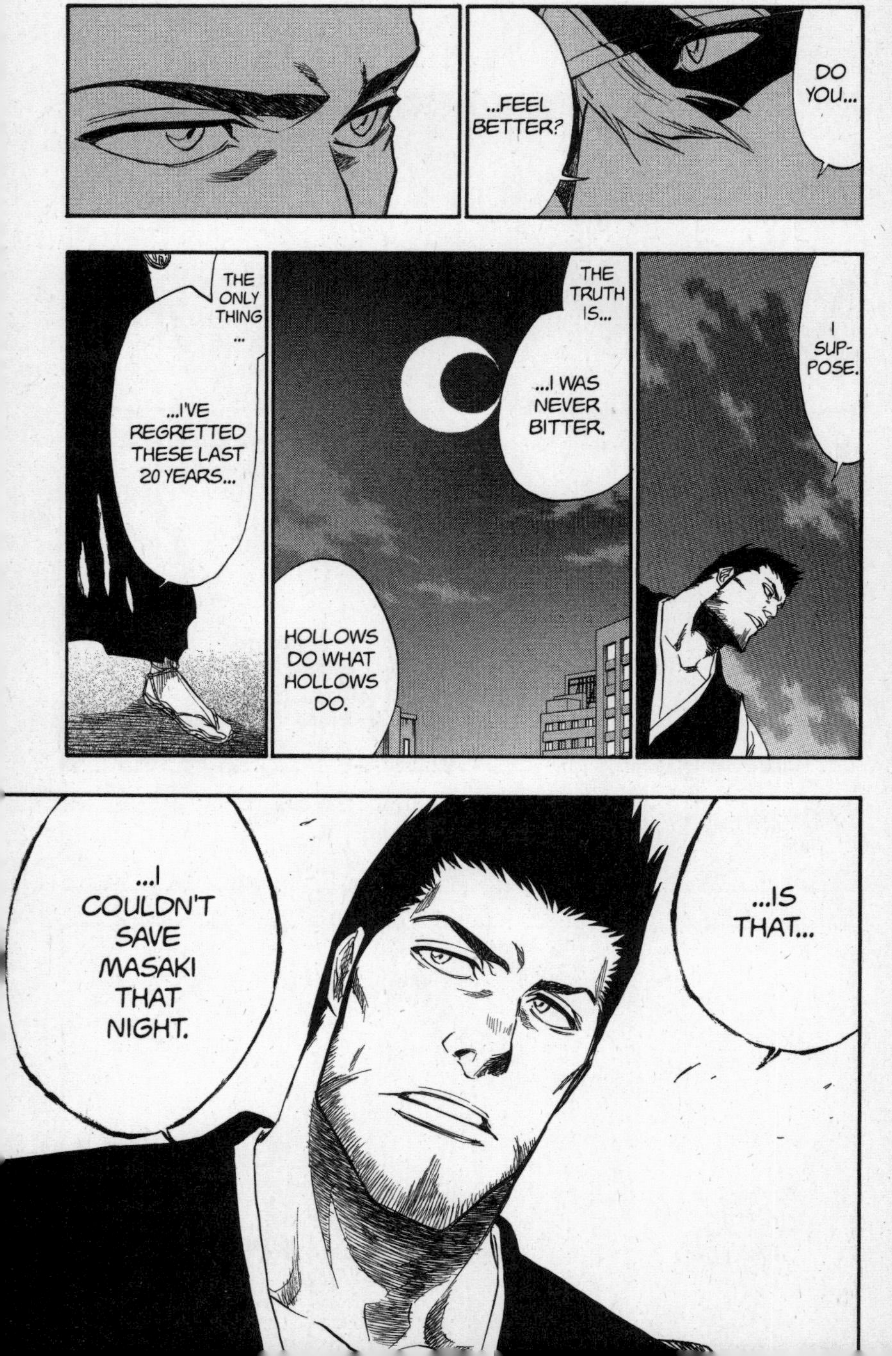
DO YOU...
...FEEL BETTER?
I SUP-POSE.
THE TRUTH IS...
...I WAS NEVER BITTER.
HOLLOWS DO WHAT HOLLOWS DO.
THE ONLY THING...
...I'VE REGRETTED THESE LAST 20 YEARS...
...IS THAT...
...I COULDN'T SAVE MASAKI THAT NIGHT.

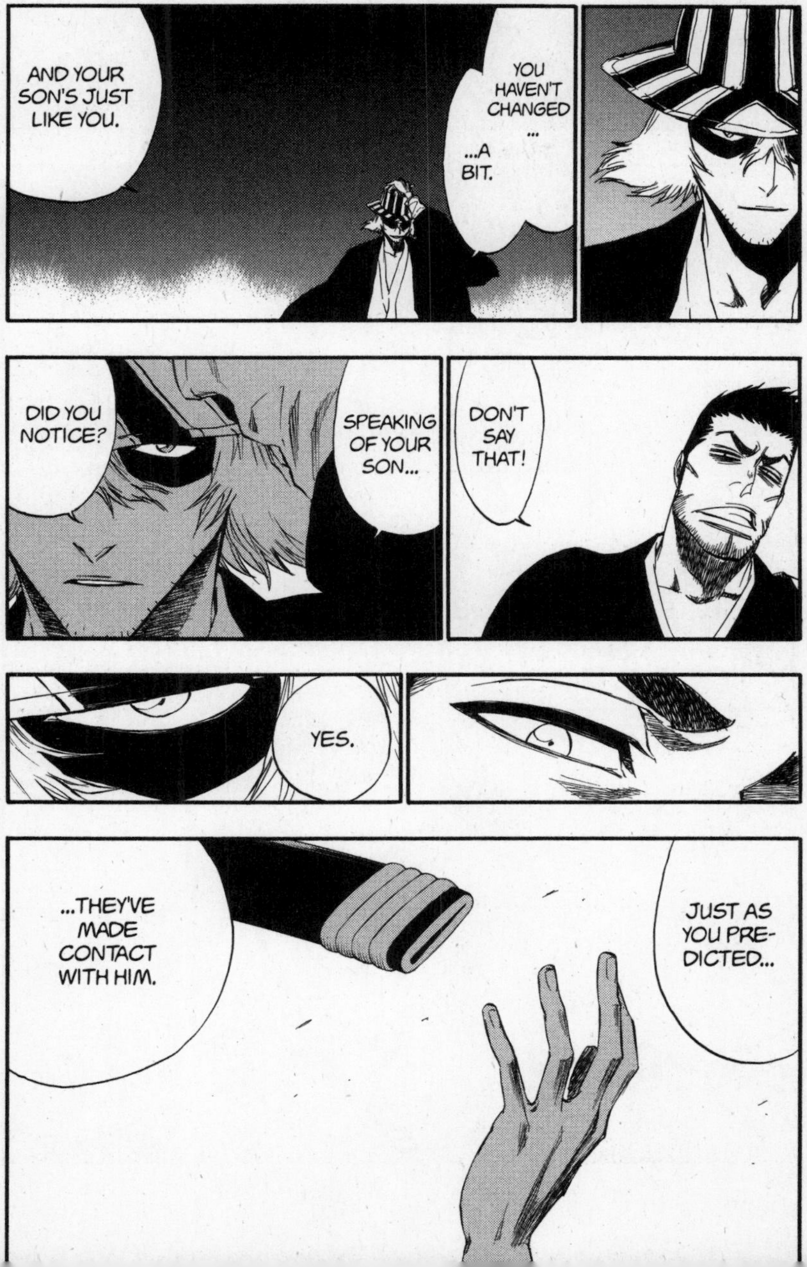
YOU HAVEN'T CHANGED ... ...A BIT.
AND YOUR SON'S JUST LIKE YOU.
DON'T SAY THAT!
SPEAKING OF YOUR SON...
DID YOU NOTICE?
YES.
JUST AS YOU PRE-DICTED...
...THEY'VE MADE CONTACT WITH HIM.

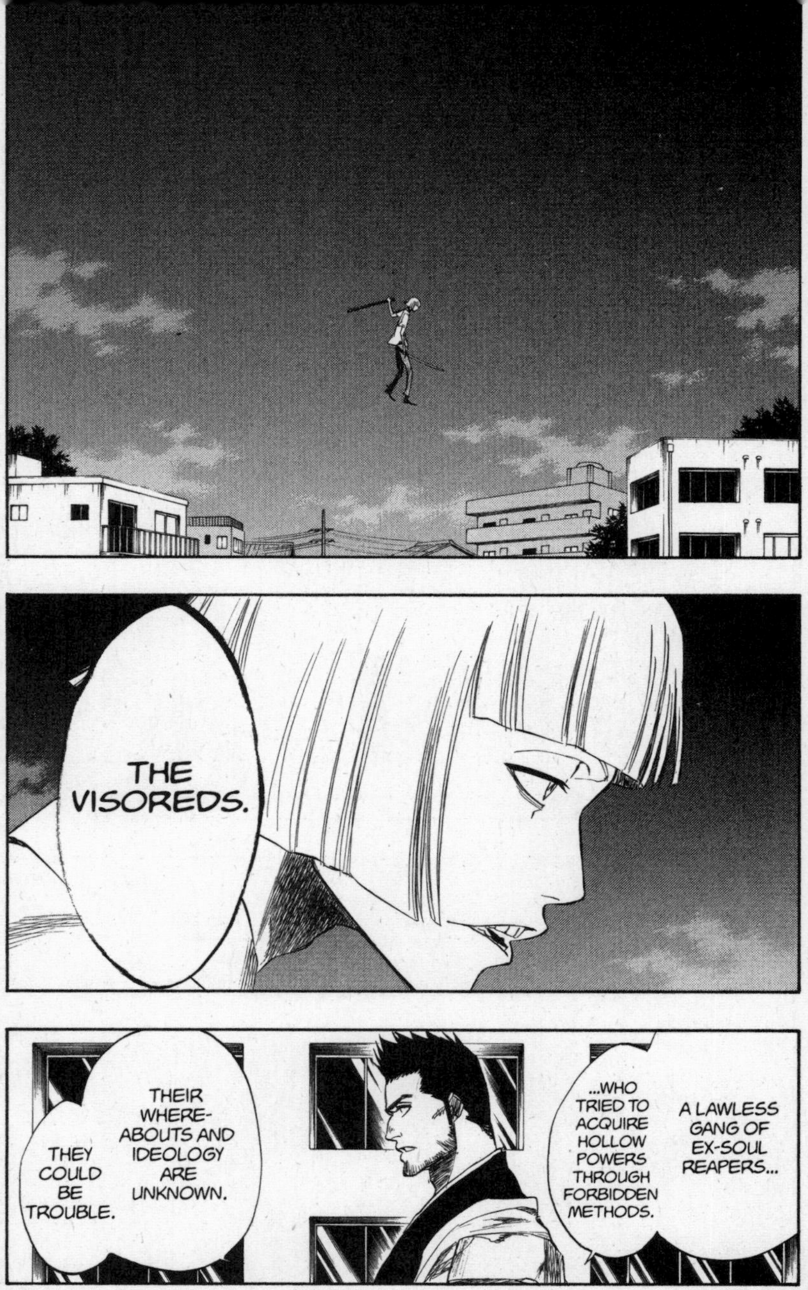
THE VISOREDS.
A LAWLESS GANG OF EX-SOUL REAPERS...
...WHO TRIED TO ACQUIRE HOLLOW POWERS THROUGH FORBIDDEN METHODS.
THEIR WHERE-ABOUTS AND IDEOLOGY ARE UNKNOWN.
THEY COULD BE TROUBLE.

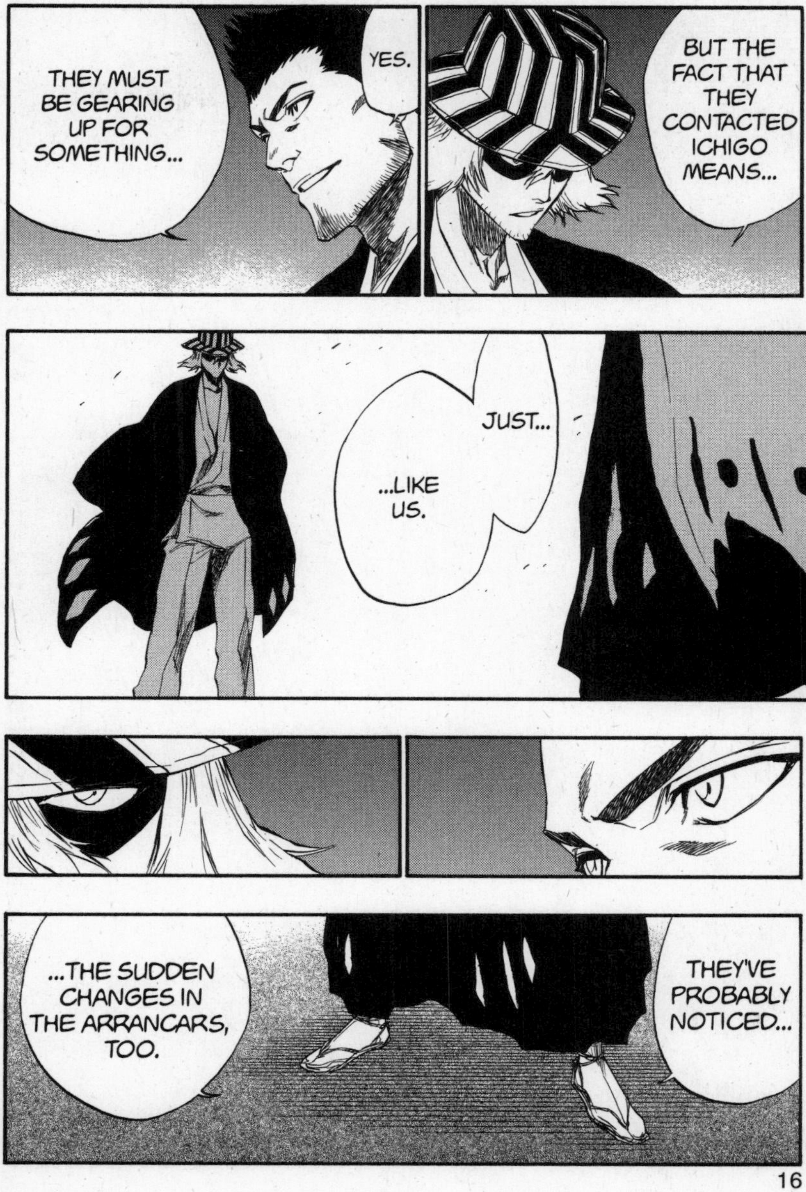
BUT THE FACT THAT THEY CONTACTED ICHIGO MEANS...
YES.
THEY MUST BE GEARING UP FOR SOMETHING...
JUST...
...LIKE US.
THEY'VE PROBABLY NOTICED...
...THE SUDDEN CHANGES IN THE ARRANCARS, TOO.

READ THIS WAY

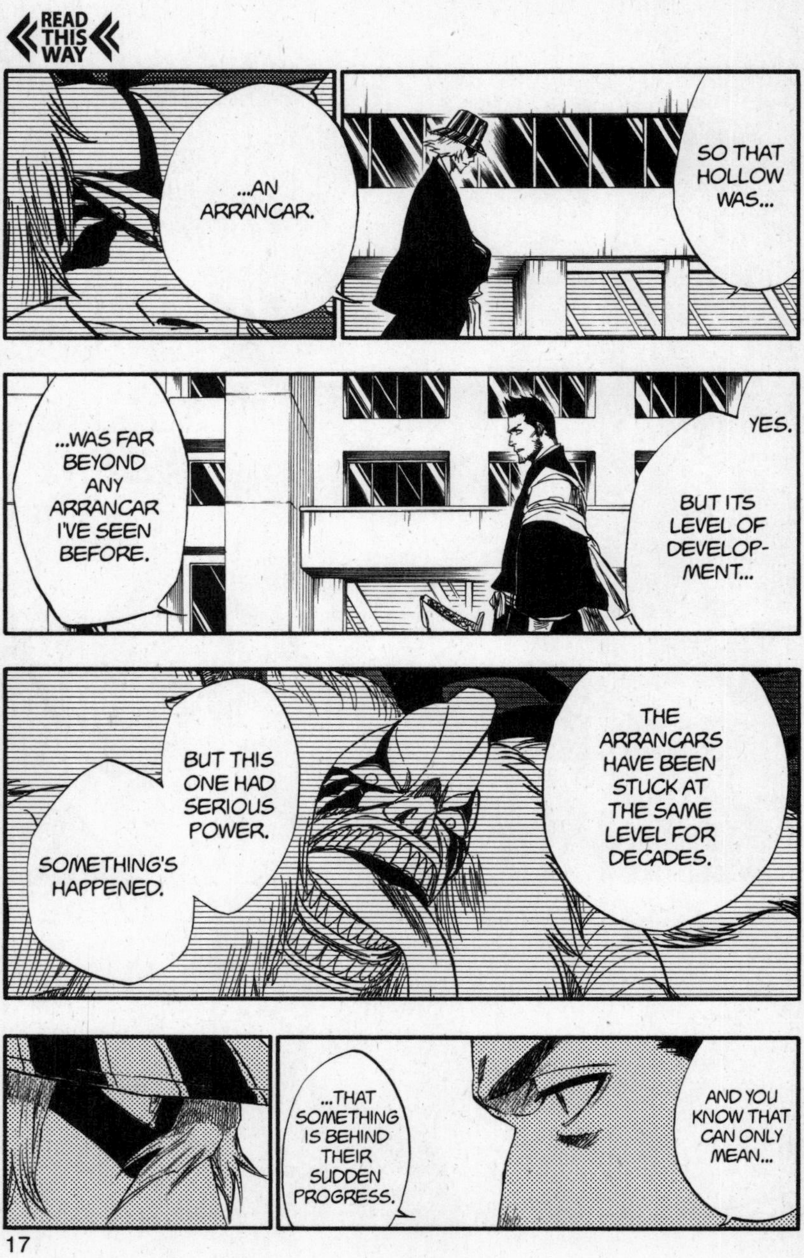
SO THAT HOLLOW WAS...
...AN ARRANCAR.
YES.
BUT ITS LEVEL OF DEVELOP-MENT...
...WAS FAR BEYOND ANY ARRANCAR I'VE SEEN BEFORE.
THE ARRANCARS HAVE BEEN STUCK AT THE SAME LEVEL FOR DECADES.
BUT THIS ONE HAD SERIOUS POWER.
SOMETHING'S HAPPENED.
AND YOU KNOW THAT CAN ONLY MEAN...
...THAT SOMETHING IS BEHIND THEIR SUDDEN PROGRESS.

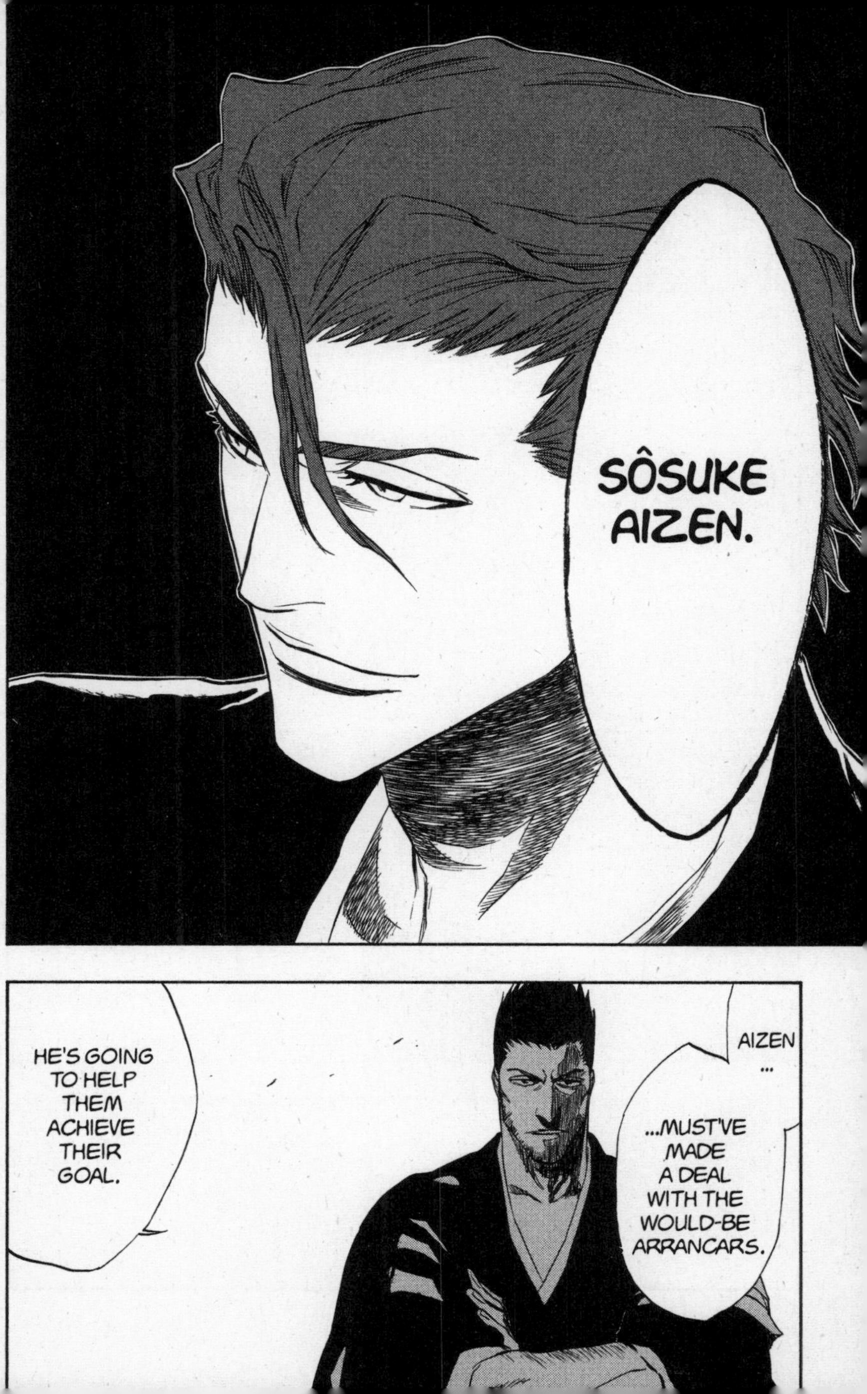
SÔSUKE AIZEN.
AIZEN ...
...MUST'VE MADE A DEAL WITH THE WOULD-BE ARRANCARS.
HE'S GOING TO HELP THEM ACHIEVE THEIR GOAL.

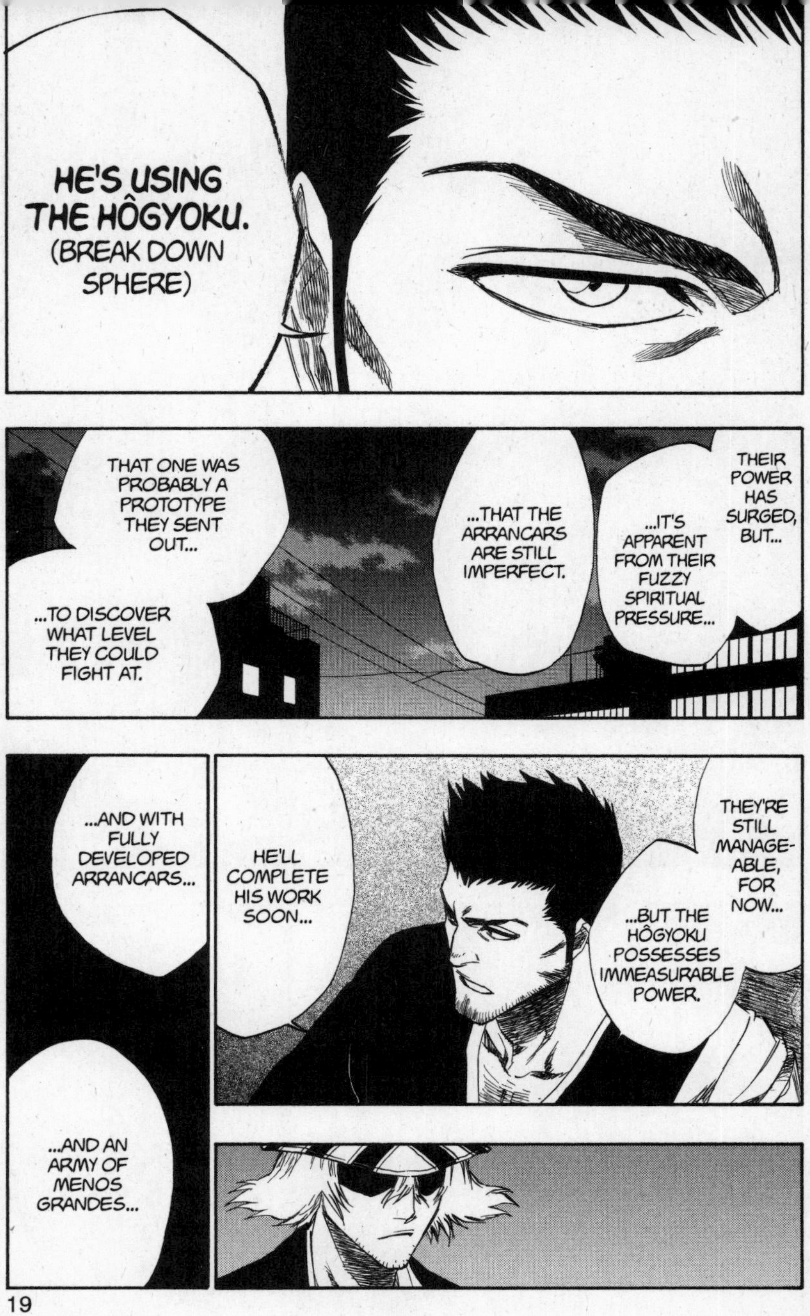
HE'S USING THE HÔGYOKU. (BREAK DOWN SPHERE)
THEIR POWER HAS SURGED, BUT...
...IT'S APPARENT FROM THEIR FUZZY SPIRITUAL PRESSURE...
...THAT THE ARRANCARS ARE STILL IMPERFECT.
THAT ONE WAS PROBABLY A PROTOTYPE THEY SENT OUT...
...TO DISCOVER WHAT LEVEL THEY COULD FIGHT AT.
THEY'RE STILL MANAGE-ABLE, FOR NOW...
...BUT THE HÔGYOKU POSSESSES IMMEASURABLE POWER.
HE'LL COMPLETE HIS WORK SOON...
...AND WITH FULLY DEVELOPED ARRANCARS...
...AND AN ARMY OF MENOS GRANDES...

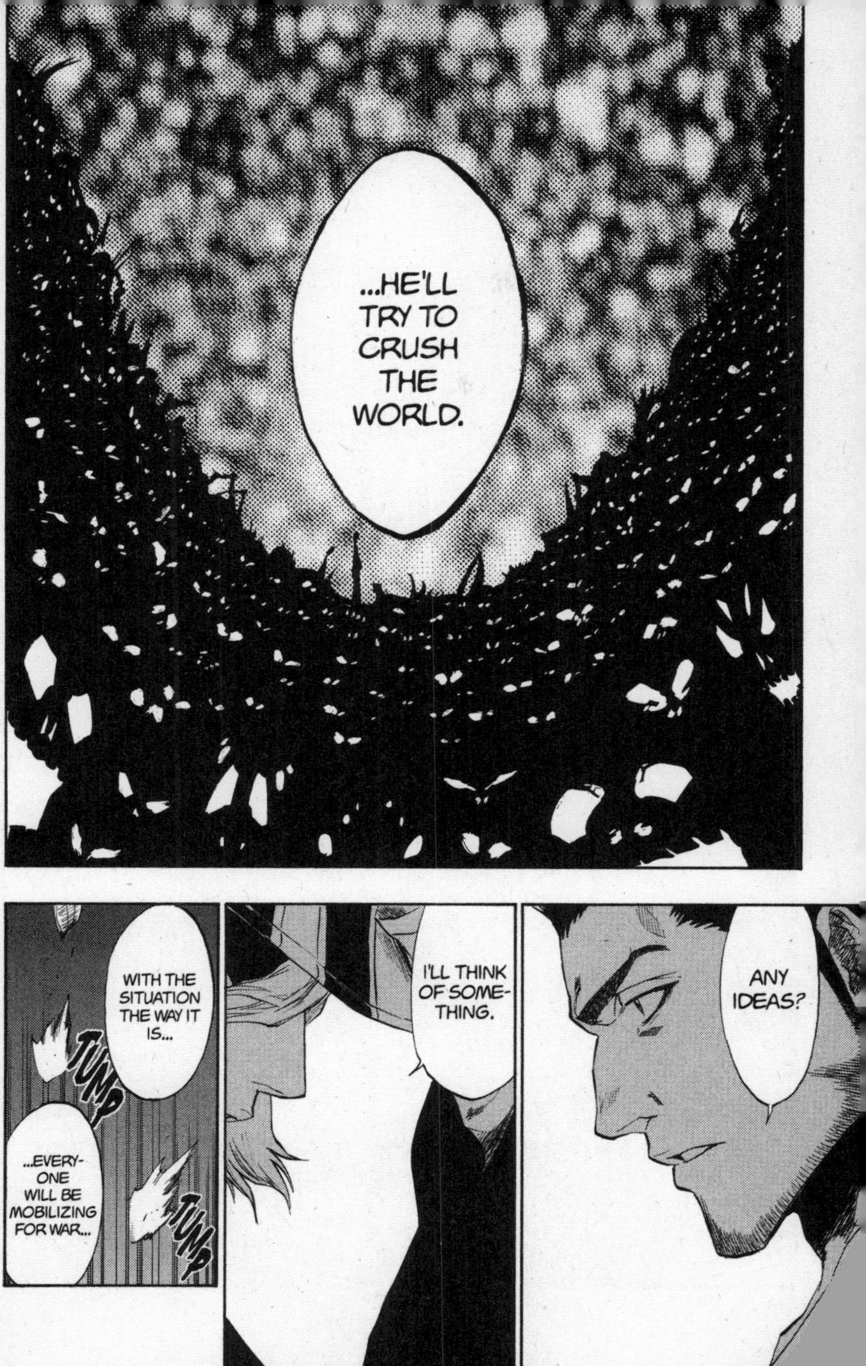
...HE'LL TRY TO CRUSH THE WORLD.
ANY IDEAS?
I'LL THINK OF SOME-THING.
WITH THE SITUATION THE WAY IT IS...
TUMP
...EVERY-ONE WILL BE MOBILIZING FOR WAR...
TUMP

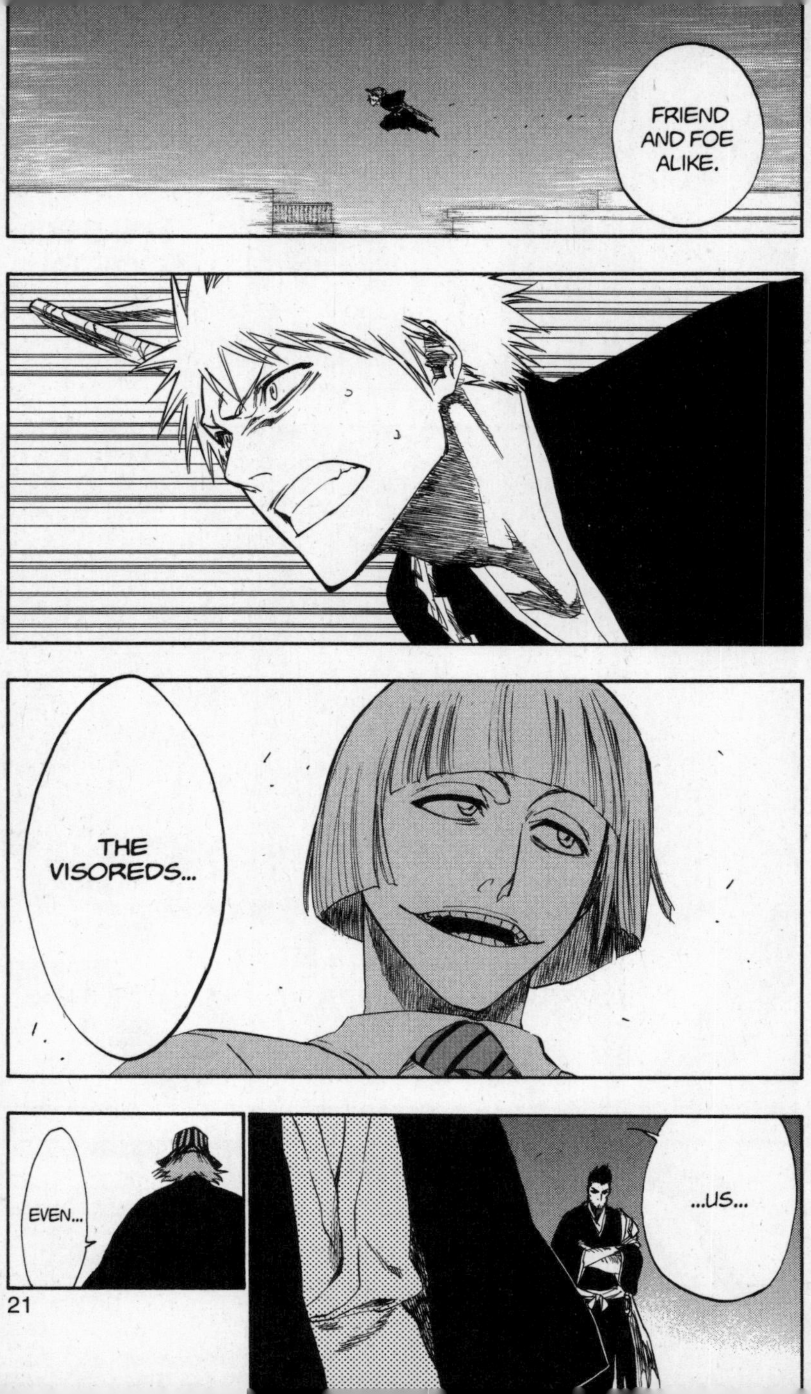
FRIEND AND FOE ALIKE.
THE VISOREDS...
...US...
EVEN...

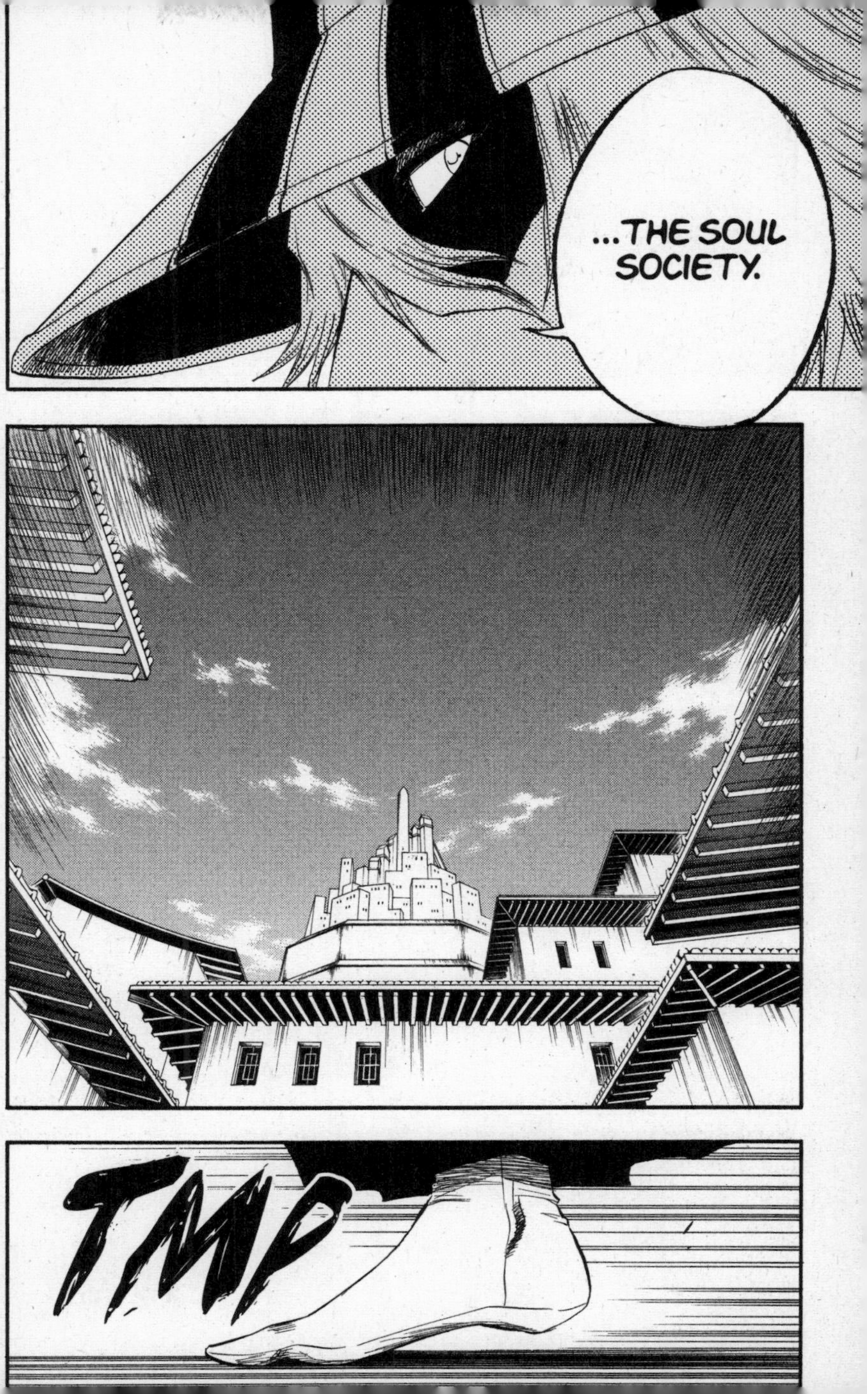
...THE SOUL SOCIETY.
TMP

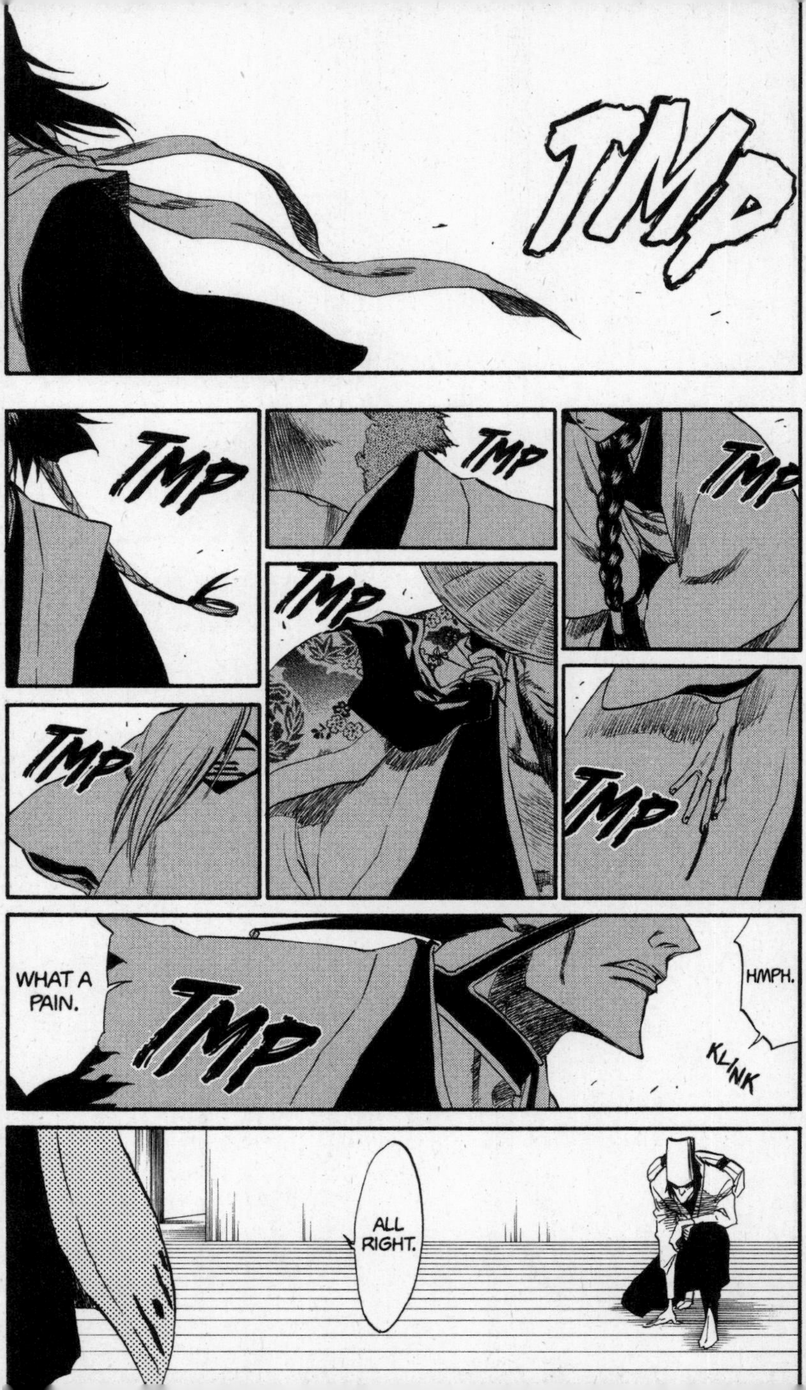
TMP
TMP
TMP
TMP
TMP
TMP
TMP
HMPH.
KLINK
TMP
WHAT A PAIN.
ALL RIGHT.

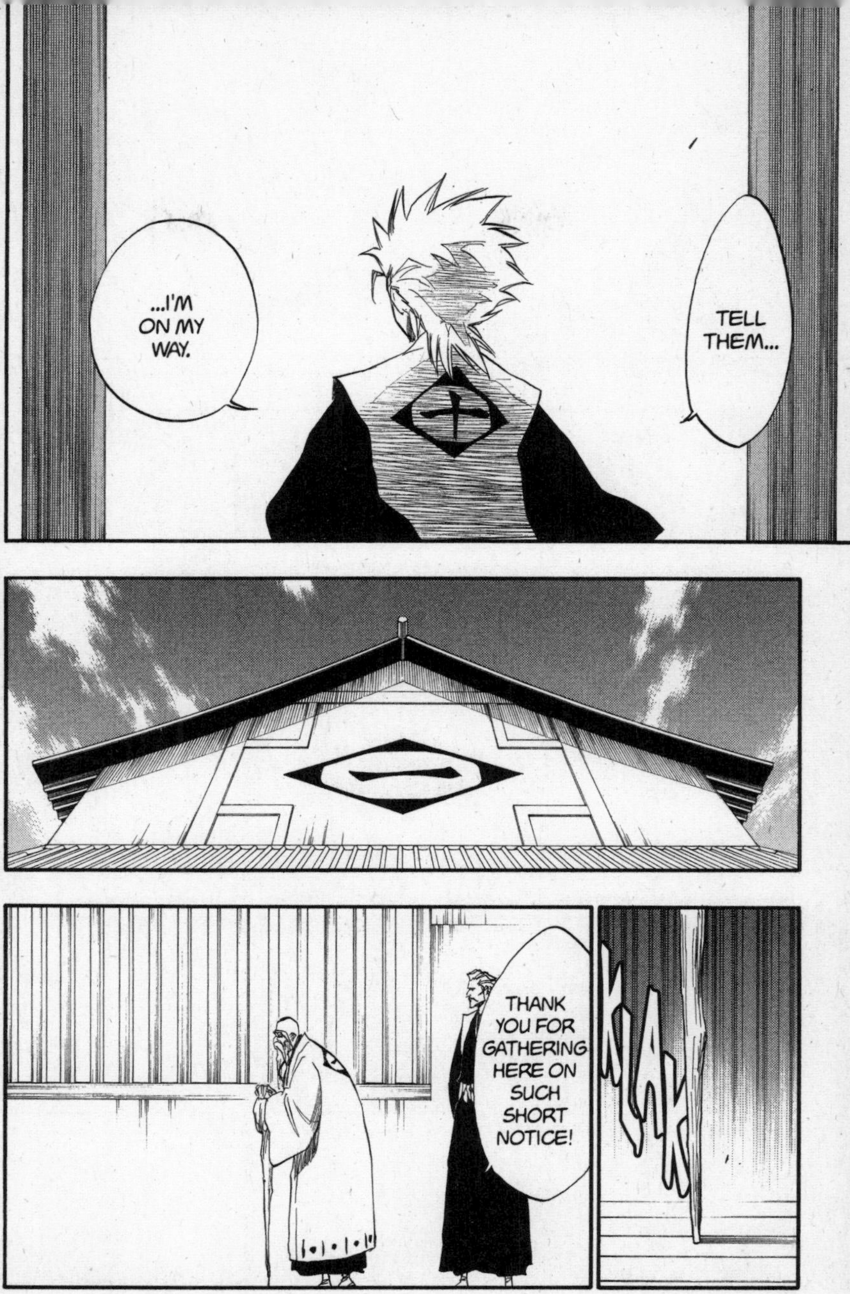
TELL THEM...
...I'M ON MY WAY.
KLAK
THANK YOU FOR GATHERING HERE ON SUCH SHORT NOTICE!

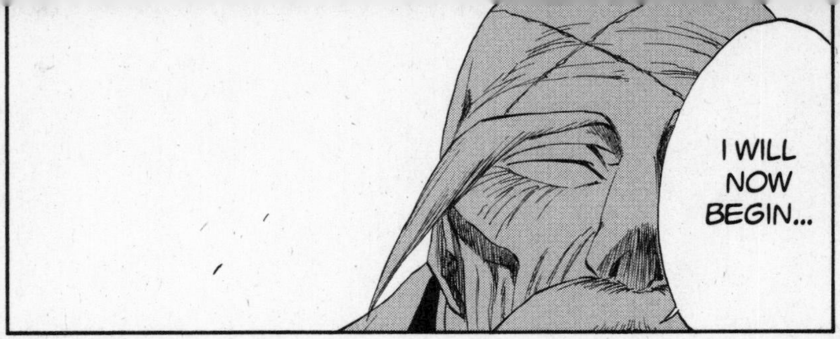
I WILL NOW BEGIN...
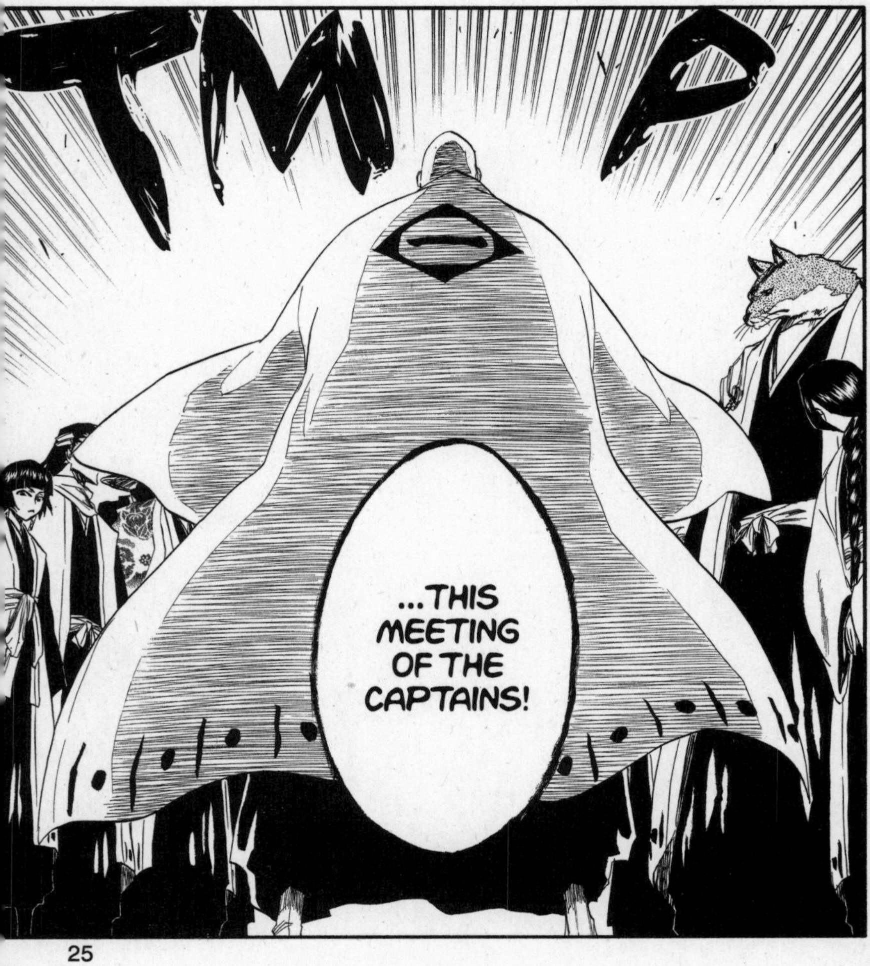
TMP
...THIS MEETING OF THE CAPTAINS!

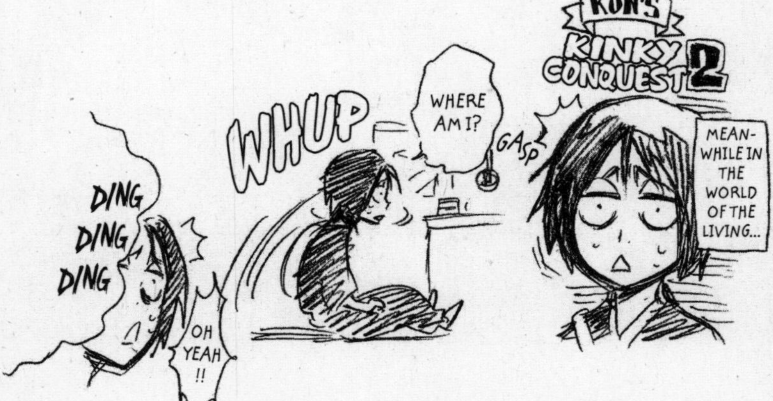
KON'S
KINKY CONQUEST 2
MEAN-WHILE IN THE WORLD OF THE LIVING...
GASP
WHERE AM I?
WHUP
DING
DING
DING
OH YEAH !!

189. RESOLVE

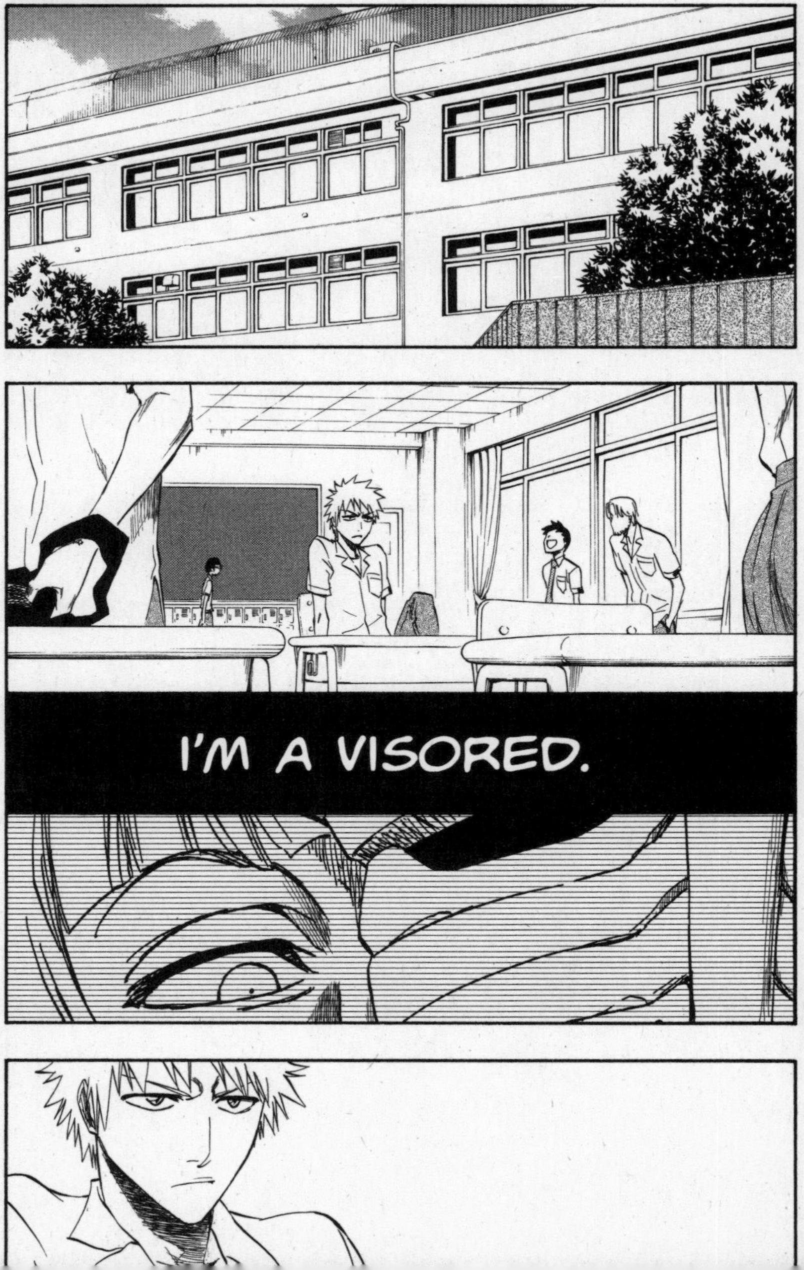
I'M A VISORED.

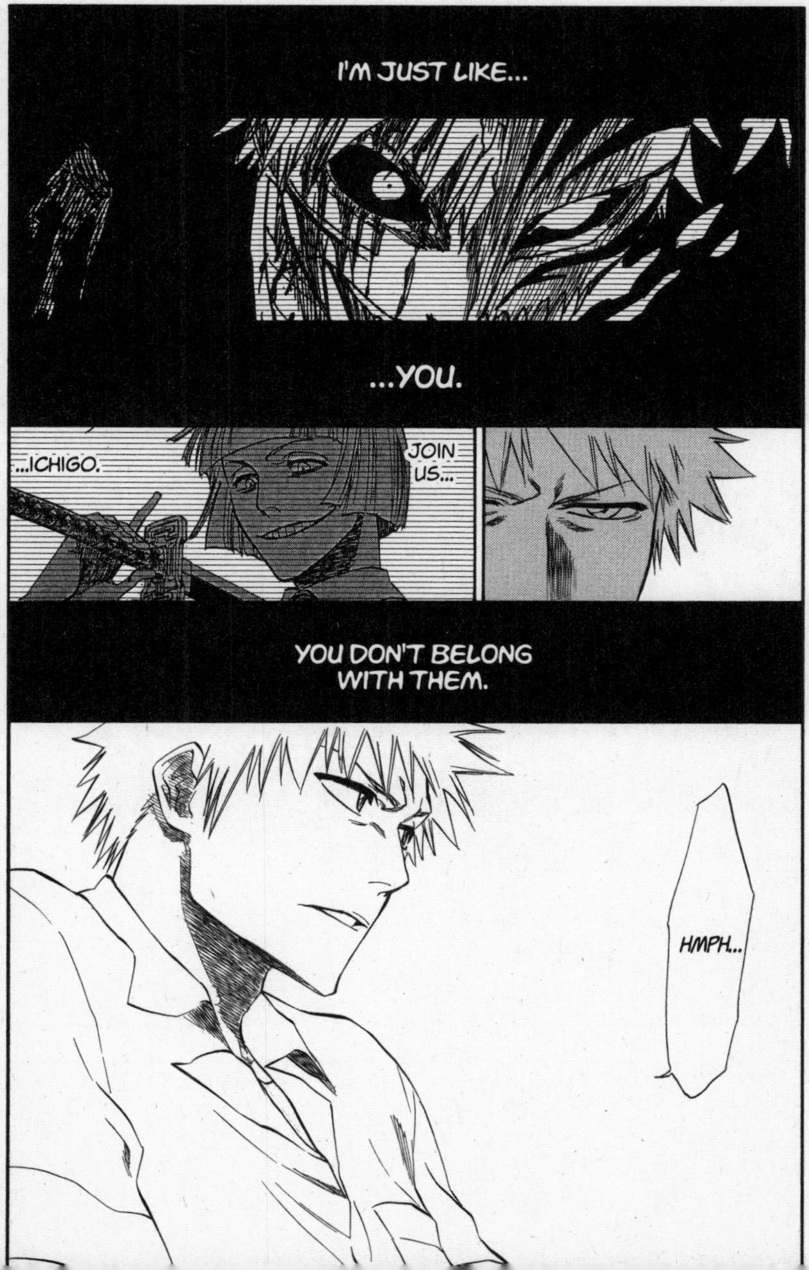
I'M JUST LIKE...
...YOU.
JOIN US...
...ICHIGO.
YOU DON'T BELONG WITH THEM.
HMPH...

READ THIS WAY

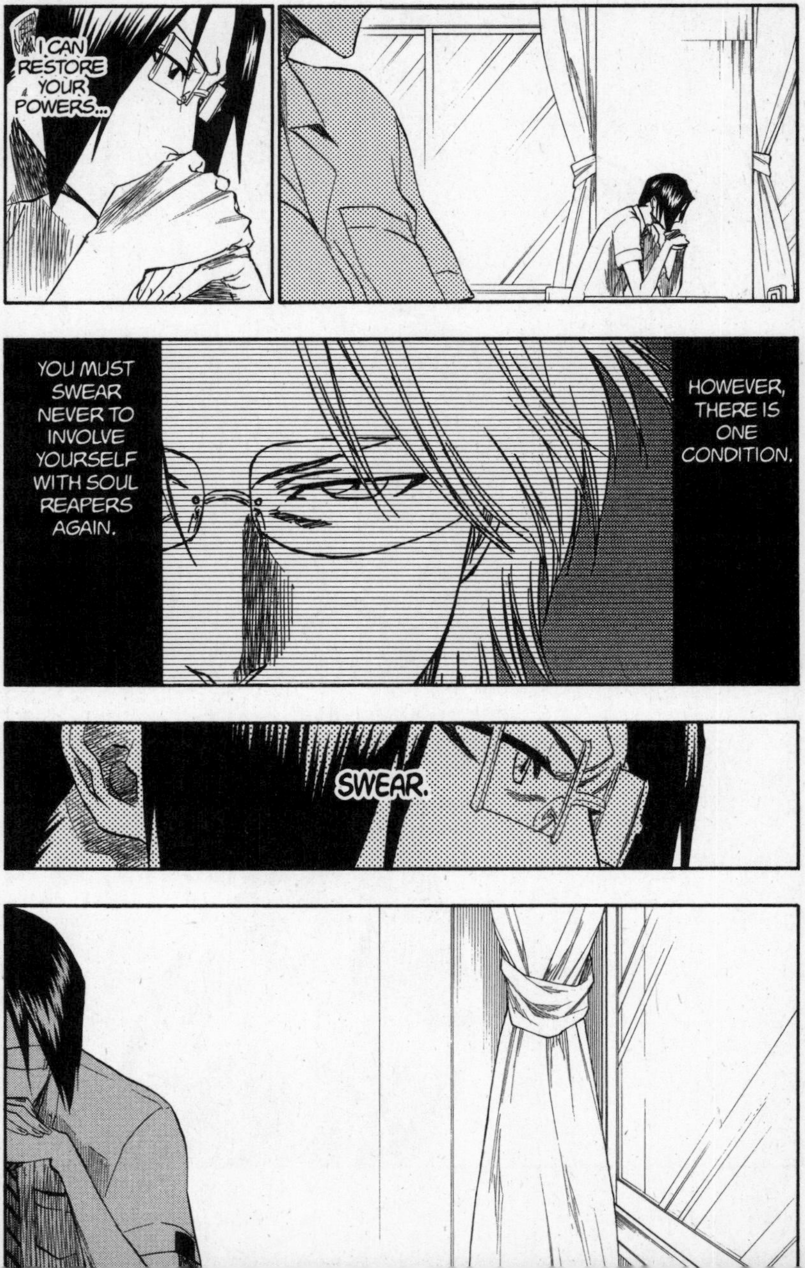
I CAN RESTORE YOUR POWERS...
HOWEVER, THERE IS ONE CONDITION.
YOU MUST SWEAR NEVER TO INVOLVE YOURSELF WITH SOUL REAPERS AGAIN.
SWEAR.

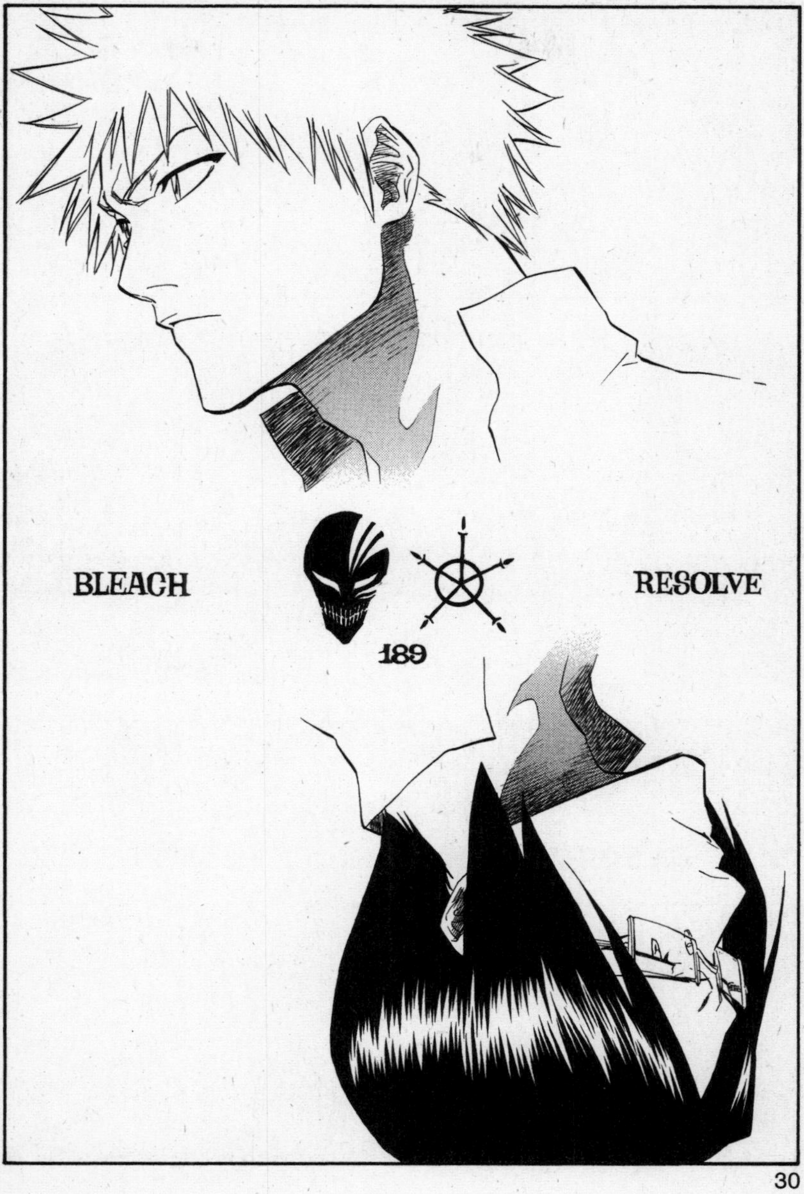
BLEACH
RESOLVE
189

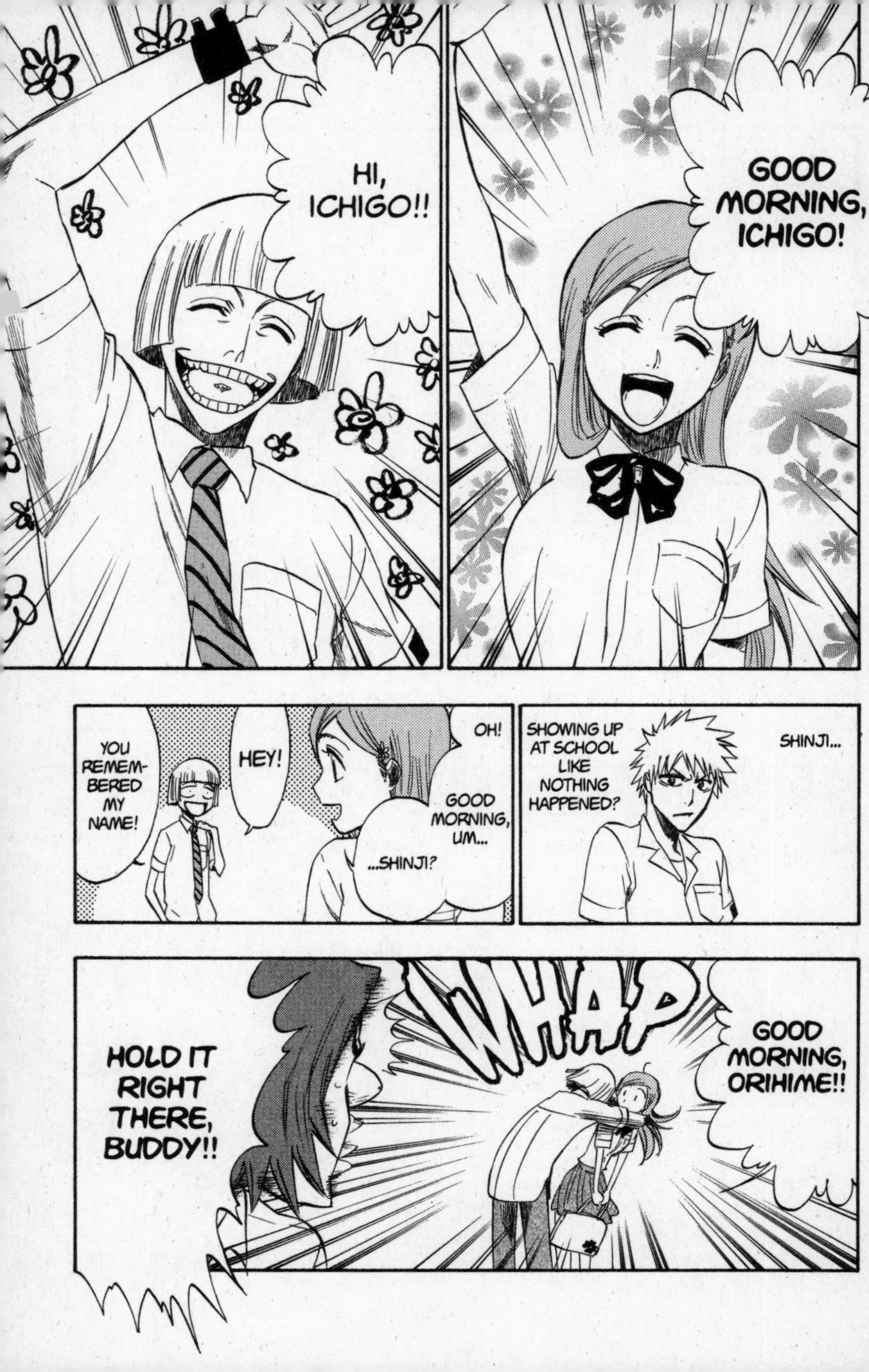
GOOD MORNING, ICHIGO!
HI, ICHIGO!!
SHINJI...
SHOWING UP AT SCHOOL LIKE NOTHING HAPPENED?
OH!
GOOD MORNING, UM...
...SHINJI?
HEY!
YOU REMEMBERED MY NAME!
GOOD MORNING, ORIHIME!!
WHAP
HOLD IT RIGHT THERE, BUDDY!!

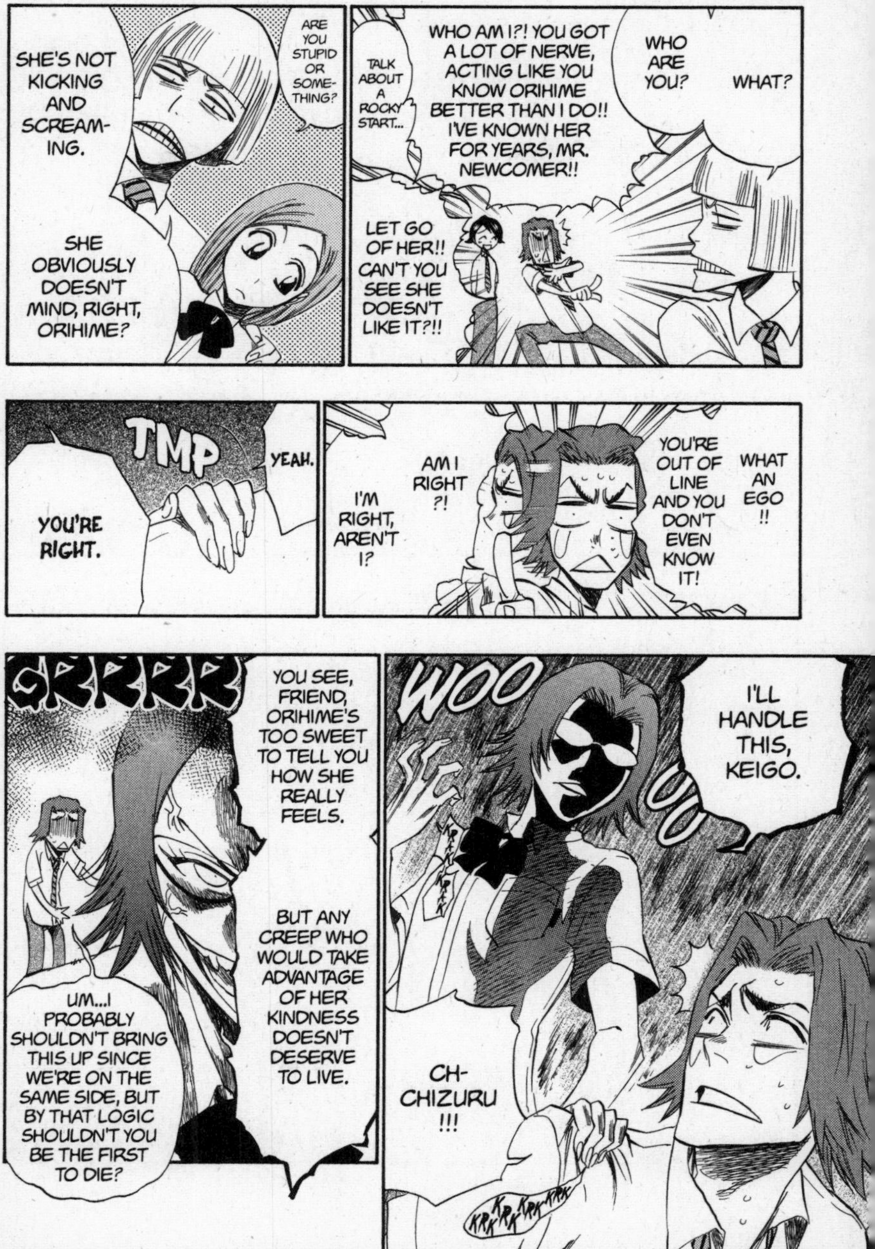
WHAT?
WHO ARE YOU?
WHO AM I?! YOU GOT A LOT OF NERVE, ACTING LIKE YOU KNOW ORIHIME BETTER THAN I DO!! I'VE KNOWN HER FOR YEARS, MR. NEWCOMER!!
TALK ABOUT A ROCKY START...
LET GO OF HER!! CAN'T YOU SEE SHE DOESN'T LIKE IT?!!
ARE YOU STUPID OR SOME-THING?
SHE'S NOT KICKING AND SCREAM-ING.
SHE OBVIOUSLY DOESN'T MIND, RIGHT, ORIHIME?
WHAT AN EGO!!
YOU'RE OUT OF LINE AND YOU DON'T EVEN KNOW IT!
AM I RIGHT?!
I'M RIGHT, AREN'T I?
YEAH.
TMP
YOU'RE RIGHT.
I'LL HANDLE THIS, KEIGO.
WOO
OO
CH-CHIZURU!!!
KRK KRK KRK KRK KRK
GRRRR
YOU SEE, FRIEND, ORIHIME'S TOO SWEET TO TELL YOU HOW SHE REALLY FEELS.
BUT ANY CREEP WHO WOULD TAKE ADVANTAGE OF HER KINDNESS DOESN'T DESERVE TO LIVE.
UM...I PROBABLY SHOULDN'T BRING THIS UP SINCE WE'RE ON THE SAME SIDE, BUT BY THAT LOGIC SHOULDN'T YOU BE THE FIRST TO DIE?

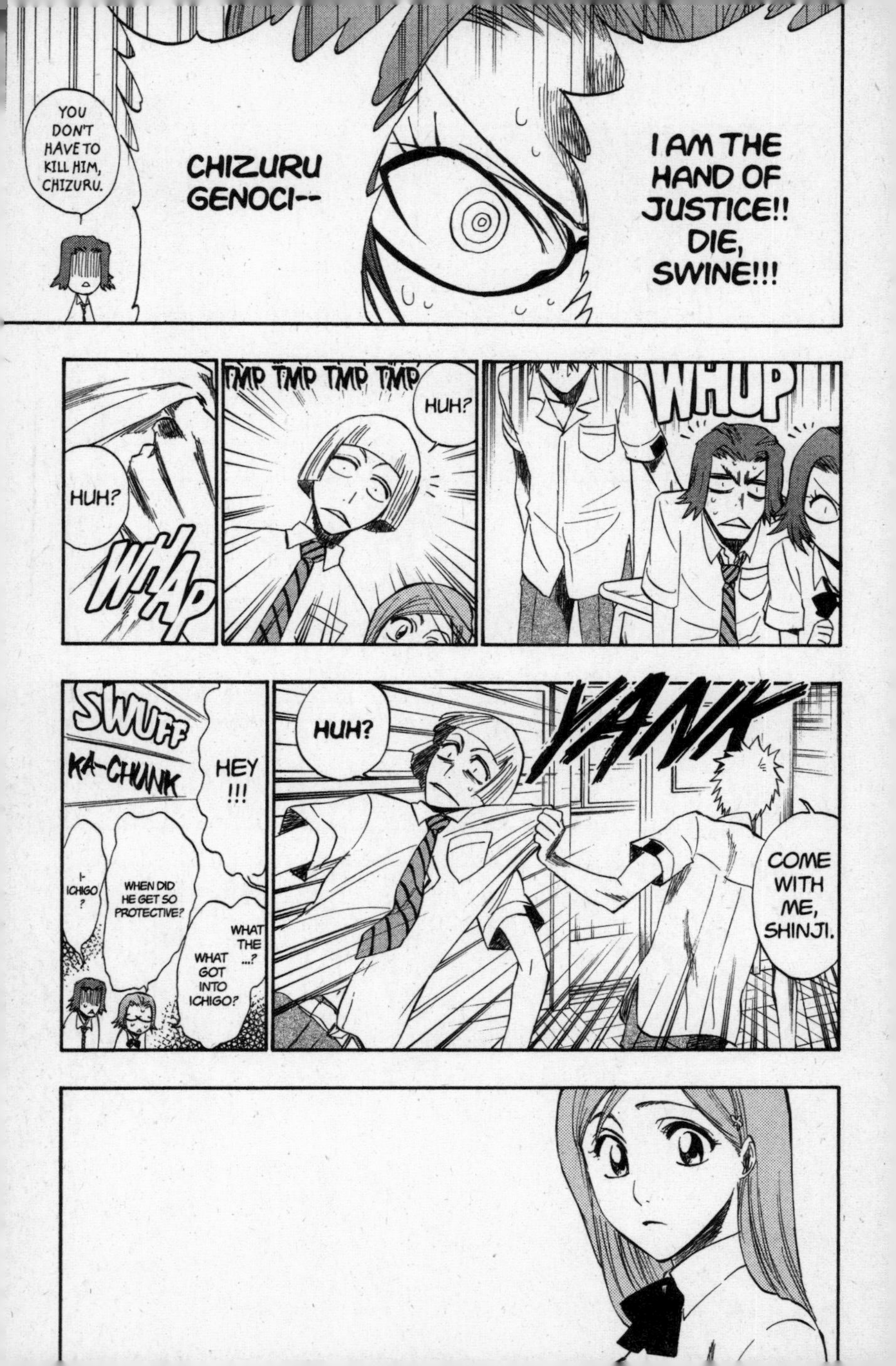
I AM THE HAND OF JUSTICE!! DIE, SWINE!!!
CHIZURU GENOCI--
YOU DON'T HAVE TO KILL HIM, CHIZURU.
WHUP
TMP TMP TMP TMP
HUH?
HUH?
WHAP
YANK
COME WITH ME, SHINJI.
HUH?
SWUFF
KA-CHUNK
HEY !!!
WHAT THE ...?
WHAT GOT INTO ICHIGO?
WHEN DID HE GET SO PROTECTIVE?
I-ICHIGO?

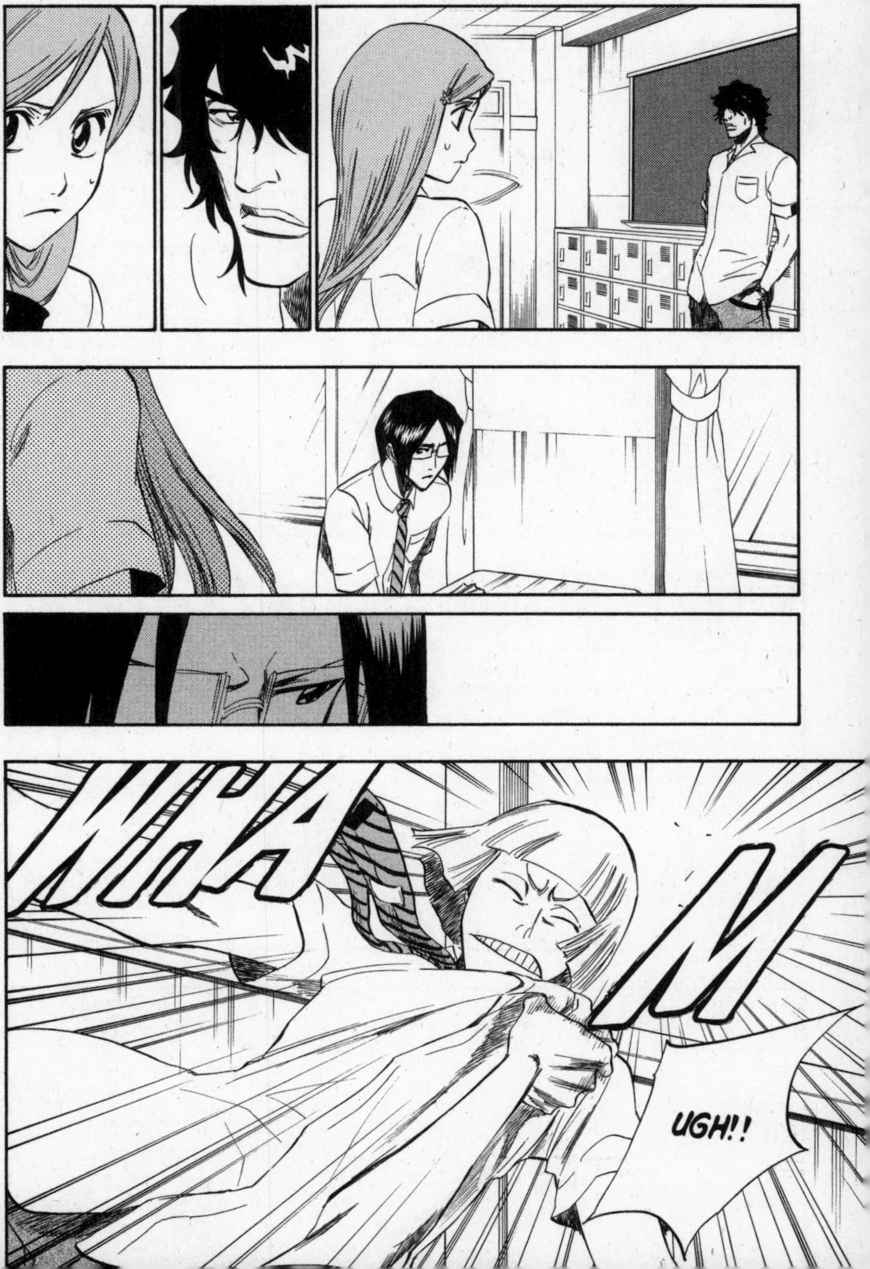
WHAM
UGH!!

READ THIS WAY

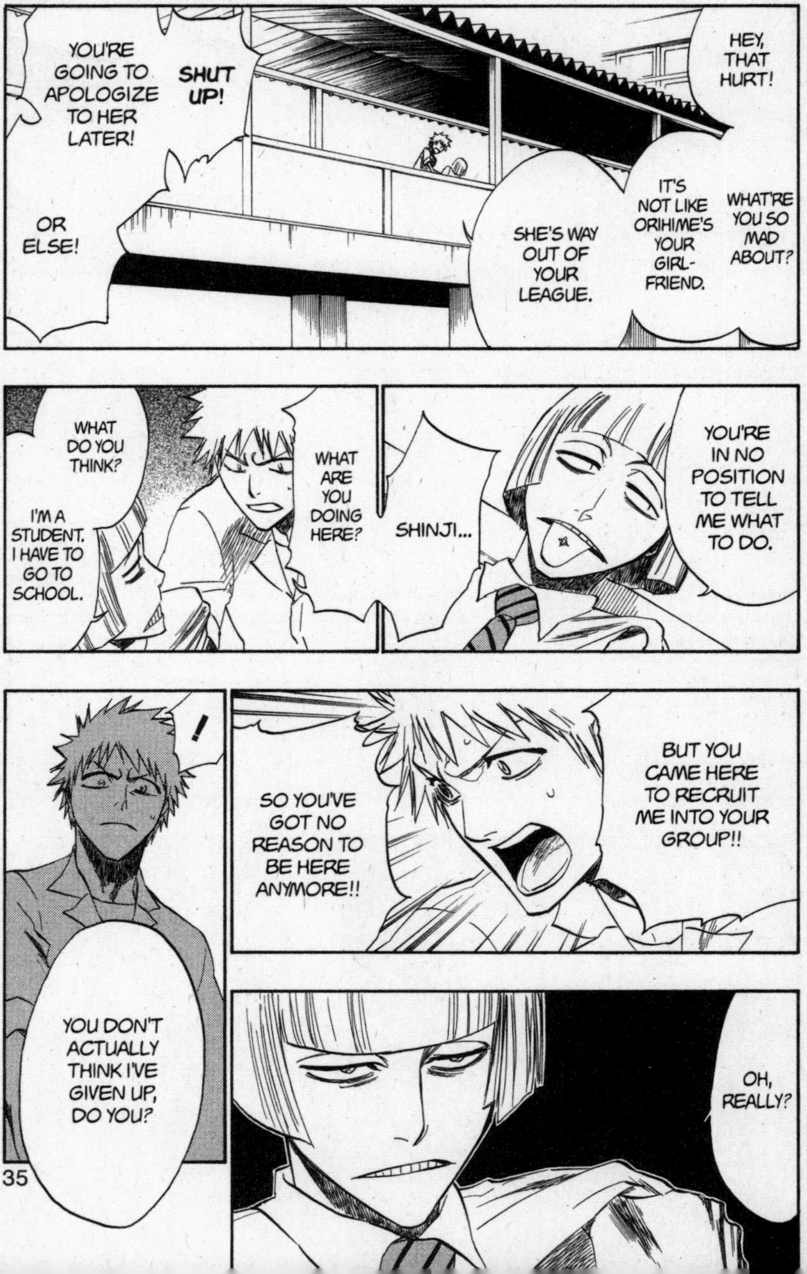
HEY, THAT HURT!
WHAT'RE YOU SO MAD ABOUT?
IT'S NOT LIKE ORIHIME'S YOUR GIRL-FRIEND.
SHE'S WAY OUT OF YOUR LEAGUE.
SHUT UP!
YOU'RE GOING TO APOLOGIZE TO HER LATER!
OR ELSE!
YOU'RE IN NO POSITION TO TELL ME WHAT TO DO.
SHINJI...
WHAT ARE YOU DOING HERE?
WHAT DO YOU THINK?
I'M A STUDENT. I HAVE TO GO TO SCHOOL.
BUT YOU CAME HERE TO RECRUIT ME INTO YOUR GROUP!!
SO YOU'VE GOT NO REASON TO BE HERE ANYMORE!!
OH, REALLY?
!
YOU DON'T ACTUALLY THINK I'VE GIVEN UP, DO YOU?

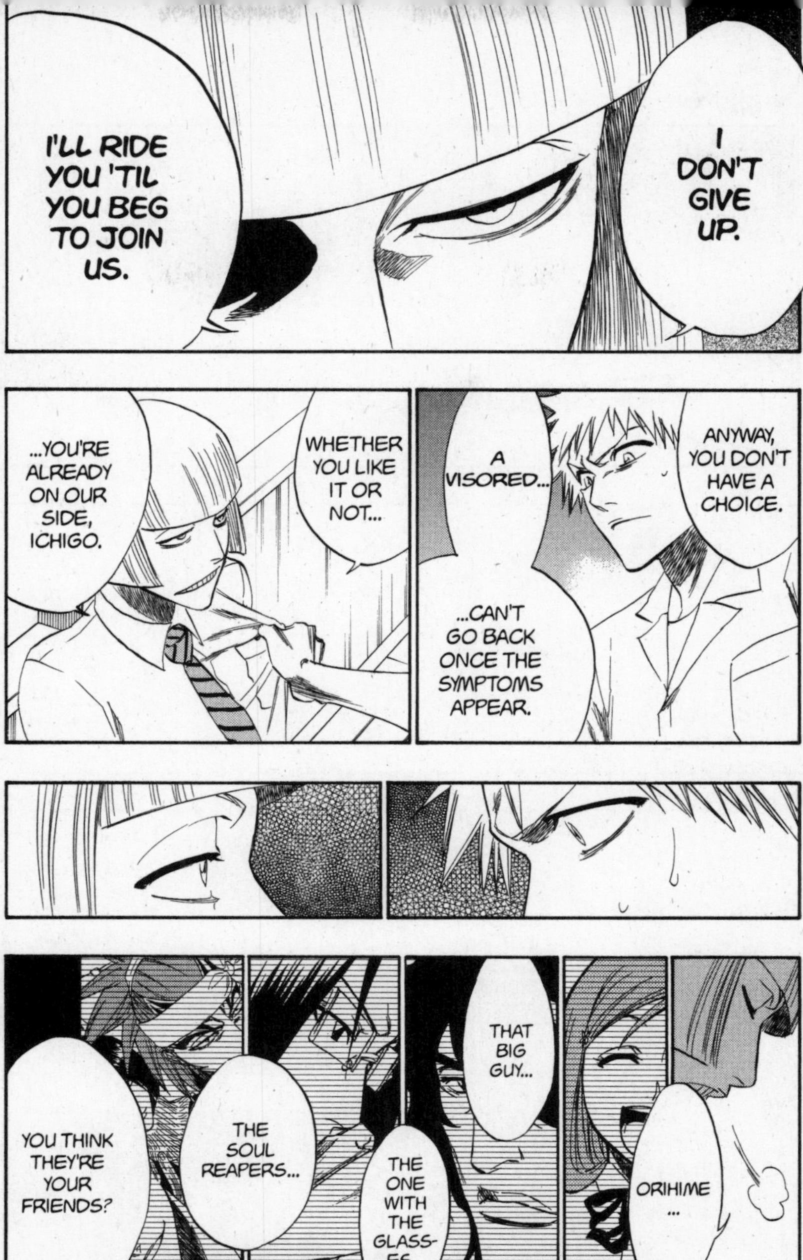
I DON'T GIVE UP.
I'LL RIDE YOU 'TIL YOU BEG TO JOIN US.
ANYWAY, YOU DON'T HAVE A CHOICE.
A VISORED...
...CAN'T GO BACK ONCE THE SYMPTOMS APPEAR.
WHETHER YOU LIKE IT OR NOT...
...YOU'RE ALREADY ON OUR SIDE, ICHIGO.
ORIHIME ...
THAT BIG GUY...
THE ONE WITH THE GLASS-ES...
THE SOUL REAPERS...
YOU THINK THEY'RE YOUR FRIENDS?

READ THIS WAY

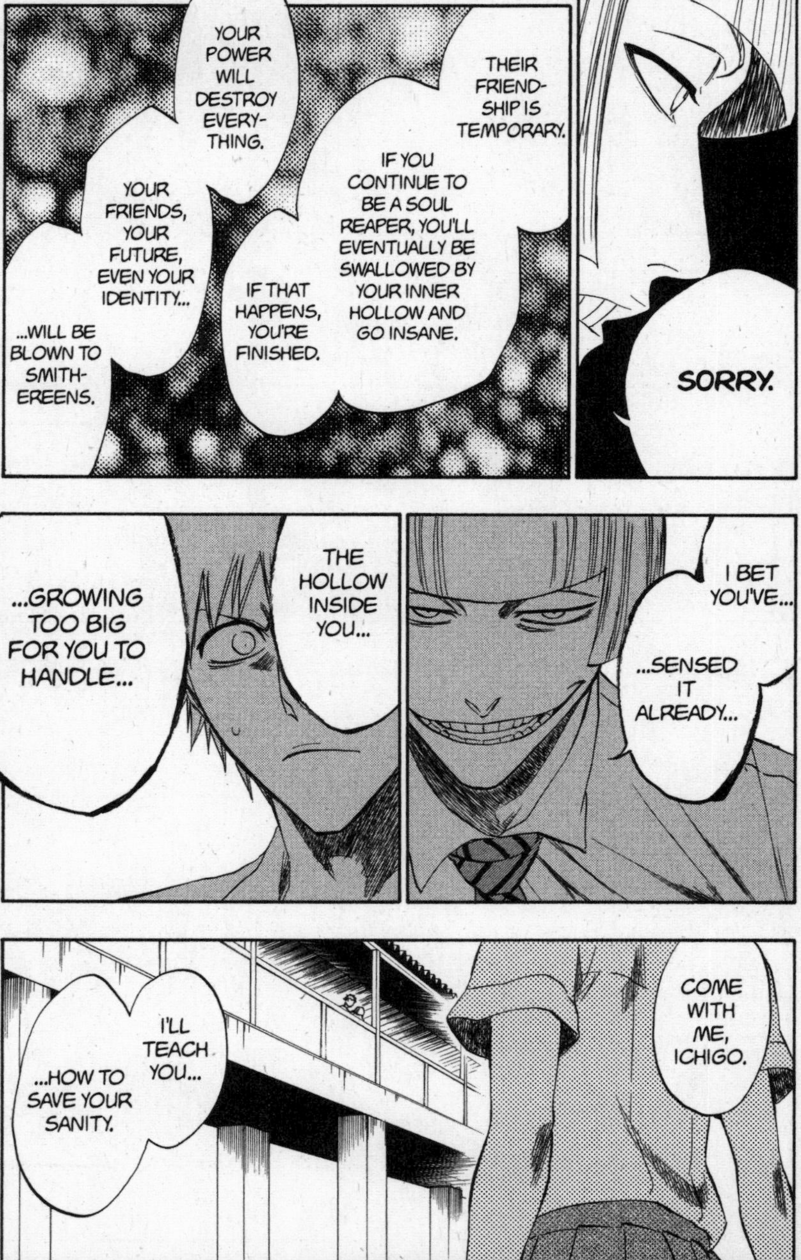

SORRY.
THEIR FRIEND-SHIP IS TEMPORARY.
IF YOU CONTINUE TO BE A SOUL REAPER, YOU'LL EVENTUALLY BE SWALLOWED BY YOUR INNER HOLLOW AND GO INSANE.
IF THAT HAPPENS, YOU'RE FINISHED.
YOUR POWER WILL DESTROY EVERY-THING.
YOUR FRIENDS, YOUR FUTURE, EVEN YOUR IDENTITY...
...WILL BE BLOWN TO SMITH-EREENS.
I BET YOU'VE...
...SENSED IT ALREADY...
THE HOLLOW INSIDE YOU...
...GROWING TOO BIG FOR YOU TO HANDLE...
COME WITH ME, ICHIGO.
I'LL TEACH YOU...
...HOW TO SAVE YOUR SANITY.

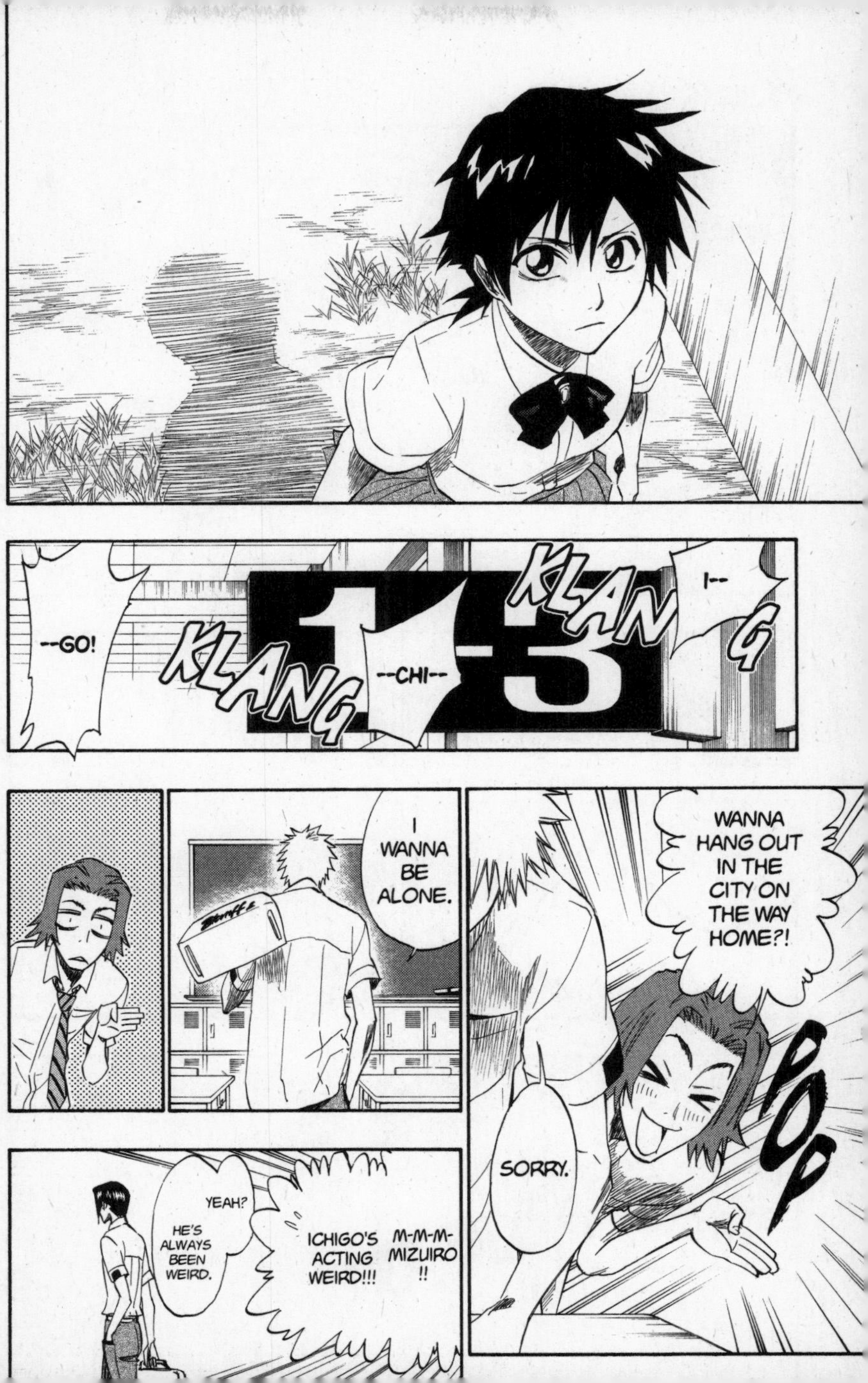
I--
KLANG
--CHI--
KLANG
--GO!
WANNA HANG OUT IN THE CITY ON THE WAY HOME?!
SORRY.
I WANNA BE ALONE.
M-M-M-MIZUIRO!!
ICHIGO'S ACTING WEIRD!!!
YEAH?
HE'S ALWAYS BEEN WEIRD.

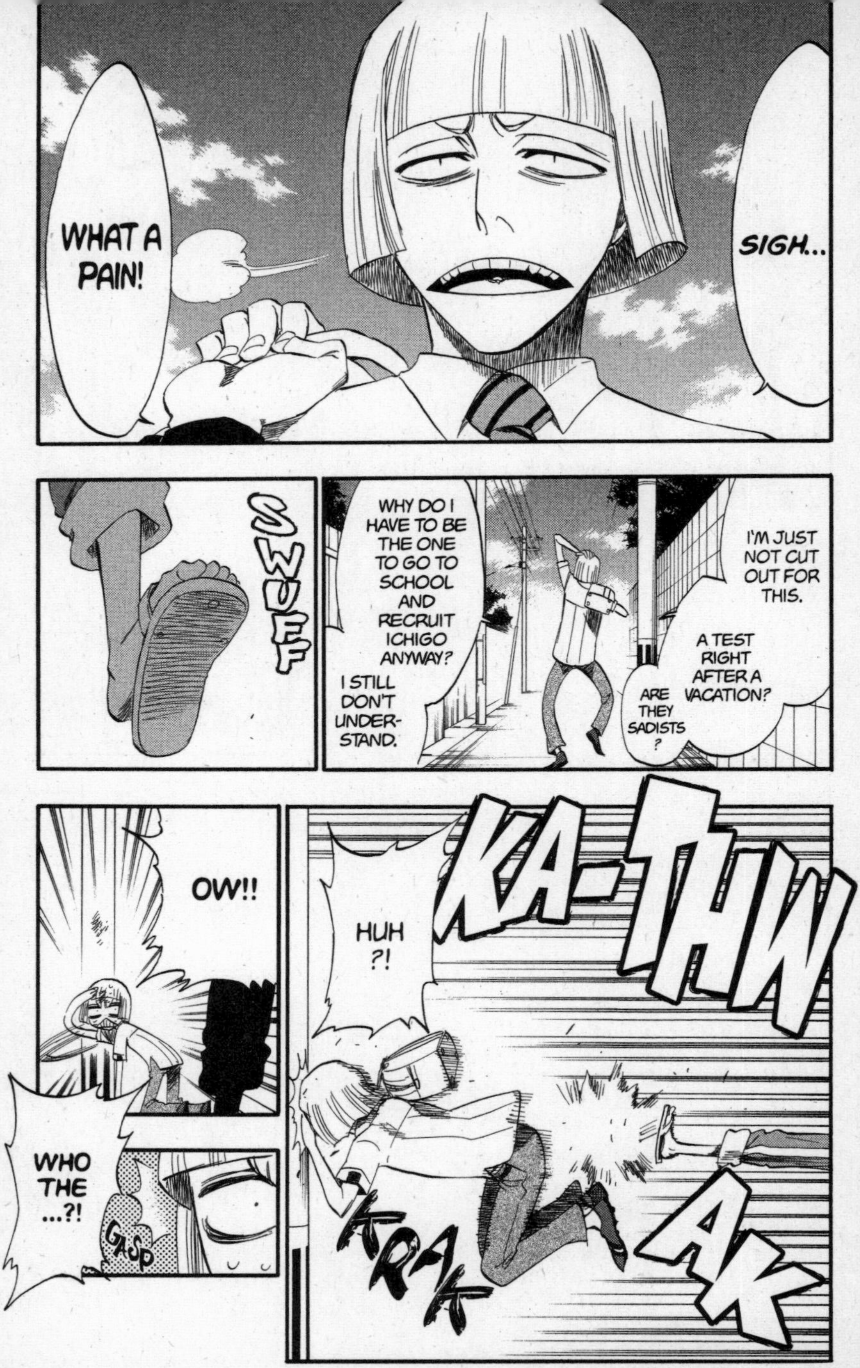
SIGH...
WHAT A PAIN!
I'M JUST NOT CUT OUT FOR THIS.
A TEST RIGHT AFTER A VACATION?
ARE THEY SADISTS?
WHY DO I HAVE TO BE THE ONE TO GO TO SCHOOL AND RECRUIT ICHIGO ANYWAY?
I STILL DON'T UNDERSTAND.
SWUFF
KA-THWAK
HUH?!
KRAK
OW!!
WHO THE ...?!
GASP

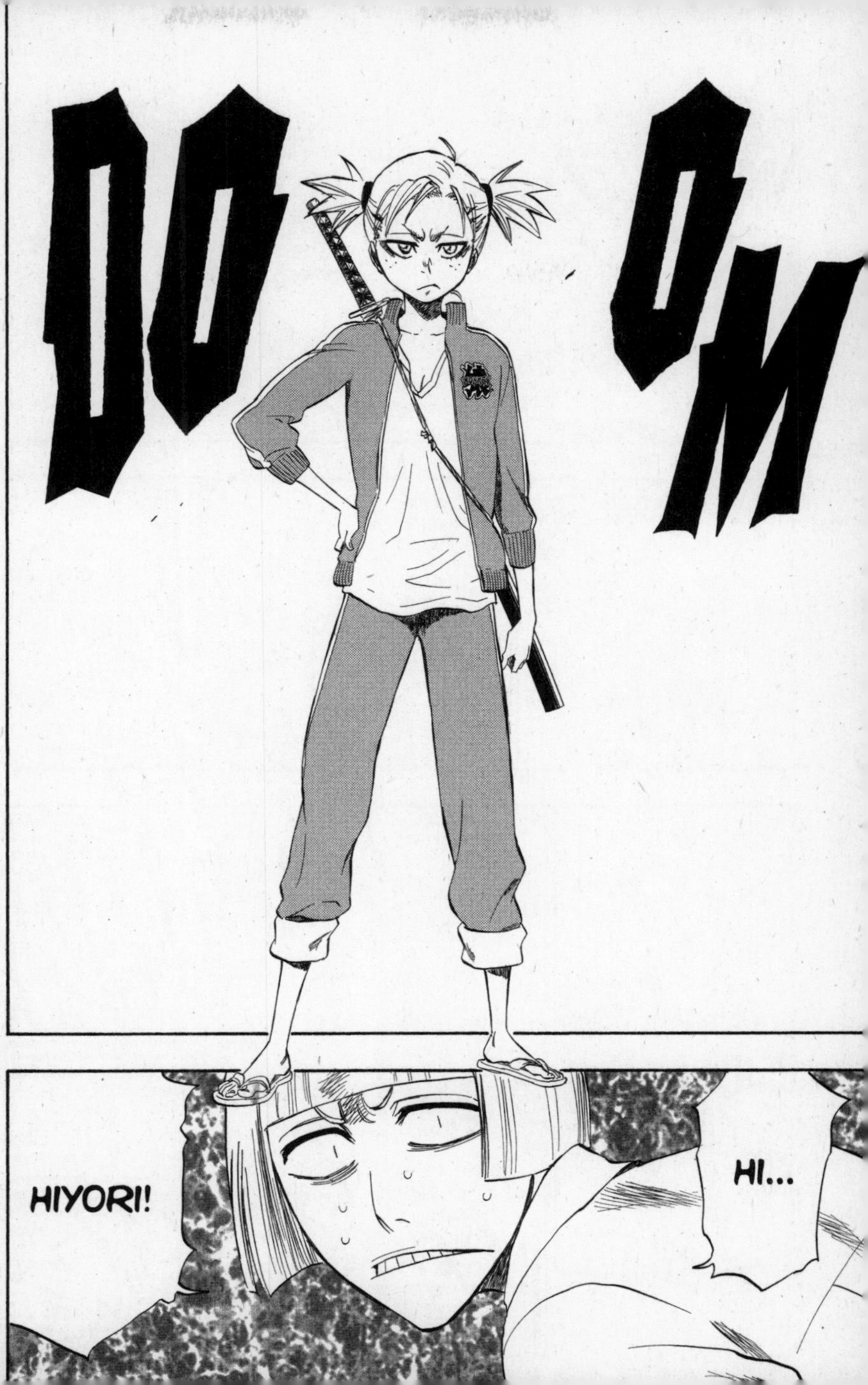
DO
OM
HI...
HIYORI!

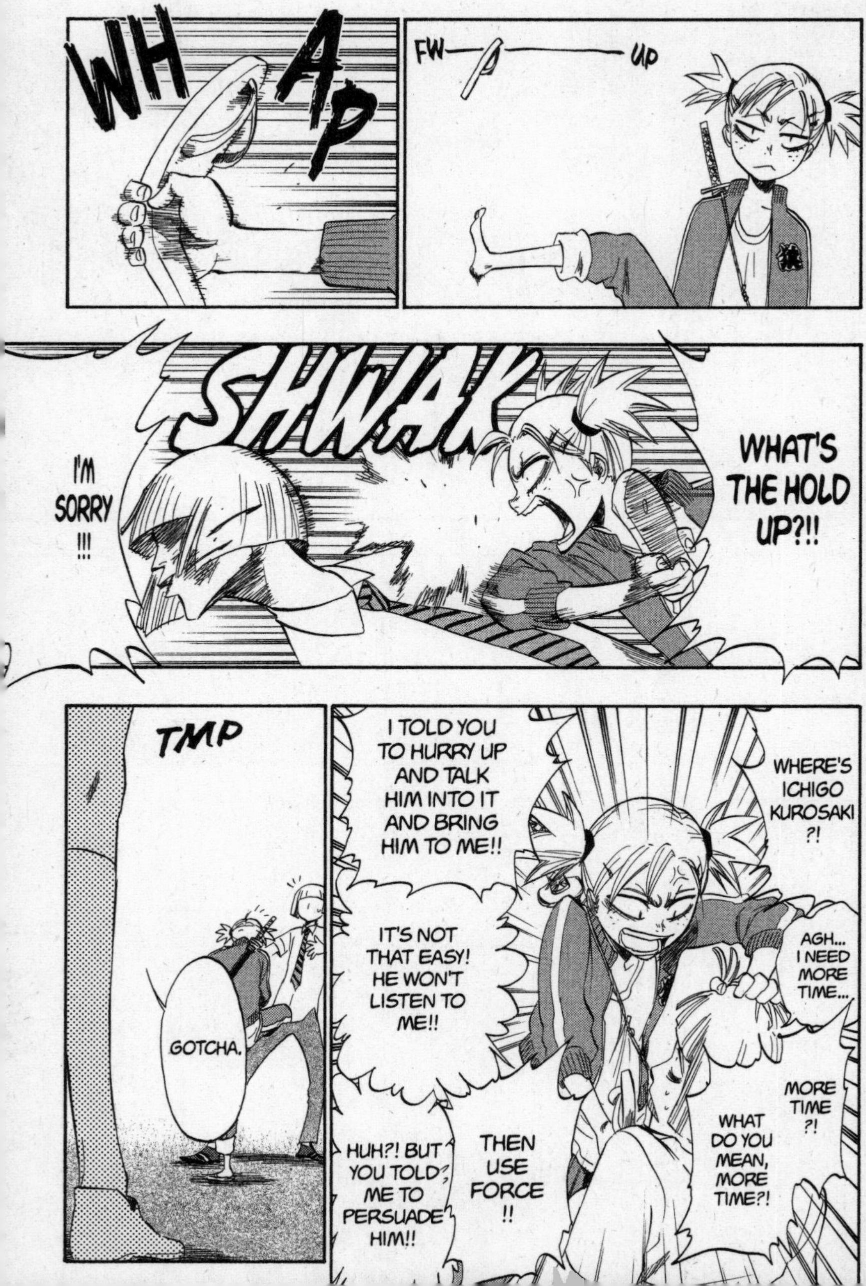
FW——UP
WHAP
SHWAK
WHAT'S THE HOLD UP?!!
I'M SORRY!!!
WHERE'S ICHIGO KUROSAKI?!
I TOLD YOU TO HURRY UP AND TALK HIM INTO IT AND BRING HIM TO ME!!
AGH... I NEED MORE TIME...
IT'S NOT THAT EASY! HE WON'T LISTEN TO ME!!
MORE TIME?!
WHAT DO YOU MEAN, MORE TIME?!
THEN USE FORCE!!
HUH?! BUT YOU TOLD ME TO PERSUADE HIM!!
TMP
GOTCHA.

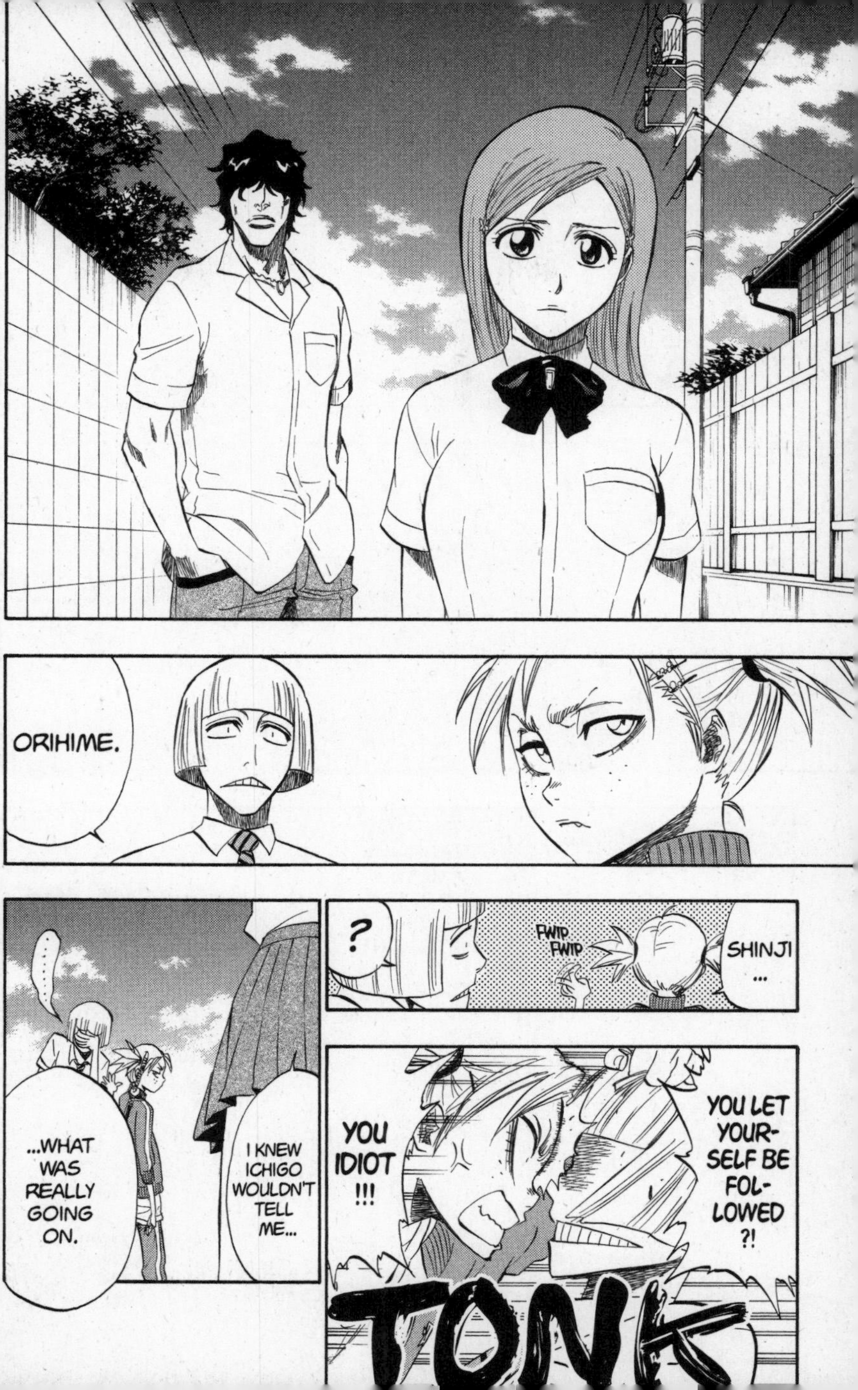
ORIHIME.
SHINJI ...
FWIP FWIP
?
YOU LET YOUR-SELF BE FOL-LOWED ?!
YOU IDIOT !!!
TONK
......
I KNEW ICHIGO WOULDN'T TELL ME...
...WHAT WAS REALLY GOING ON.

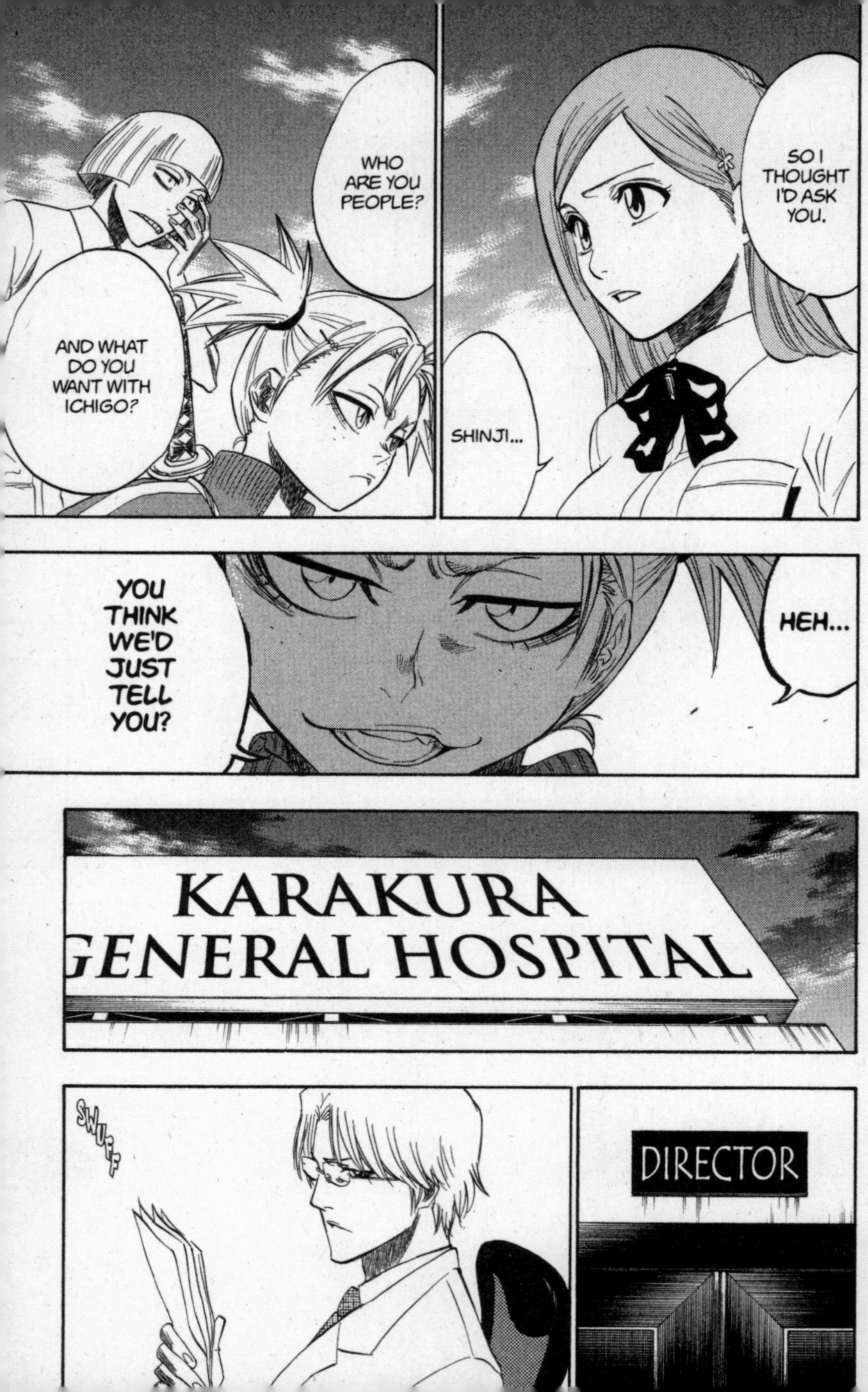
SO I THOUGHT I'D ASK YOU.
SHINJI...
WHO ARE YOU PEOPLE?
AND WHAT DO YOU WANT WITH ICHIGO?
HEH...
YOU THINK WE'D JUST TELL YOU?
KARAKURA GENERAL HOSPITAL
DIRECTOR
SWUFF

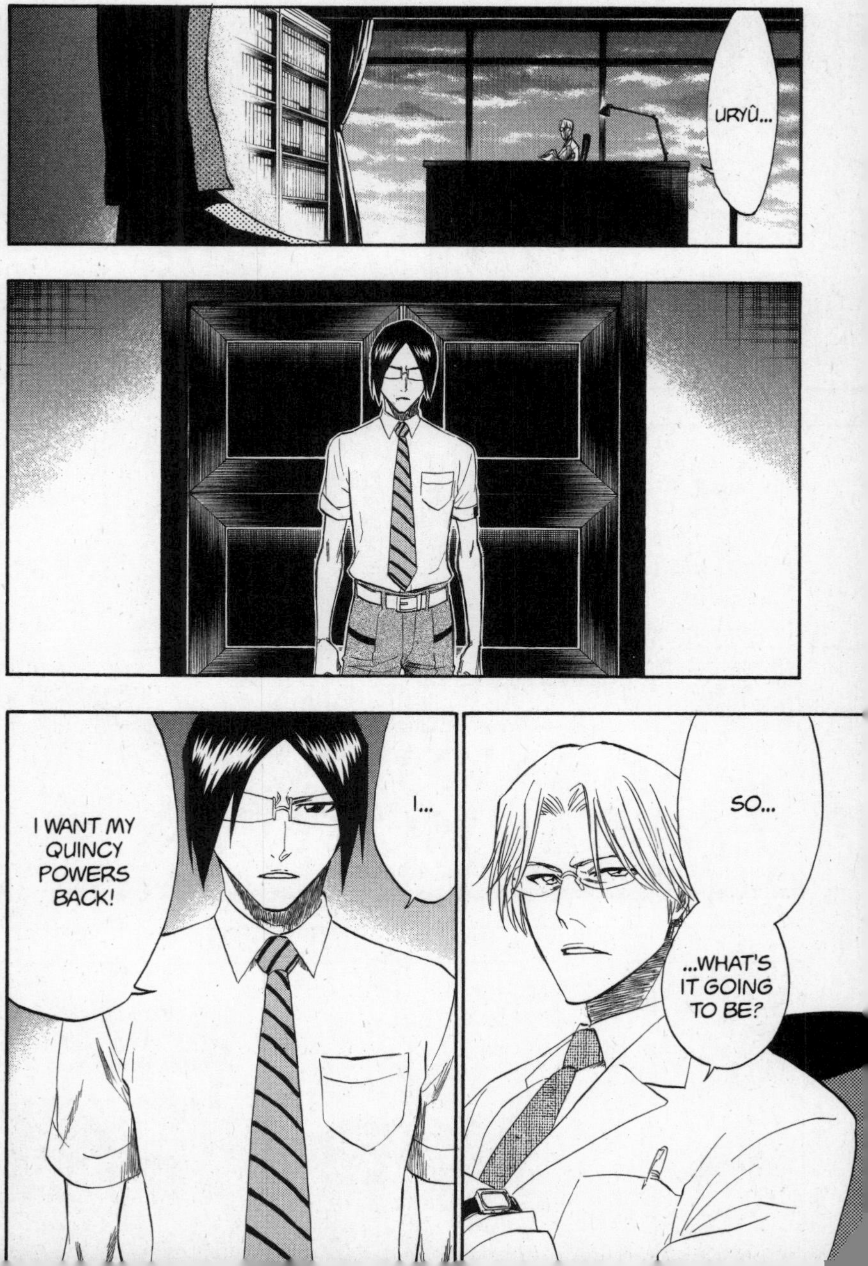
URYÛ...
SO...
...WHAT'S IT GOING TO BE?
I...
I WANT MY QUINCY POWERS BACK!

AND?

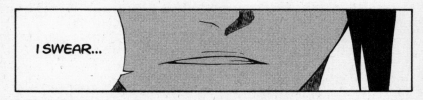

I SWEAR...

...WITH THE SOUL REAPERS AGAIN.

...GET INVOLVED...

...I'LL NEVER...

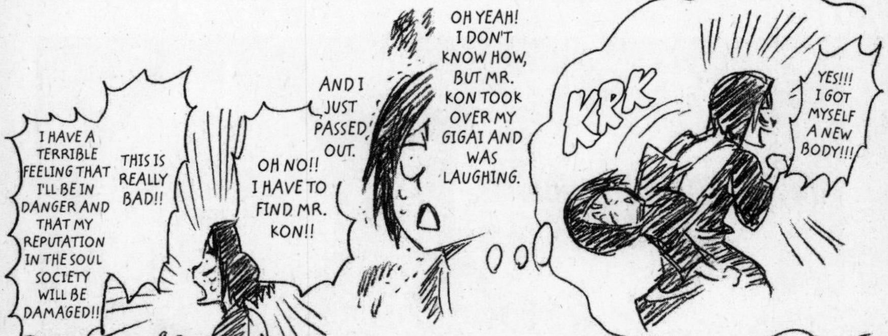
YES!!! I GOT MYSELF A NEW BODY!!!
KRK
OH YEAH! I DON'T KNOW HOW, BUT MR. KON TOOK OVER MY GIGAI AND WAS LAUGHING.
AND I JUST PASSED OUT.
OH NO!! I HAVE TO FIND MR. KON!!
THIS IS REALLY BAD!!
I HAVE A TERRIBLE FEELING THAT I'LL BE IN DANGER AND THAT MY REPUTATION IN THE SOUL SOCIETY WILL BE DAMAGED!!

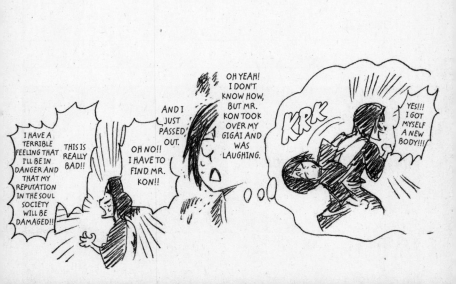

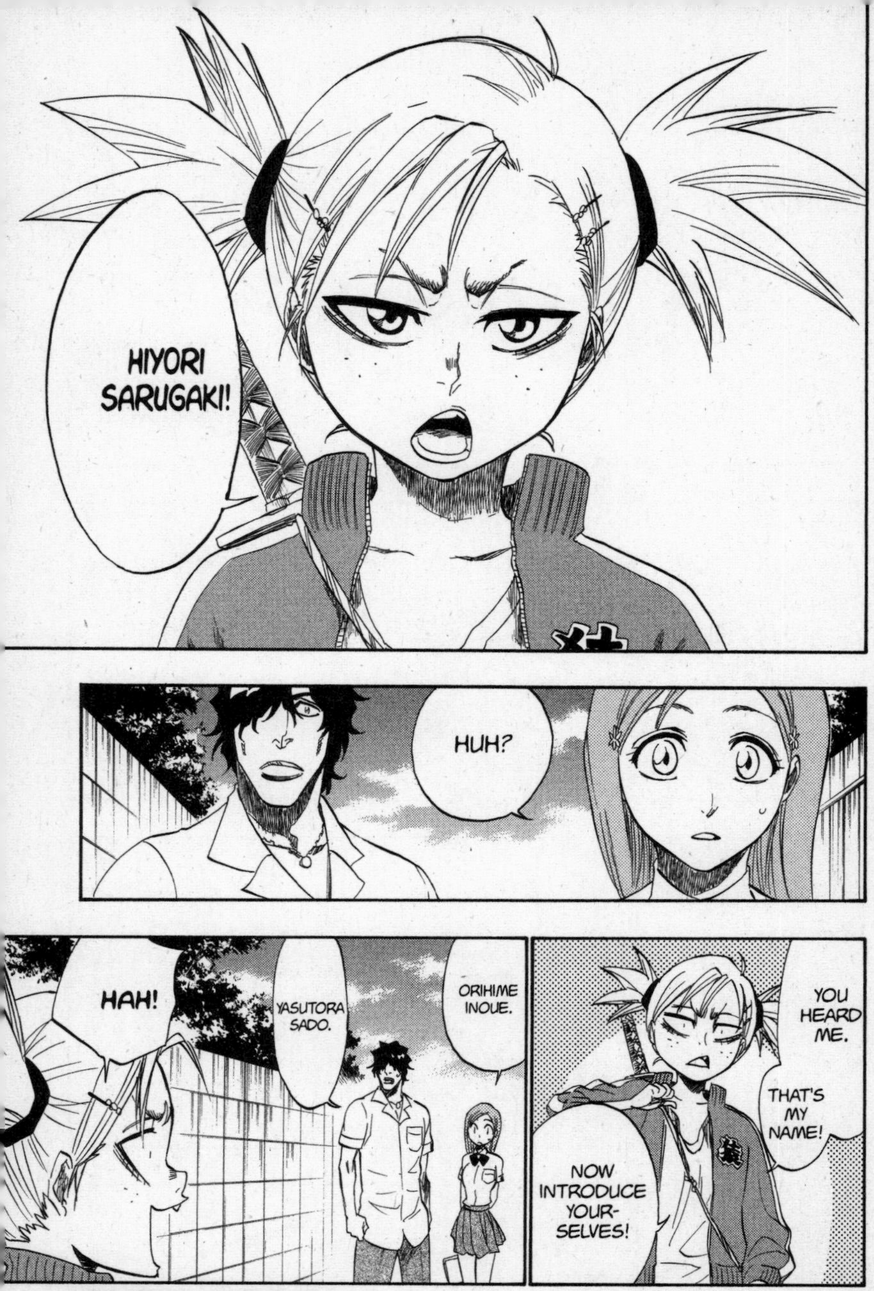
HIYORI SARUGAKI!
HUH?
YOU HEARD ME.
THAT'S MY NAME!
NOW INTRODUCE YOUR-SELVES!
ORIHIME INOUE.
YASUTORA SADO.
HAH!

190. Conquistadores

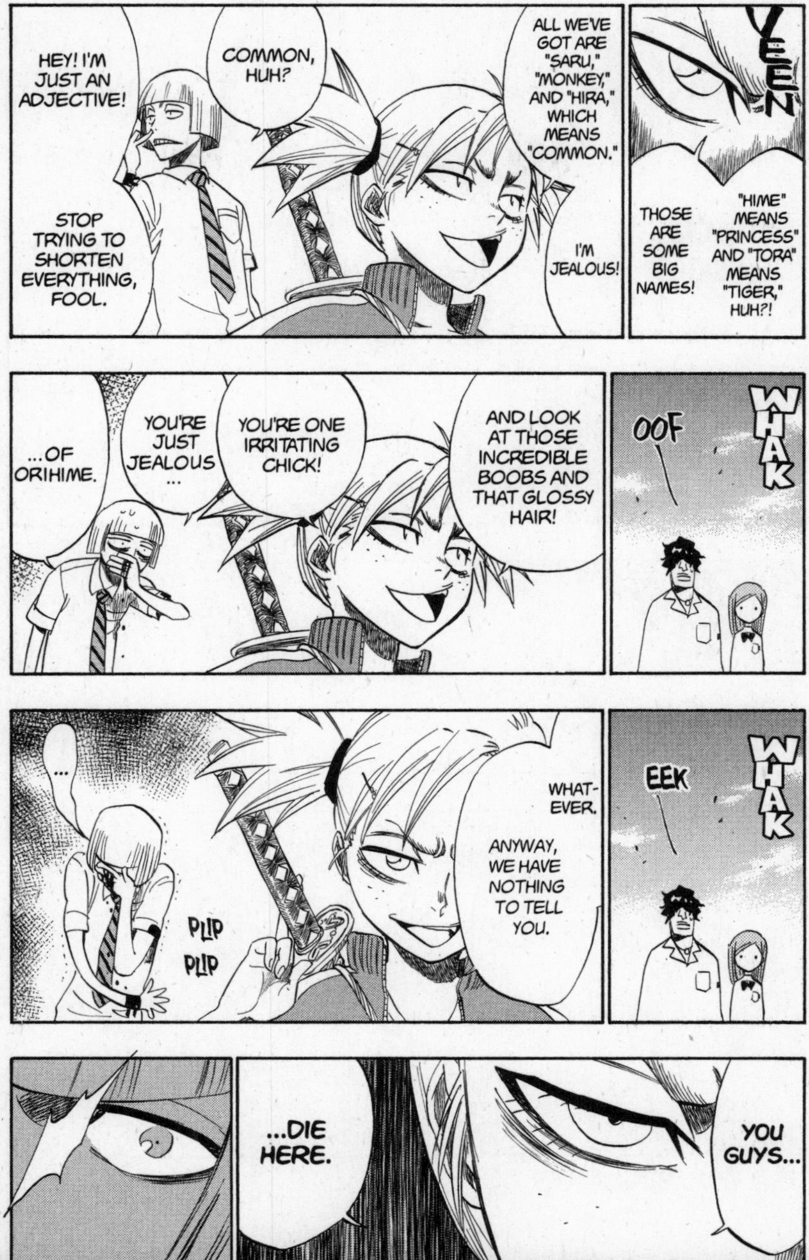
YEEN
"HIME" MEANS "PRINCESS" AND "TORA" MEANS "TIGER," HUH?!
THOSE ARE SOME BIG NAMES!
ALL WE'VE GOT ARE "SARU," "MONKEY," AND "HIRA," WHICH MEANS "COMMON."
I'M JEALOUS!
COMMON, HUH?
HEY! I'M JUST AN ADJECTIVE!
STOP TRYING TO SHORTEN EVERYTHING, FOOL.
WHAK
OOF
AND LOOK AT THOSE INCREDIBLE BOOBS AND THAT GLOSSY HAIR!
YOU'RE ONE IRRITATING CHICK!
YOU'RE JUST JEALOUS ...
...OF ORIHIME.
WHAK
EEK
WHAT-EVER.
ANYWAY, WE HAVE NOTHING TO TELL YOU.
...
PLIP
PLIP
YOU GUYS...
...DIE HERE.

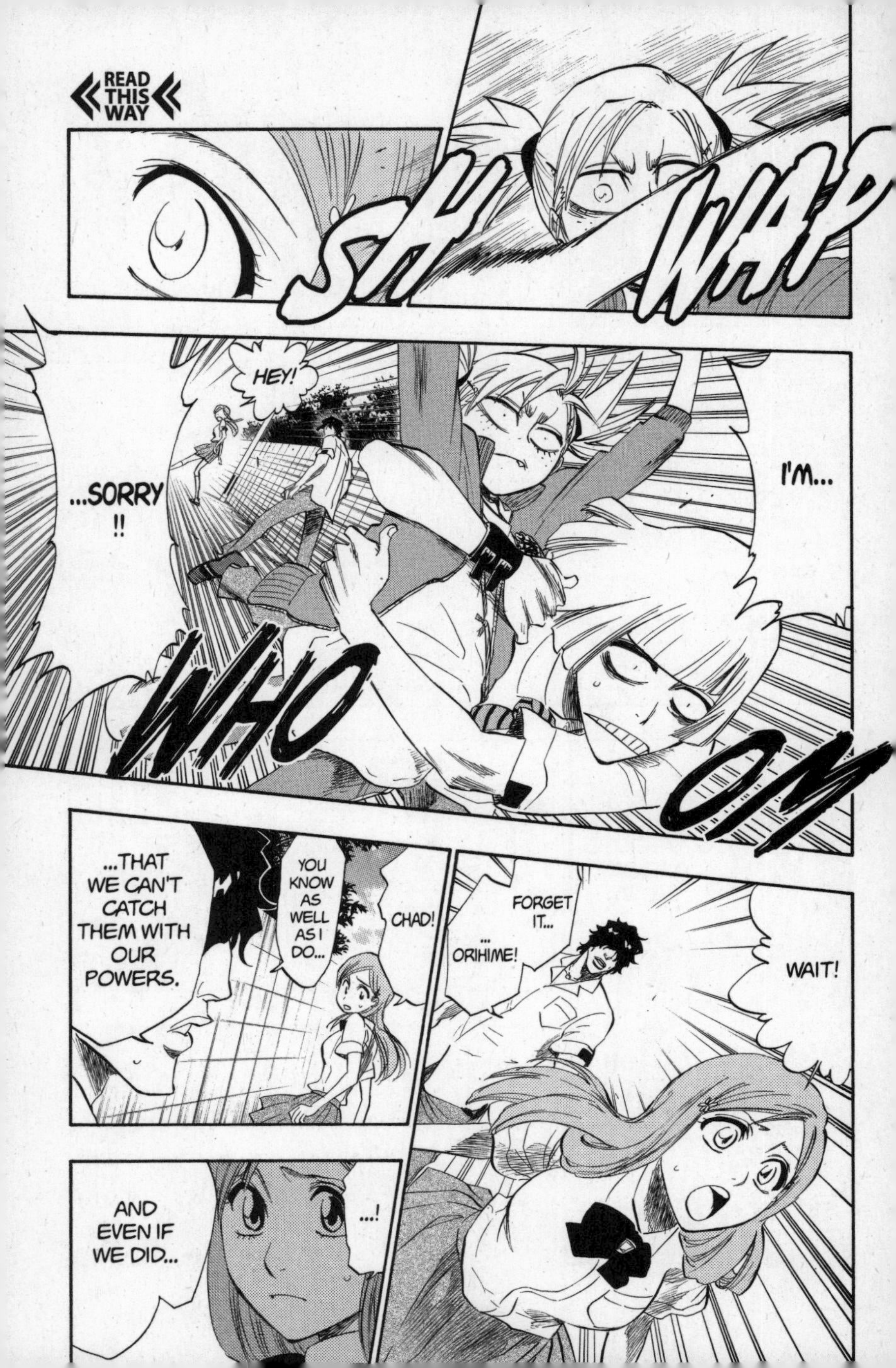
READ THIS WAY
SH WAP
HEY!
I'M...
...SORRY !!
WHO OM
WAIT!
FORGET IT... ...ORIHIME!
CHAD!
YOU KNOW AS WELL AS I DO...
...THAT WE CAN'T CATCH THEM WITH OUR POWERS.
...!
AND EVEN IF WE DID...

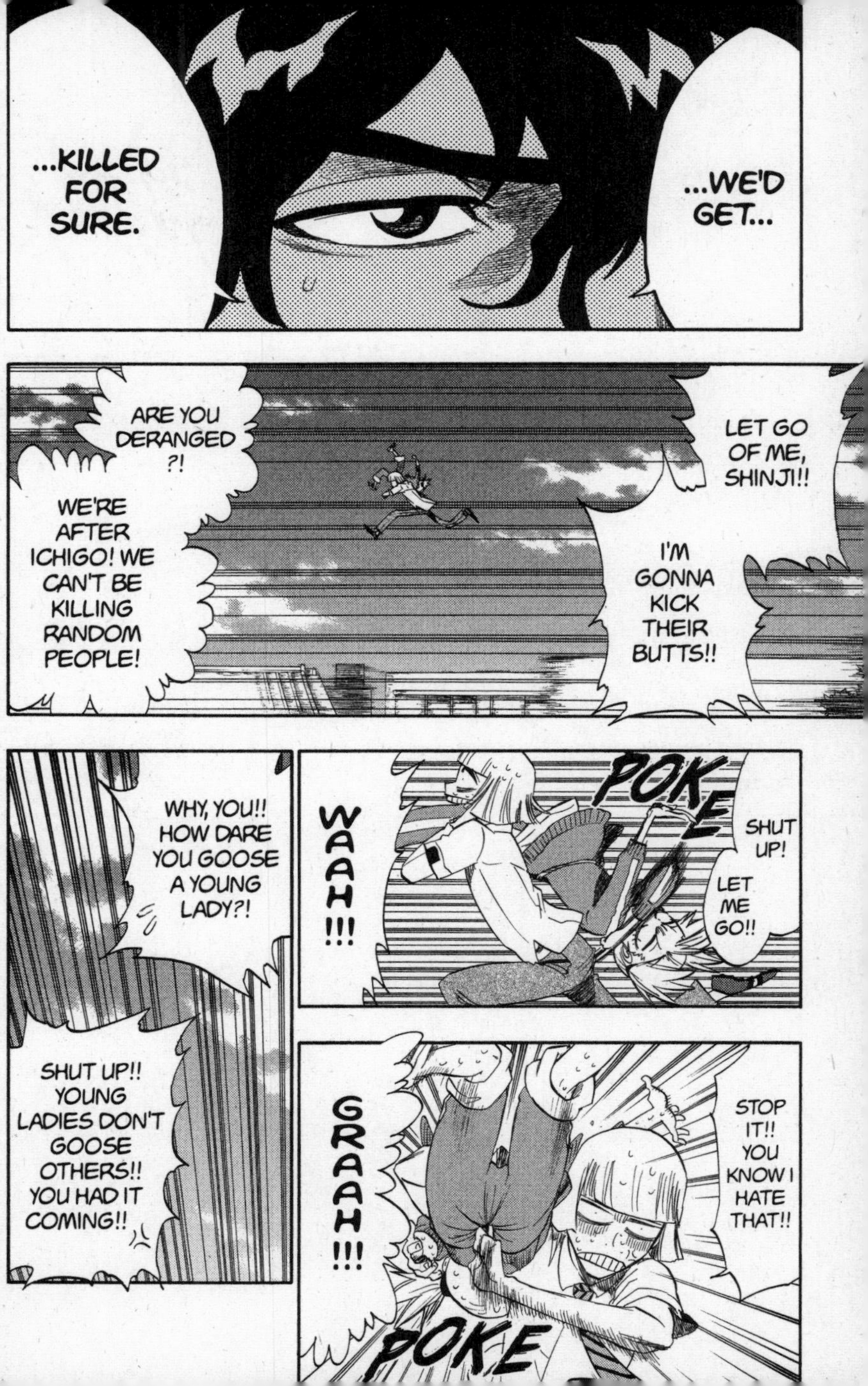
...WE'D GET...
...KILLED FOR SURE.
LET GO OF ME, SHINJI!!
I'M GONNA KICK THEIR BUTTS!!
ARE YOU DERANGED?!
WE'RE AFTER ICHIGO! WE CAN'T BE KILLING RANDOM PEOPLE!
POKE
SHUT UP!
LET ME GO!!
WAAAH!!!
STOP IT!! YOU KNOW I HATE THAT!!
GRAAAH!!!
POKE
WHY, YOU!! HOW DARE YOU GOOSE A YOUNG LADY?!
SHUT UP!! YOUNG LADIES DON'T GOOSE OTHERS!! YOU HAD IT COMING!!

READ THIS WAY

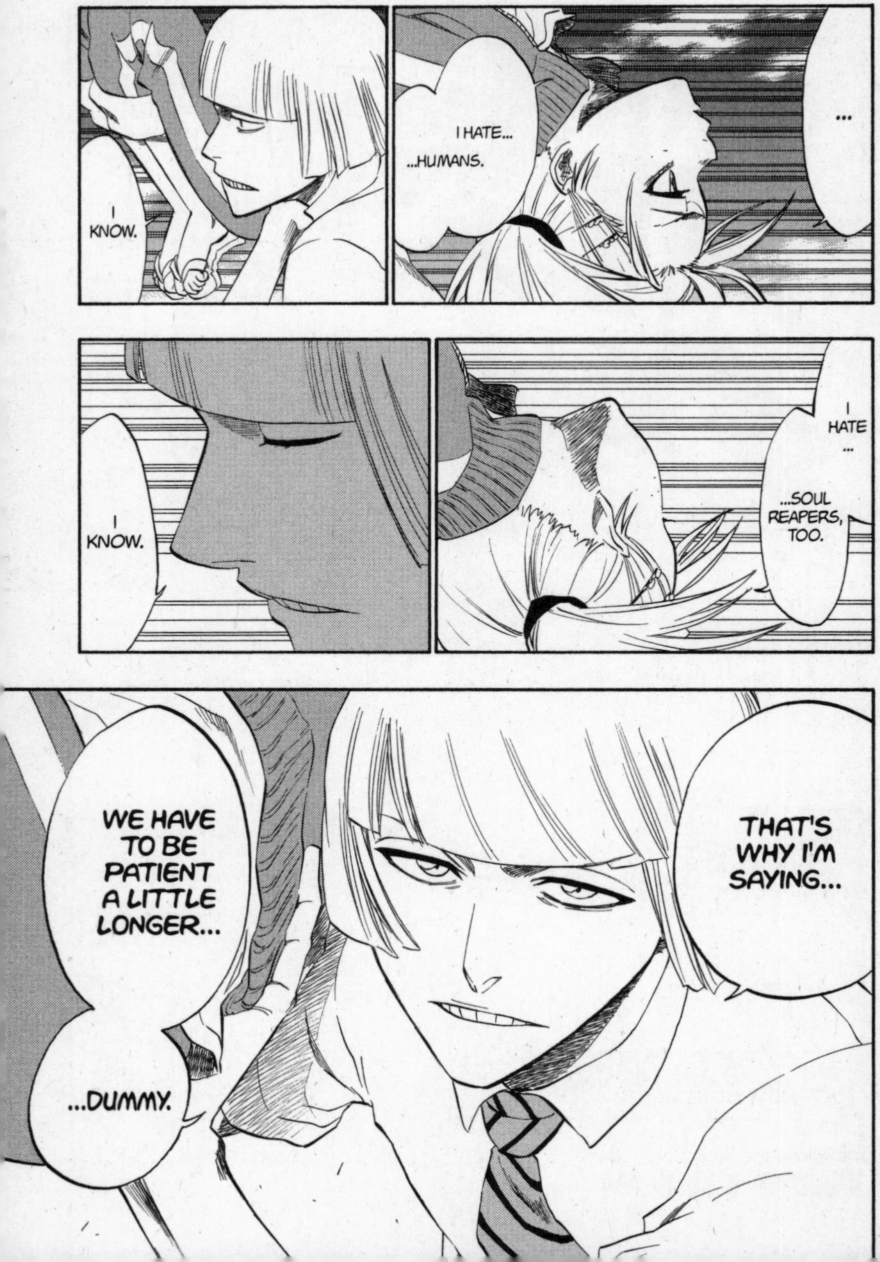
...
I HATE... ...HUMANS.
I KNOW.
I HATE ... ...SOUL REAPERS, TOO.
I KNOW.
THAT'S WHY I'M SAYING...
WE HAVE TO BE PATIENT A LITTLE LONGER...
...DUMMY.

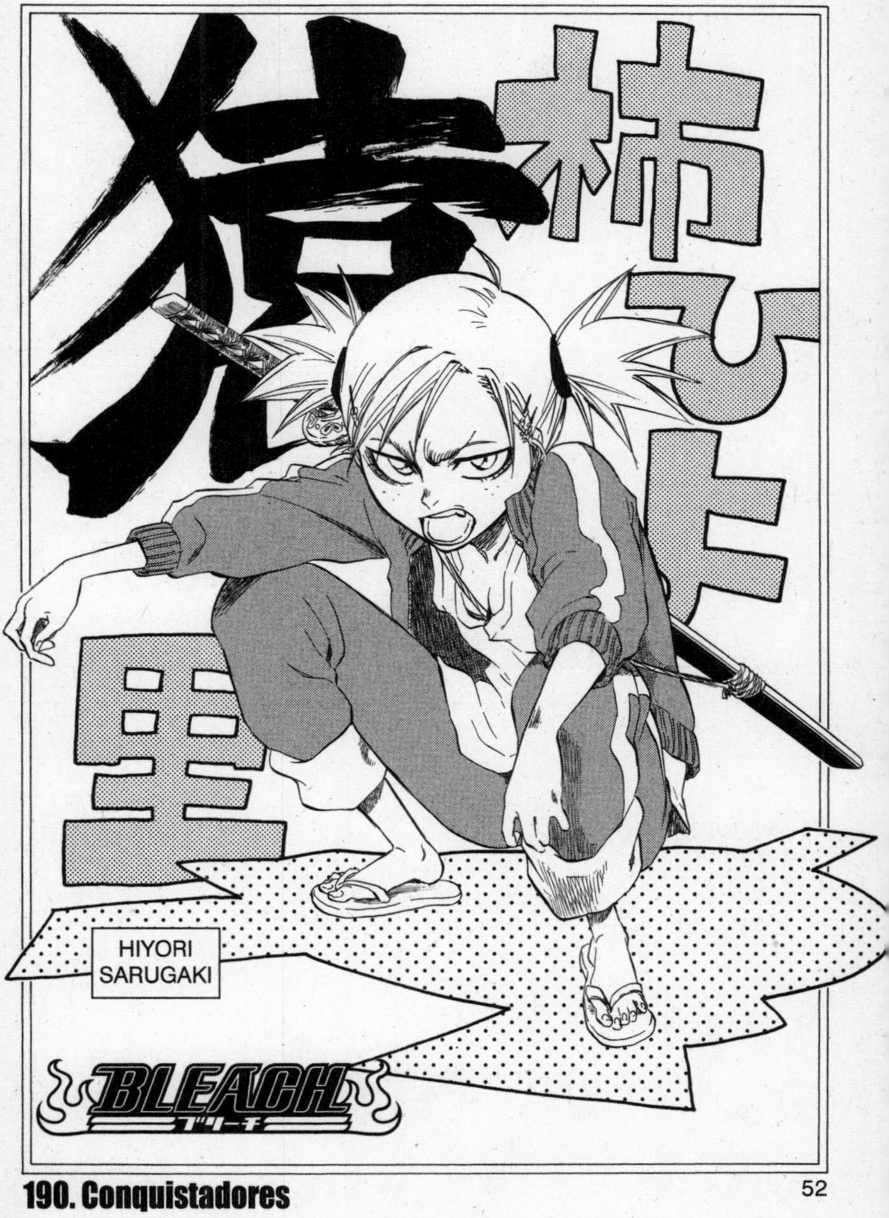
猿柿ひよ里
HIYORI SARUGAKI
BLEACH
ブリーチ

190. Conquistadores

READ THIS WAY

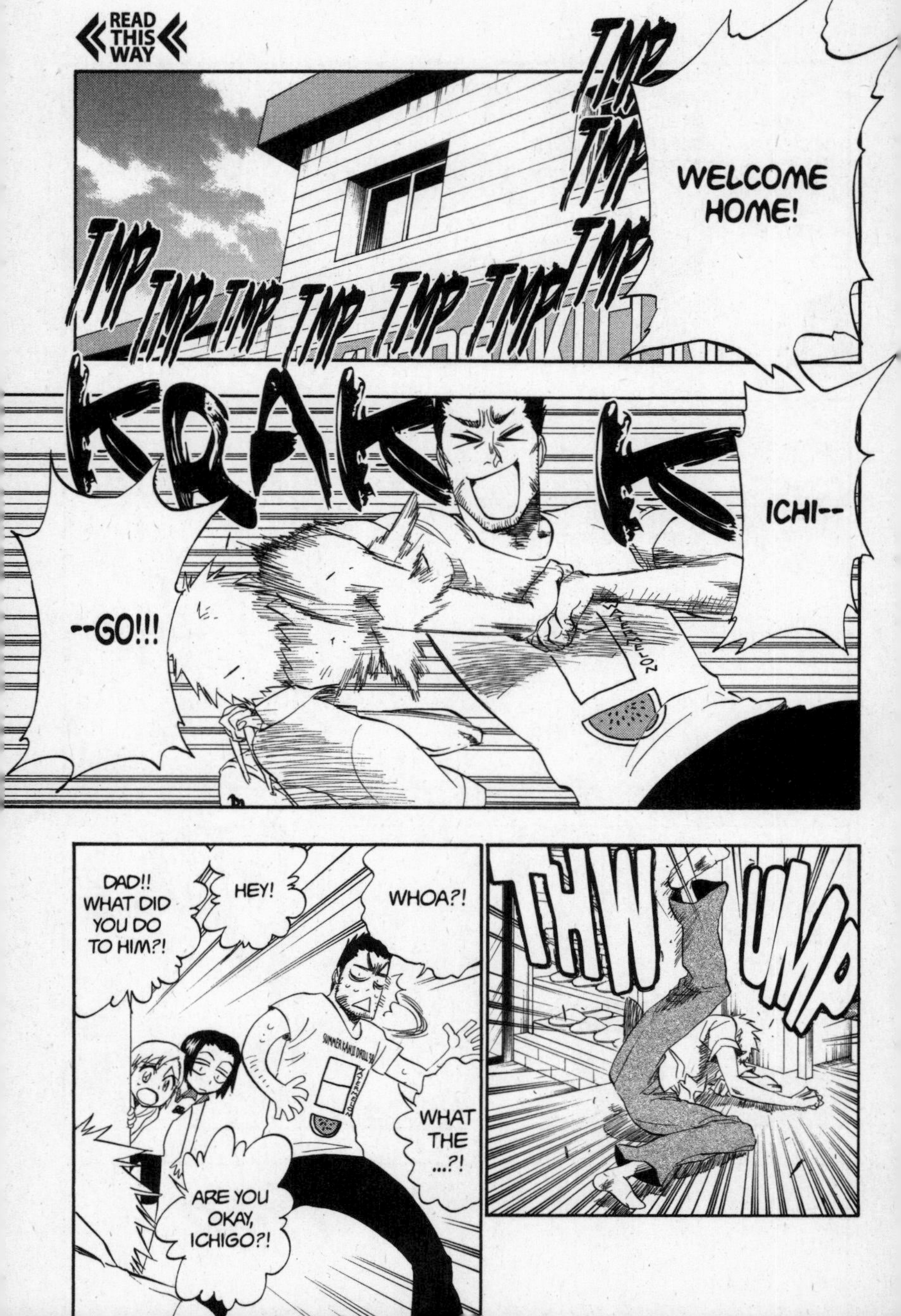
TMP TMP TMP TMP TMP TMP TMP TMP TMP TMP TMP
WELCOME HOME!
ICHI--
KRAKK
--GO!!!
WATERMELON
THWUMP
WHOA?!
HEY!
DAD!! WHAT DID YOU DO TO HIM?!
WHAT THE ...?!
ARE YOU OKAY, ICHIGO?!

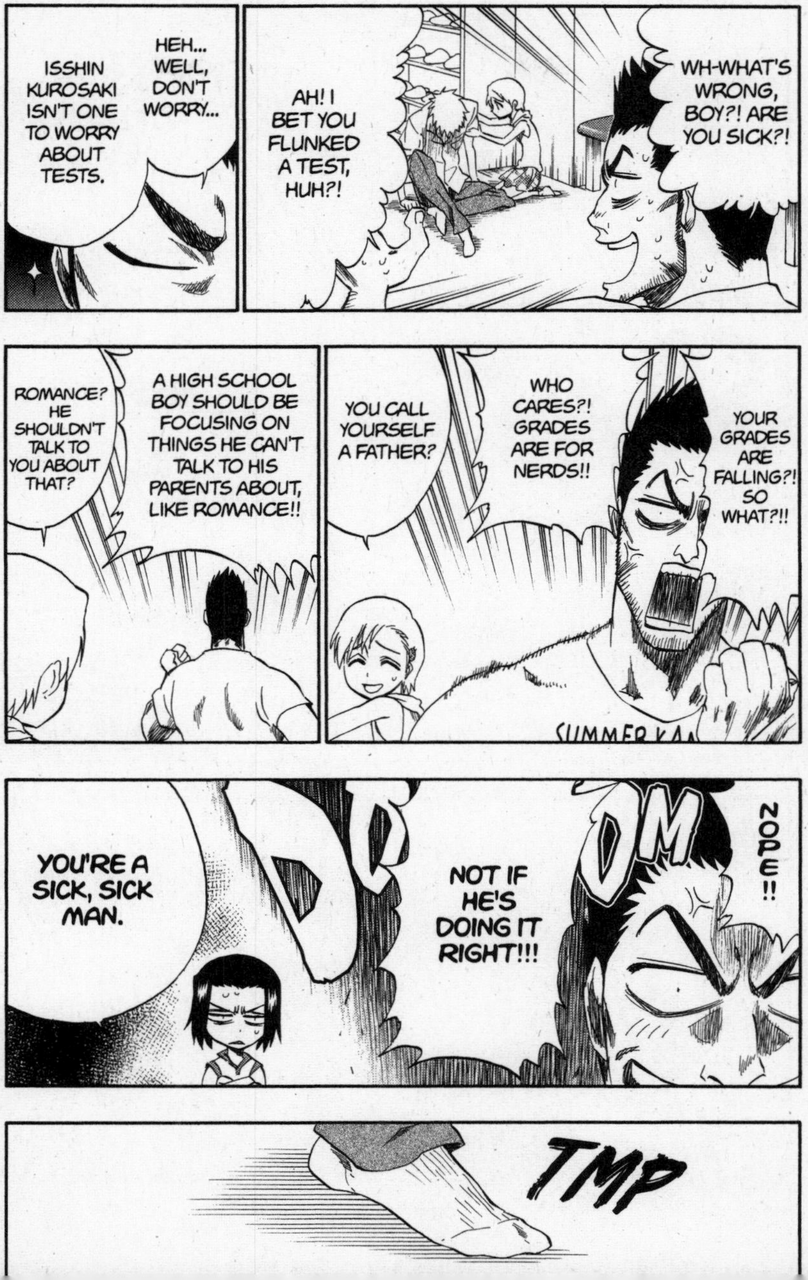
WH-WHAT'S WRONG, BOY?! ARE YOU SICK?!
AH! I BET YOU FLUNKED A TEST, HUH?!
HEH... WELL, DON'T WORRY...
ISSHIN KUROSAKI ISN'T ONE TO WORRY ABOUT TESTS.
YOUR GRADES ARE FALLING?! SO WHAT?!!
WHO CARES?! GRADES ARE FOR NERDS!!
YOU CALL YOURSELF A FATHER?
A HIGH SCHOOL BOY SHOULD BE FOCUSING ON THINGS HE CAN'T TALK TO HIS PARENTS ABOUT, LIKE ROMANCE!!
ROMANCE? HE SHOULDN'T TALK TO YOU ABOUT THAT?
NOPE!!
DOM
NOT IF HE'S DOING IT RIGHT!!!
YOU'RE A SICK, SICK MAN.
TMP

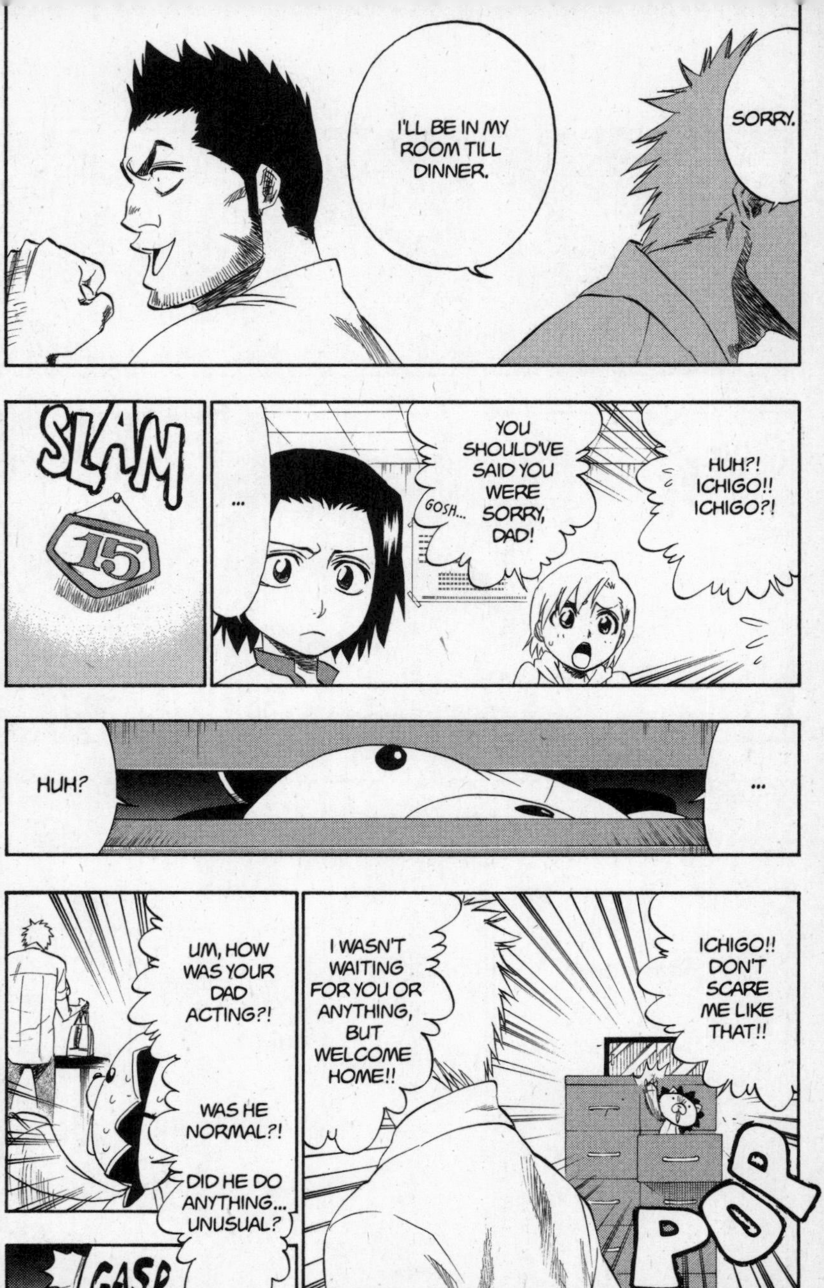
SORRY.
I'LL BE IN MY ROOM TILL DINNER.
HUH?! ICHIGO!! ICHIGO?!
YOU SHOULD'VE SAID YOU WERE SORRY, DAD!
GOSH...
...
SLAM
15
...
HUH?
ICHIGO!! DON'T SCARE ME LIKE THAT!!
I WASN'T WAITING FOR YOU OR ANYTHING, BUT WELCOME HOME!!
POP
UM, HOW WAS YOUR DAD ACTING?!
WAS HE NORMAL?!
DID HE DO ANYTHING... UNUSUAL?
GASP

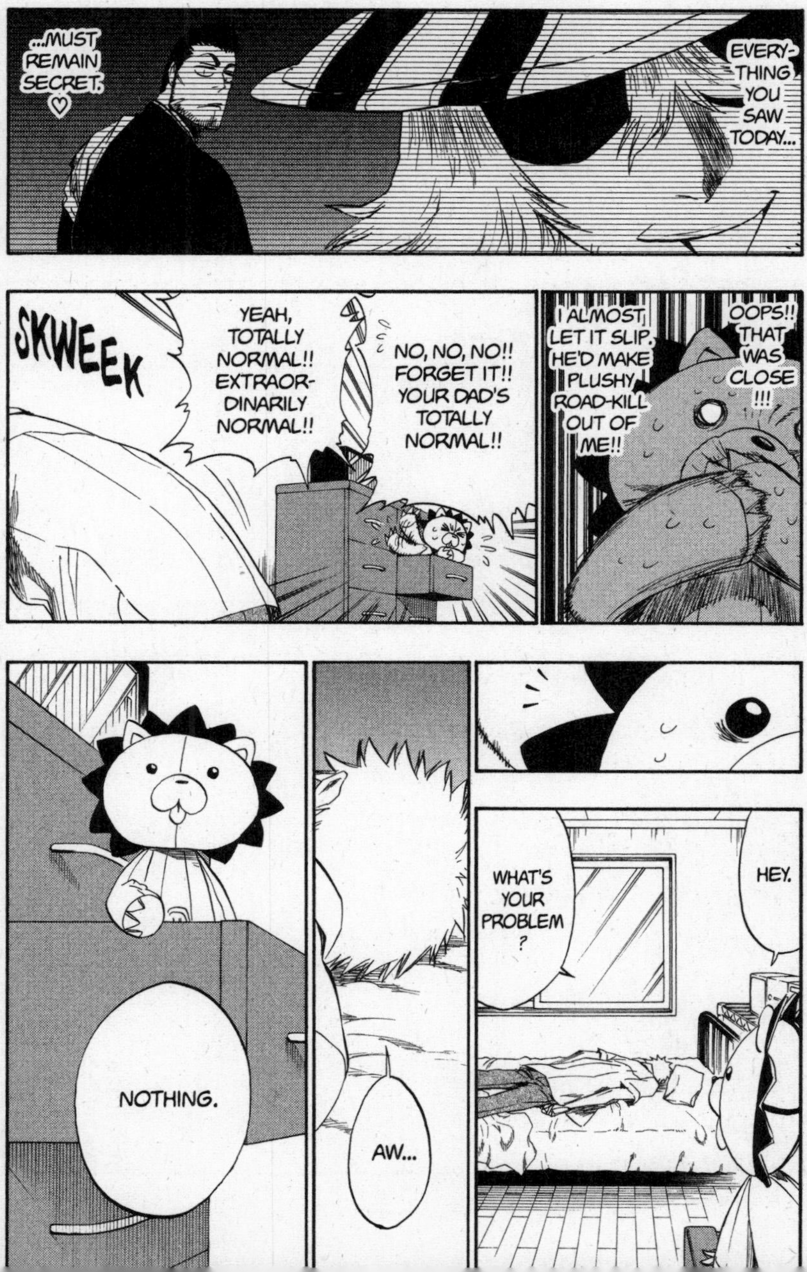
EVERY-THING YOU SAW TODAY...
...MUST REMAIN SECRET. ♡
OOPS!! THAT WAS CLOSE!!!
I ALMOST LET IT SLIP. HE'D MAKE PLUSHY ROAD-KILL OUT OF ME!!
NO, NO, NO!! FORGET IT!! YOUR DAD'S TOTALLY NORMAL!!
YEAH, TOTALLY NORMAL!! EXTRAOR-DINARILY NORMAL!!
SKWEEK
HEY.
WHAT'S YOUR PROBLEM?
AW...
NOTHING.

READ THIS WAY

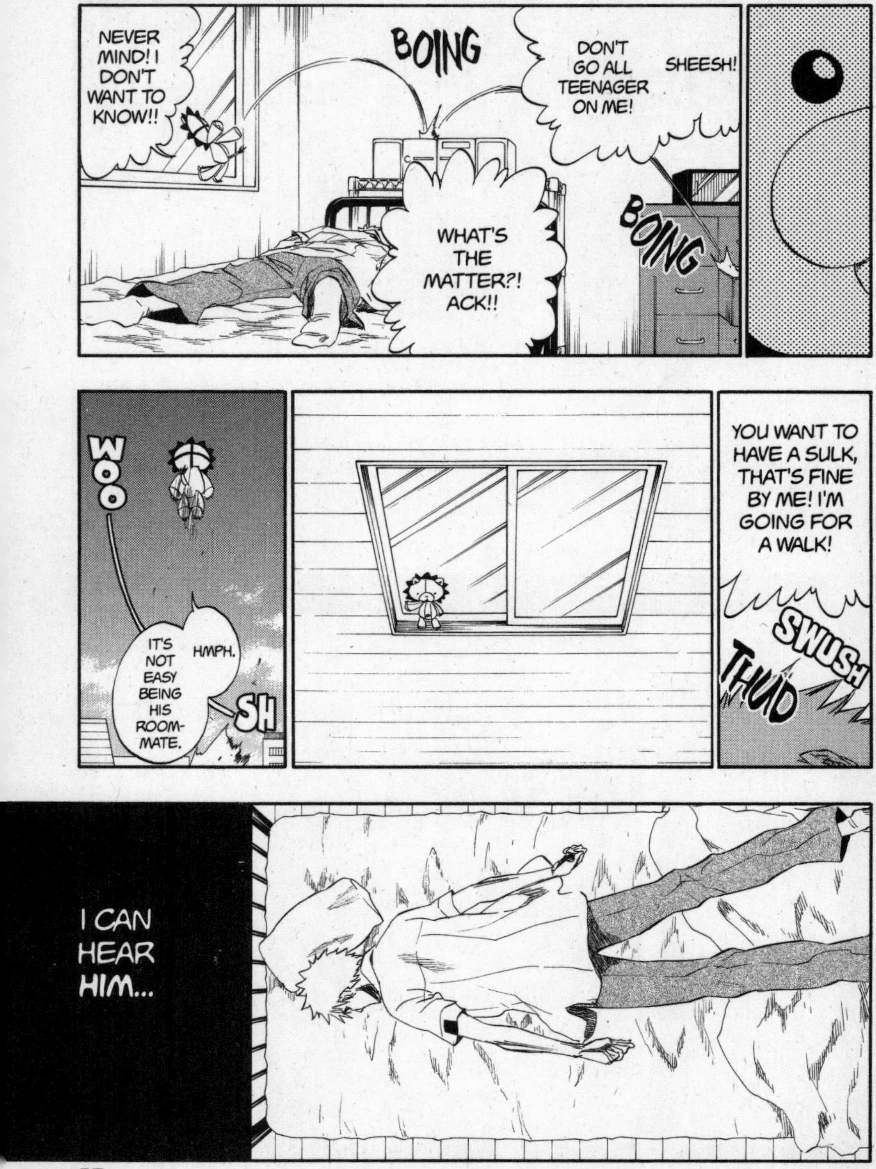
SHEESH!
DON'T GO ALL TEENAGER ON ME!
BOING
BOING
WHAT'S THE MATTER?! ACK!!
NEVER MIND!! I DON'T WANT TO KNOW!!
YOU WANT TO HAVE A SULK, THAT'S FINE BY ME! I'M GOING FOR A WALK!
SWUSH
THUD
WOOSH
HMPH.
IT'S NOT EASY BEING HIS ROOMMATE.
I CAN HEAR HIM...

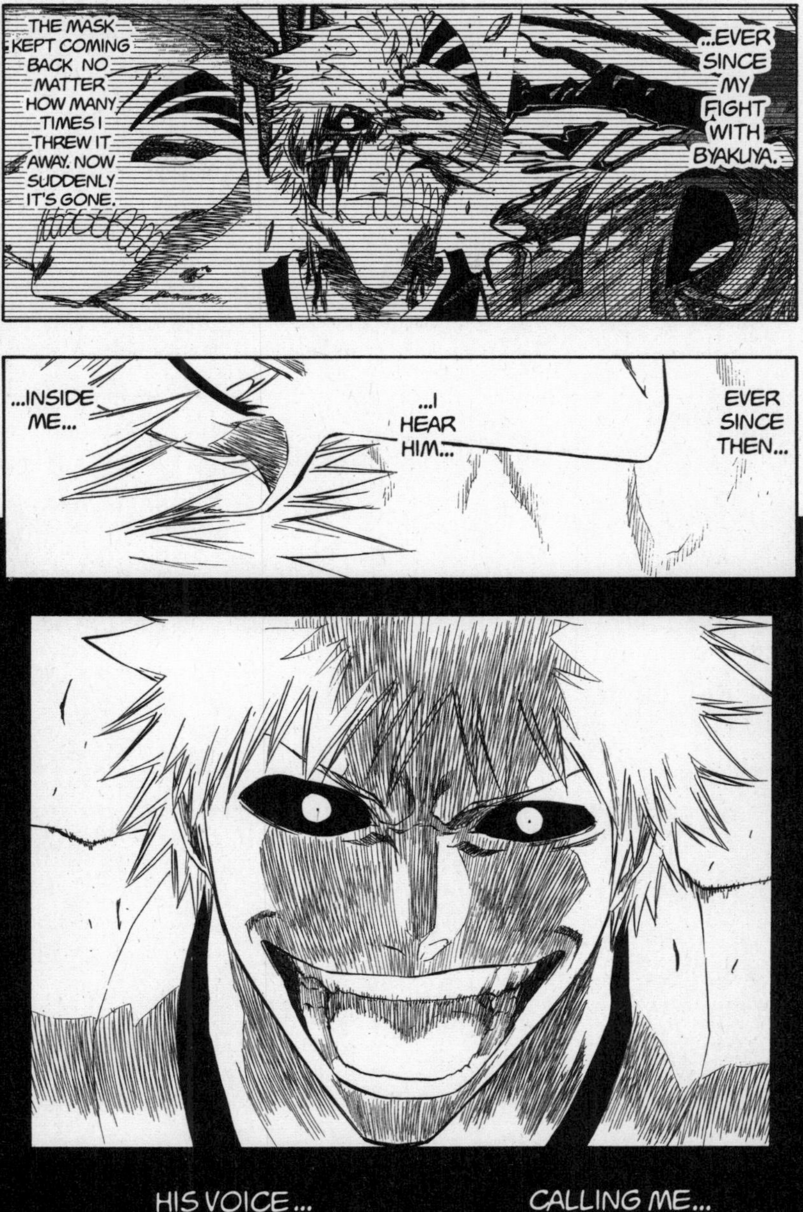
...EVER SINCE MY FIGHT WITH BYAKUYA.
THE MASK KEPT COMING BACK NO MATTER HOW MANY TIMES I THREW IT AWAY. NOW SUDDENLY IT'S GONE.
EVER SINCE THEN...
...I HEAR HIM...
...INSIDE ME...
CALLING ME...
HIS VOICE...

READ THIS WAY

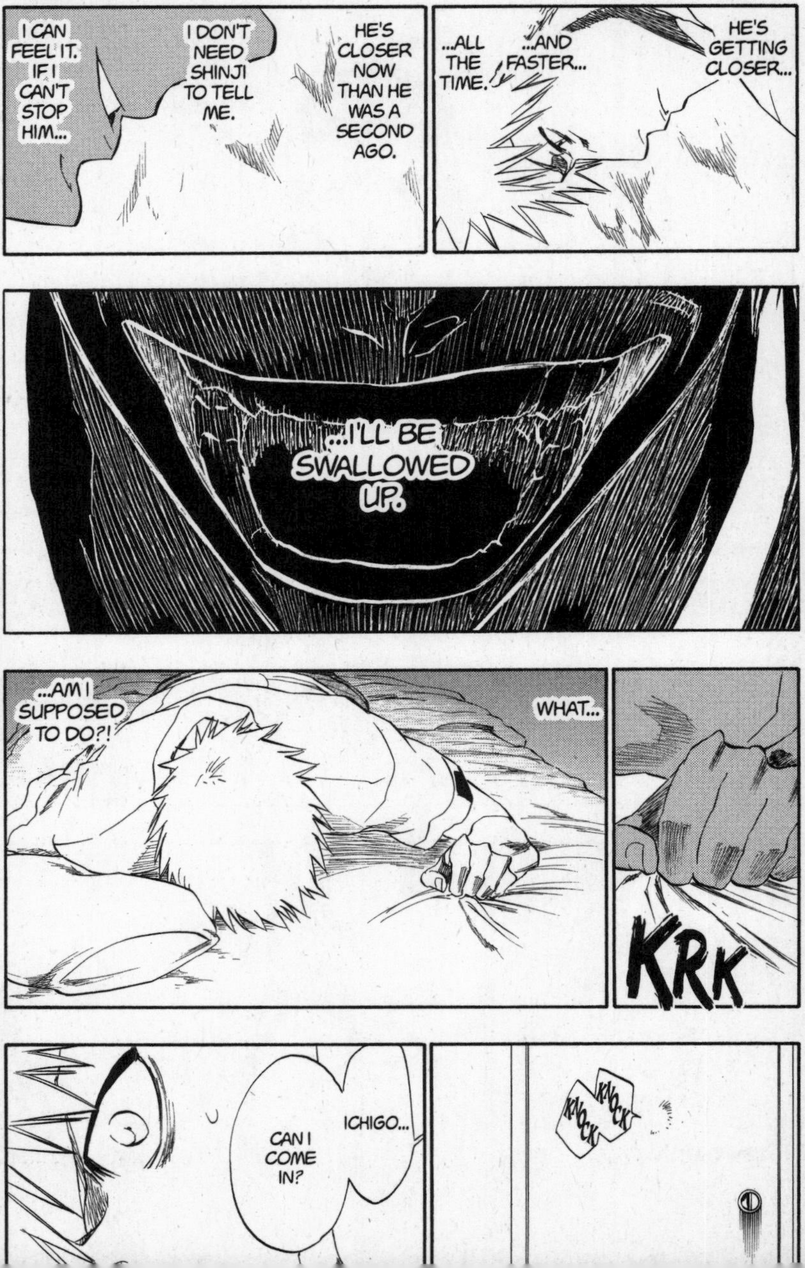

HE'S GETTING CLOSER...
...AND FASTER...
...ALL THE TIME.
HE'S CLOSER NOW THAN HE WAS A SECOND AGO.
I DON'T NEED SHINJI TO TELL ME.
I CAN FEEL IT. IF I CAN'T STOP HIM...
...I'LL BE SWALLOWED UP.
KRK
WHAT...
...AM I SUPPOSED TO DO?!
KNOCK
KNOCK
ICHIGO...
CAN I COME IN?

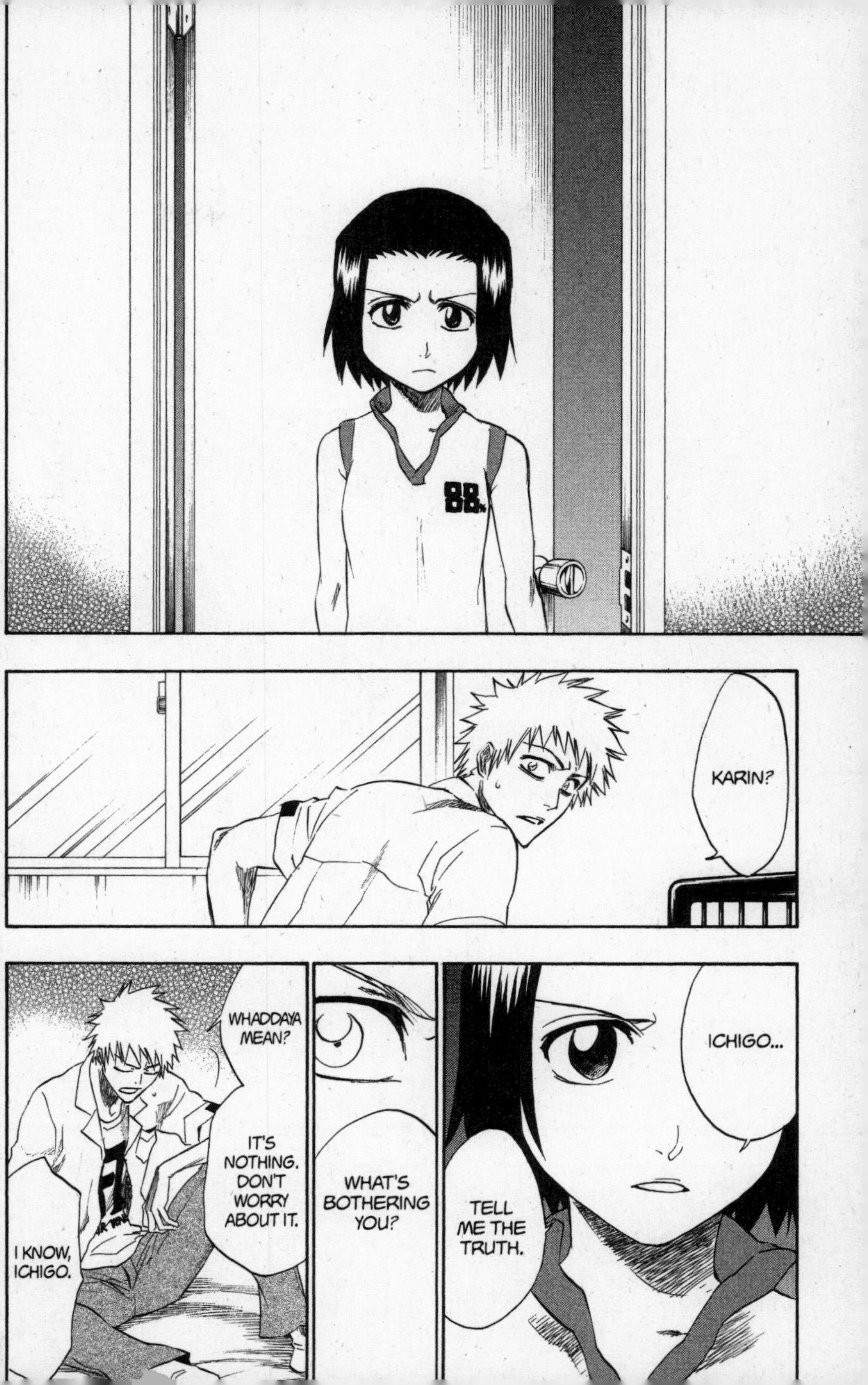
KARIN?
ICHIGO...
TELL ME THE TRUTH.
WHAT'S BOTHERING YOU?
WHADDAYA MEAN?
IT'S NOTHING. DON'T WORRY ABOUT IT.
I KNOW, ICHIGO.

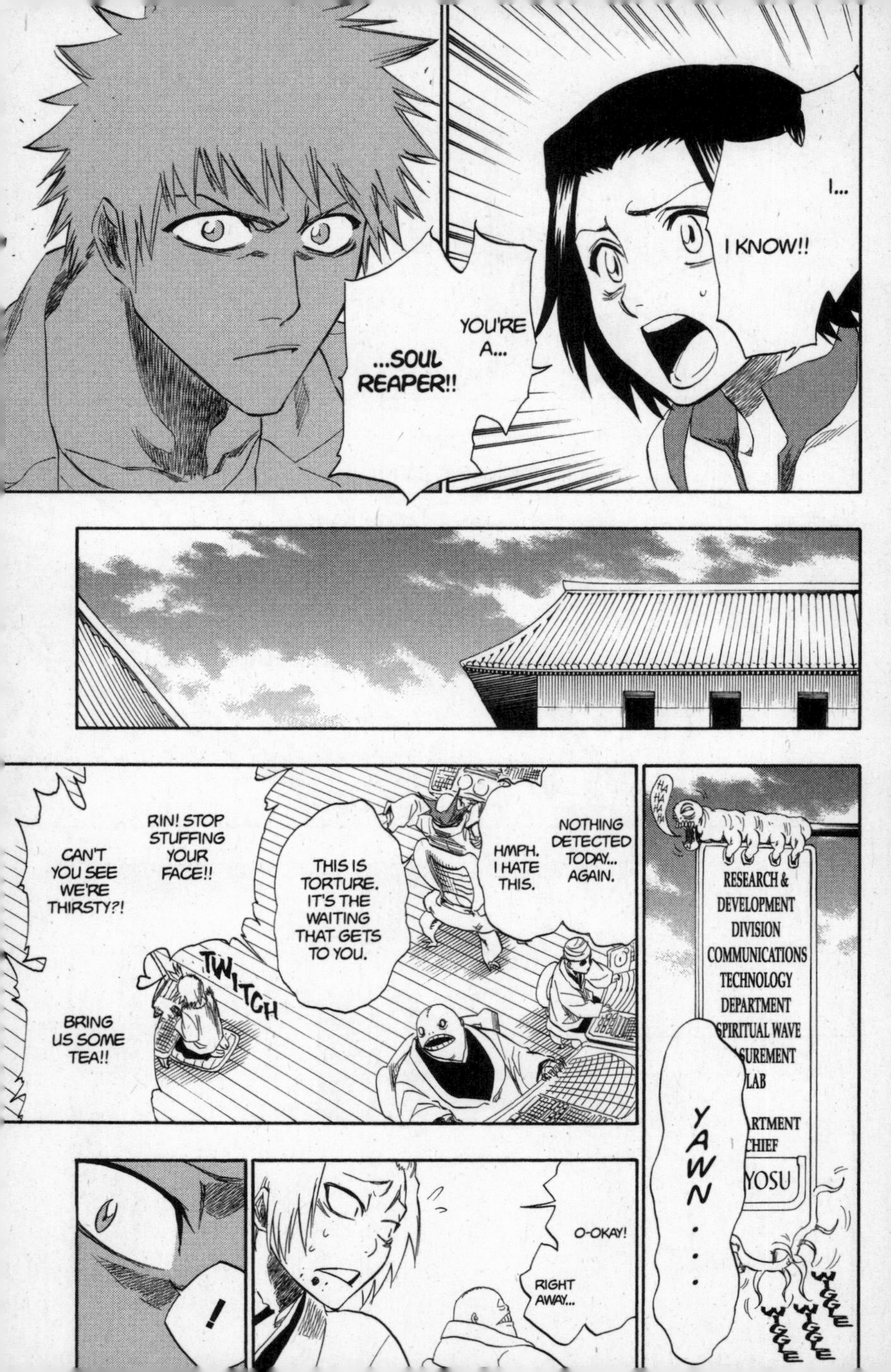
I...
I KNOW!!
YOU'RE A...
...SOUL REAPER!!
HA HA HA HA
RESEARCH & DEVELOPMENT DIVISION COMMUNICATIONS TECHNOLOGY DEPARTMENT SPIRITUAL WAVE
LAB
CHIEF
YAWN...
WIGGLE WIGGLE WIGGLE WIGGLE
NOTHING DETECTED TODAY... AGAIN.
HMPH. I HATE THIS.
THIS IS TORTURE. IT'S THE WAITING THAT GETS TO YOU.
RIN! STOP STUFFING YOUR FACE!!
CAN'T YOU SEE WE'RE THIRSTY?!
TWITCH
BRING US SOME TEA!!
O-OKAY!
RIGHT AWAY...
!

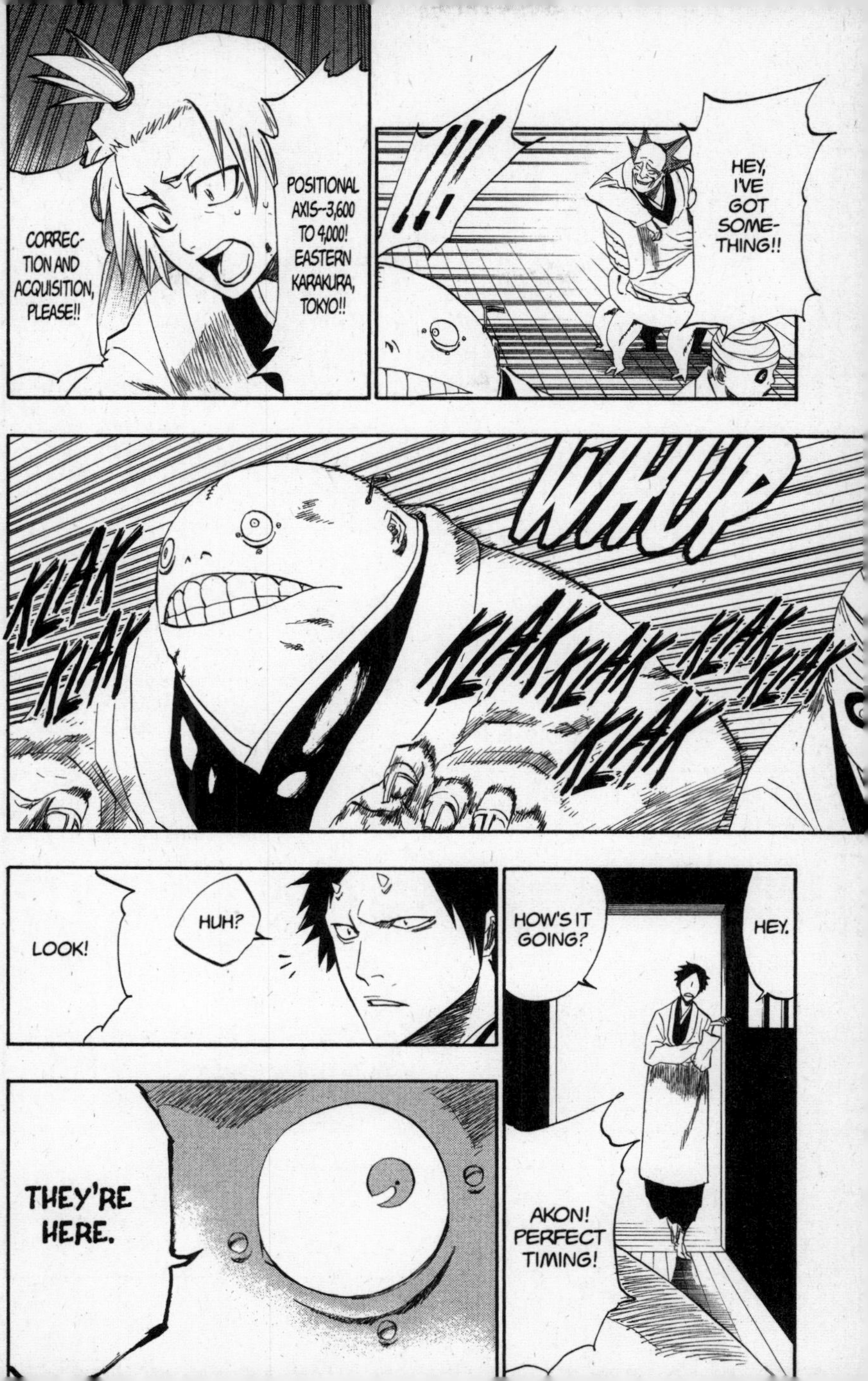
HEY, I'VE GOT SOME-THING!!
!!
POSITIONAL AXIS--3,600 TO 4,000! EASTERN KARAKURA, TOKYO!!
CORREC-TION AND ACQUISITION, PLEASE!!
WHUP
KLAK KLAK KLAK
KLAK KLAK KLAK
KLAK KLAK
HEY.
HOW'S IT GOING?
AKON! PERFECT TIMING!
HUH?
LOOK!
THEY'RE HERE.

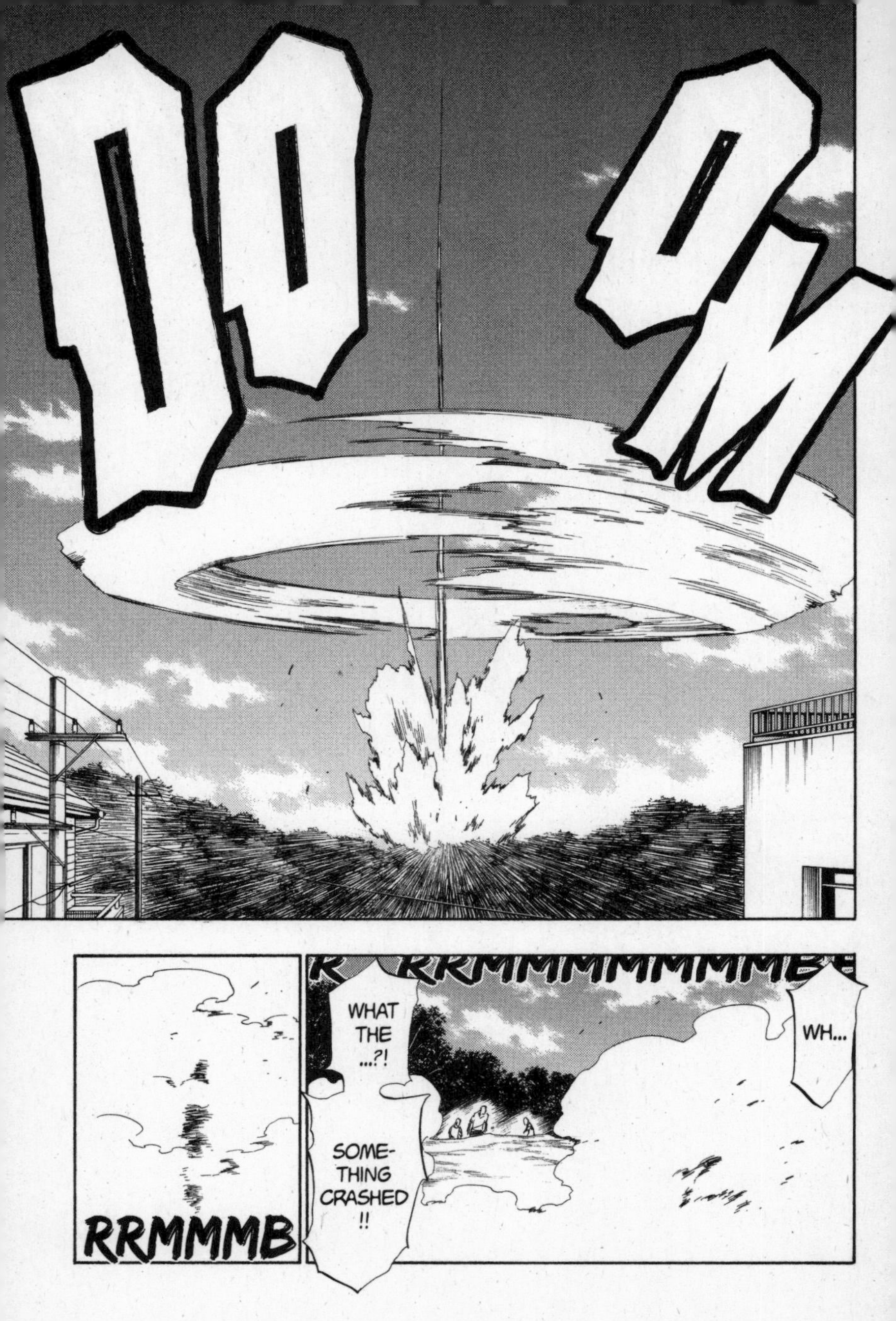
DOOM
R RRMMMMMMMMMB
WH...
WHAT THE ...?!
SOME-THING CRASHED !!
RRMMMB

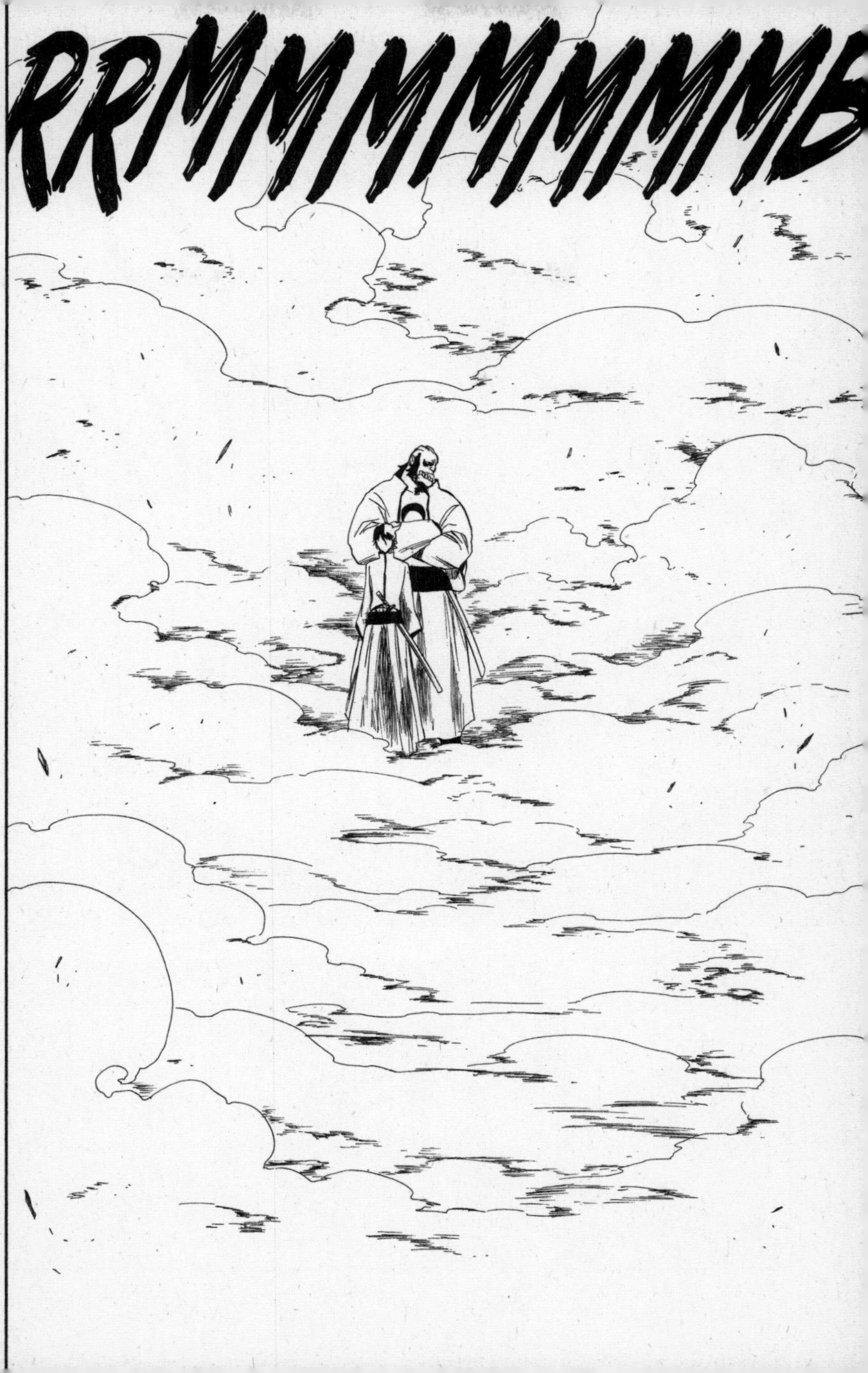
RRMMMMMMMB

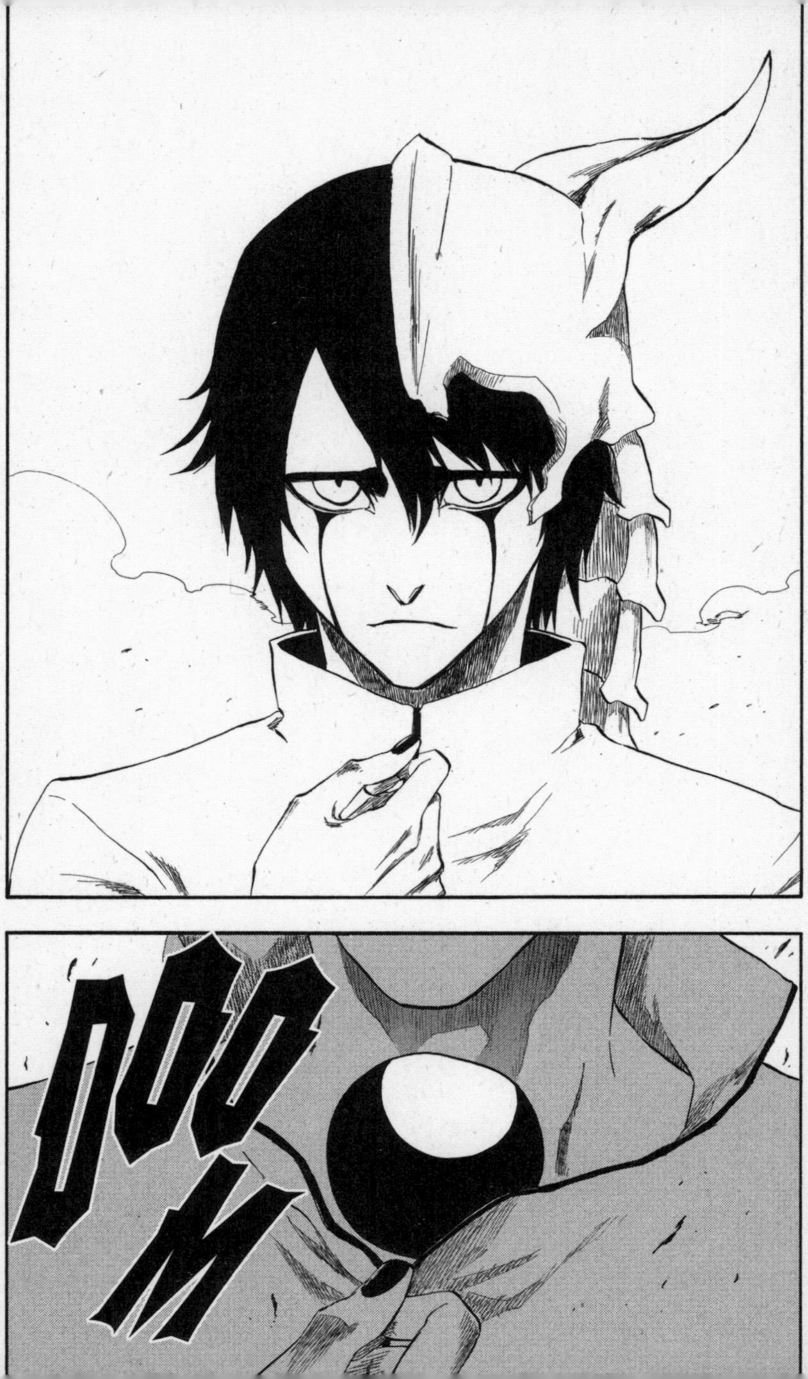
DOOM

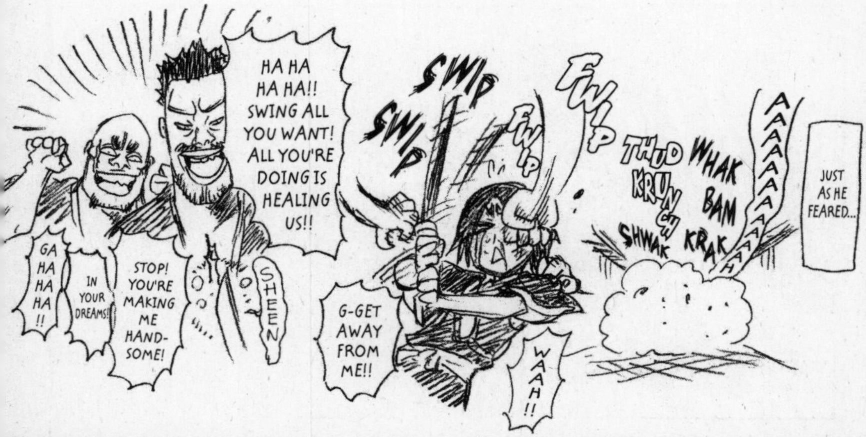
JUST AS HE FEARED...
AAAAAAAAAAAAAH
WHAK
BAM
KRAK
THUD
KRUNCH
SHWAK
FWIP
WAAH!!
FWIP
SWIP
SWIP
G-GET AWAY FROM ME!!
HA HA HA HA!! SWING ALL YOU WANT! ALL YOU'RE DOING IS HEALING US!!
SHEEN
STOP! YOU'RE MAKING ME HAND-SOME!
IN YOUR DREAMS!
GA HA HA HA!!

191. Conquistadores 2 (Screaming Symphony)

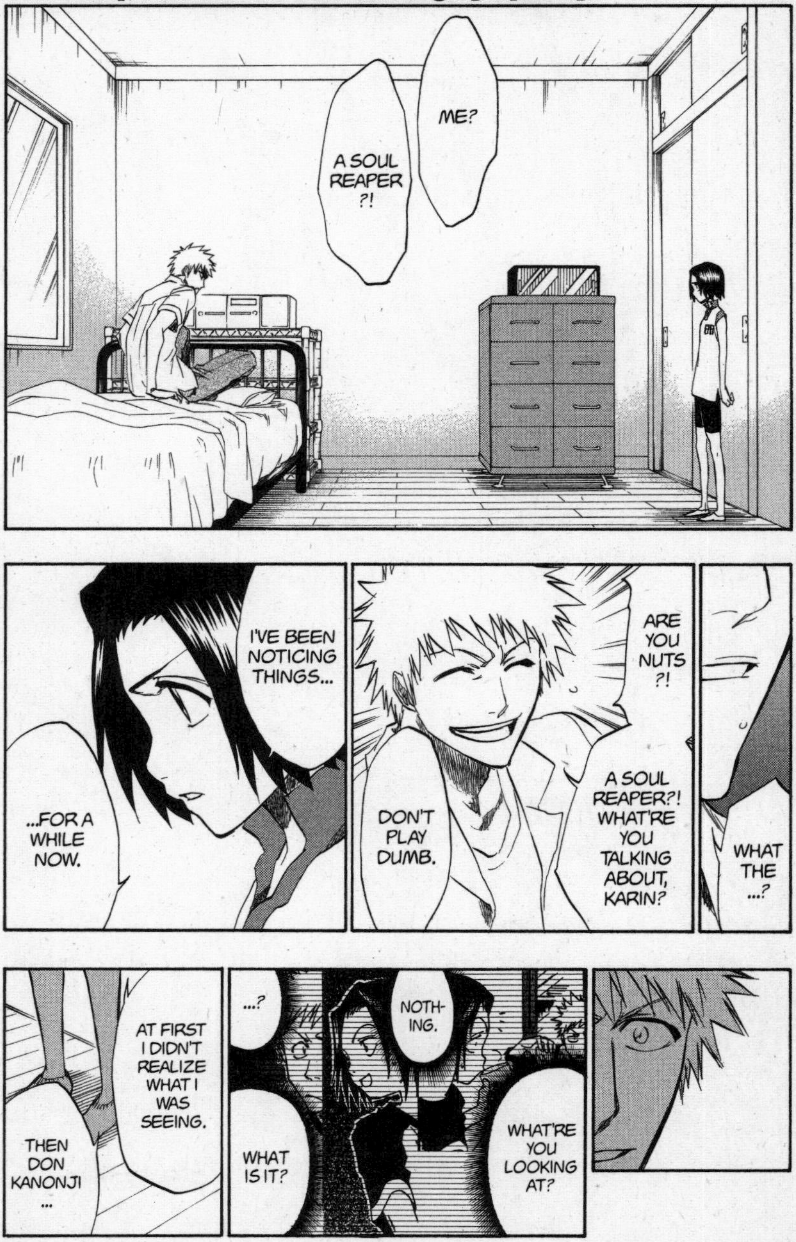
ME?
A SOUL REAPER ?!
WHAT THE ...?
ARE YOU NUTS ?!
A SOUL REAPER?! WHAT'RE YOU TALKING ABOUT, KARIN?
DON'T PLAY DUMB.
I'VE BEEN NOTICING THINGS...
...FOR A WHILE NOW.
WHAT'RE YOU LOOKING AT?
...?
WHAT IS IT?
NOTH-ING.
AT FIRST I DIDN'T REALIZE WHAT I WAS SEEING.
THEN DON KANONJI ...

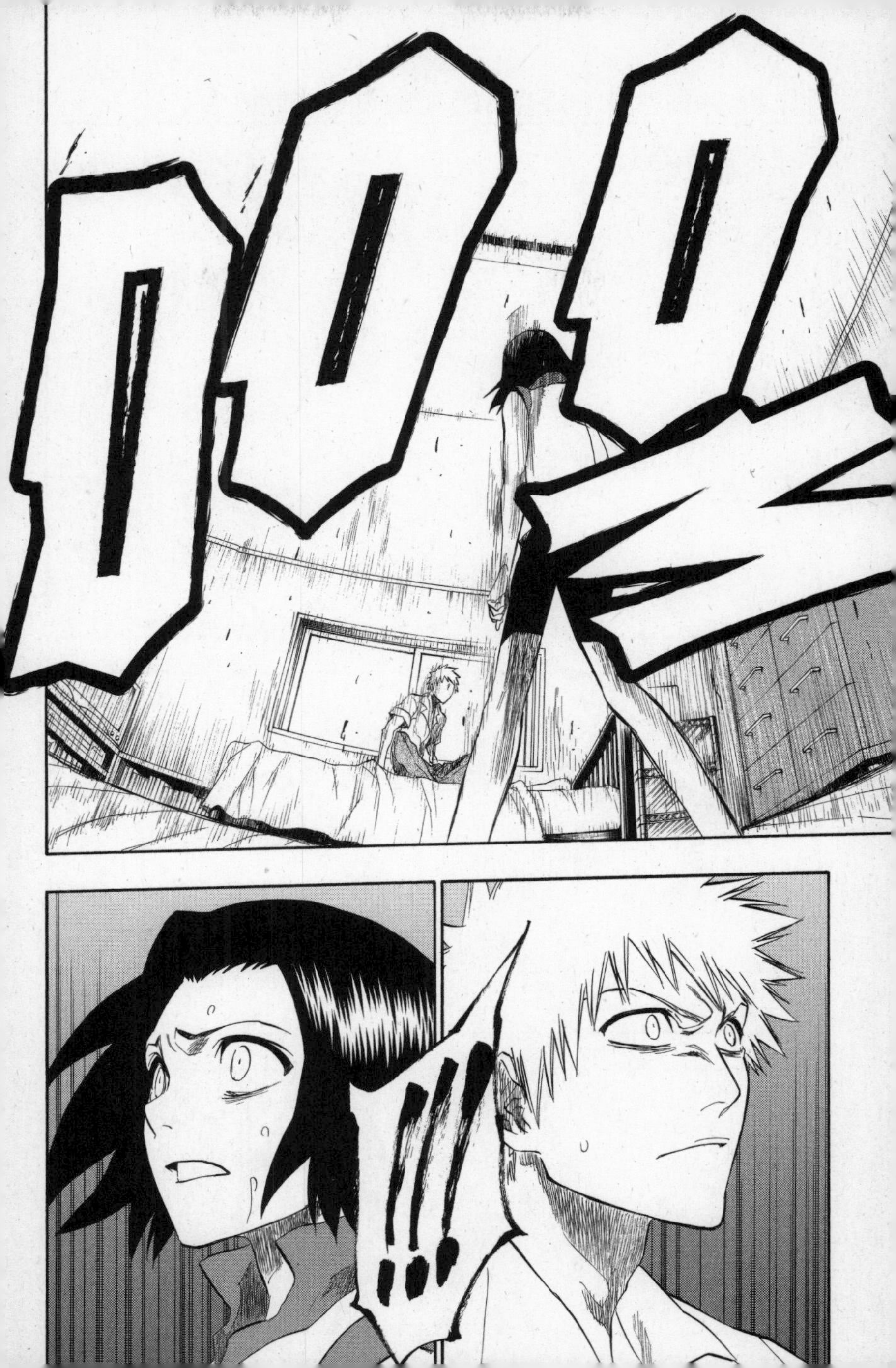

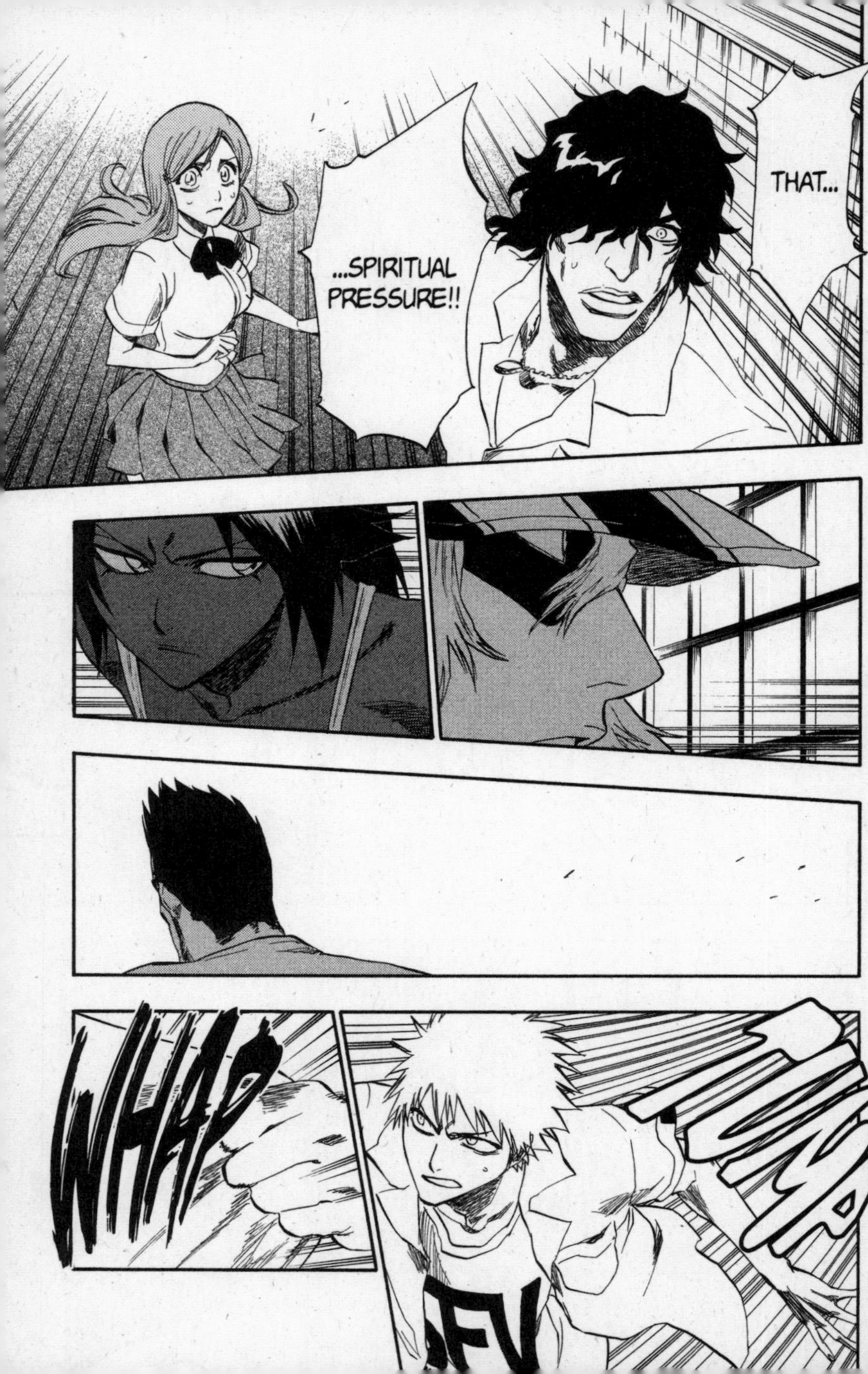
THAT...
...SPIRITUAL PRESSURE!!
THUMP
WHAP

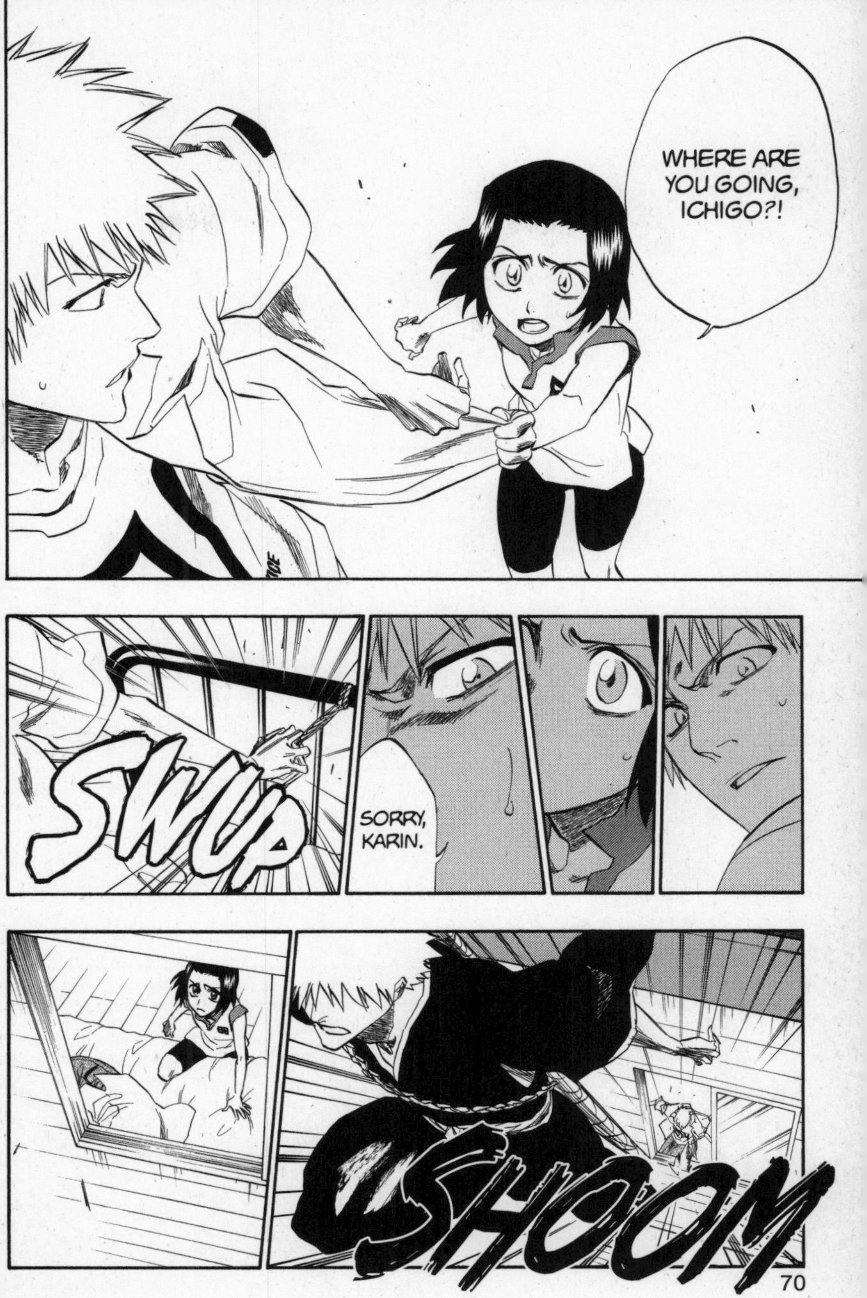
WHERE ARE YOU GOING, ICHIGO?!
SORRY, KARIN.
SWUP
SHOOM

191. Conquistadores 2

(Screaming Symphony)

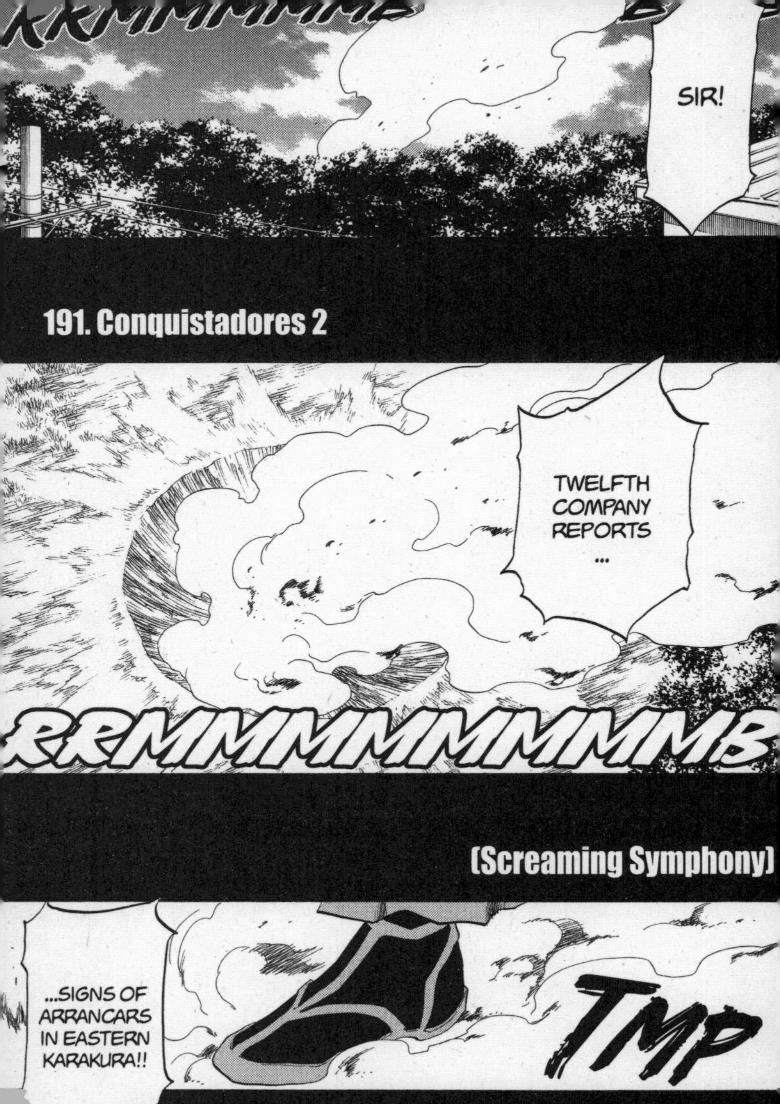
SIR!
TWELFTH COMPANY REPORTS ...
RRMMMMMMMMMMB
TMP
...SIGNS OF ARRANCARS IN EASTERN KARAKURA!!

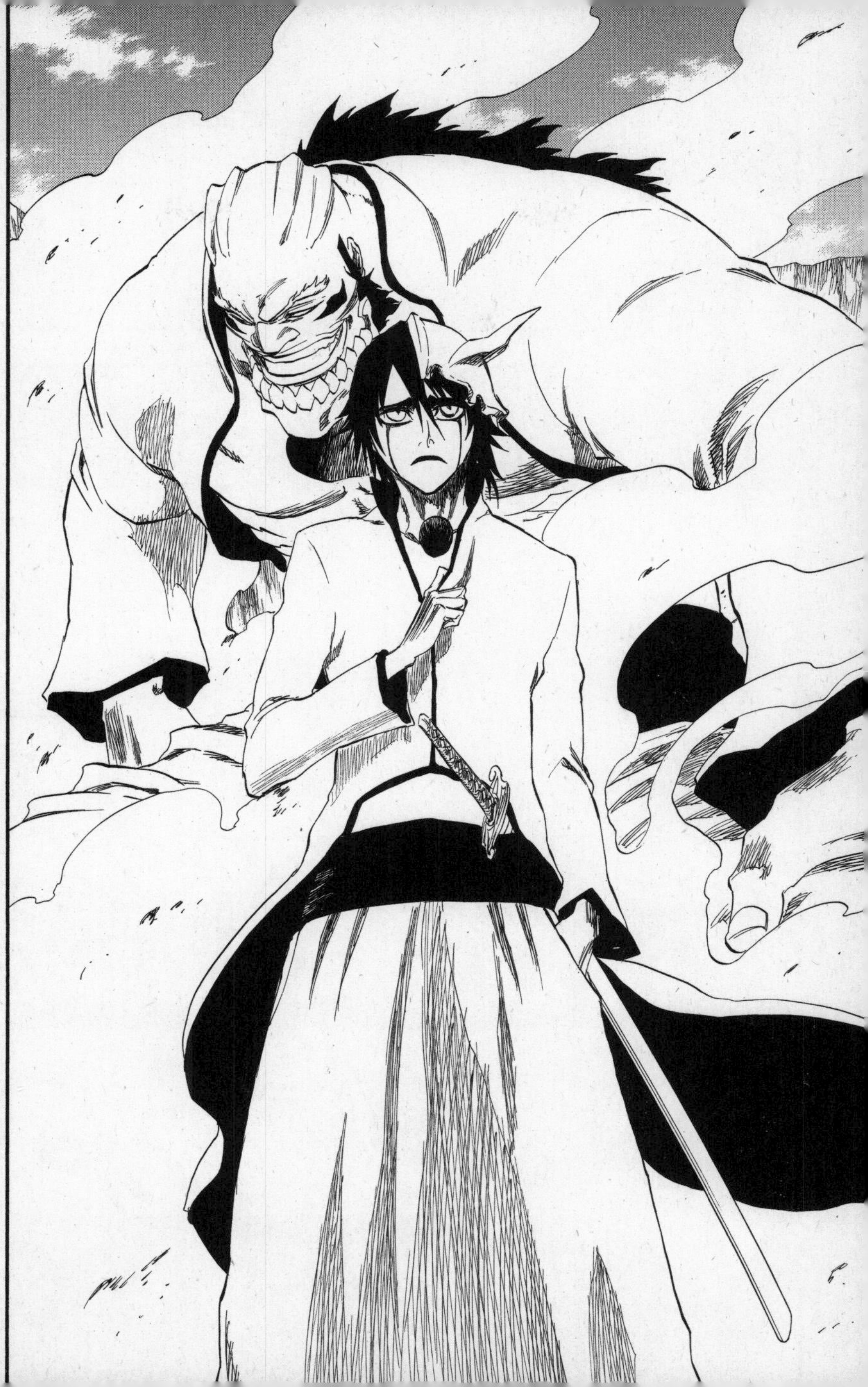

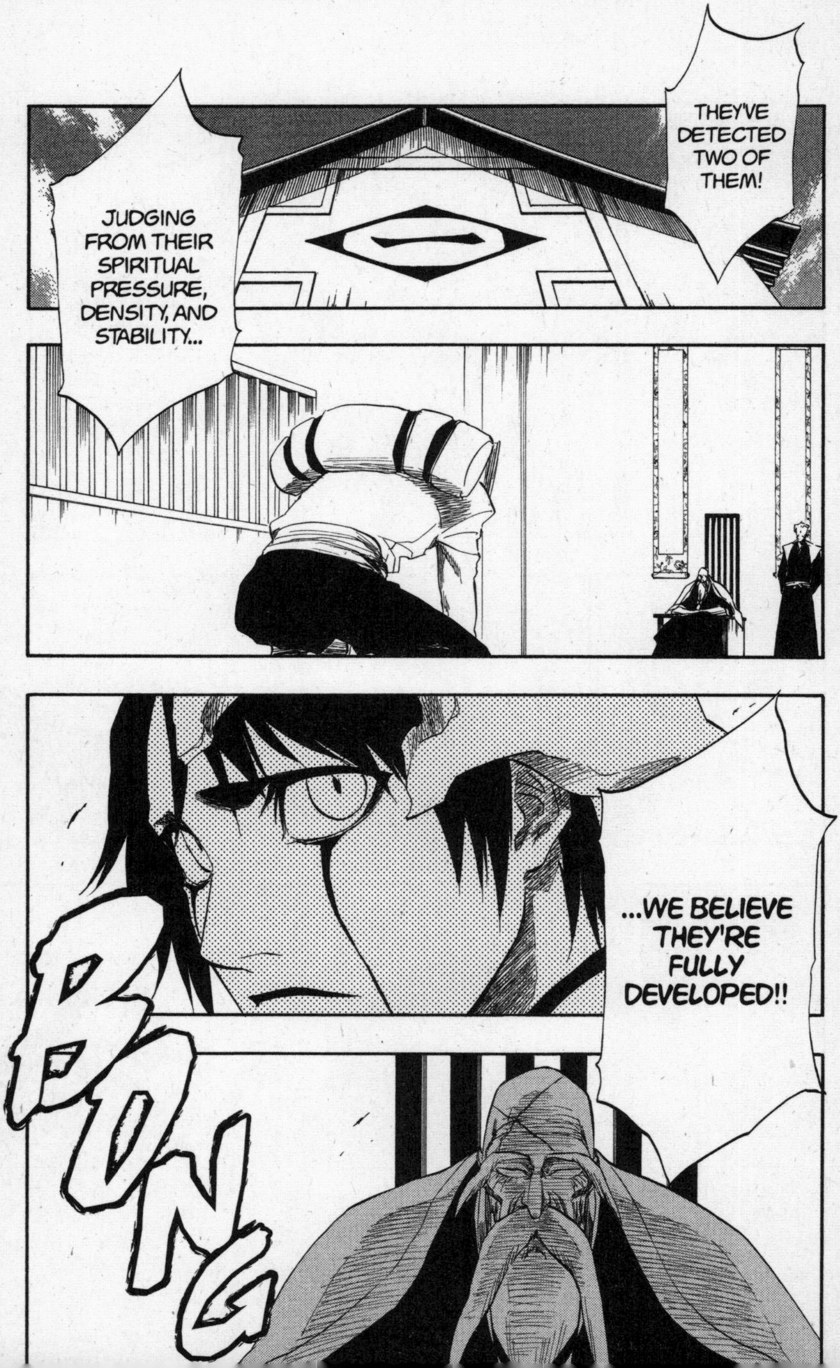
THEY'VE DETECTED TWO OF THEM!
JUDGING FROM THEIR SPIRITUAL PRESSURE, DENSITY, AND STABILITY...
...WE BELIEVE THEY'RE FULLY DEVELOPED!!
BONG

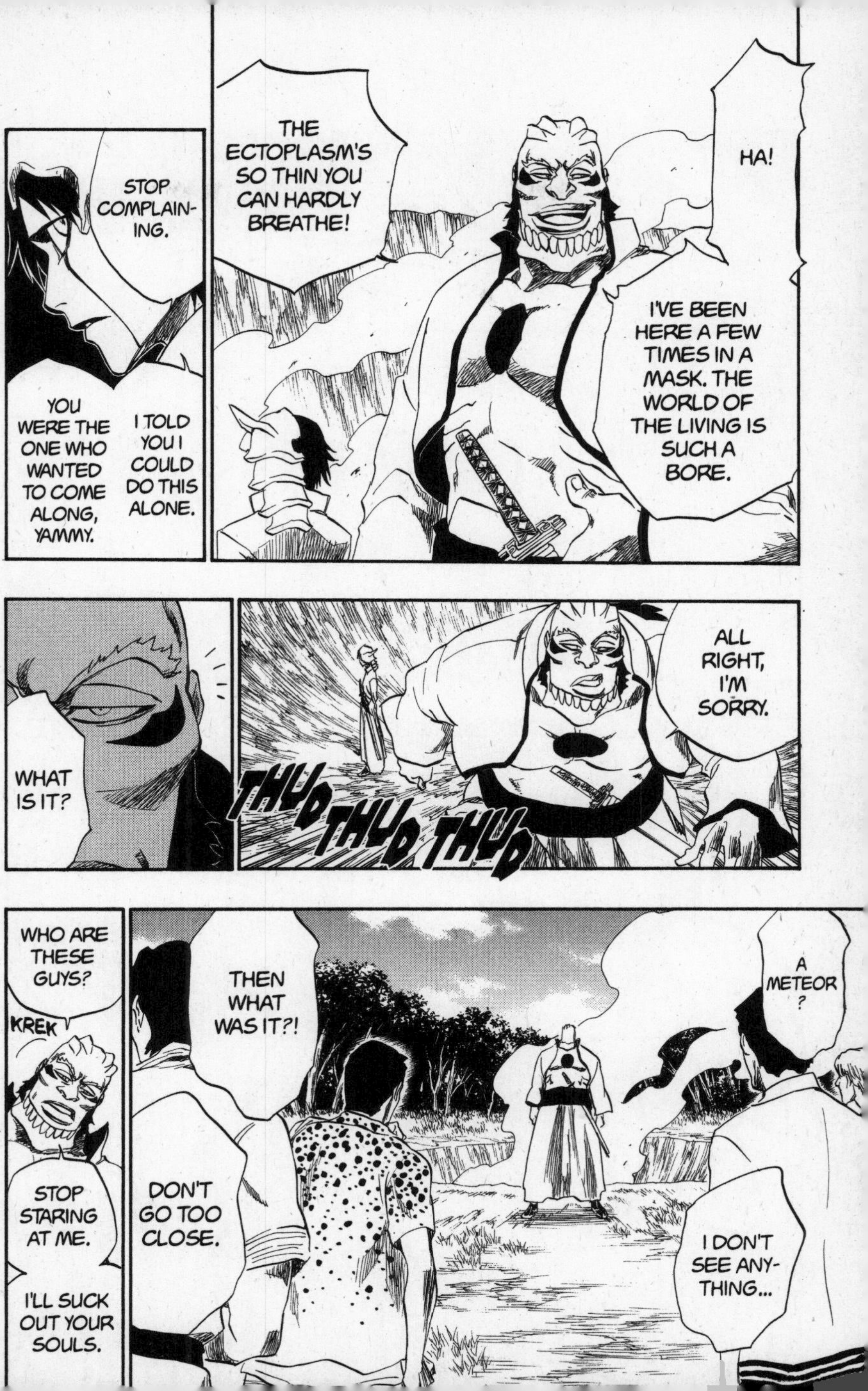
HA!
THE ECTOPLASM'S SO THIN YOU CAN HARDLY BREATHE!
I'VE BEEN HERE A FEW TIMES IN A MASK. THE WORLD OF THE LIVING IS SUCH A BORE.
STOP COMPLAINING.
I TOLD YOU I COULD DO THIS ALONE.
YOU WERE THE ONE WHO WANTED TO COME ALONG, YAMMY.
ALL RIGHT, I'M SORRY.
THUD THUD THUD
WHAT IS IT?
A METEOR?
THEN WHAT WAS IT?!
I DON'T SEE ANYTHING...
DON'T GO TOO CLOSE.
WHO ARE THESE GUYS?
KREK
STOP STARING AT ME.
I'LL SUCK OUT YOUR SOULS.

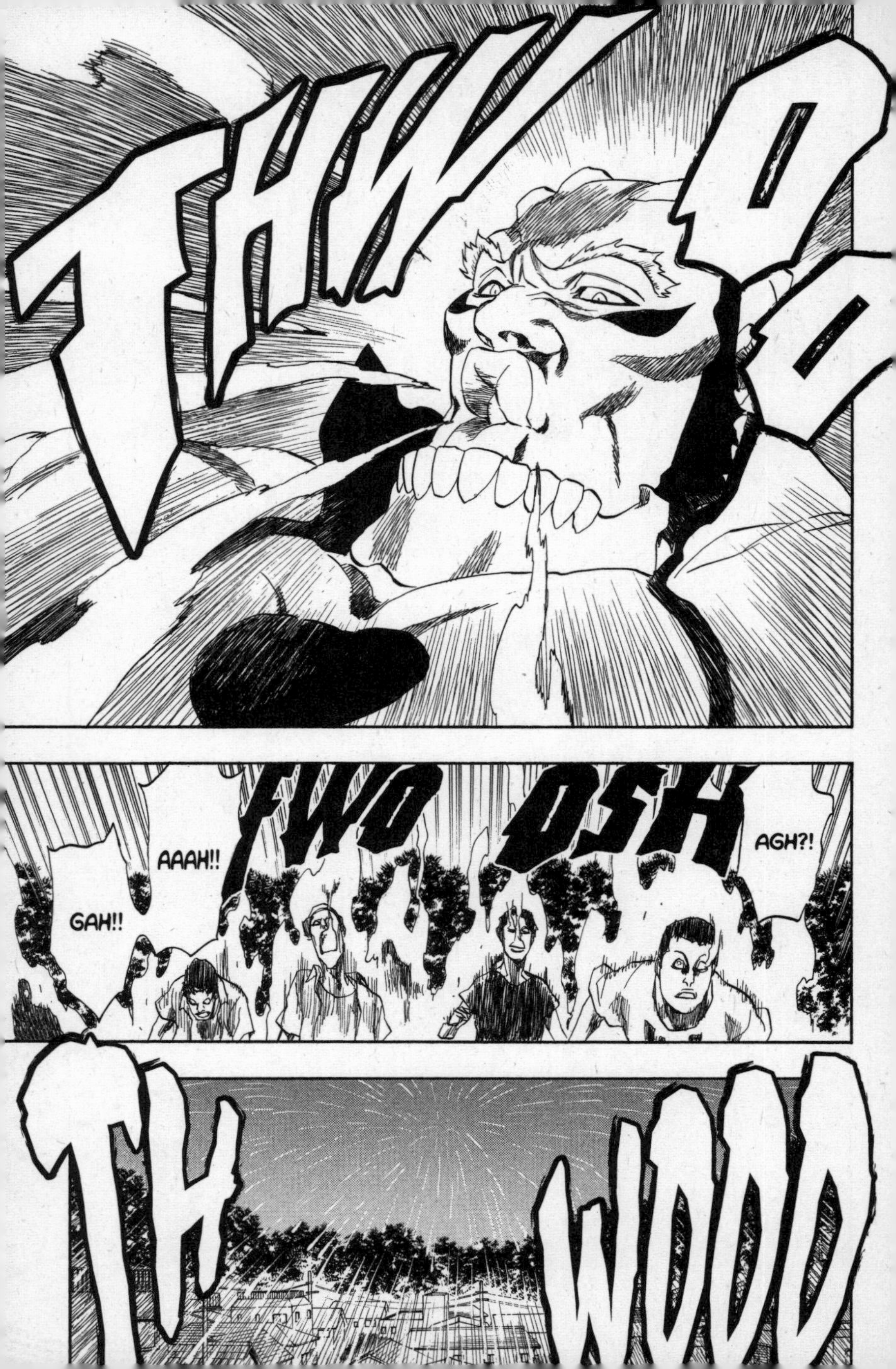
THWOOD
TWOOSH
AGH?!
AAAH!!
GAH!!
THWOOD

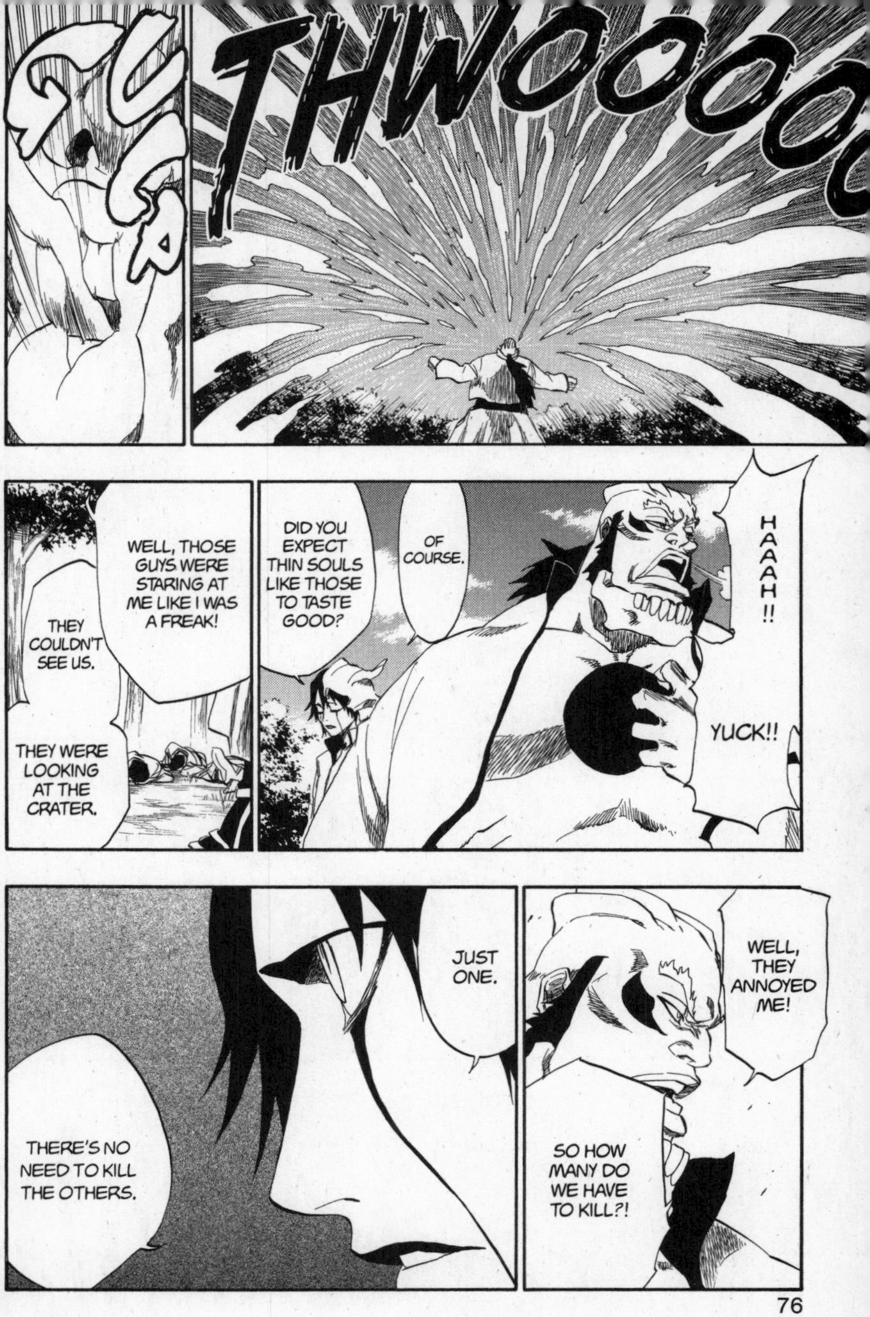
THWOOOO
GULP
HAAAH!!
YUCK!!
OF COURSE.
DID YOU EXPECT THIN SOULS LIKE THOSE TO TASTE GOOD?
WELL, THOSE GUYS WERE STARING AT ME LIKE I WAS A FREAK!
THEY COULDN'T SEE US.
THEY WERE LOOKING AT THE CRATER.
WELL, THEY ANNOYED ME!
SO HOW MANY DO WE HAVE TO KILL?!
JUST ONE.
THERE'S NO NEED TO KILL THE OTHERS.

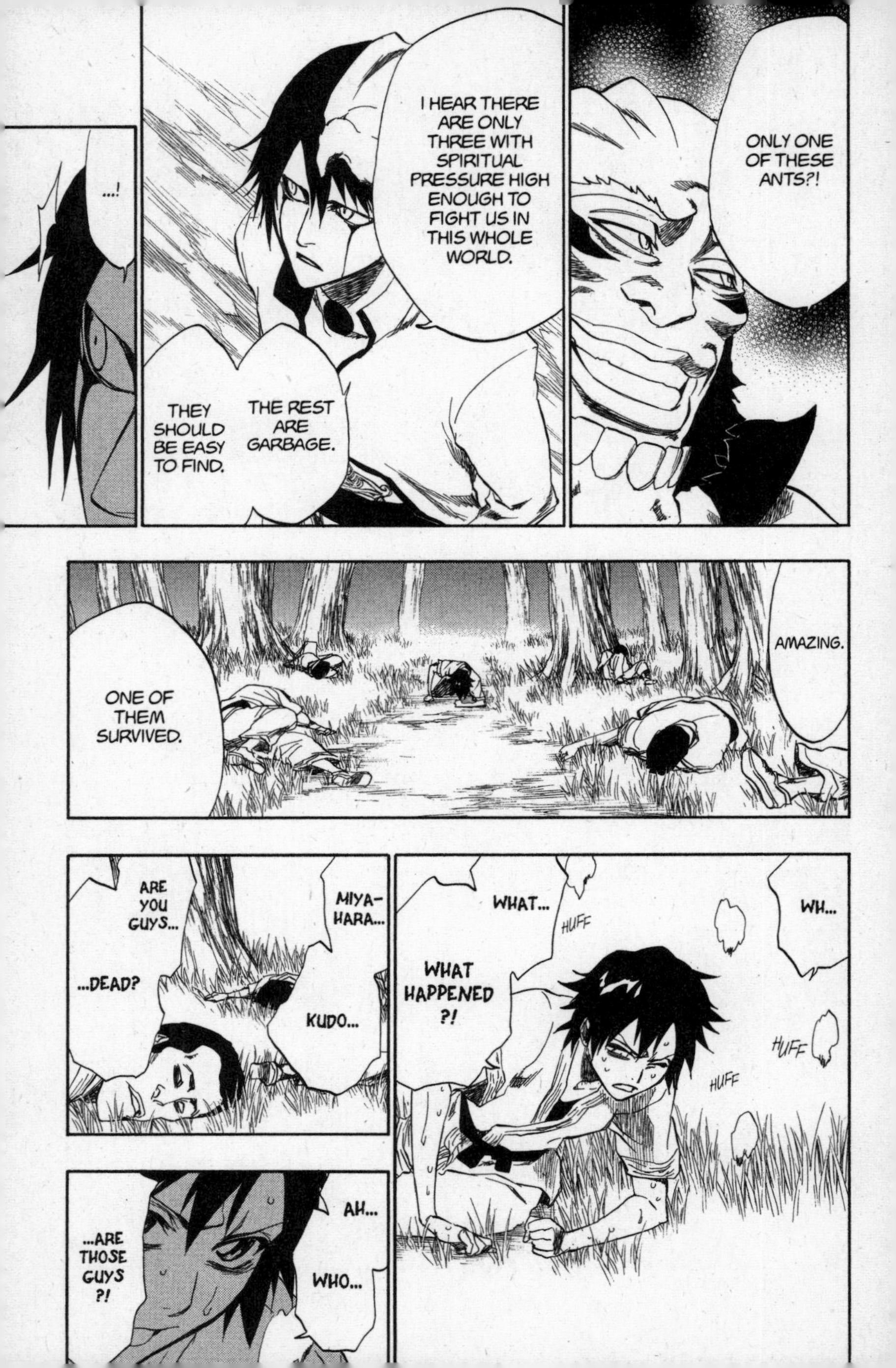
ONLY ONE OF THESE ANTS?!
I HEAR THERE ARE ONLY THREE WITH SPIRITUAL PRESSURE HIGH ENOUGH TO FIGHT US IN THIS WHOLE WORLD.
THE REST ARE GARBAGE.
THEY SHOULD BE EASY TO FIND.
...!
AMAZING.
ONE OF THEM SURVIVED.
WH...
WHAT...
HUFF
WHAT HAPPENED ?!
HUFF
HUFF
MIYA-HARA...
KUDO...
ARE YOU GUYS...
...DEAD?
AH...
WHO...
...ARE THOSE GUYS ?!

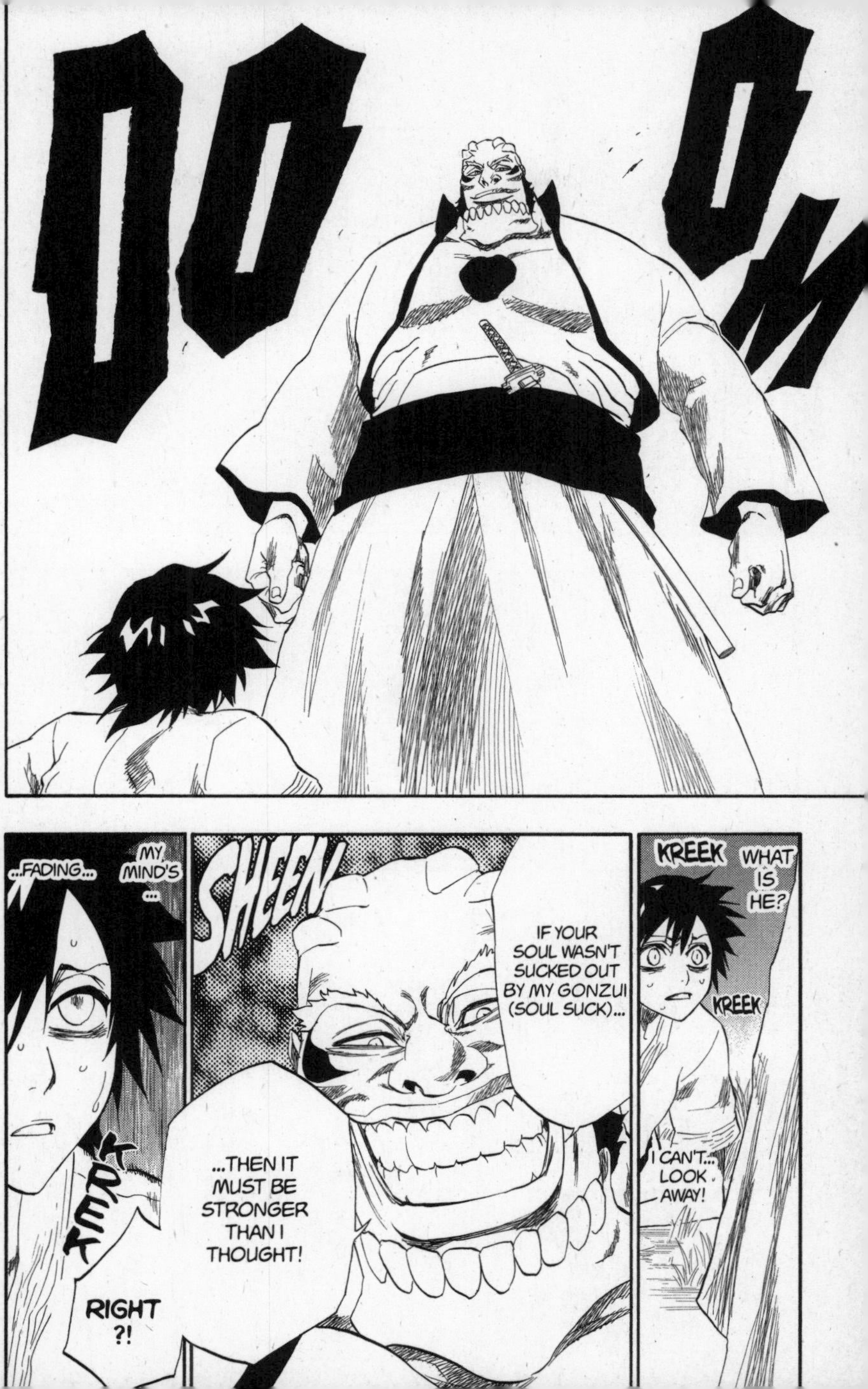
DOOM
KREEK
WHAT IS HE?
KREEK
I CAN'T... LOOK AWAY!
SHEEN
IF YOUR SOUL WASN'T SUCKED OUT BY MY GONZUI (SOUL SUCK)...
...THEN IT MUST BE STRONGER THAN I THOUGHT!
MY MIND'S ...
...FADING...
KREEK
RIGHT ?!

READ THIS WAY

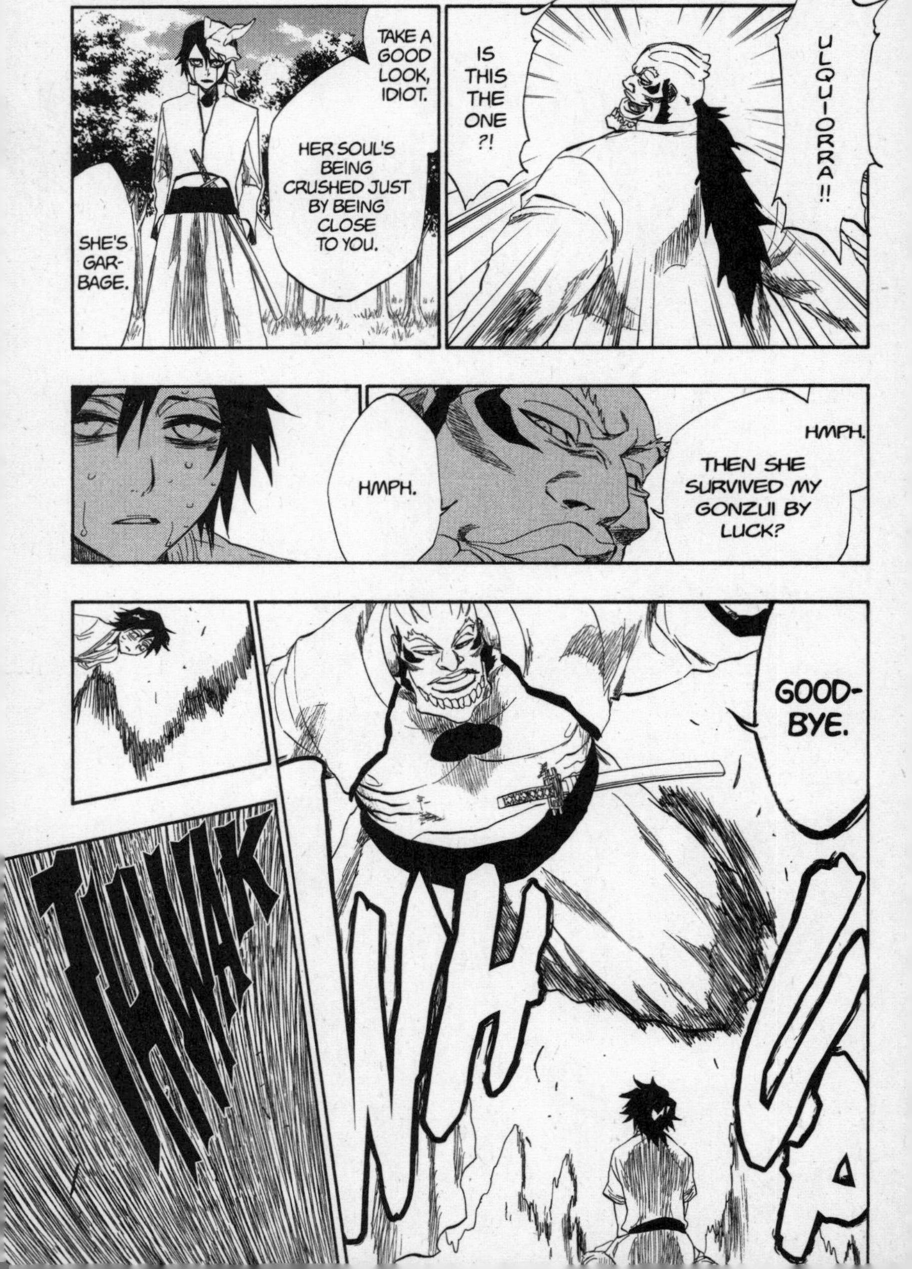
ULQUIORRA!!
IS THIS THE ONE?!
TAKE A GOOD LOOK, IDIOT.
HER SOUL'S BEING CRUSHED JUST BY BEING CLOSE TO YOU.
SHE'S GAR-BAGE.
HMPH.
THEN SHE SURVIVED MY GONZUI BY LUCK?
HMPH.
GOOD-BYE.
THWAK

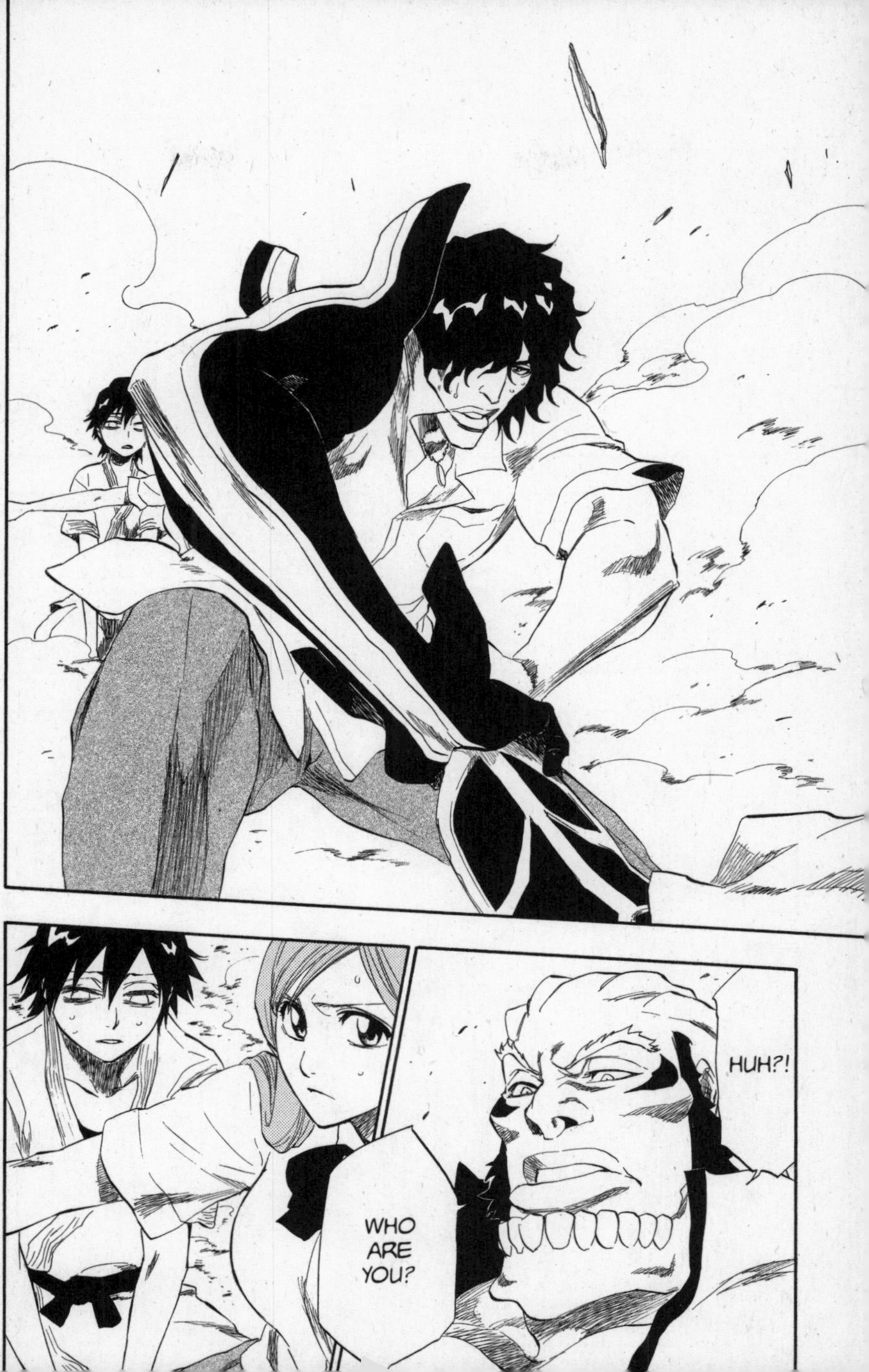
HUH?!
WHO ARE YOU?

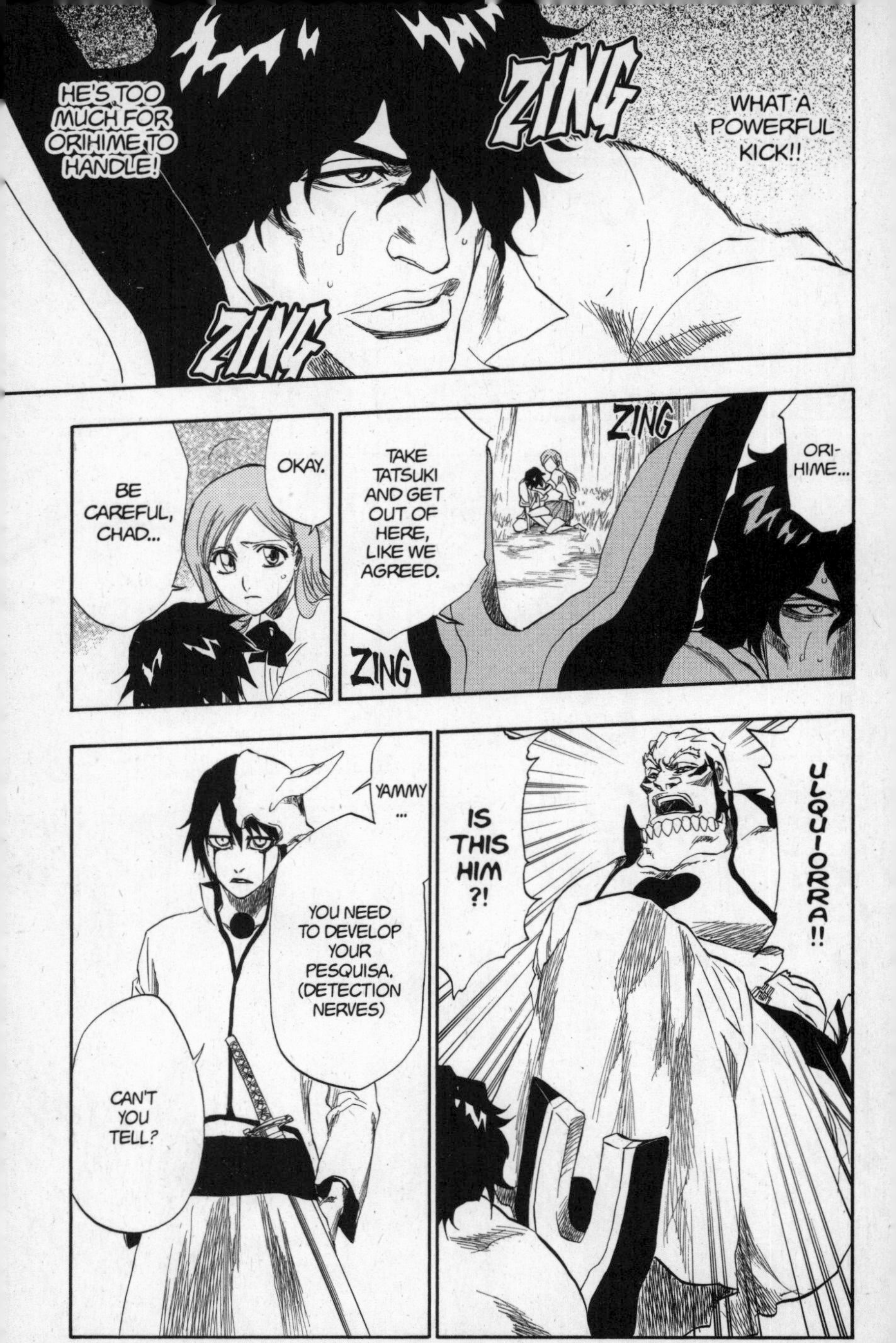
WHAT A POWERFUL KICK!!
ZING
HE'S TOO MUCH FOR ORIHIME TO HANDLE!
ZING
ORI-HIME...
ZING
TAKE TATSUKI AND GET OUT OF HERE, LIKE WE AGREED.
ZING
OKAY.
BE CAREFUL, CHAD...
ULQUIORRA!!
IS THIS HIM?!
YAMMY...
YOU NEED TO DEVELOP YOUR PESQUISA. (DETECTION NERVES)
CAN'T YOU TELL?

HE'S GARBAGE, TOO.

HE IS?!

THO

FWO

OM

OSH

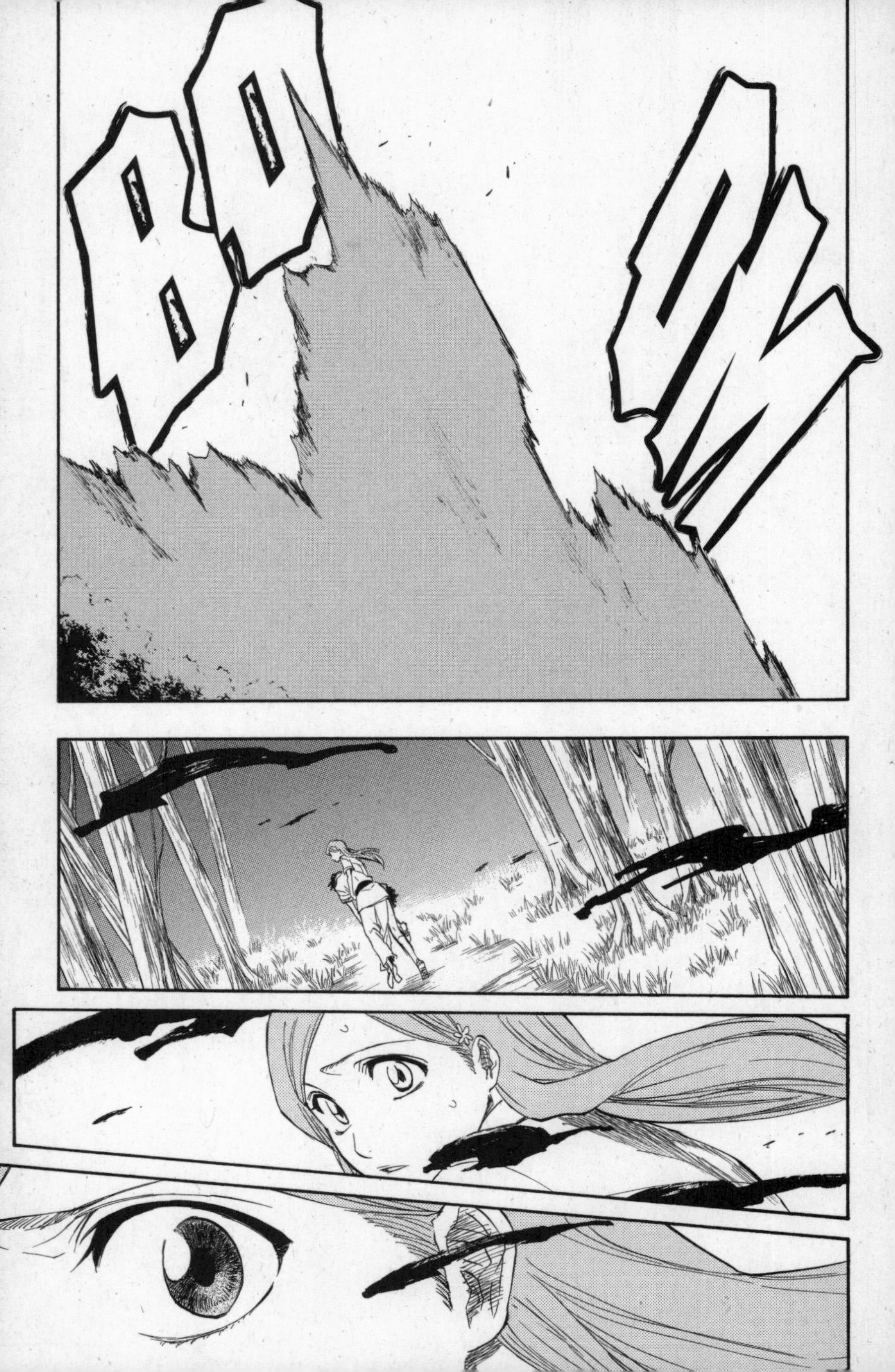
BOOM

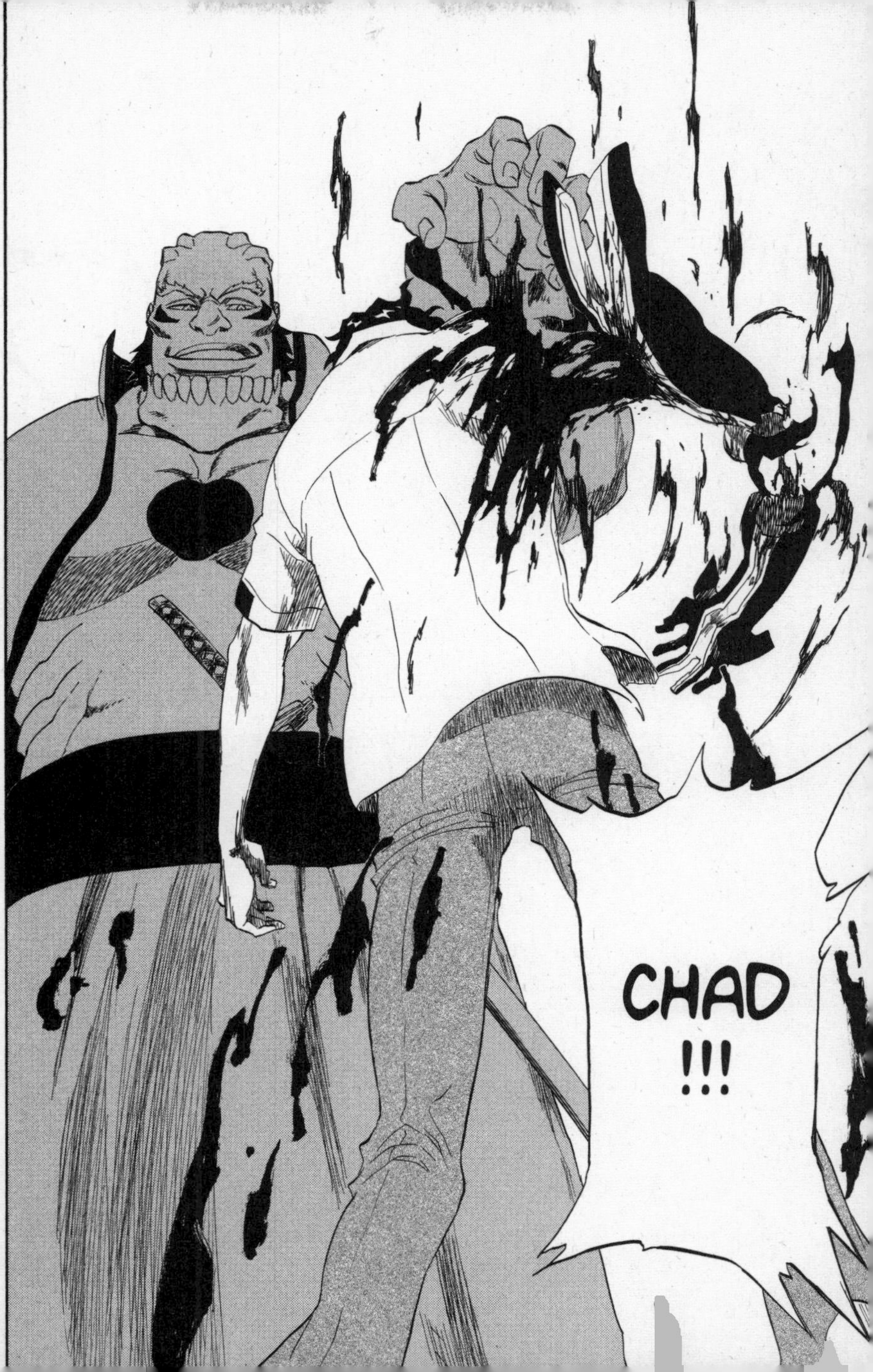
CHAD
!!!

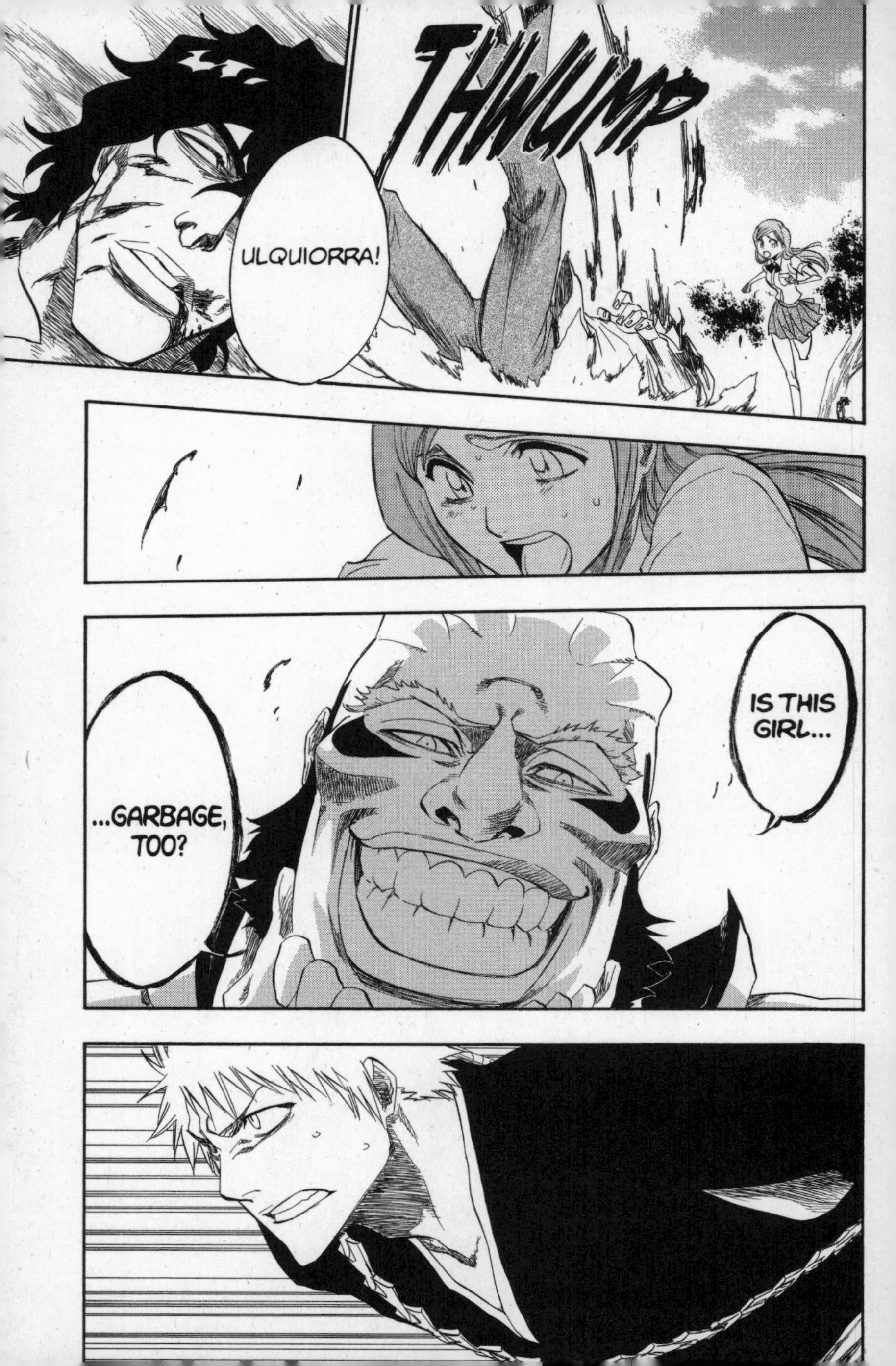
THWUMP
ULQUIORRA!
IS THIS GIRL...
...GARBAGE, TOO?

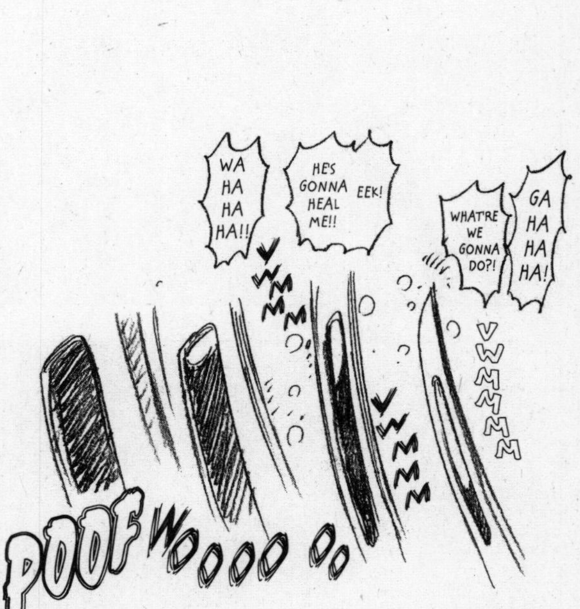
GA HA HA HA!
WHAT'RE WE GONNA DO?!
EEK!
HE'S GONNA HEAL ME!!
WA HA HA HA!!
VWMMMM
VWMMM
VWMMM
POOF
WOOOO OO

192. Conquistadores 3 (Hounded Priestess)

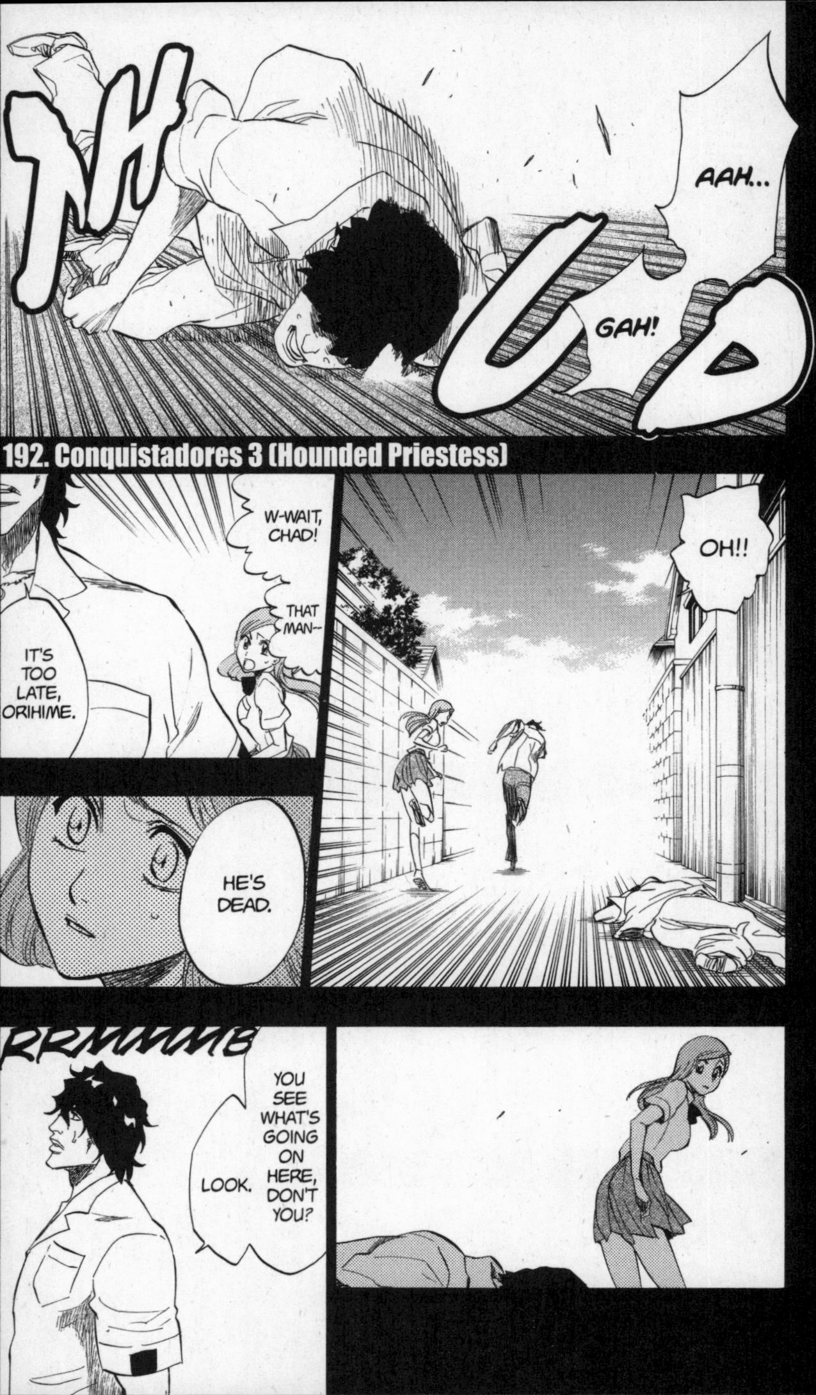

AAH...
GAH!
THUD
OH!!
W-WAIT, CHAD!
THAT MAN--
IT'S TOO LATE, ORIHIME.
HE'S DEAD.
RRMMMB
YOU SEE WHAT'S GOING ON HERE, DON'T YOU?
LOOK.

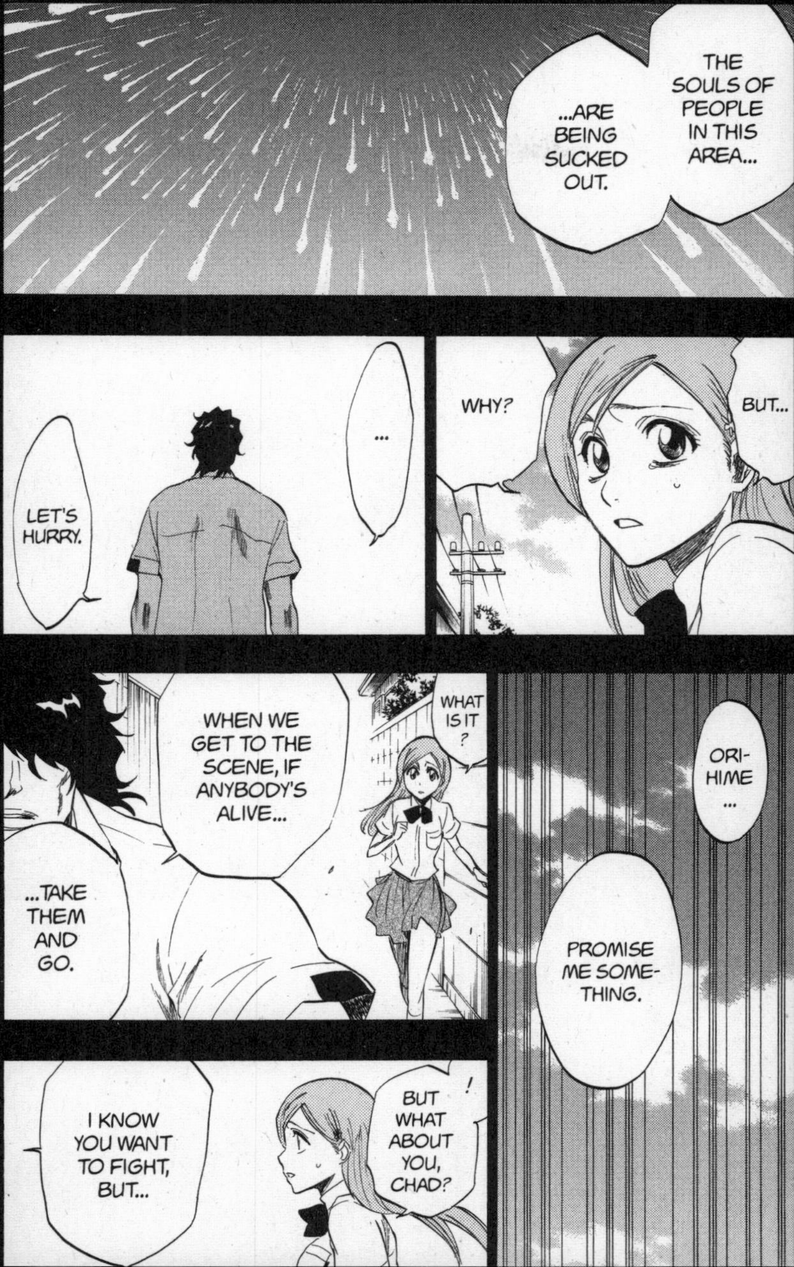
THE SOULS OF PEOPLE IN THIS AREA...
...ARE BEING SUCKED OUT.
BUT...
WHY?
...
LET'S HURRY.
ORI-HIME...
PROMISE ME SOME-THING.
WHAT IS IT?
WHEN WE GET TO THE SCENE, IF ANYBODY'S ALIVE...
...TAKE THEM AND GO.
!
BUT WHAT ABOUT YOU, CHAD?
I KNOW YOU WANT TO FIGHT, BUT...

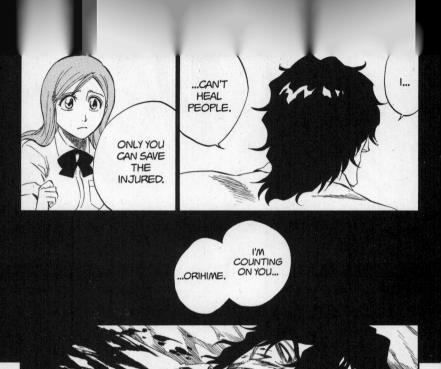

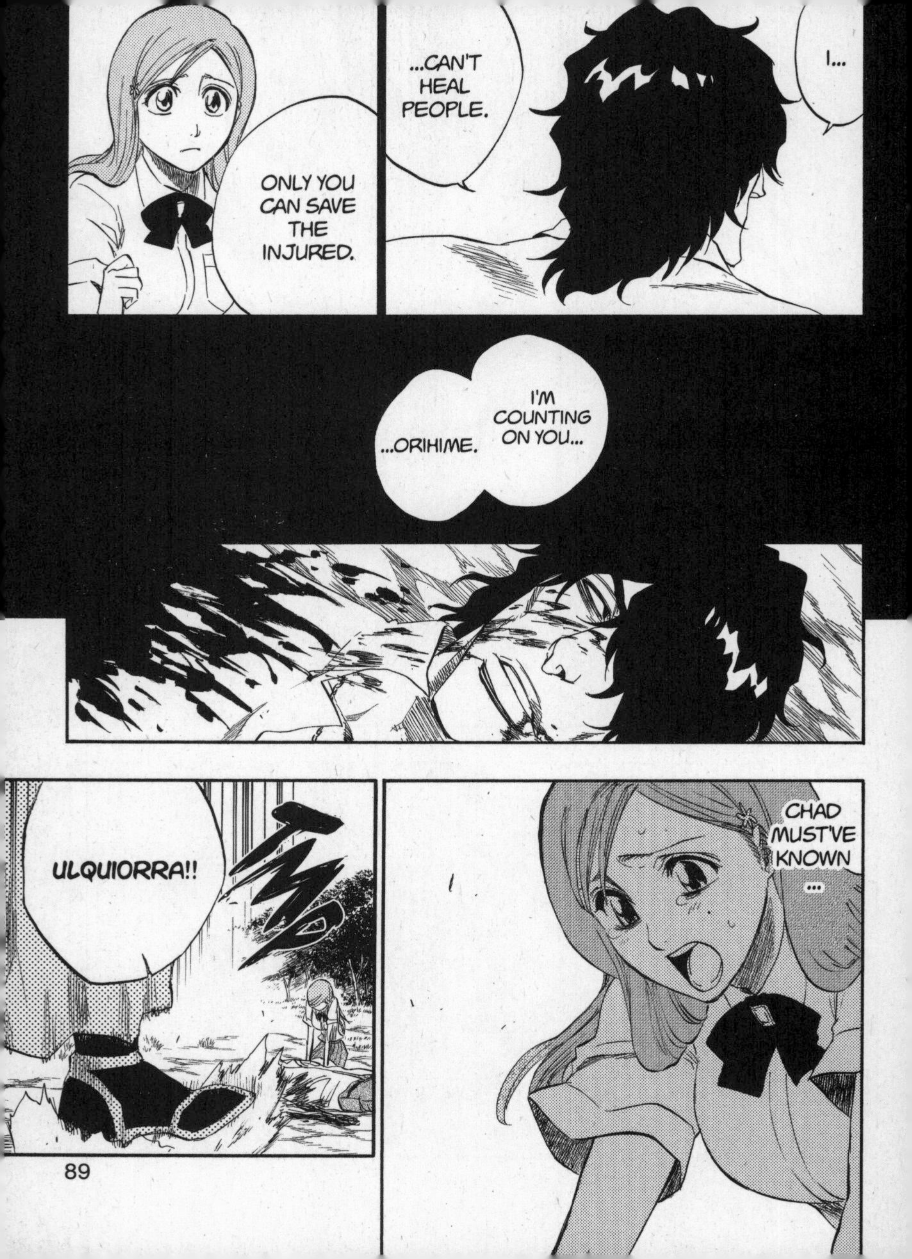
I...
...CAN'T HEAL PEOPLE.
ONLY YOU CAN SAVE THE INJURED.
I'M COUNTING ON YOU...
...ORIHIME.
CHAD MUST'VE KNOWN ...
ULQUIORRA!!

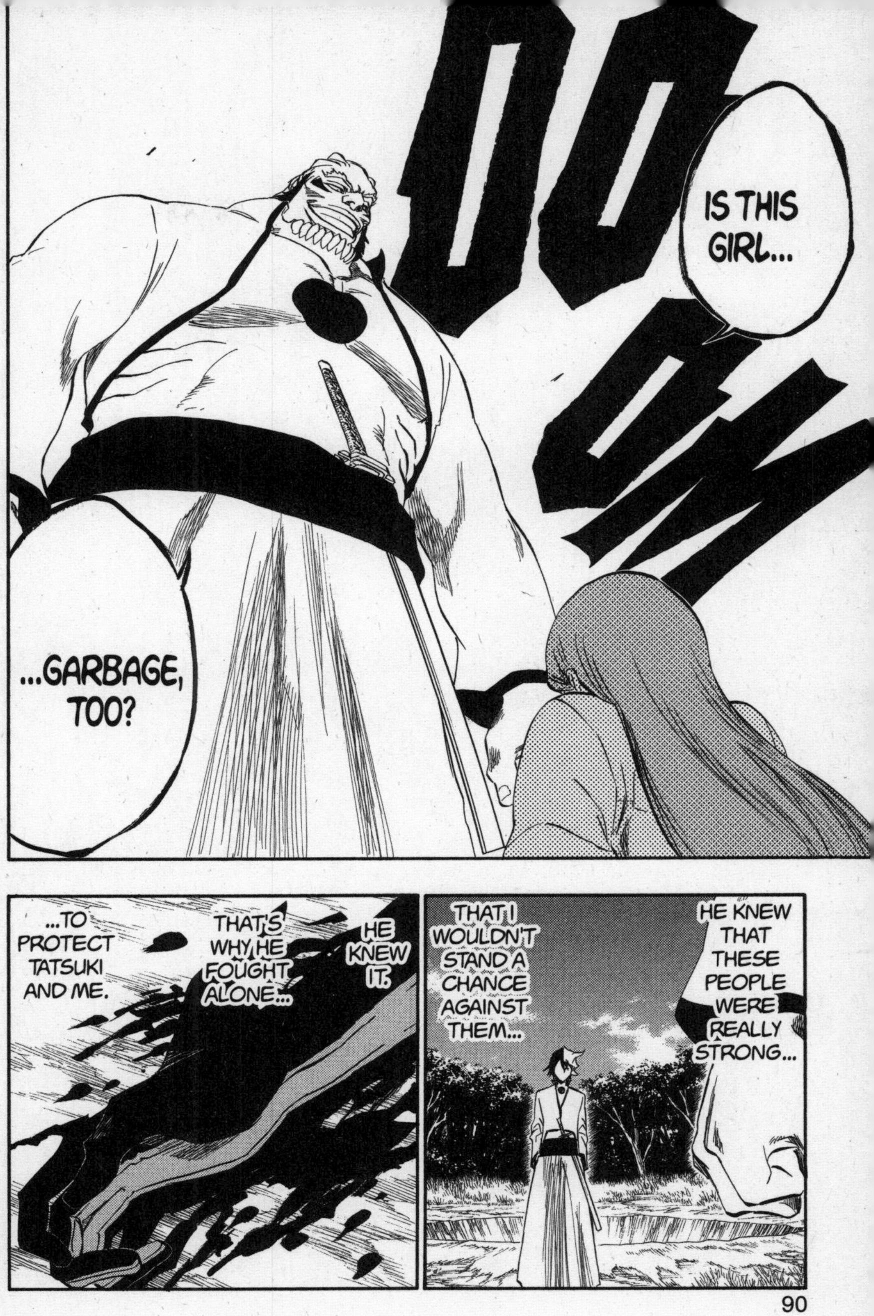
IS THIS GIRL...
DOOM
...GARBAGE, TOO?
HE KNEW THAT THESE PEOPLE WERE REALLY STRONG...
THAT I WOULDN'T STAND A CHANCE AGAINST THEM...
HE KNEW IT.
THAT'S WHY HE FOUGHT ALONE...
...TO PROTECT TATSUKI AND ME.

UH-
HUH.

GARBAGE.

REALLY
?!

WHOOOM

SANTEN
KESSHUN.
(THREE-
GOD
SHIELD)

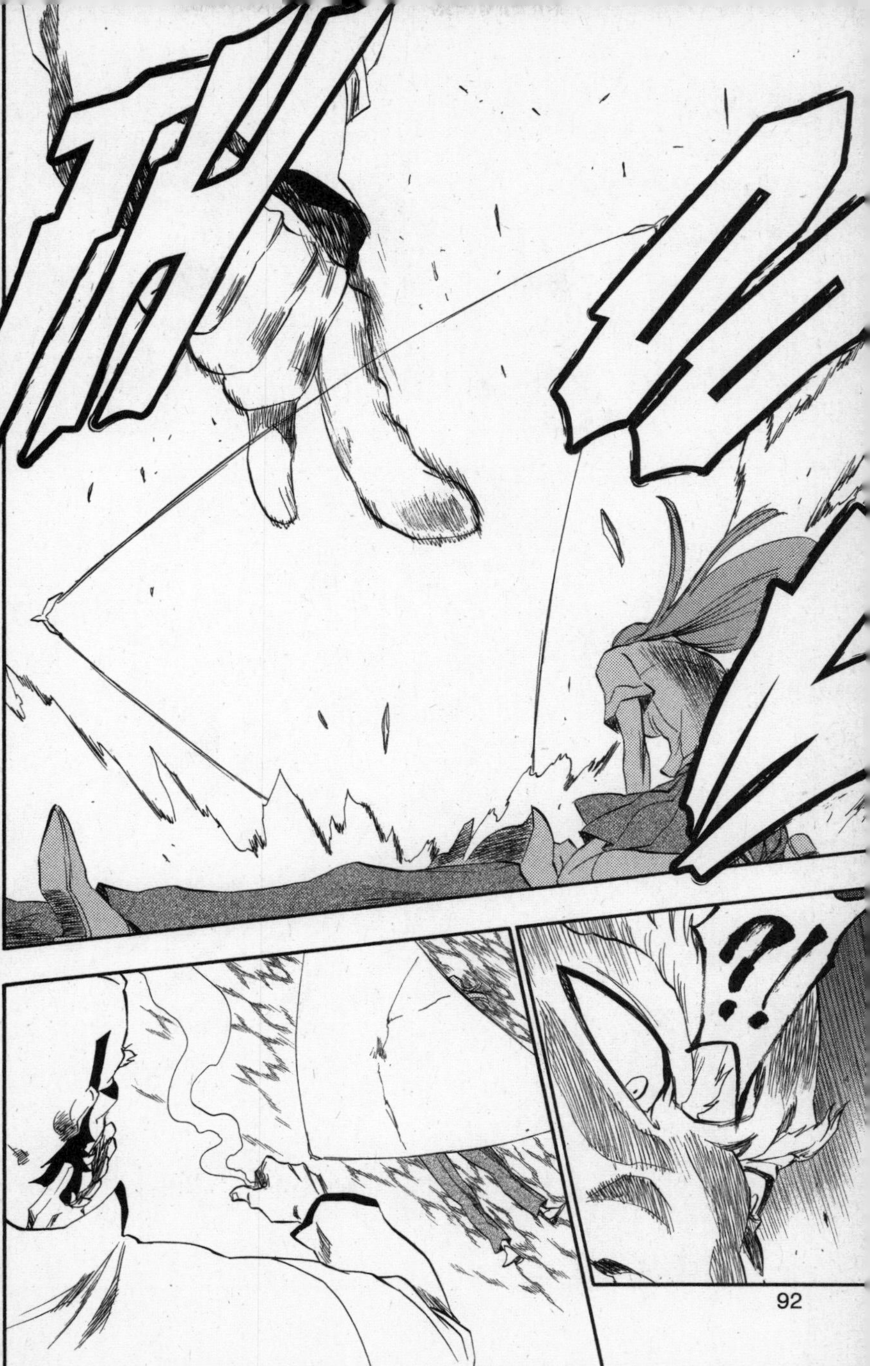
?!

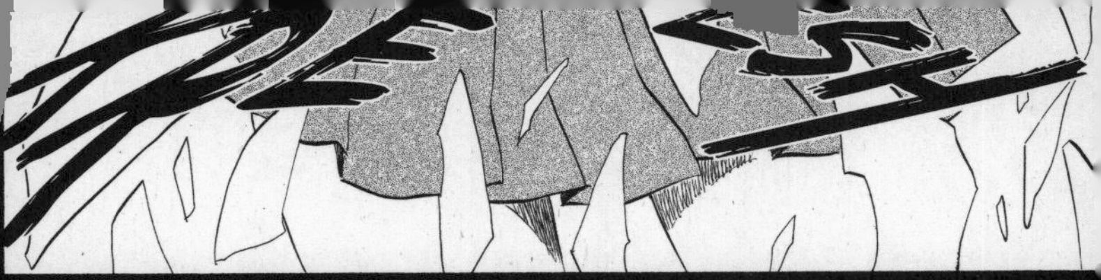

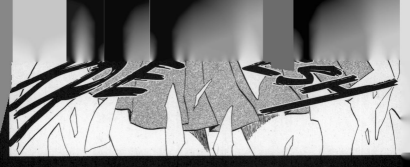

192. Conquistadores 3 (Hounded Priestess)

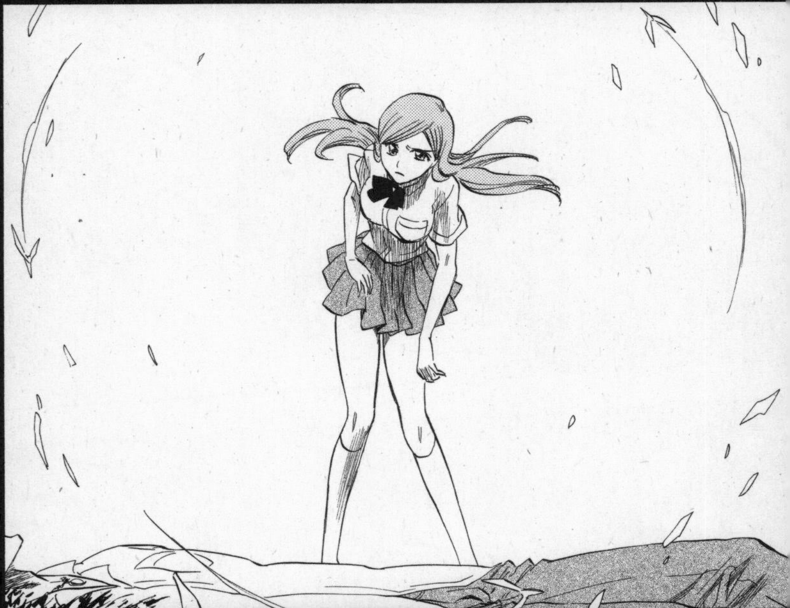

BLEACH —ブリーチ—

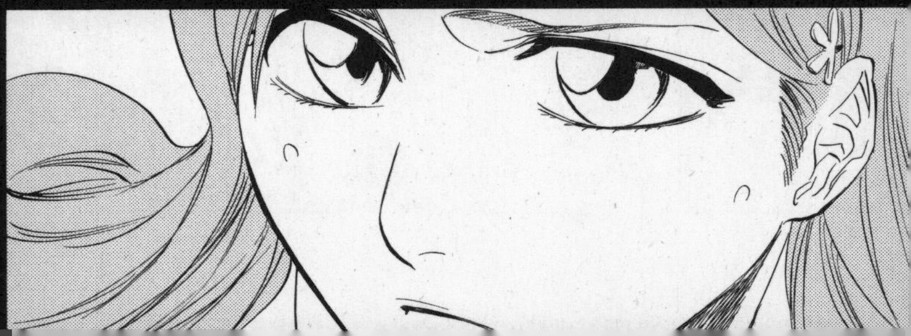

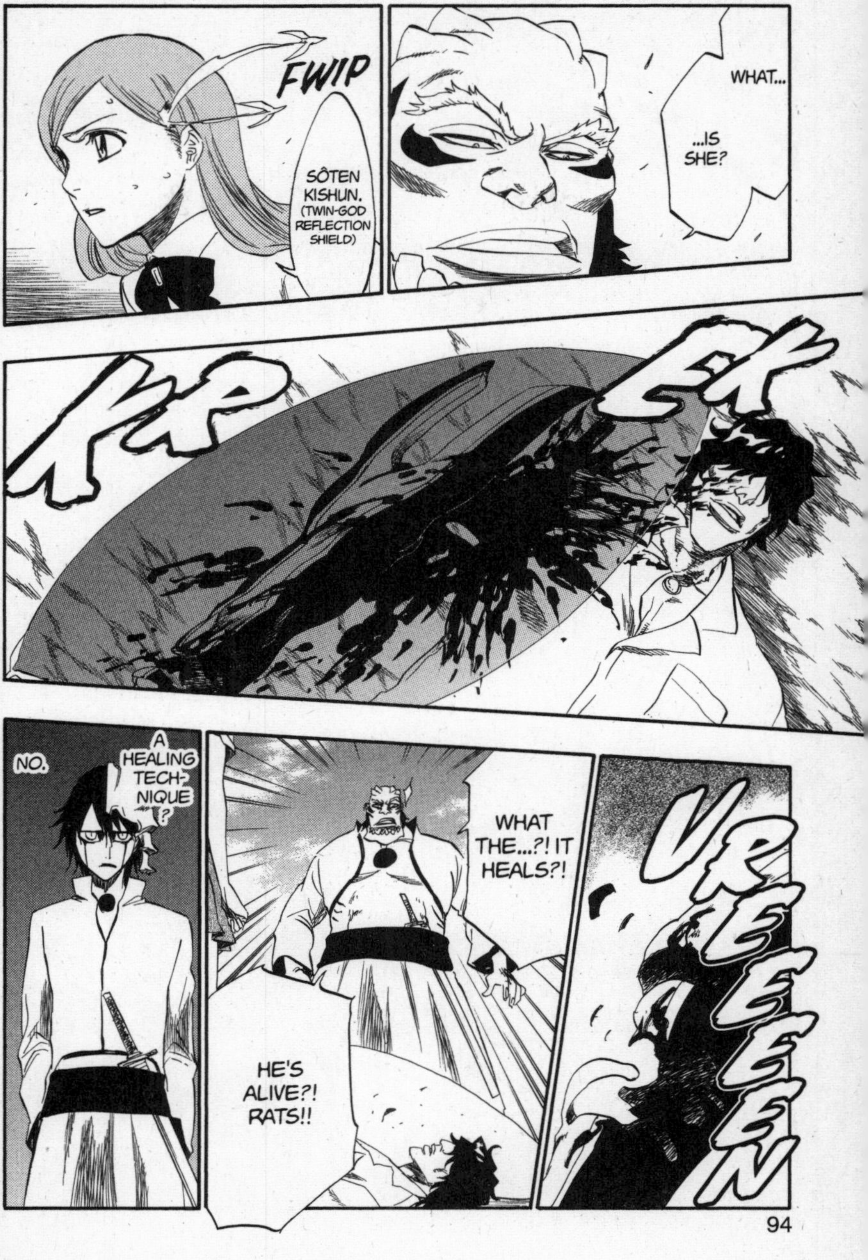
WHAT...
...IS SHE?
FWIP
SÔTEN KISHUN. (TWIN-GOD REFLECTION SHIELD)
KIP
EK
VREEEEEN
WHAT THE...?! IT HEALS?!
HE'S ALIVE?! RATS!!
A HEALING TECH-NIQUE?
NO.

READ THIS WAY

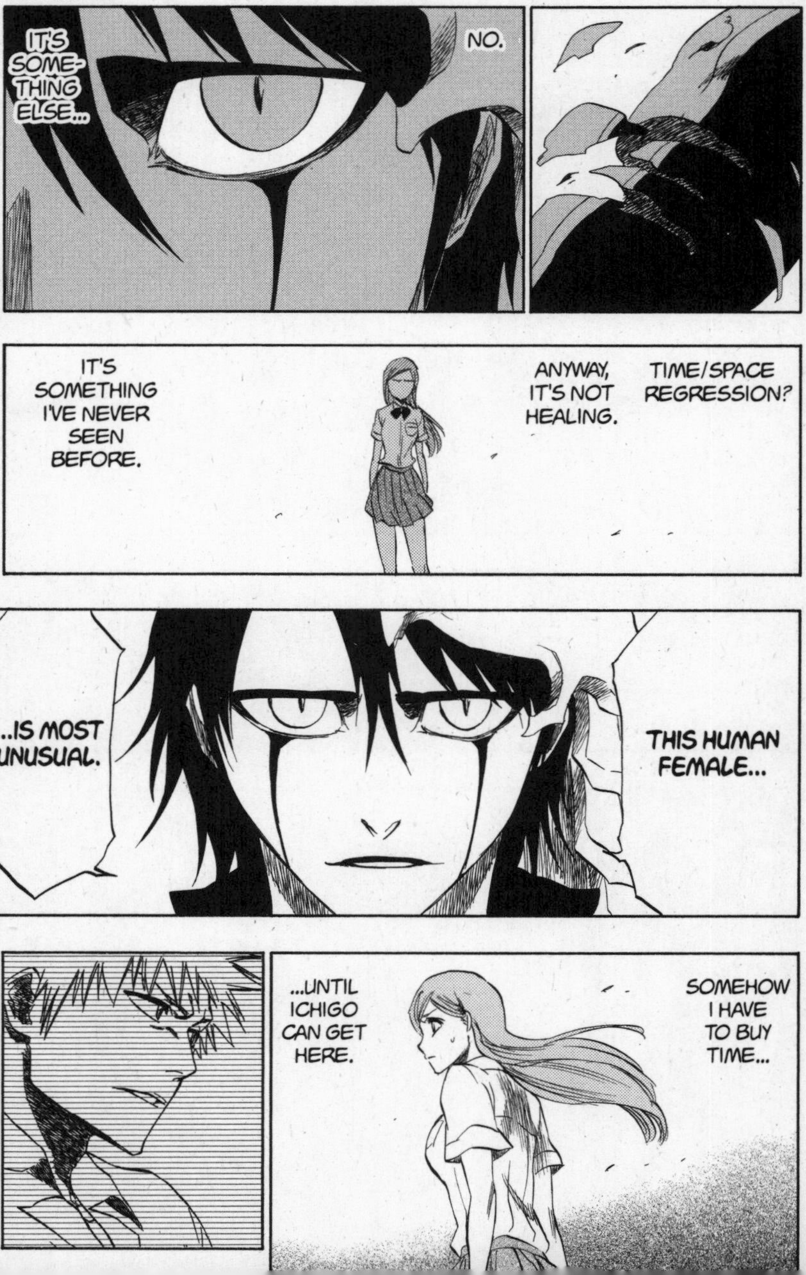
NO.
IT'S SOMETHING ELSE...
TIME/SPACE REGRESSION?
ANYWAY, IT'S NOT HEALING.
IT'S SOMETHING I'VE NEVER SEEN BEFORE.
THIS HUMAN FEMALE...
...IS MOST UNUSUAL.
SOMEHOW I HAVE TO BUY TIME...
...UNTIL ICHIGO CAN GET HERE.

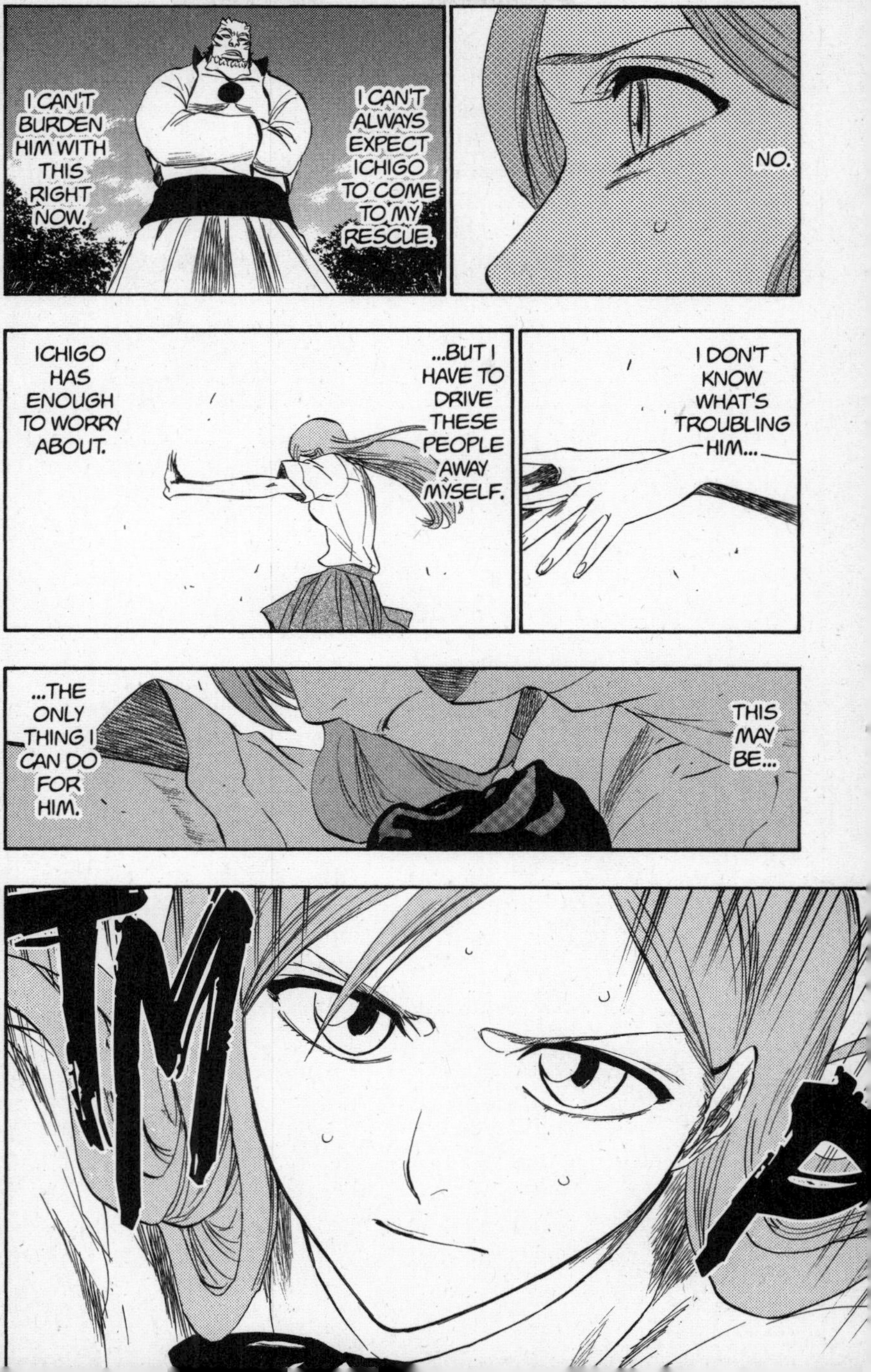
NO.
I CAN'T ALWAYS EXPECT ICHIGO TO COME TO MY RESCUE.
I CAN'T BURDEN HIM WITH THIS RIGHT NOW.
I DON'T KNOW WHAT'S TROUBLING HIM...
...BUT I HAVE TO DRIVE THESE PEOPLE AWAY MYSELF.
ICHIGO HAS ENOUGH TO WORRY ABOUT.
THIS MAY BE...
...THE ONLY THING I CAN DO FOR HIM.

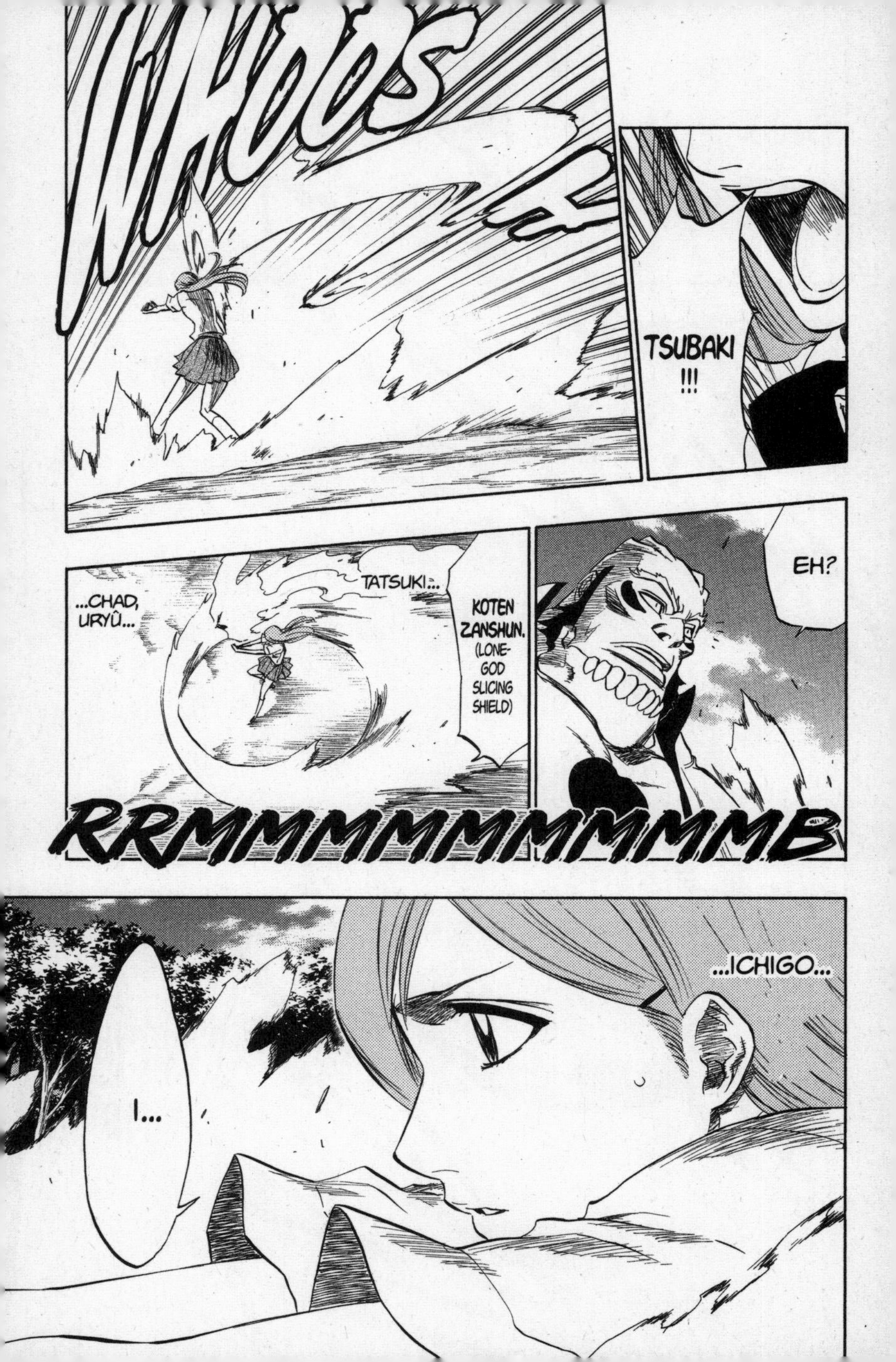
TSUBAKI !!!
WHOOSH
EH?
KOTEN ZANSHUN. (LONE-GOD SLICING SHIELD)
TATSUKI...
...CHAD, URYÛ...
RRMMMMMMMMMMB
...ICHIGO...
I...

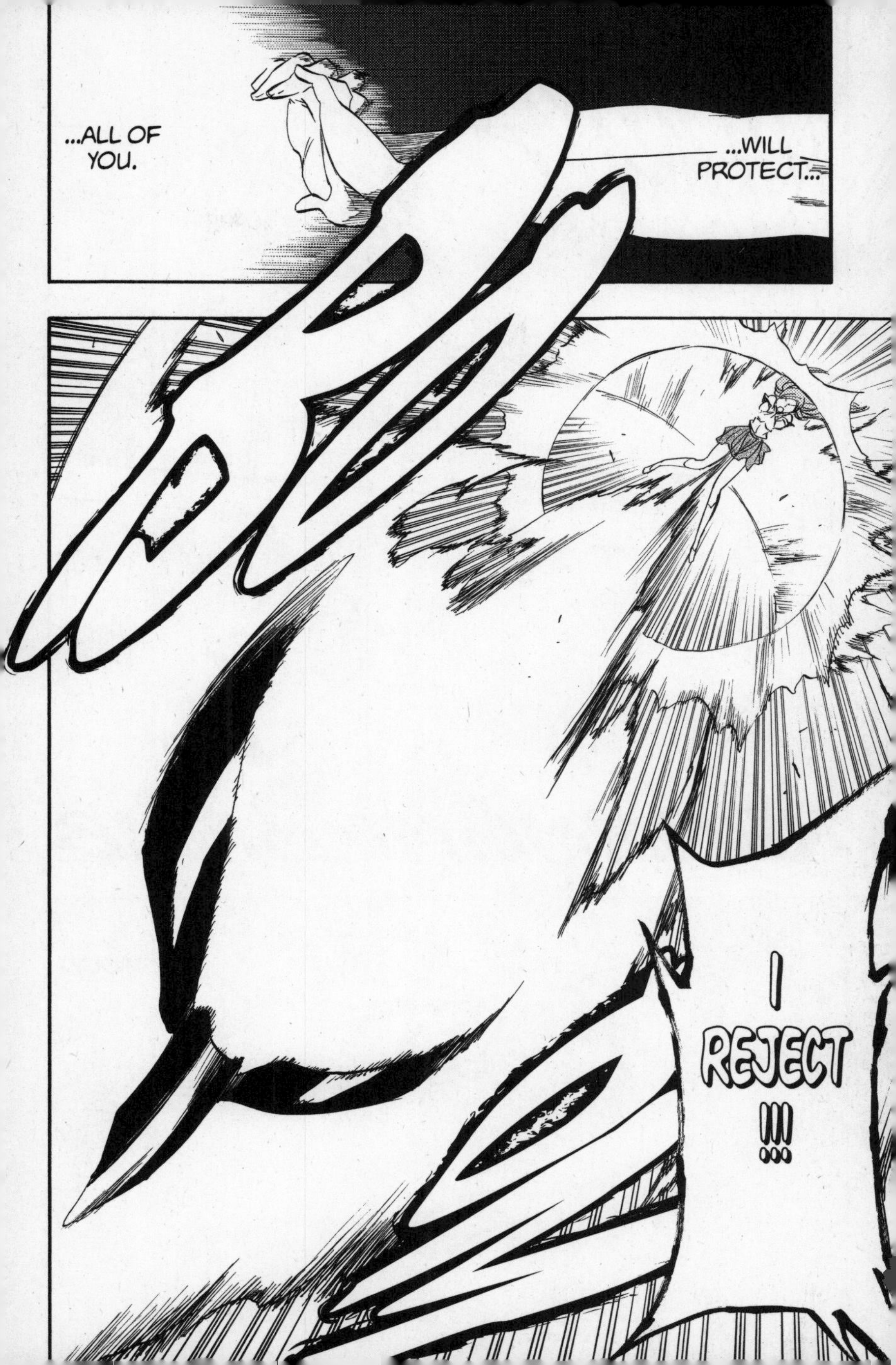
...WILL PROTECT...
...ALL OF YOU.
I REJECT!!!

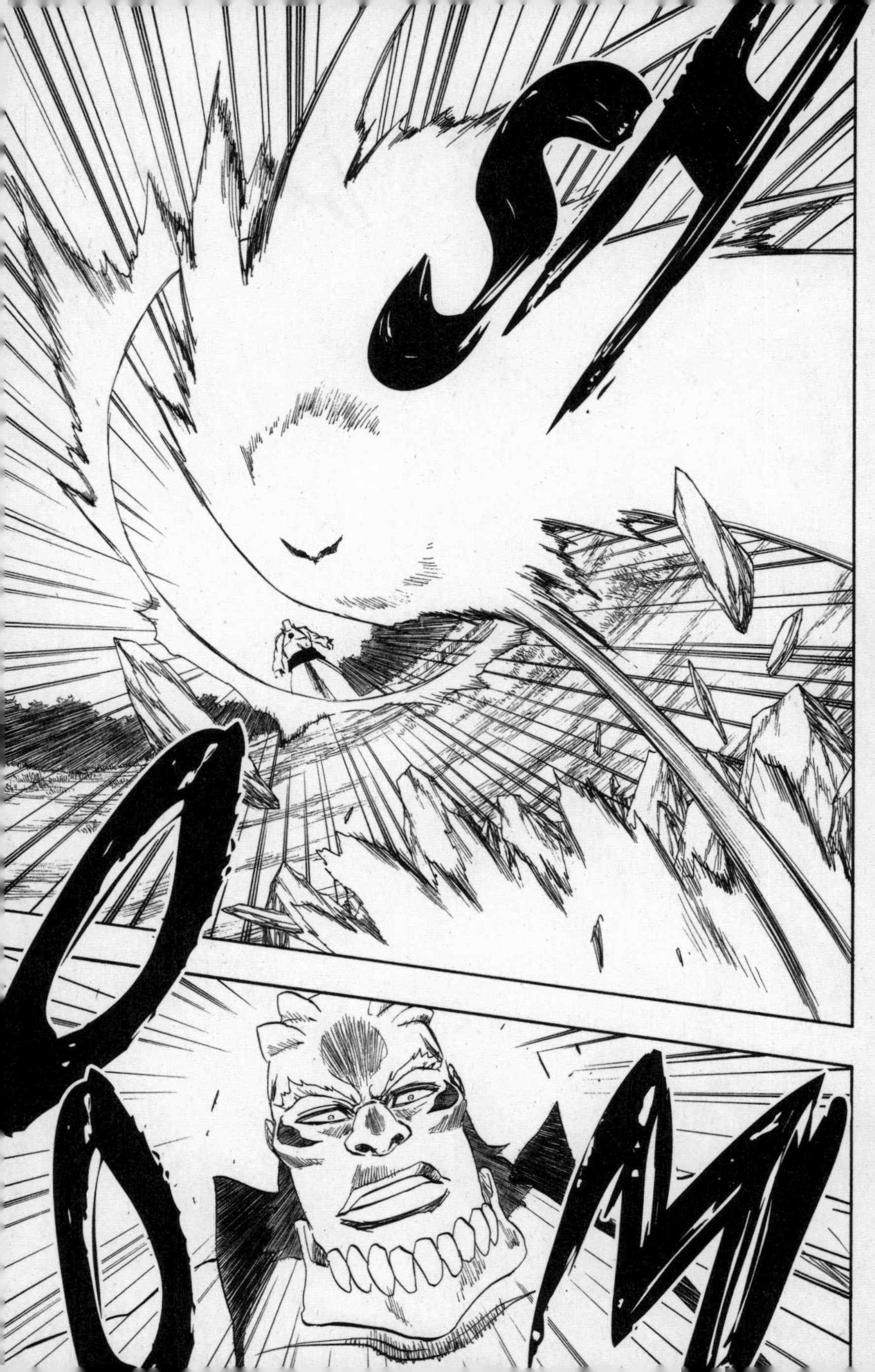
SH
OOM

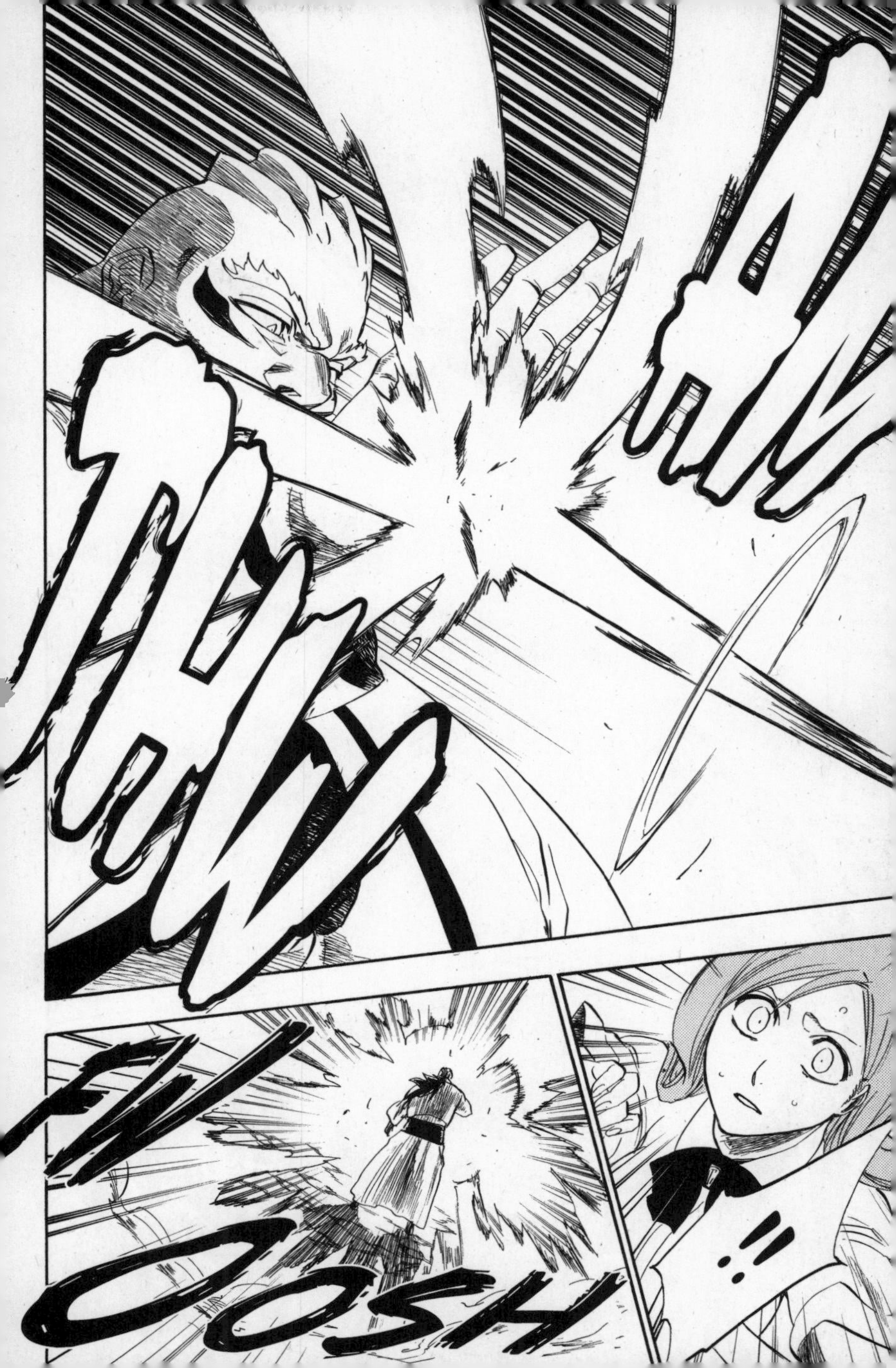
FWOOSH
!!

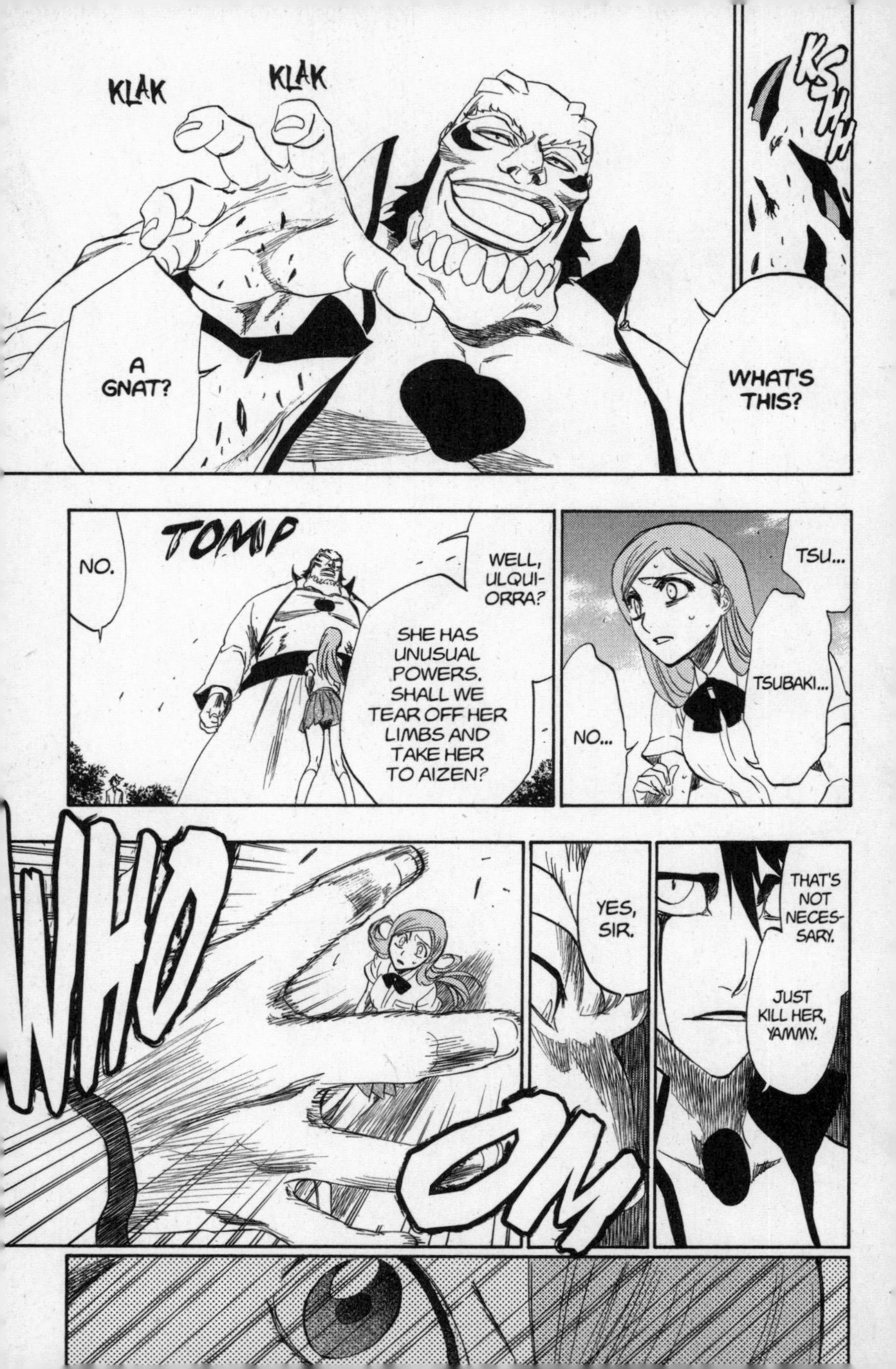
KSHH
KLAK
KLAK
WHAT'S THIS?
A GNAT?
TSU...
TSUBAKI...
NO...
WELL, ULQUI-ORRA?
SHE HAS UNUSUAL POWERS. SHALL WE TEAR OFF HER LIMBS AND TAKE HER TO AIZEN?
TOMP
NO.
THAT'S NOT NECES-SARY.
JUST KILL HER, YAMMY.
YES, SIR.
WHOOM

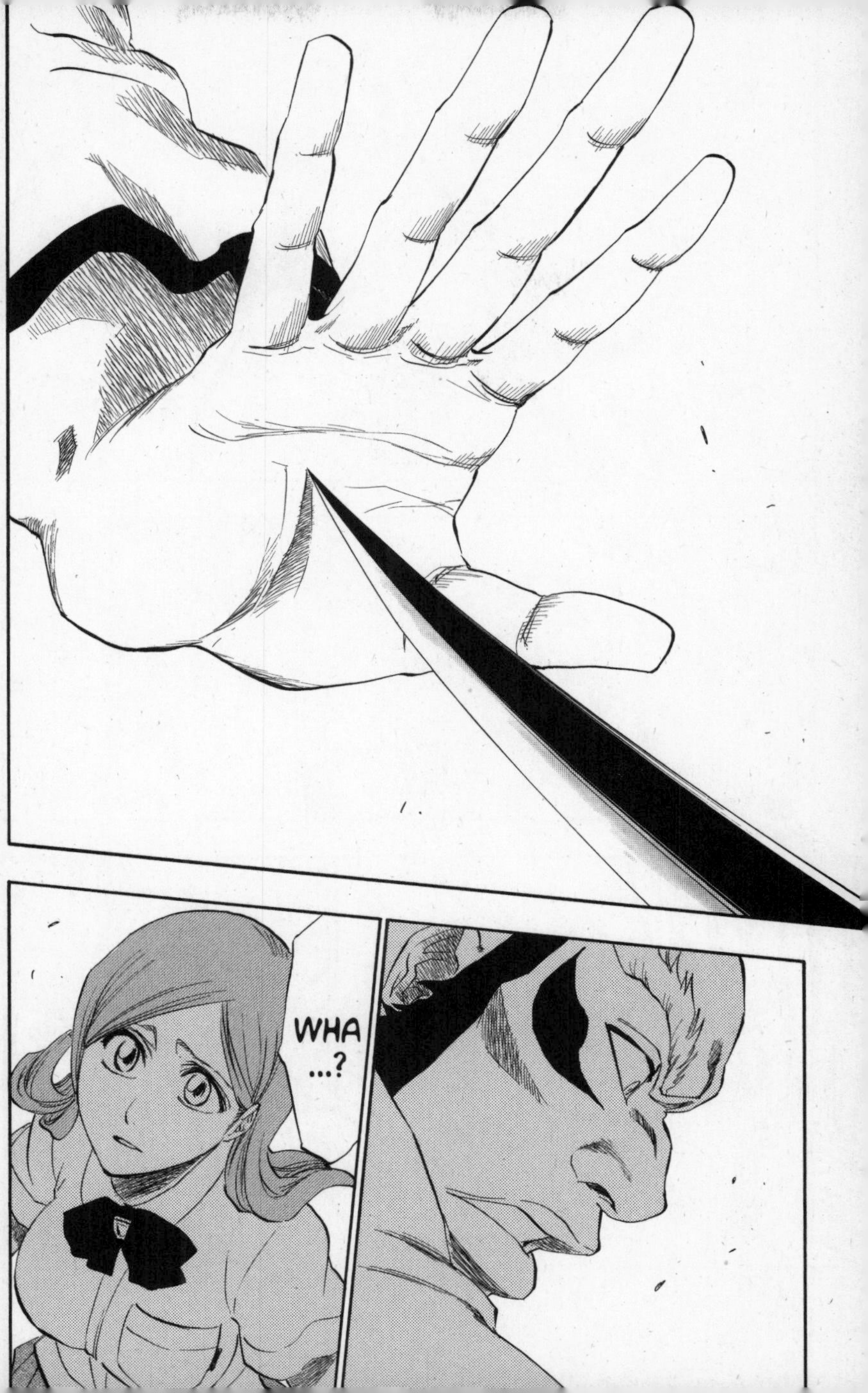
WHA ...?

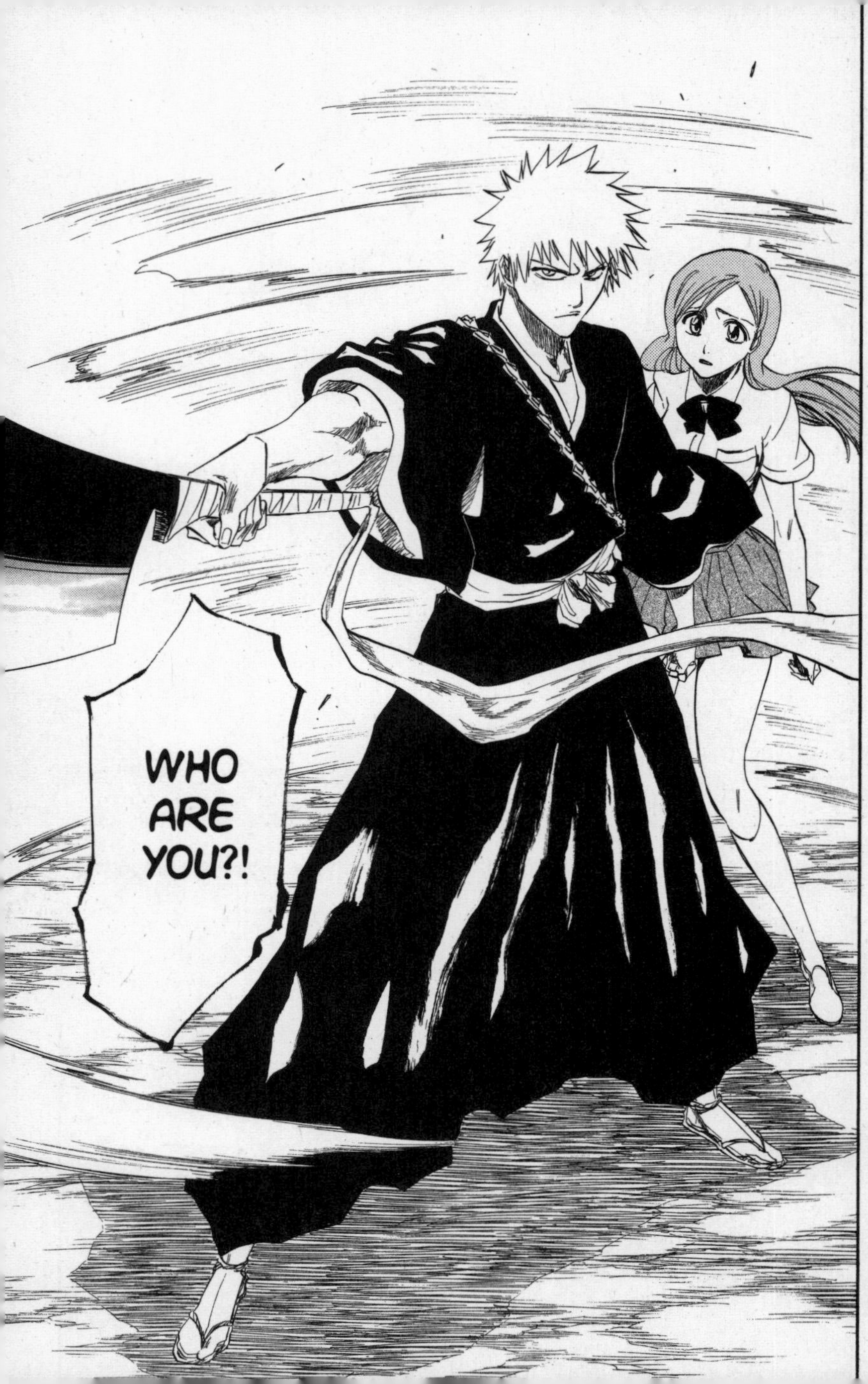
WHO ARE YOU?!

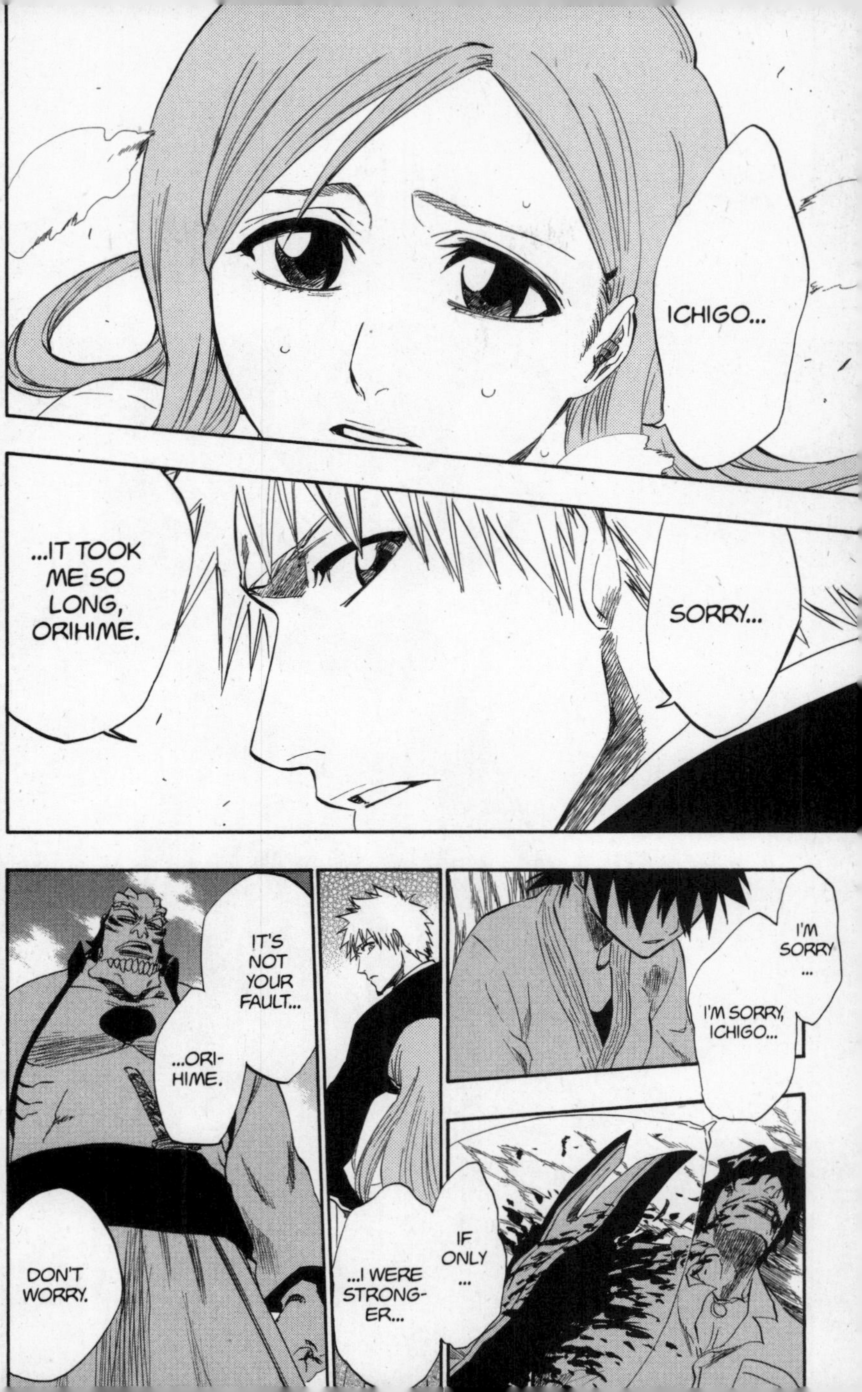
ICHIGO...
SORRY...
...IT TOOK ME SO LONG, ORIHIME.
I'M SORRY ...
I'M SORRY, ICHIGO...
IF ONLY ...
...I WERE STRONG-ER...
IT'S NOT YOUR FAULT...
...ORI-HIME.
DON'T WORRY.

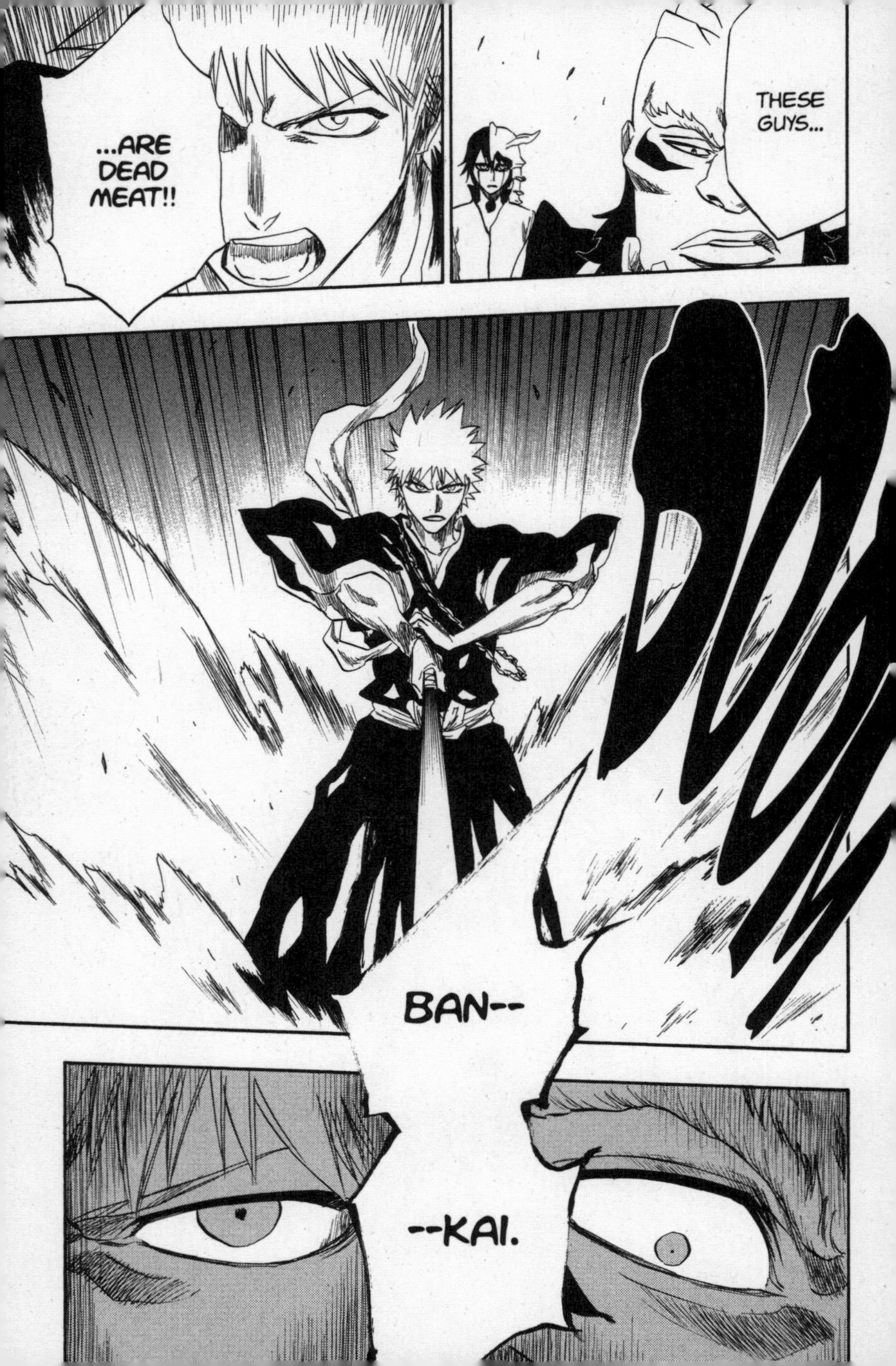
THESE GUYS...
...ARE DEAD MEAT!!
BAN--
--KAI.

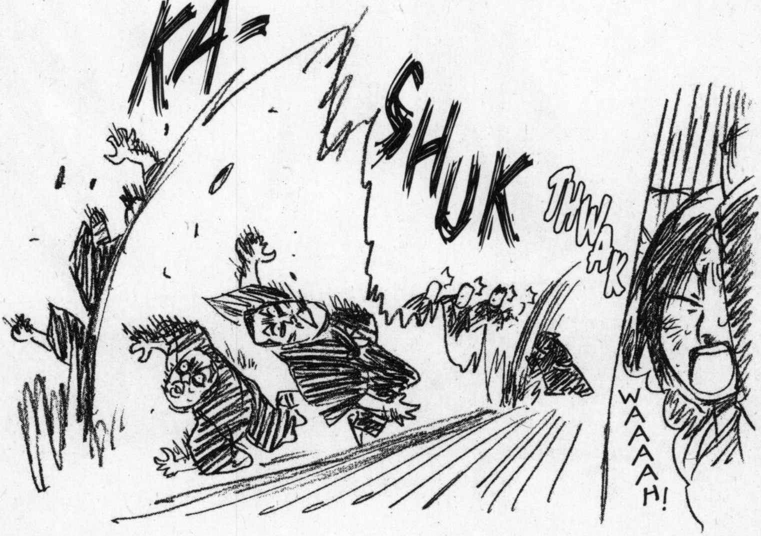
WAAAAAH!
KA-SHUK
THWAK

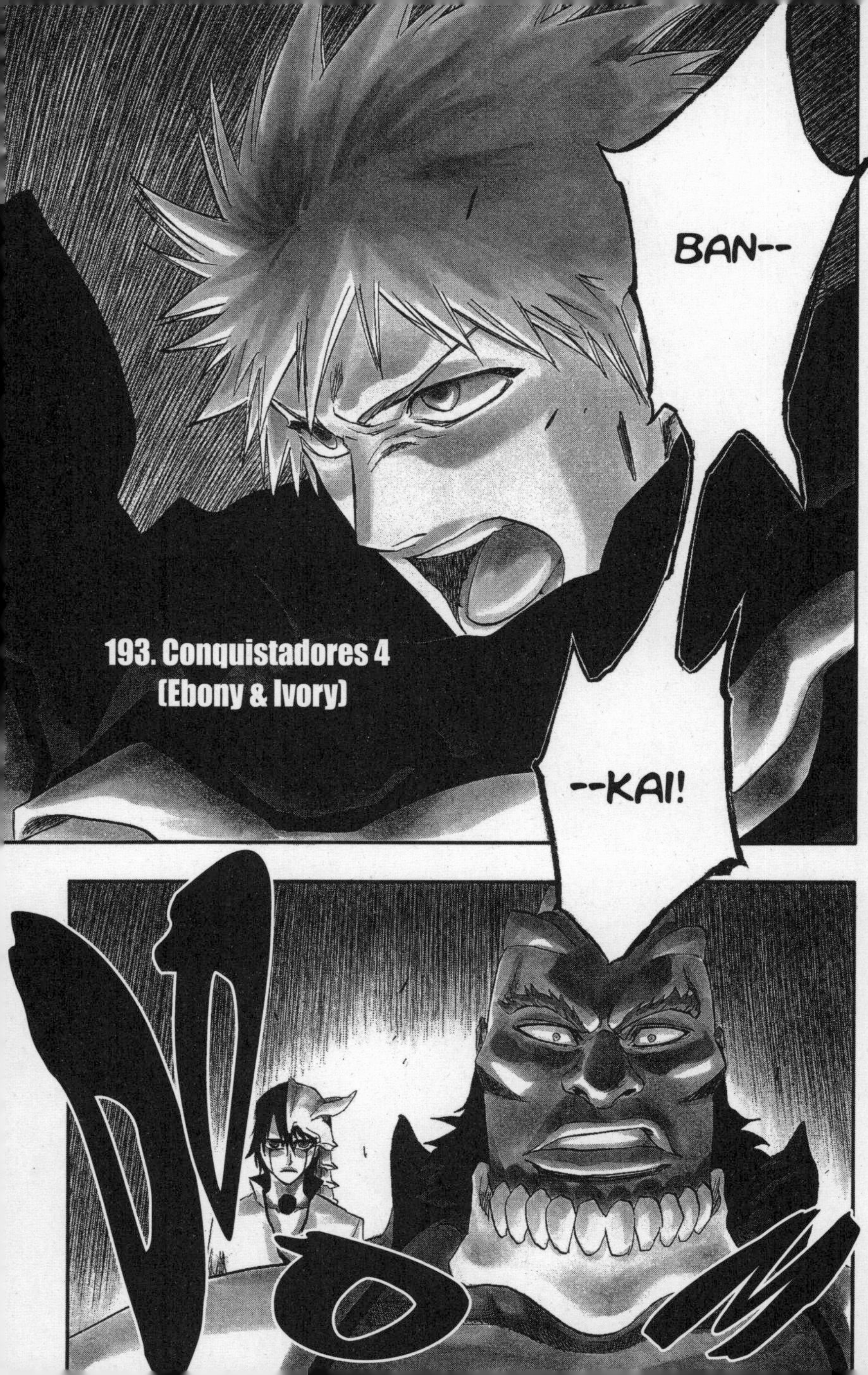
BAN--
193. Conquistadores 4
(Ebony & Ivory)
--KAI!

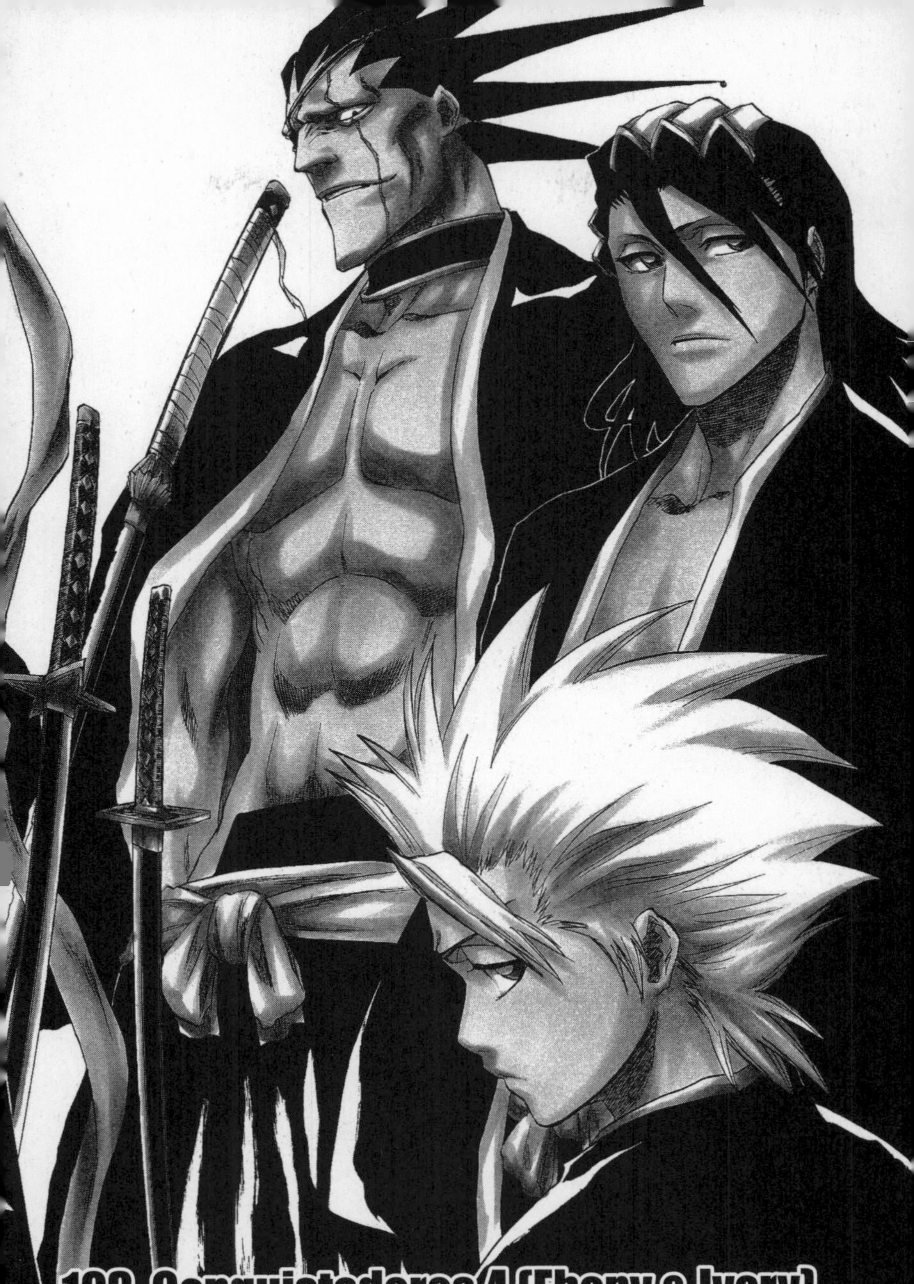

193. Conquistadores 4 (Ebony & Ivory)

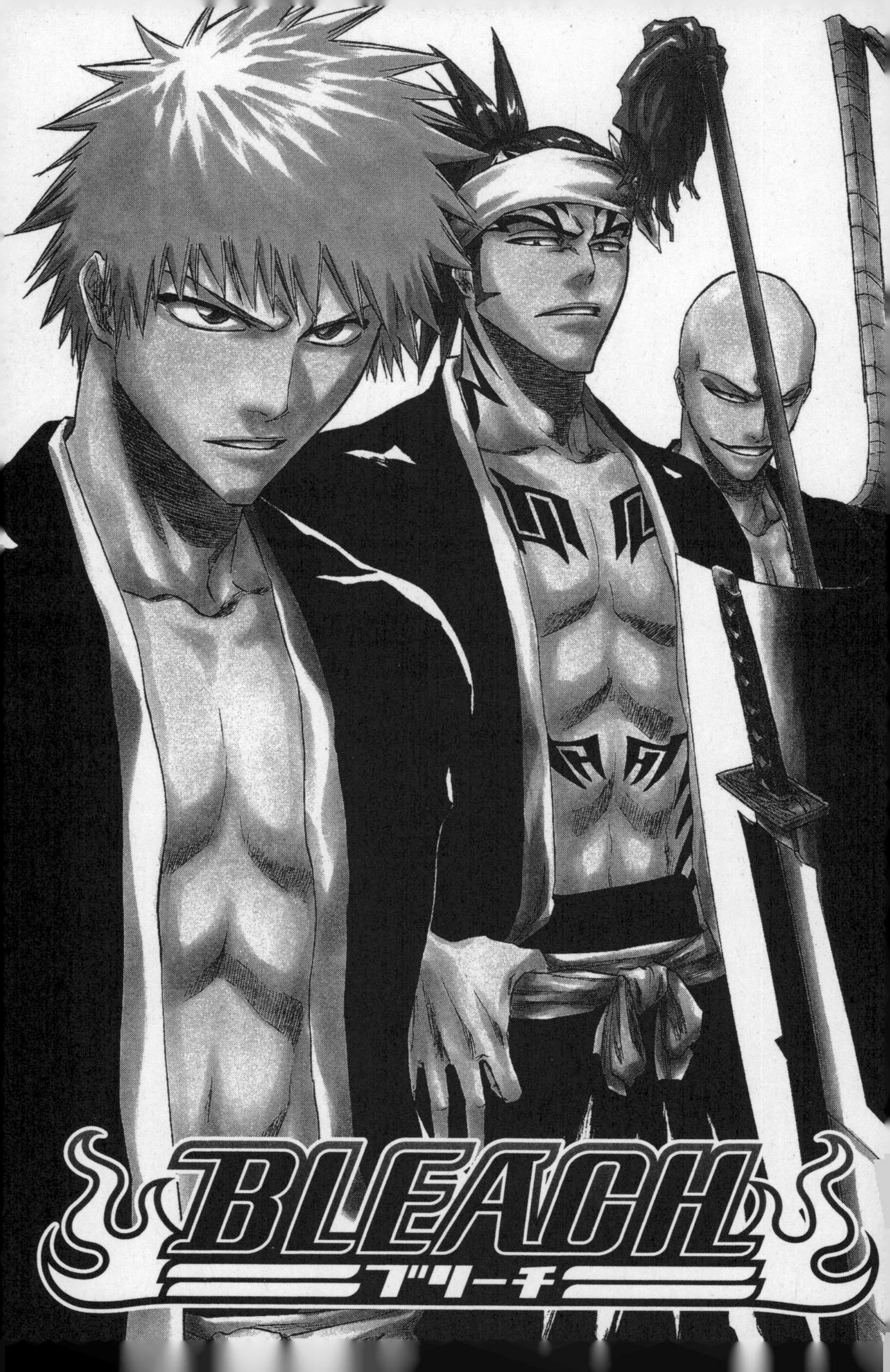
BLEACH
ブリーチ

BLEACH
ブリーチ

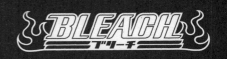

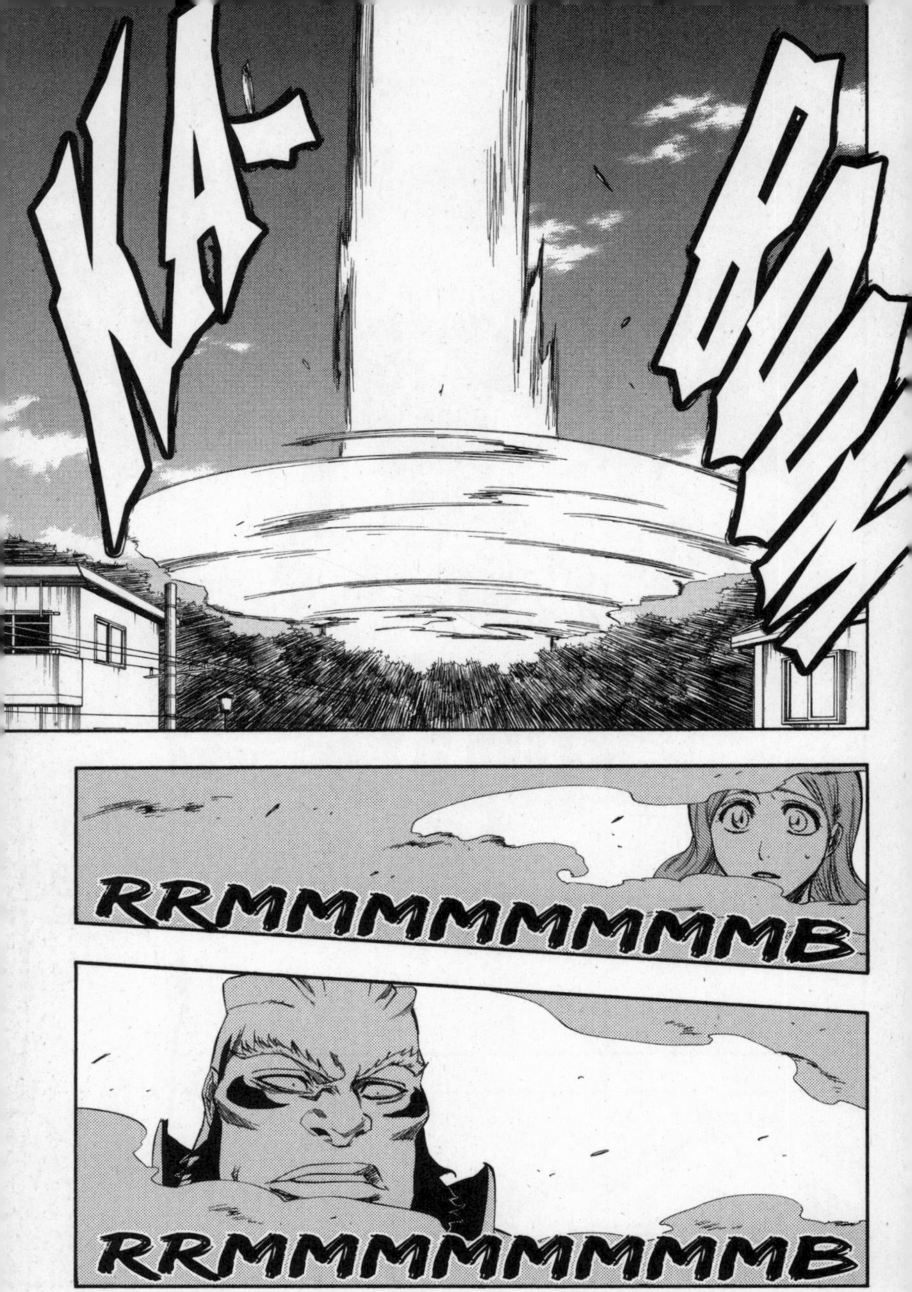
KA-
BOOM
RRMMMMMMMMMB
RRMMMMMMMMMMB

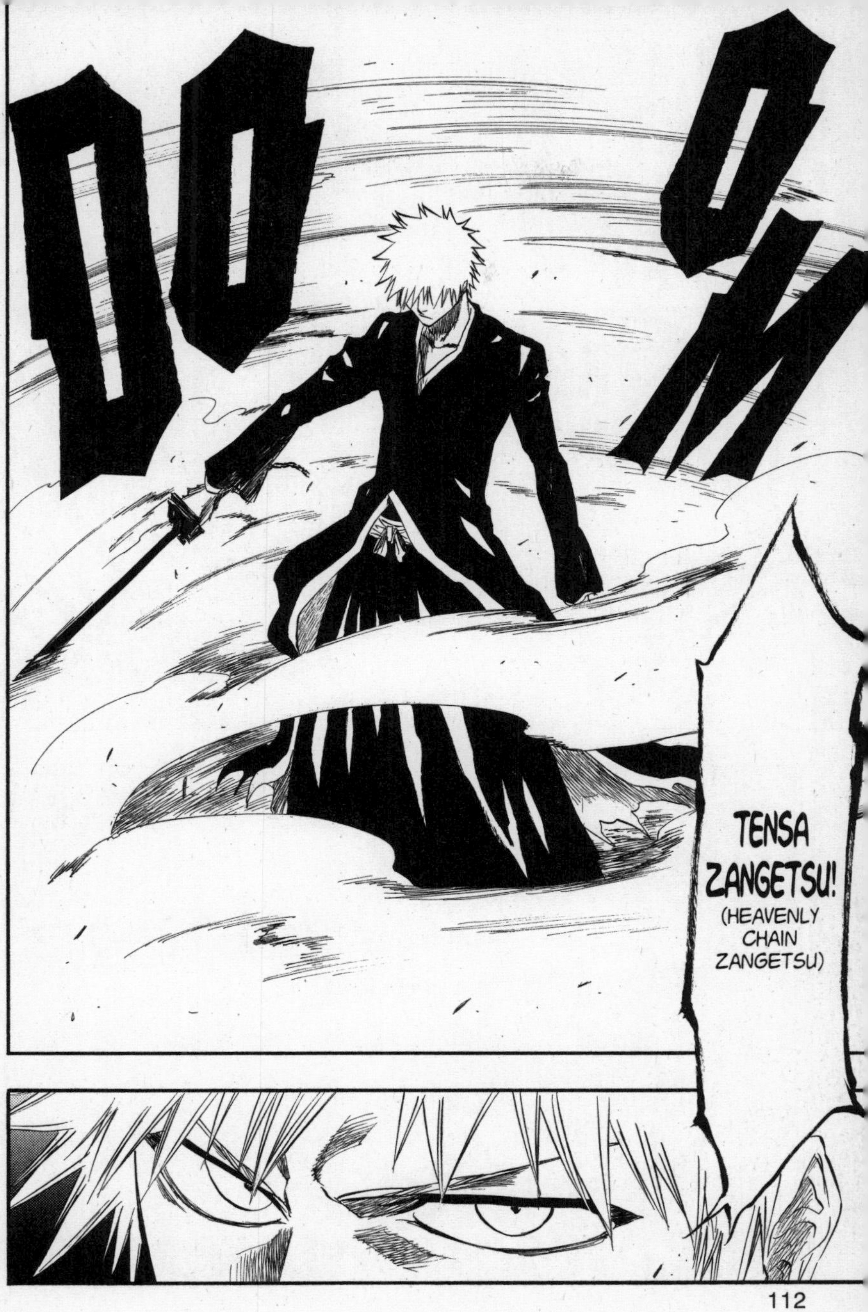
DOOOM
TENSA ZANGETSU!
(HEAVENLY CHAIN ZANGETSU)

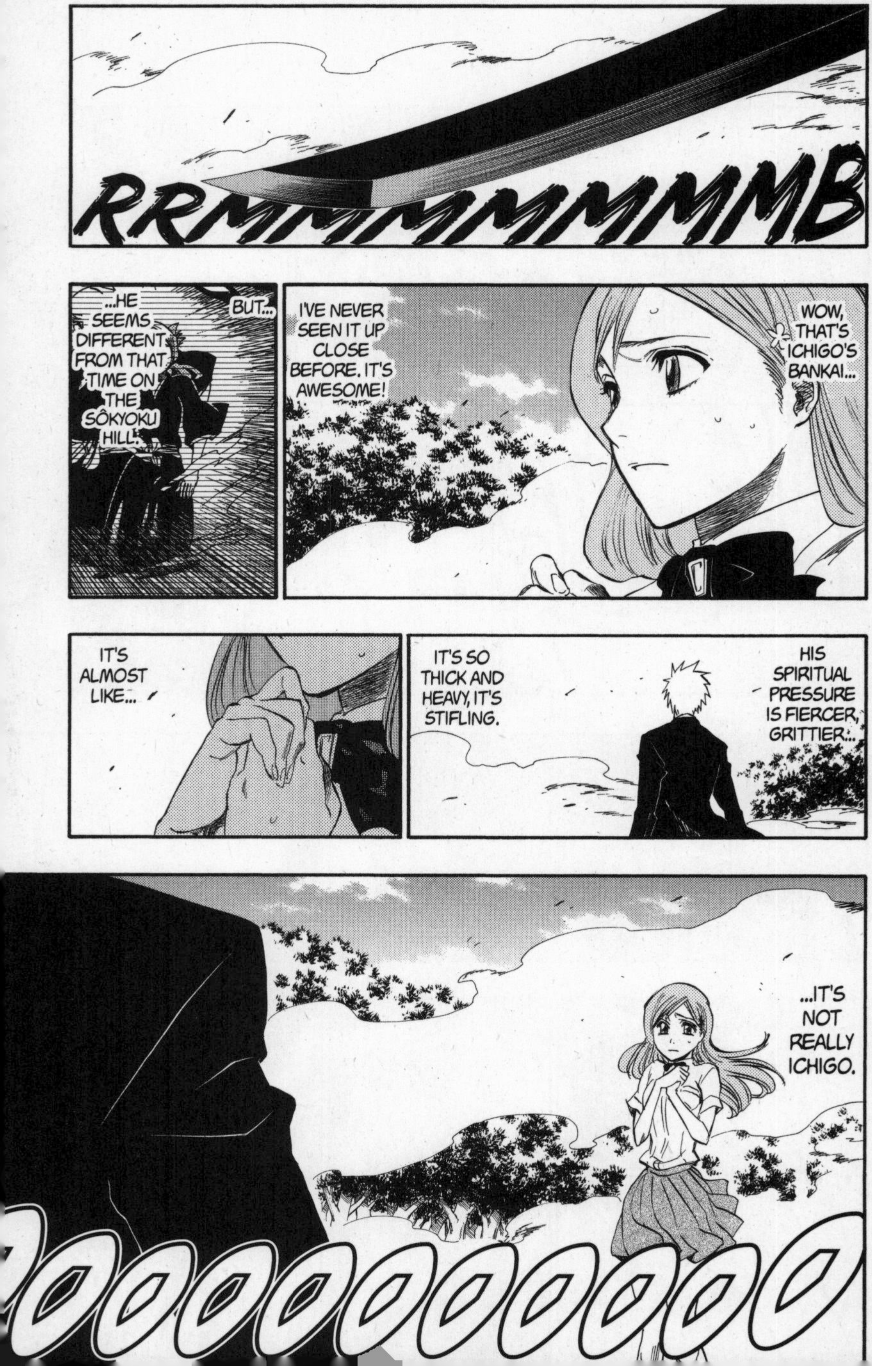
RRMMMMMMMMMB
WOW, THAT'S ICHIGO'S BANKAI...
I'VE NEVER SEEN IT UP CLOSE BEFORE. IT'S AWESOME!
BUT...
...HE SEEMS DIFFERENT FROM THAT TIME ON THE SÔKYOKU HILL.
HIS SPIRITUAL PRESSURE IS FIERCER, GRITTIER...
IT'S SO THICK AND HEAVY, IT'S STIFLING.
IT'S ALMOST LIKE...
...IT'S NOT REALLY ICHIGO.
OOOOOOOOOOO

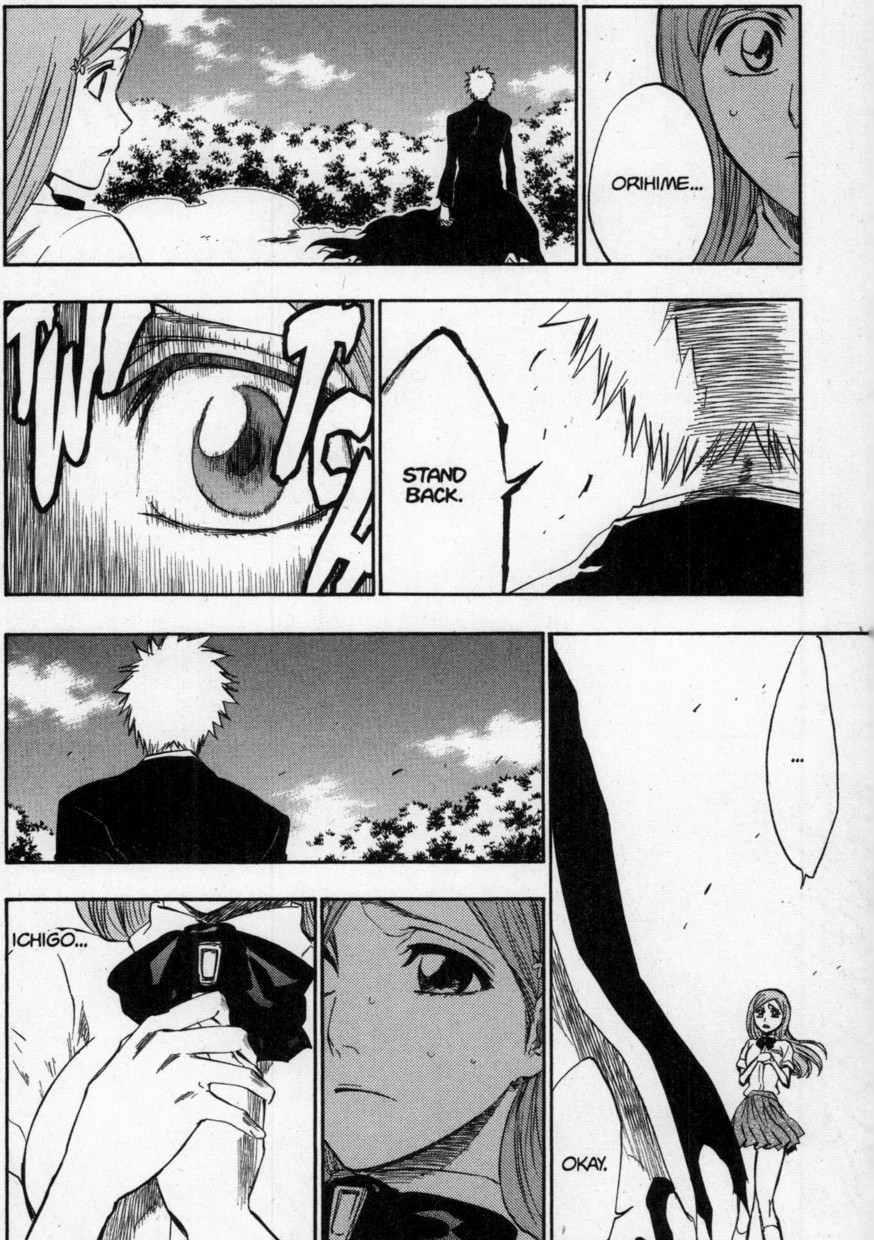
ORIHIME...
STAND BACK.
TWITCH
...
OKAY.
ICHIGO...

READ THIS WAY

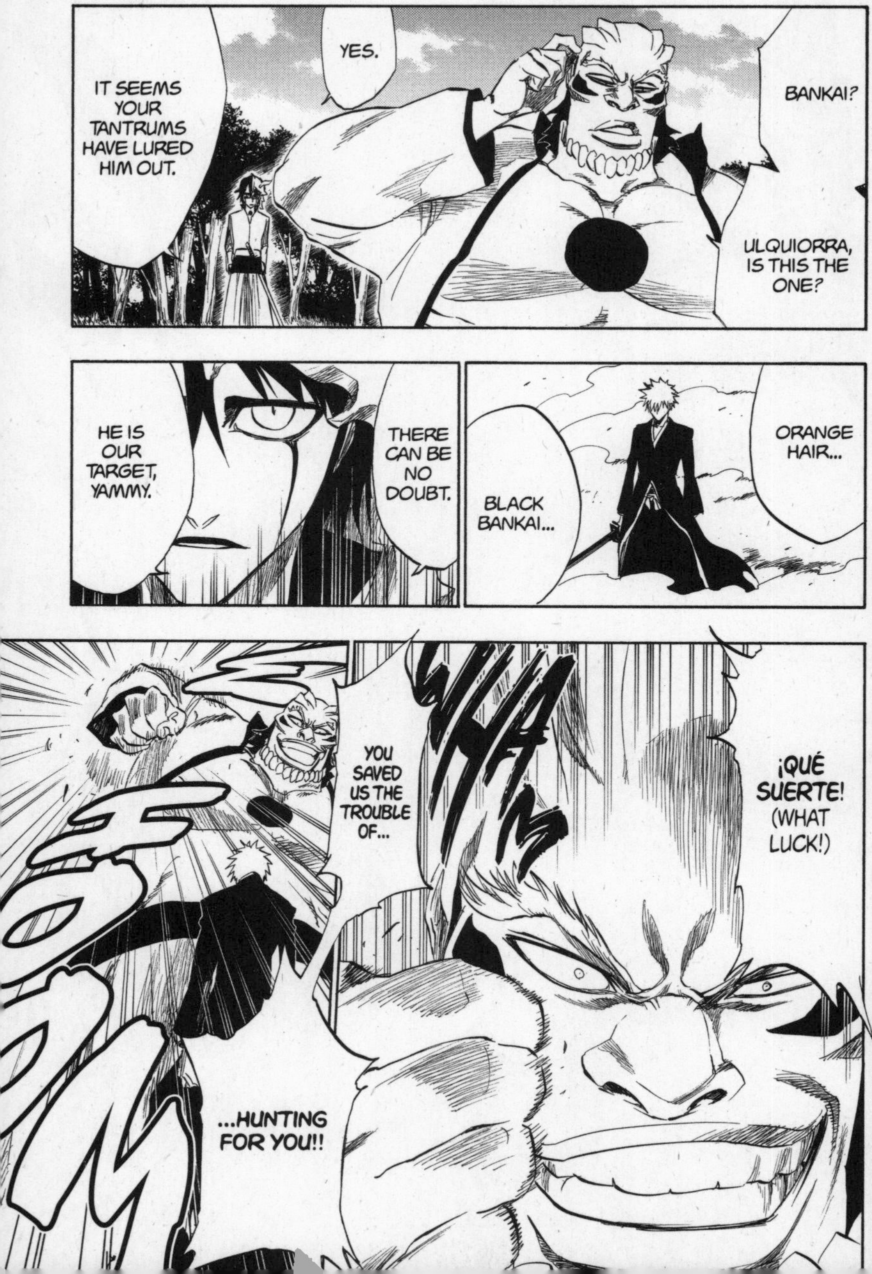
BANKAI?
ULQUIORRA, IS THIS THE ONE?
YES.
IT SEEMS YOUR TANTRUMS HAVE LURED HIM OUT.
ORANGE HAIR...
BLACK BANKAI...
THERE CAN BE NO DOUBT.
HE IS OUR TARGET, YAMMY.
¡QUÉ SUERTE! (WHAT LUCK!)
YOU SAVED US THE TROUBLE OF...
...HUNTING FOR YOU!!

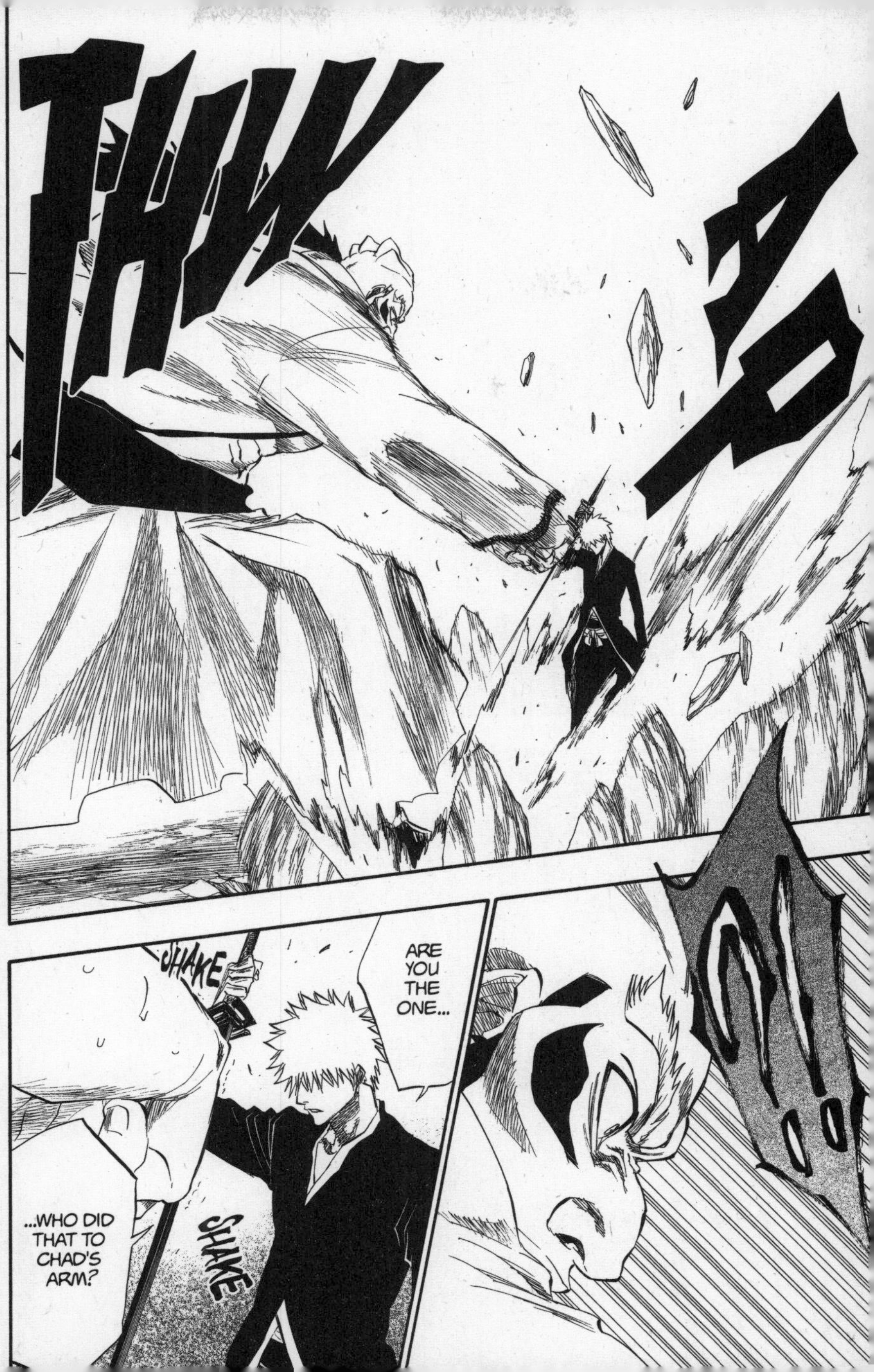
!?
ARE YOU THE ONE...
SHAKE
...WHO DID THAT TO CHAD'S ARM?
SHAKE

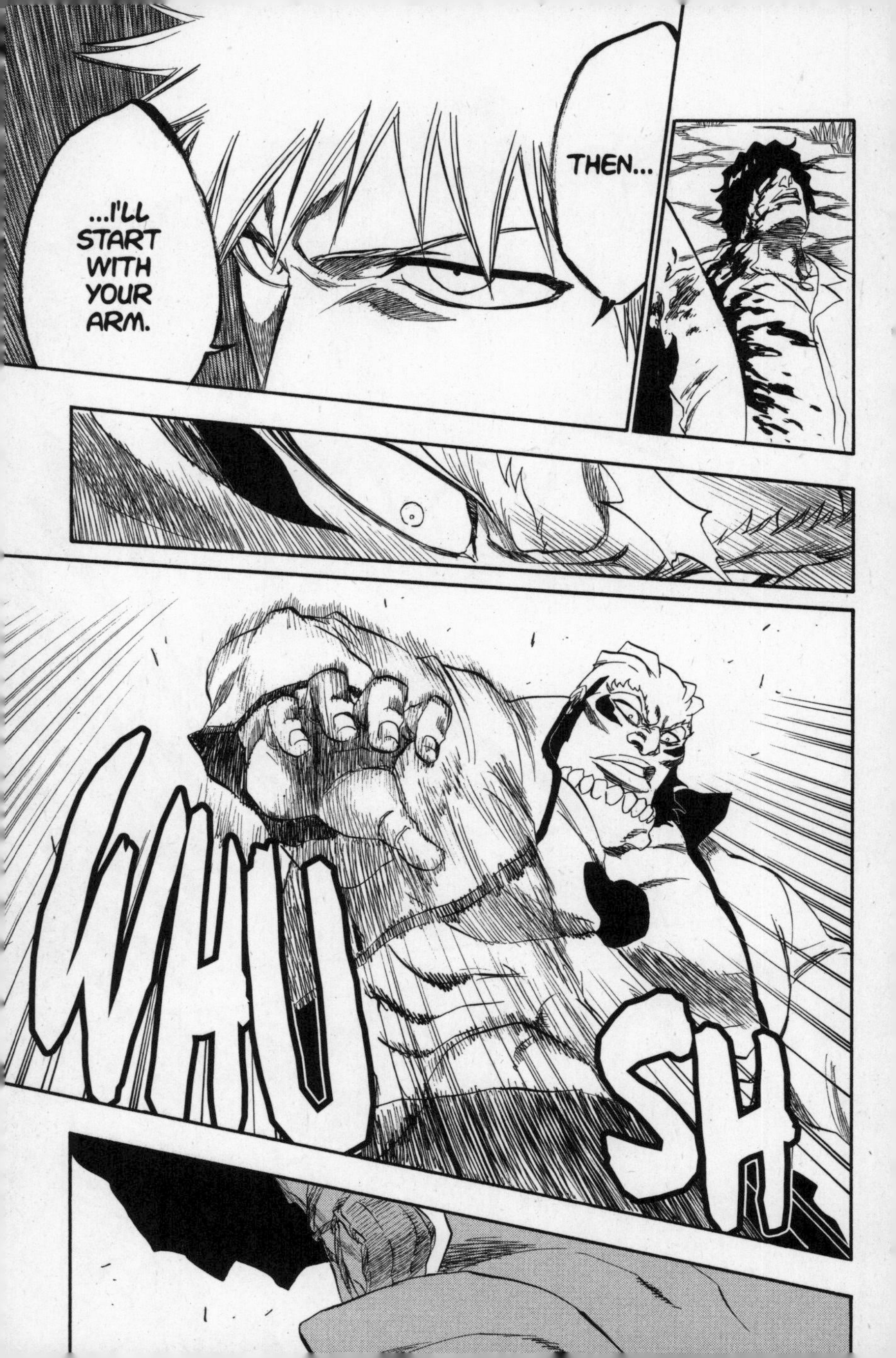
THEN...
...I'LL START WITH YOUR ARM.
WHOOSH

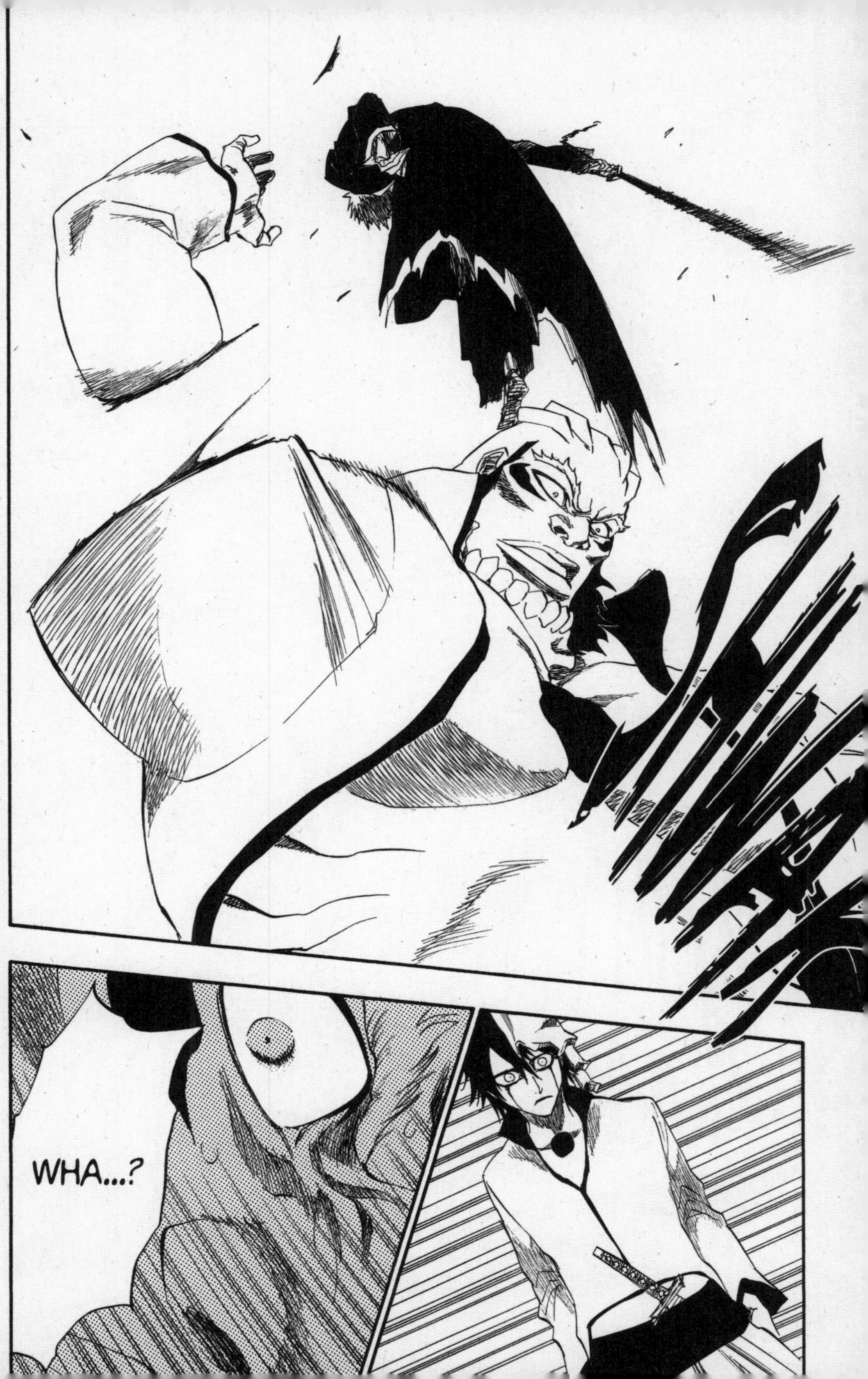
WHA...?

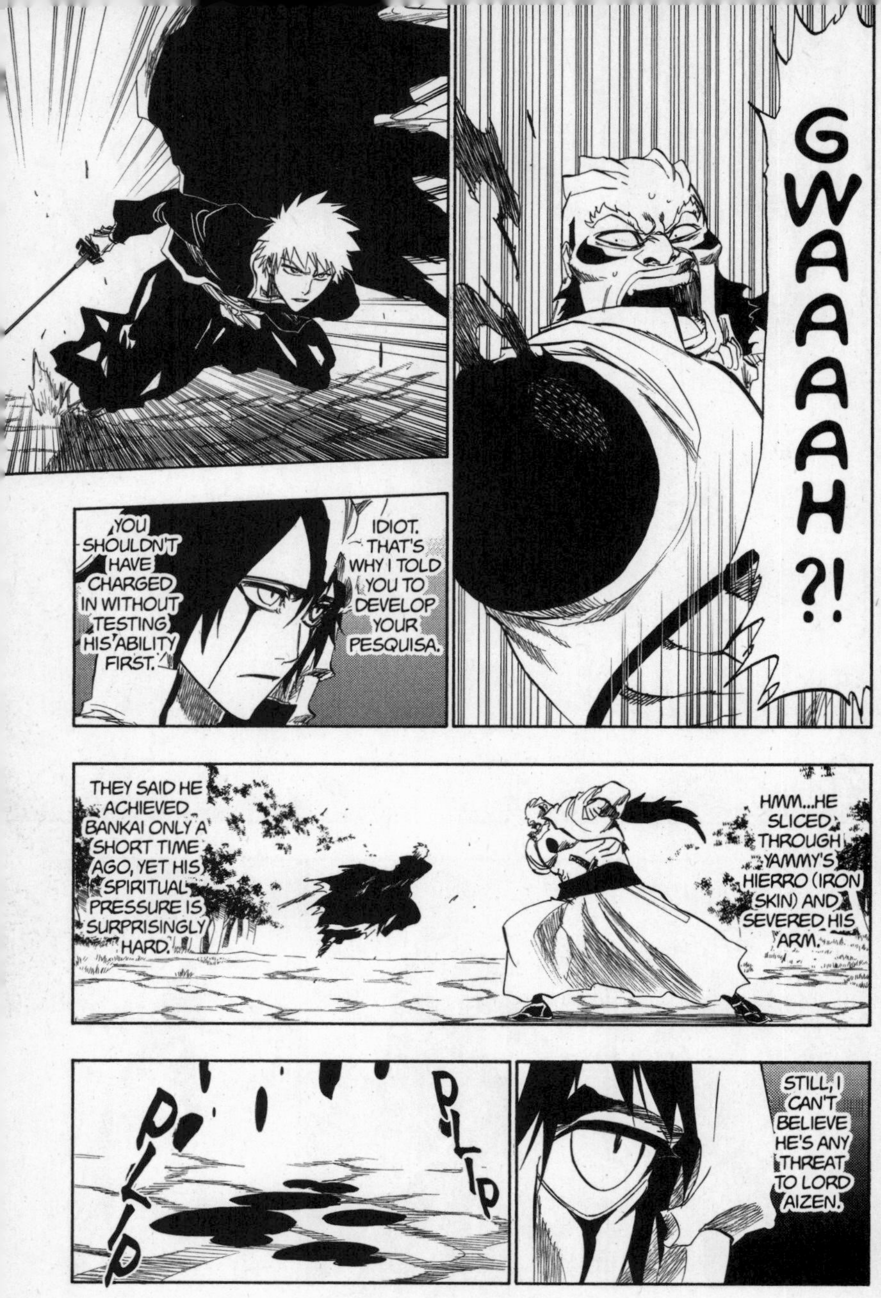
GWAAAAH ?!
IDIOT. THAT'S WHY I TOLD YOU TO DEVELOP YOUR PESQUISA.
YOU SHOULDN'T HAVE CHARGED IN WITHOUT TESTING HIS ABILITY FIRST.
HMM...HE SLICED THROUGH YAMMY'S HIERRO (IRON SKIN) AND SEVERED HIS ARM.
THEY SAID HE ACHIEVED BANKAI ONLY A SHORT TIME AGO, YET HIS SPIRITUAL PRESSURE IS SURPRISINGLY HARD.
STILL, I CAN'T BELIEVE HE'S ANY THREAT TO LORD AIZEN.
PLIP
PLIP

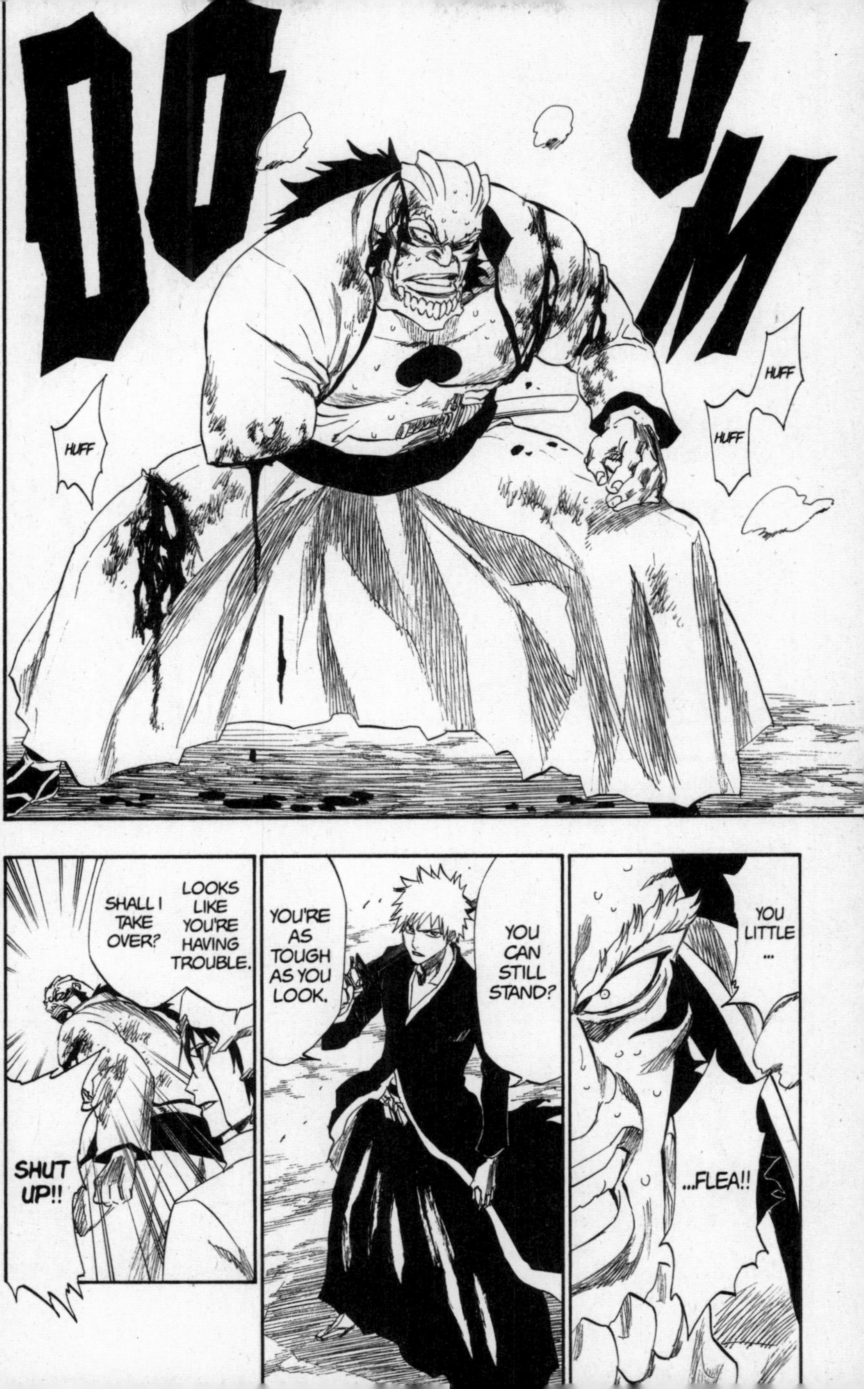
DO
OM
HUFF
HUFF
HUFF
YOU LITTLE ...
...FLEA!!
YOU CAN STILL STAND?
YOU'RE AS TOUGH AS YOU LOOK.
LOOKS LIKE YOU'RE HAVING TROUBLE.
SHALL I TAKE OVER?
SHUT UP!!

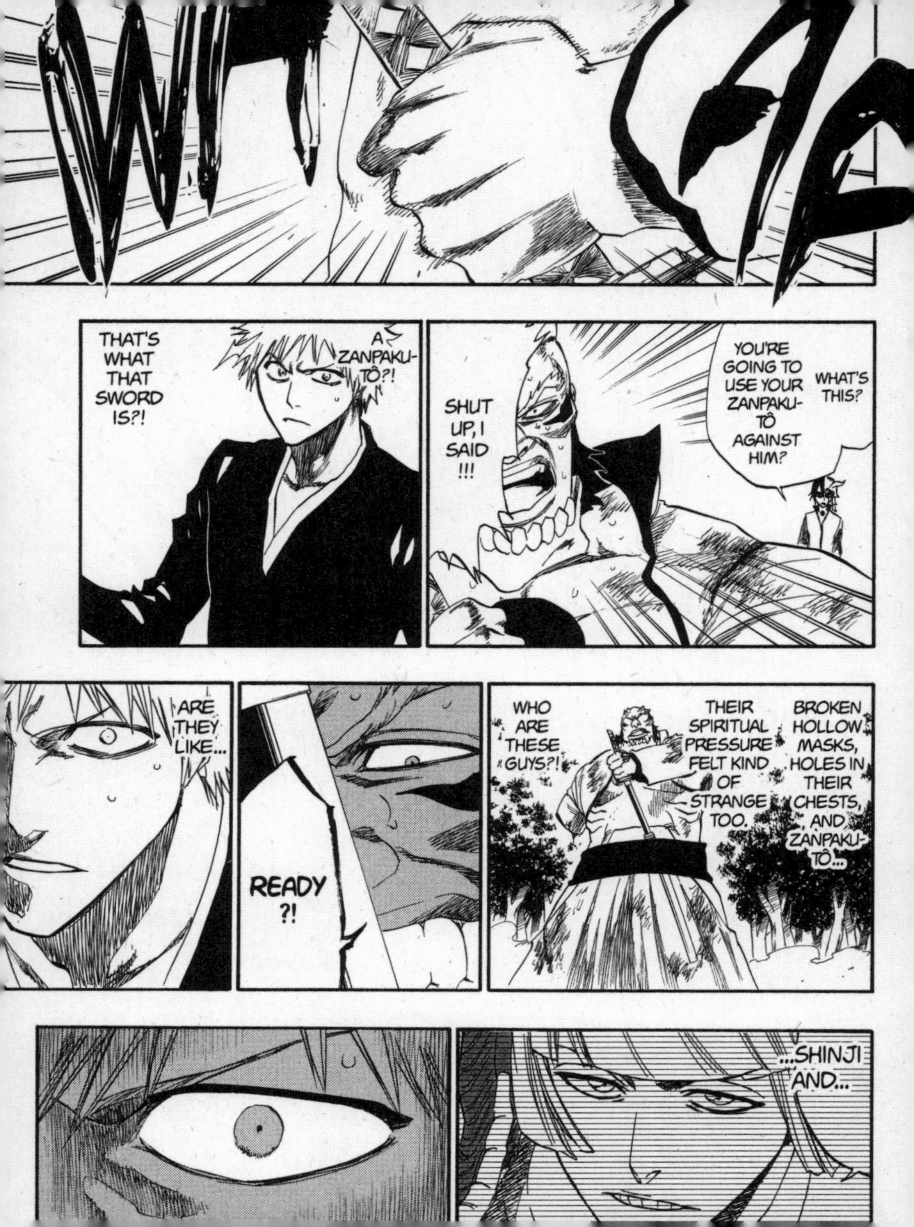
WHAP
WHAT'S THIS?
YOU'RE GOING TO USE YOUR ZANPAKU-TÔ AGAINST HIM?
SHUT UP, I SAID !!!
A ZANPAKU-TÔ?!
THAT'S WHAT THAT SWORD IS?!
BROKEN HOLLOW MASKS, HOLES IN THEIR CHESTS, AND ZANPAKU-TÔ...
THEIR SPIRITUAL PRESSURE FELT KIND OF STRANGE TOO.
WHO ARE THESE GUYS?!
READY ?!
ARE THEY LIKE...
...SHINJI AND...

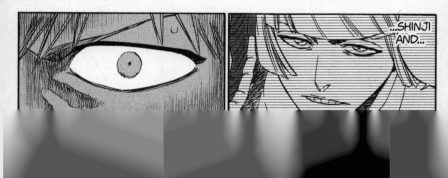

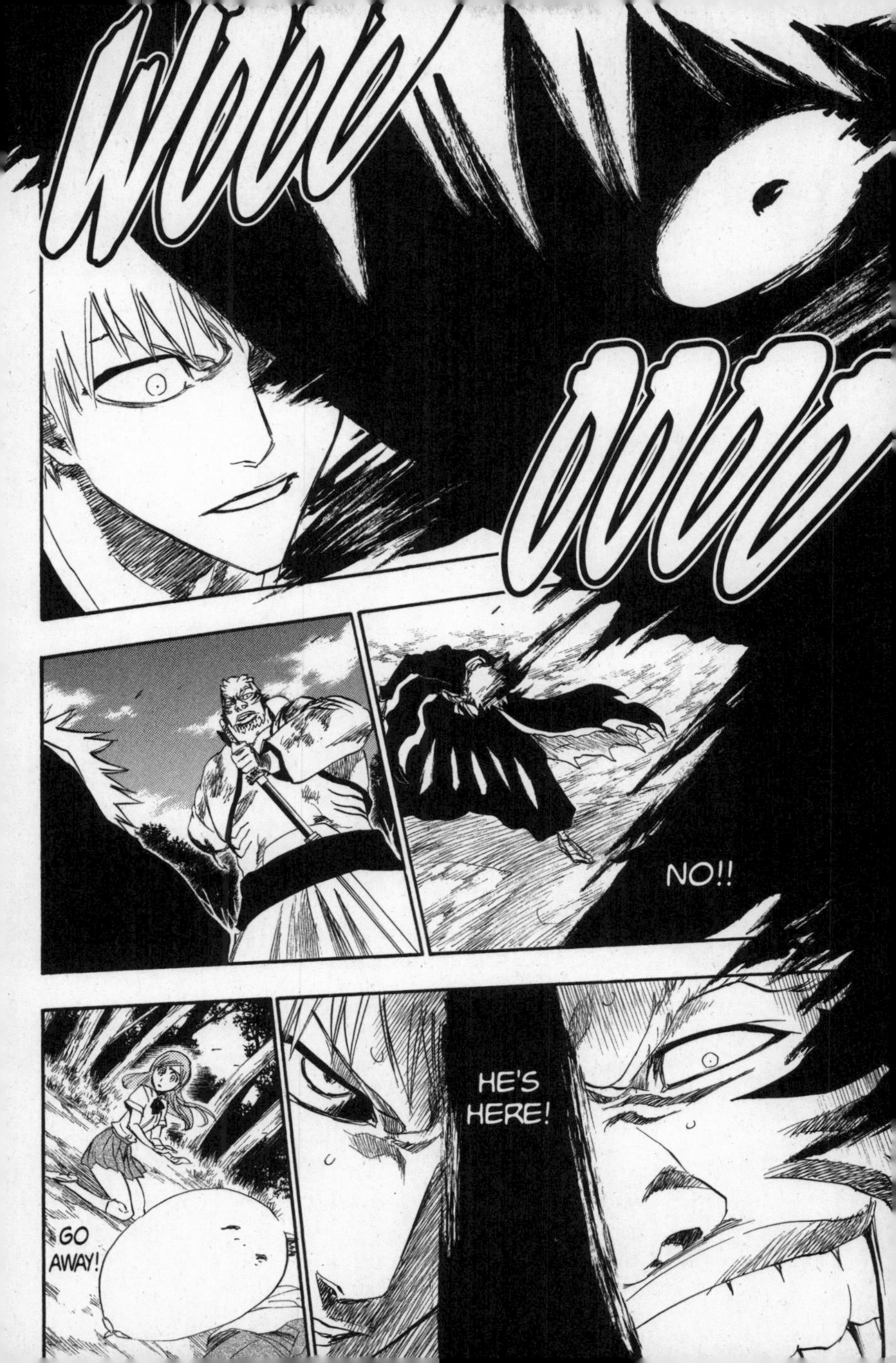
NO!!
HE'S HERE!
GO AWAY!

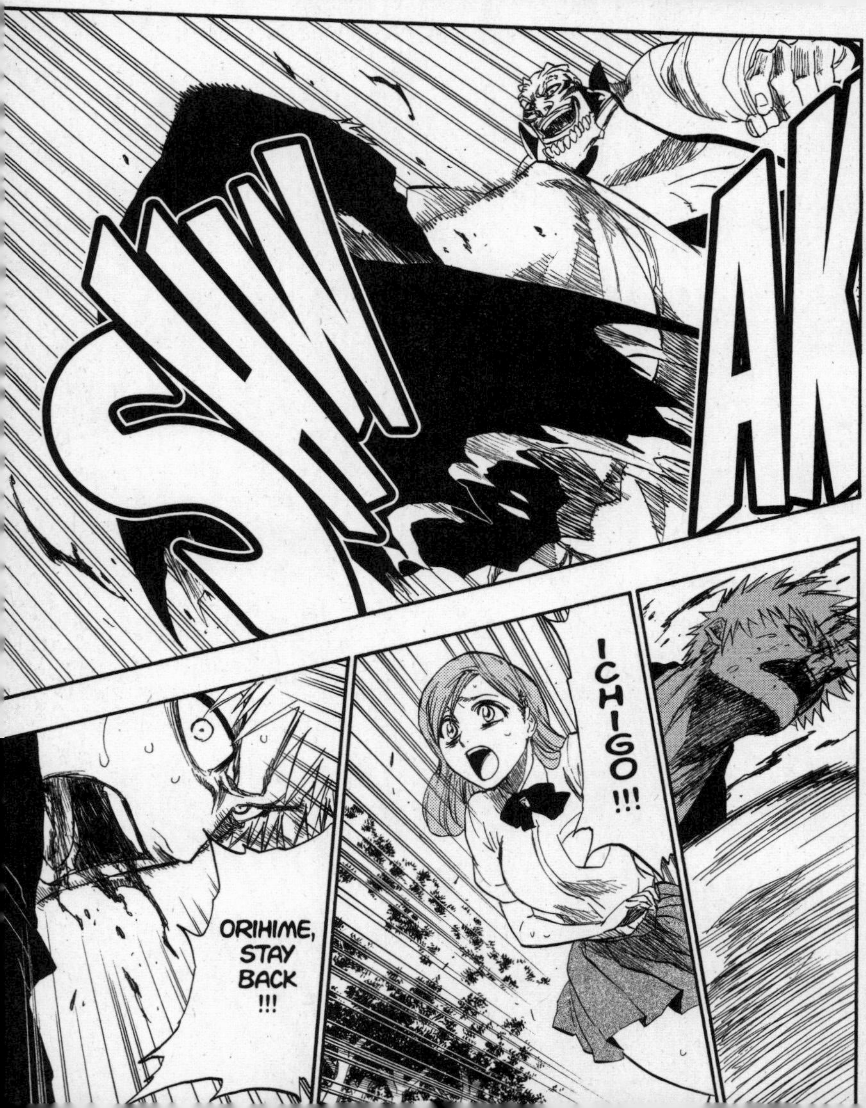
SHWAK
ICHIGO!!!
ORIHIME, STAY BACK!!!

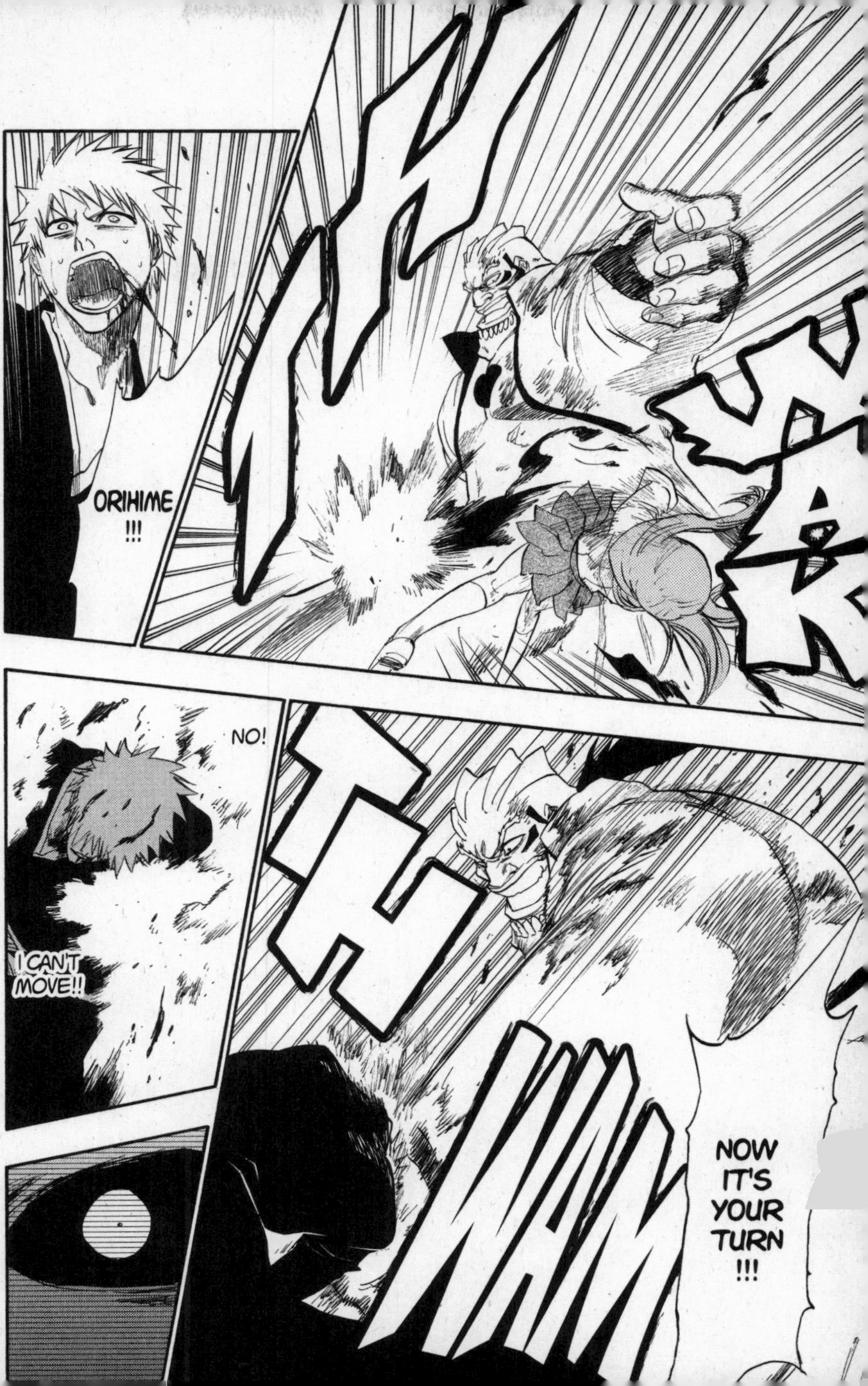
ORIHIME !!!
NOW IT'S YOUR TURN !!!
WHAM
NO!
I CAN'T MOVE!!

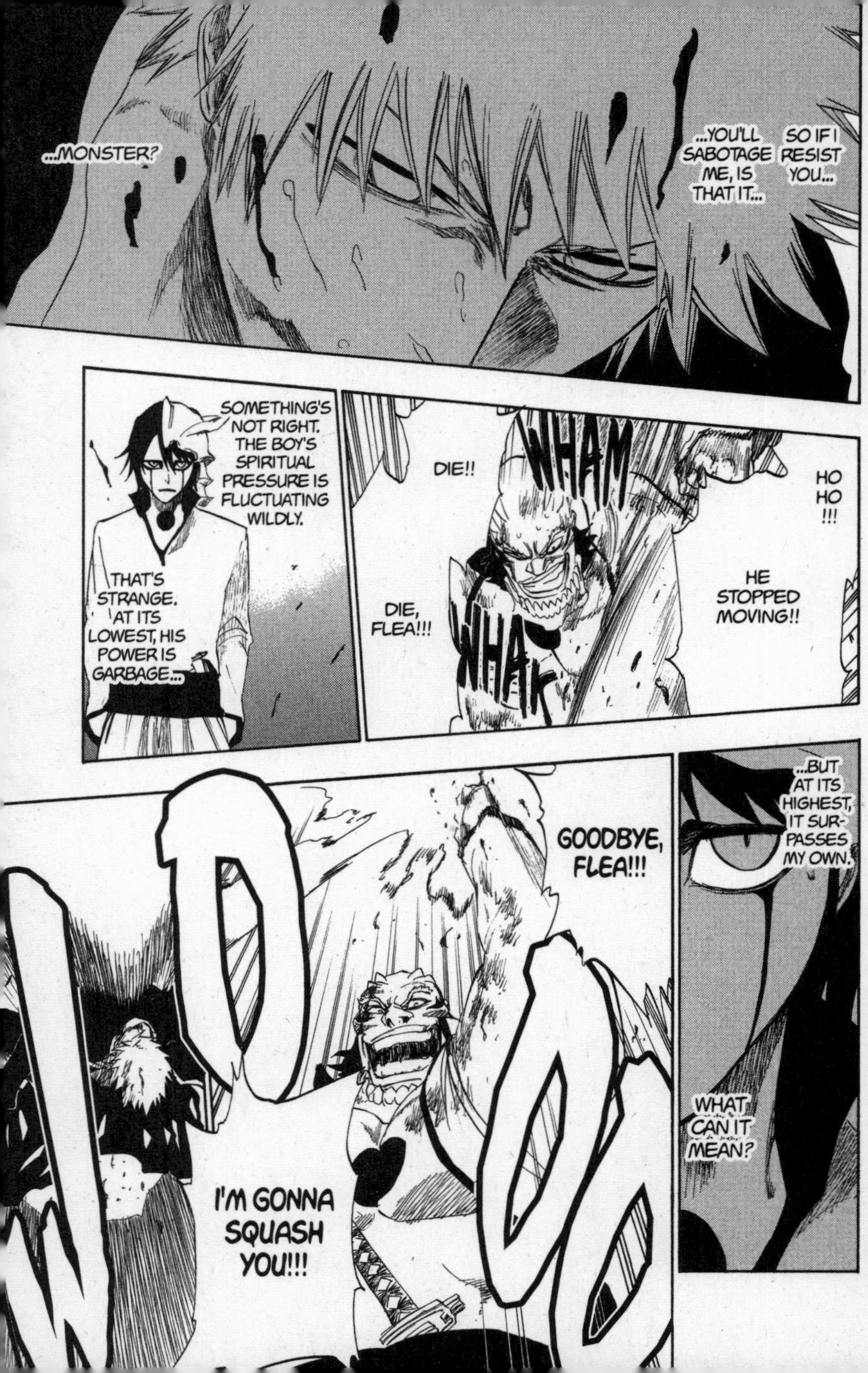
SO IF I RESIST YOU...
...YOU'LL SABOTAGE ME, IS THAT IT...
...MONSTER?
HO HO !!!
HE STOPPED MOVING!!
WHAM
DIE!!
WHAK
DIE, FLEA!!!
SOMETHING'S NOT RIGHT. THE BOY'S SPIRITUAL PRESSURE IS FLUCTUATING WILDLY.
THAT'S STRANGE. AT ITS LOWEST, HIS POWER IS GARBAGE...
...BUT AT ITS HIGHEST, IT SURPASSES MY OWN.
WHAT CAN IT MEAN?
GOODBYE, FLEA!!!
I'M GONNA SQUASH YOU!!!

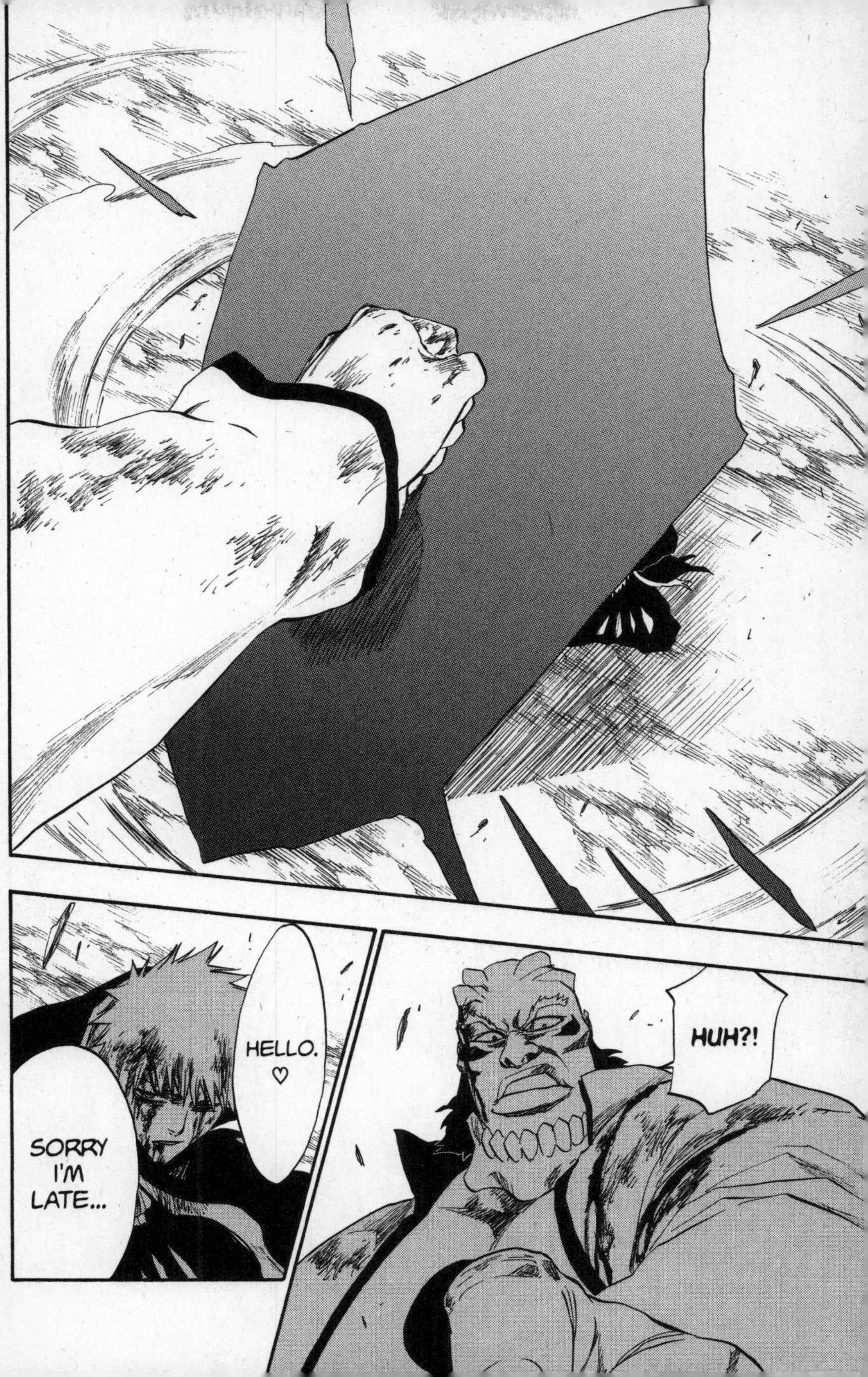
HUH?!
HELLO. ♡
SORRY I'M LATE...

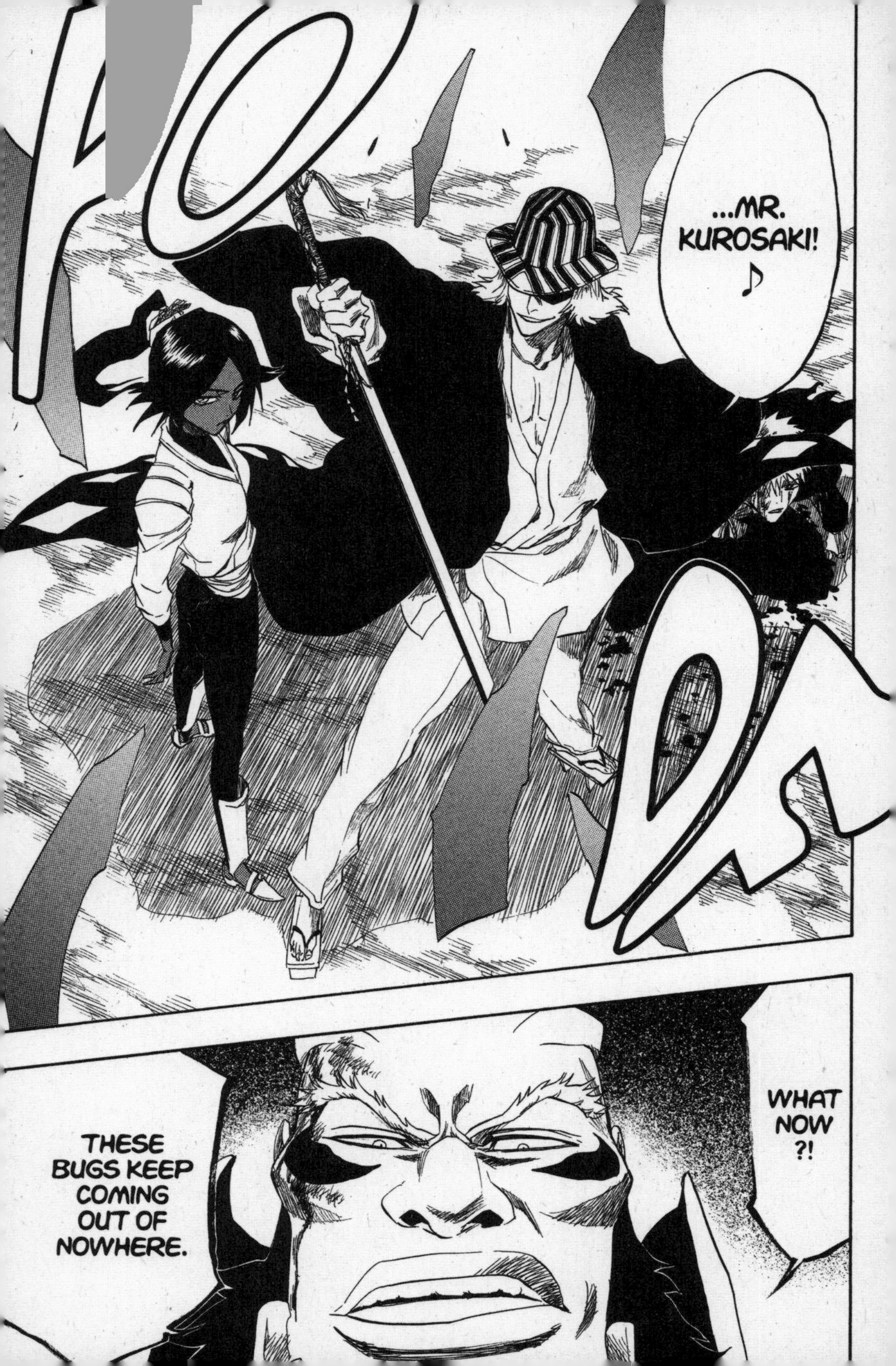
...MR. KUROSAKI! ♪
WHAT NOW ?!
THESE BUGS KEEP COMING OUT OF NOWHERE.

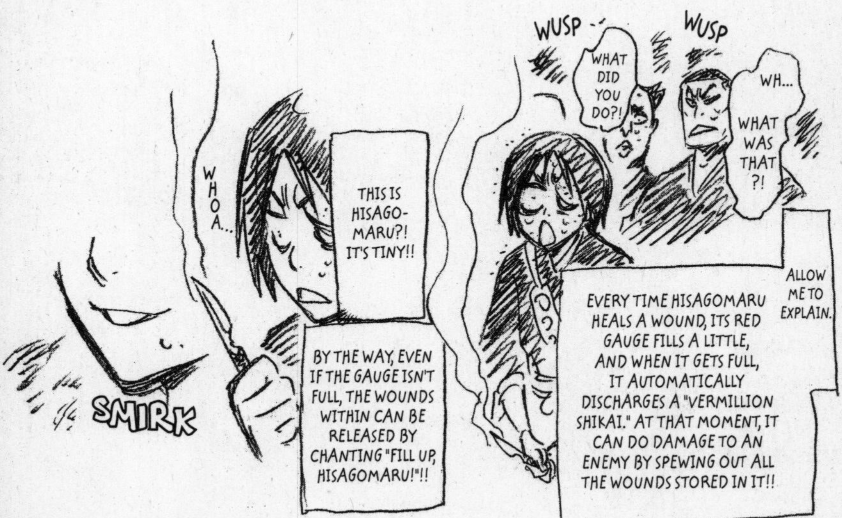
WUSP
WH... WHAT WAS THAT?!
WHAT DID YOU DO?!
WUSP
ALLOW ME TO EXPLAIN.
EVERY TIME HISAGOMARU HEALS A WOUND, ITS RED GAUGE FILLS A LITTLE, AND WHEN IT GETS FULL, IT AUTOMATICALLY DISCHARGES A "VERMILLION SHIKAI." AT THAT MOMENT, IT CAN DO DAMAGE TO AN ENEMY BY SPEWING OUT ALL THE WOUNDS STORED IN IT!!
THIS IS HISAGOMARU?! IT'S TINY!!
WHOA...
BY THE WAY, EVEN IF THE GAUGE ISN'T FULL, THE WOUNDS WITHIN CAN BE RELEASED BY CHANTING "FILL UP, HISAGOMARU!"!!
SMIRK

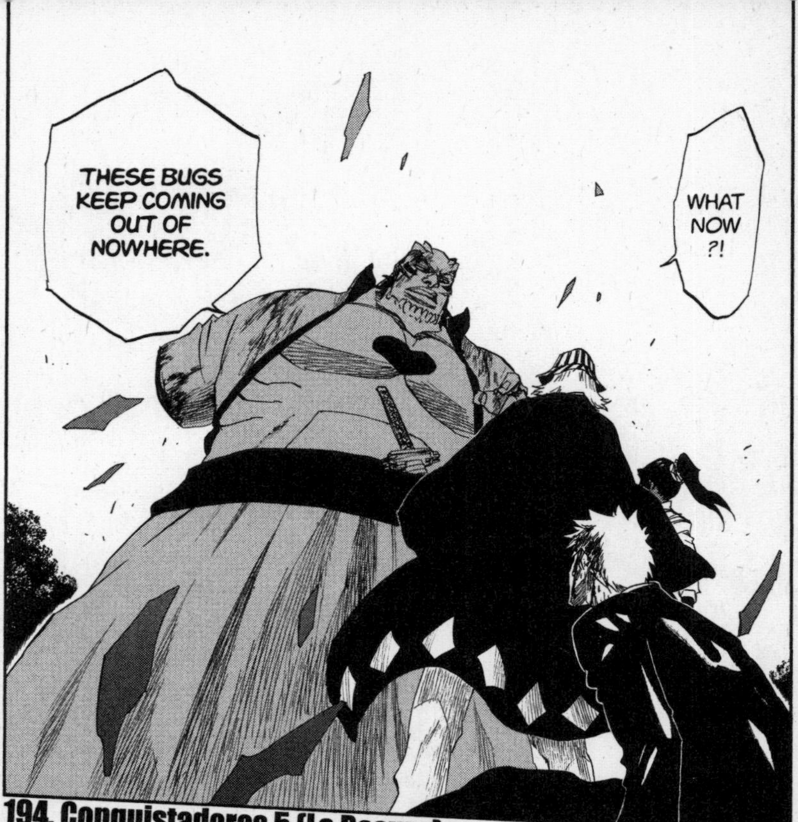
WHAT NOW?!
THESE BUGS KEEP COMING OUT OF NOWHERE.

194. Conquistadores 5 (La Basura)

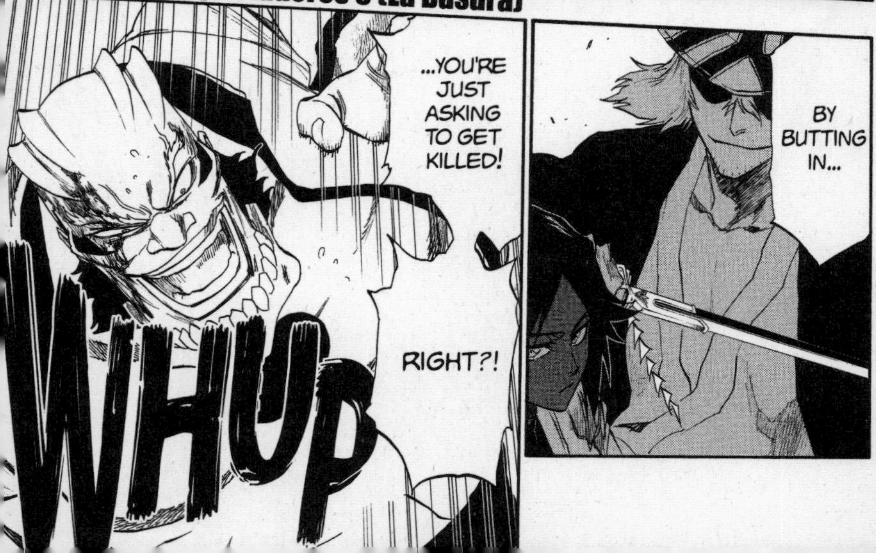
BY BUTTING IN...
...YOU'RE JUST ASKING TO GET KILLED!
RIGHT?!
WHUP

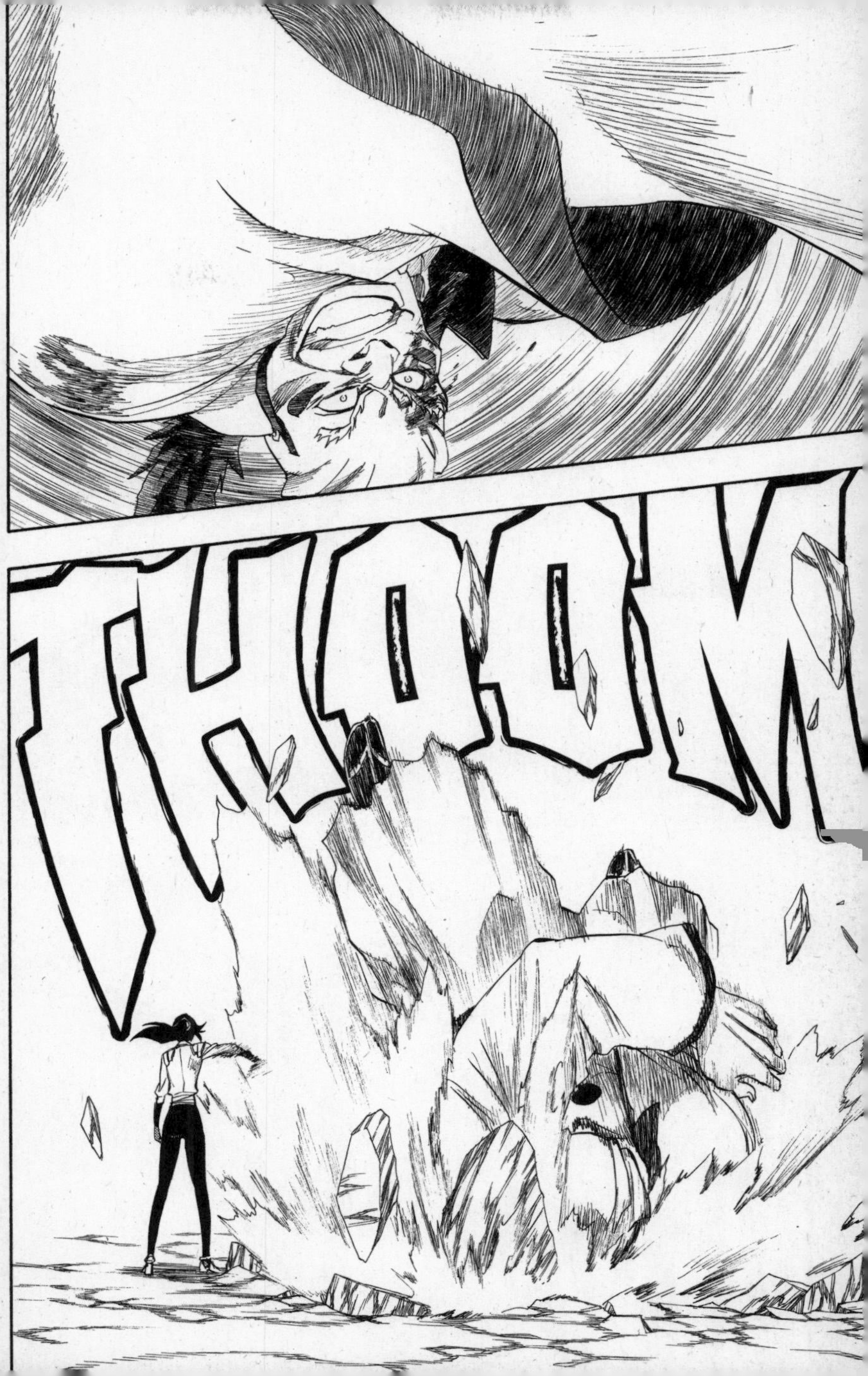
THOOM

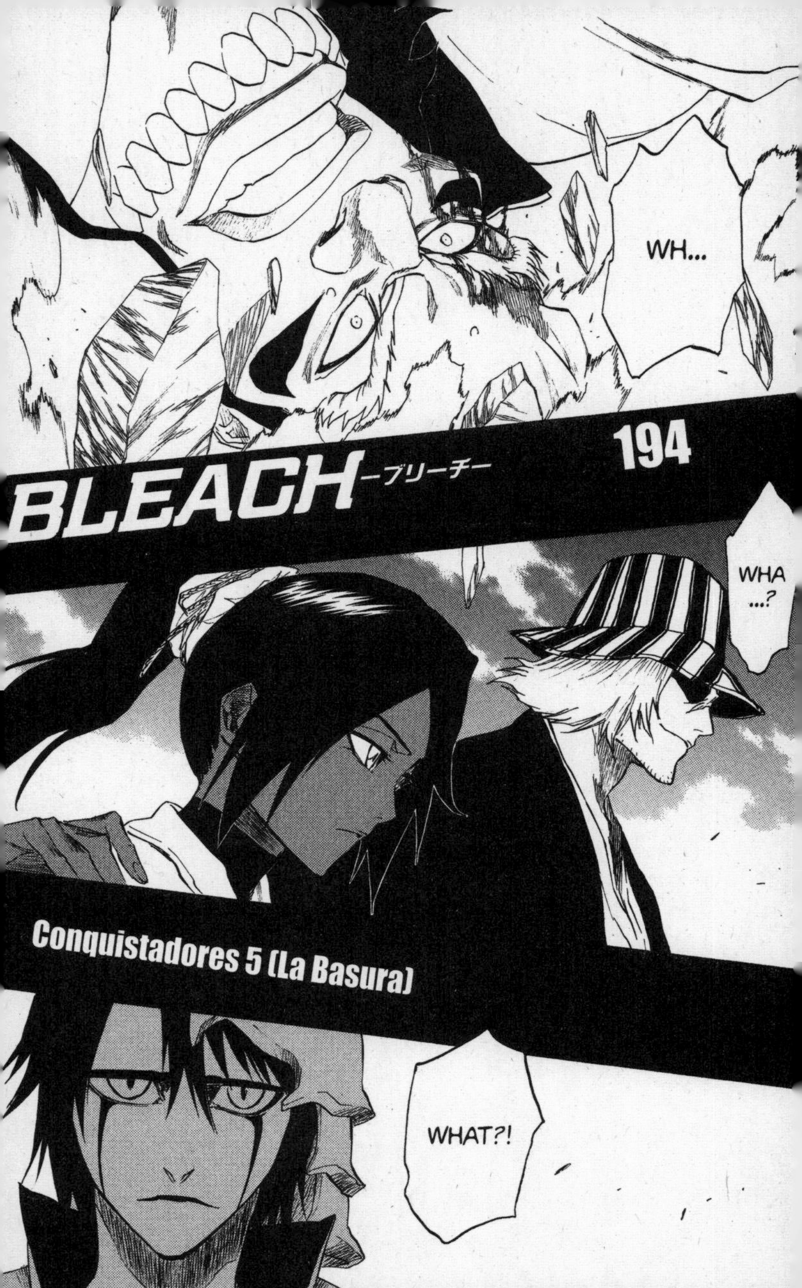
WH...
194
BLEACH
ーブリーチー
WHA ...?
Conquistadores 5 (La Basura)
WHAT?!

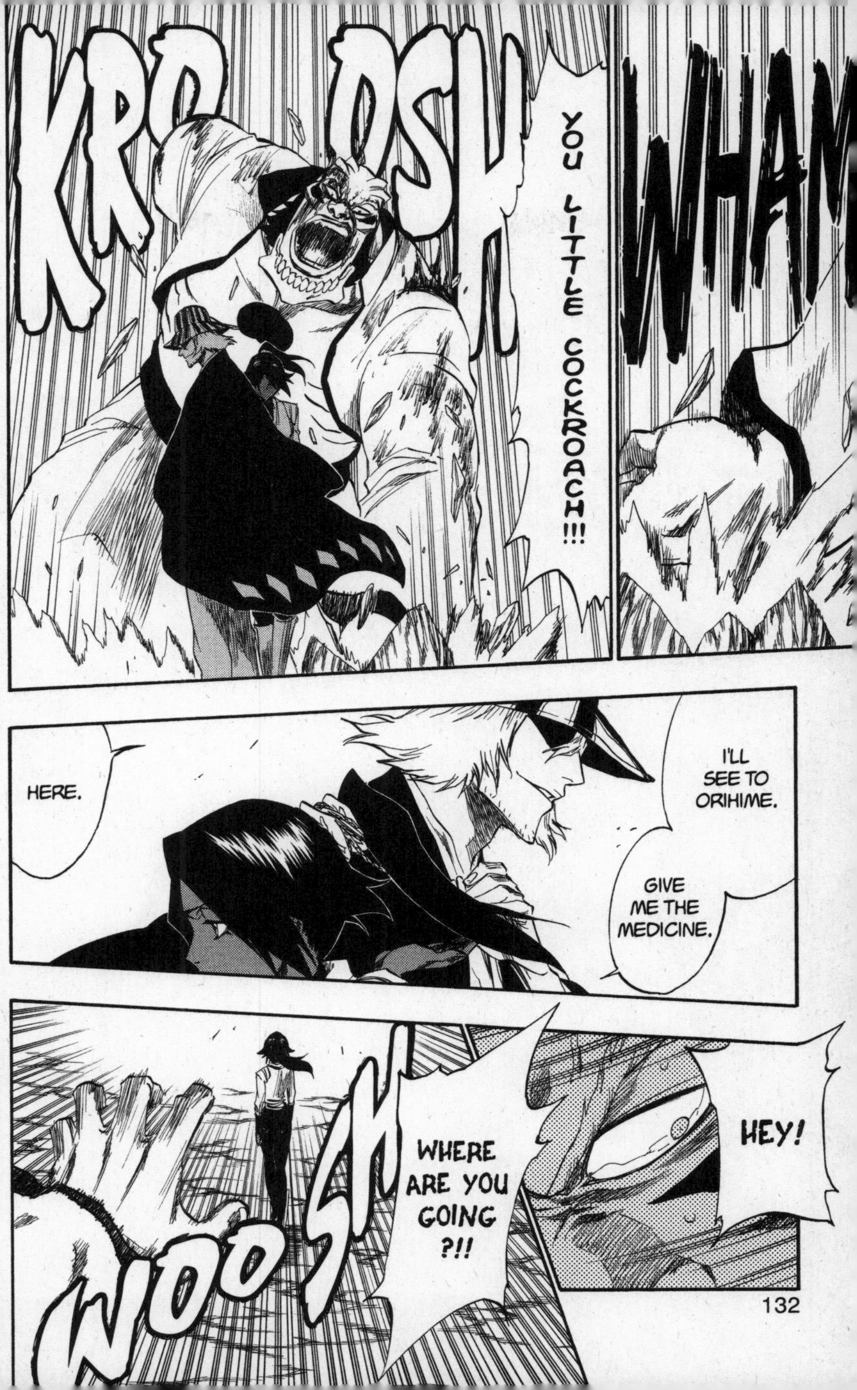
WHAM
YOU LITTLE COCKROACH!!!
KRO OSH
I'LL SEE TO ORIHIME.
GIVE ME THE MEDICINE.
HERE.
HEY!
WHERE ARE YOU GOING ?!!
WOOSH

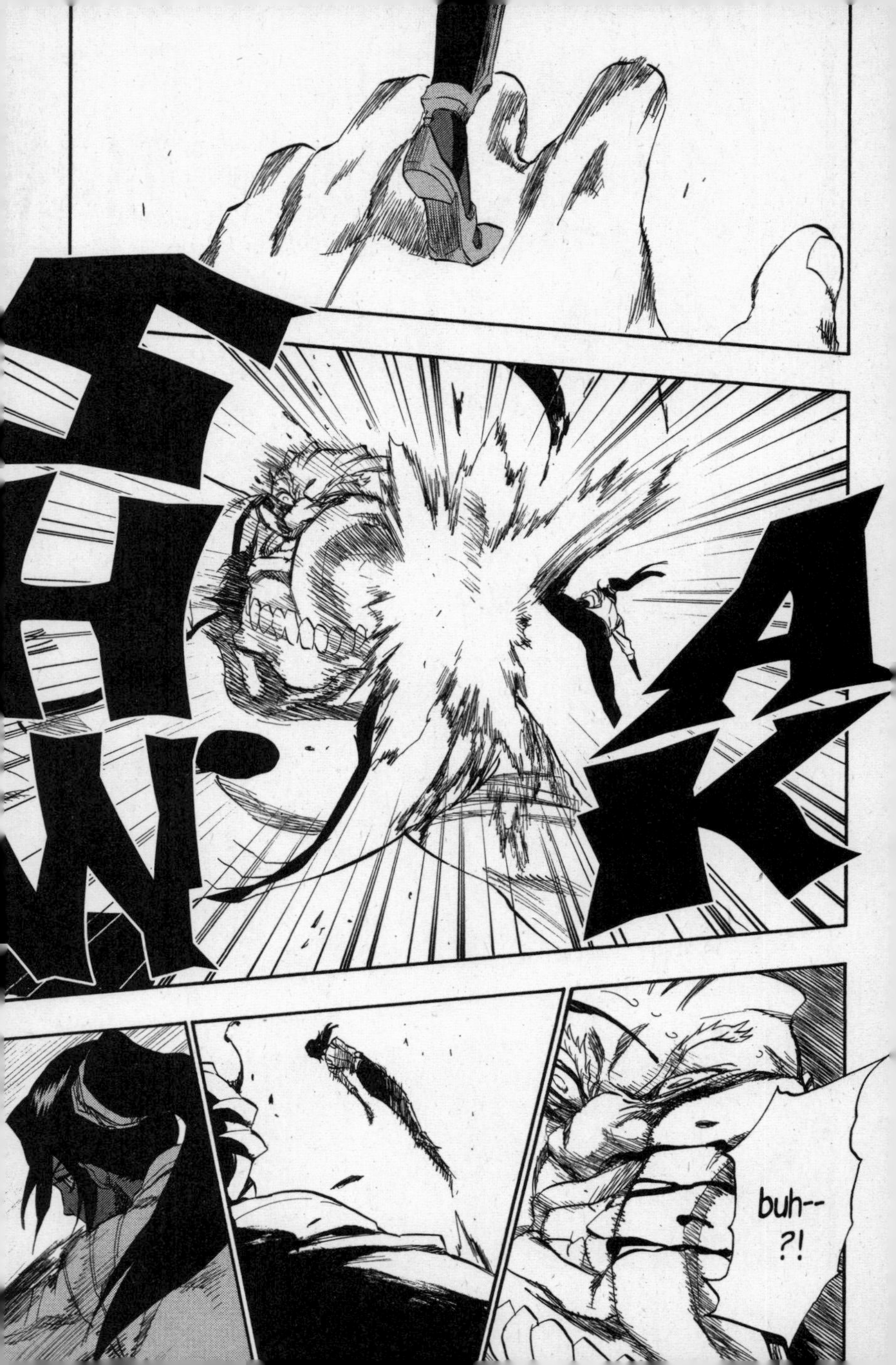
THWAK
buh--
?!

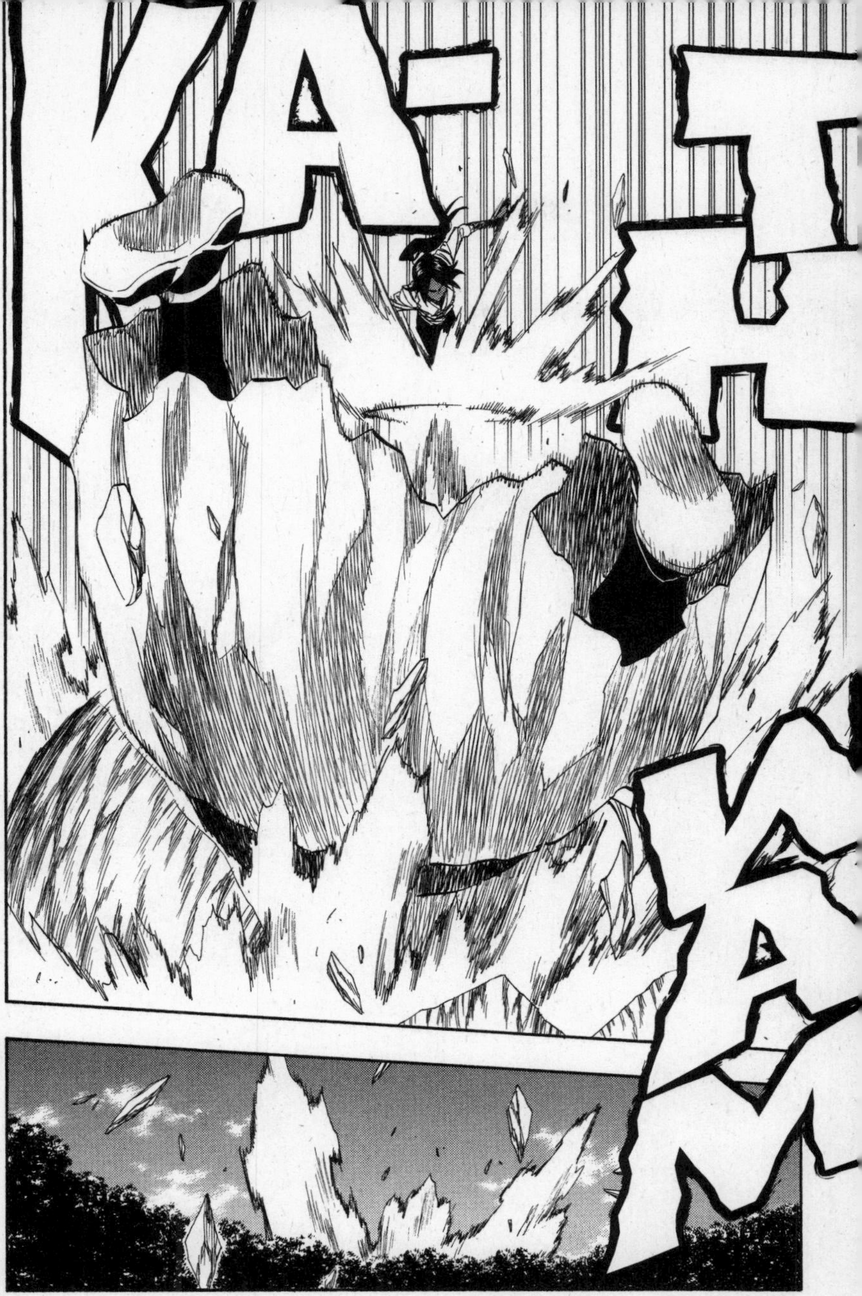
KA-T
KAM

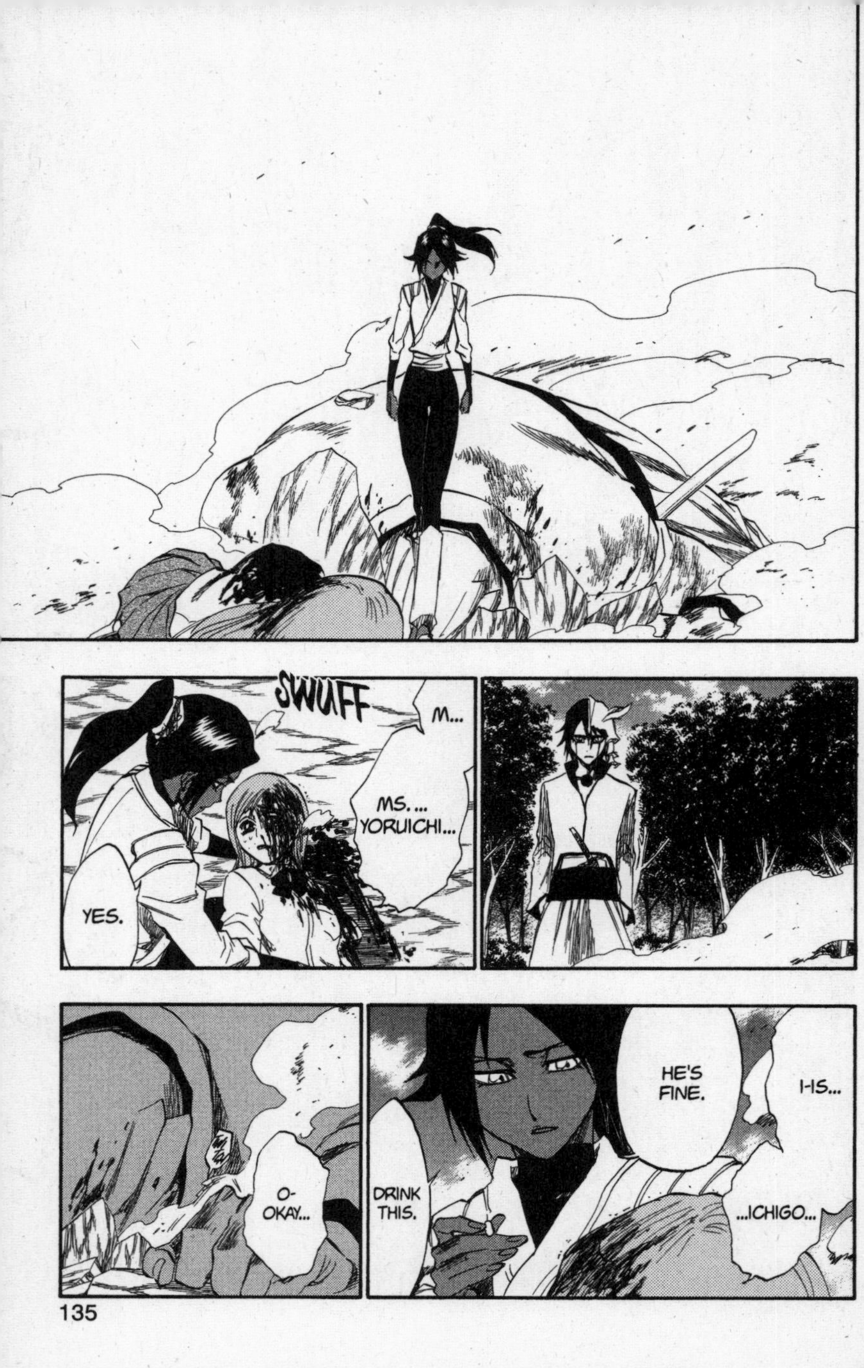
M...
MS. ... YORUICHI...
SWUFF
YES.
I-IS...
...ICHIGO...
HE'S FINE.
DRINK THIS.
O-OKAY...

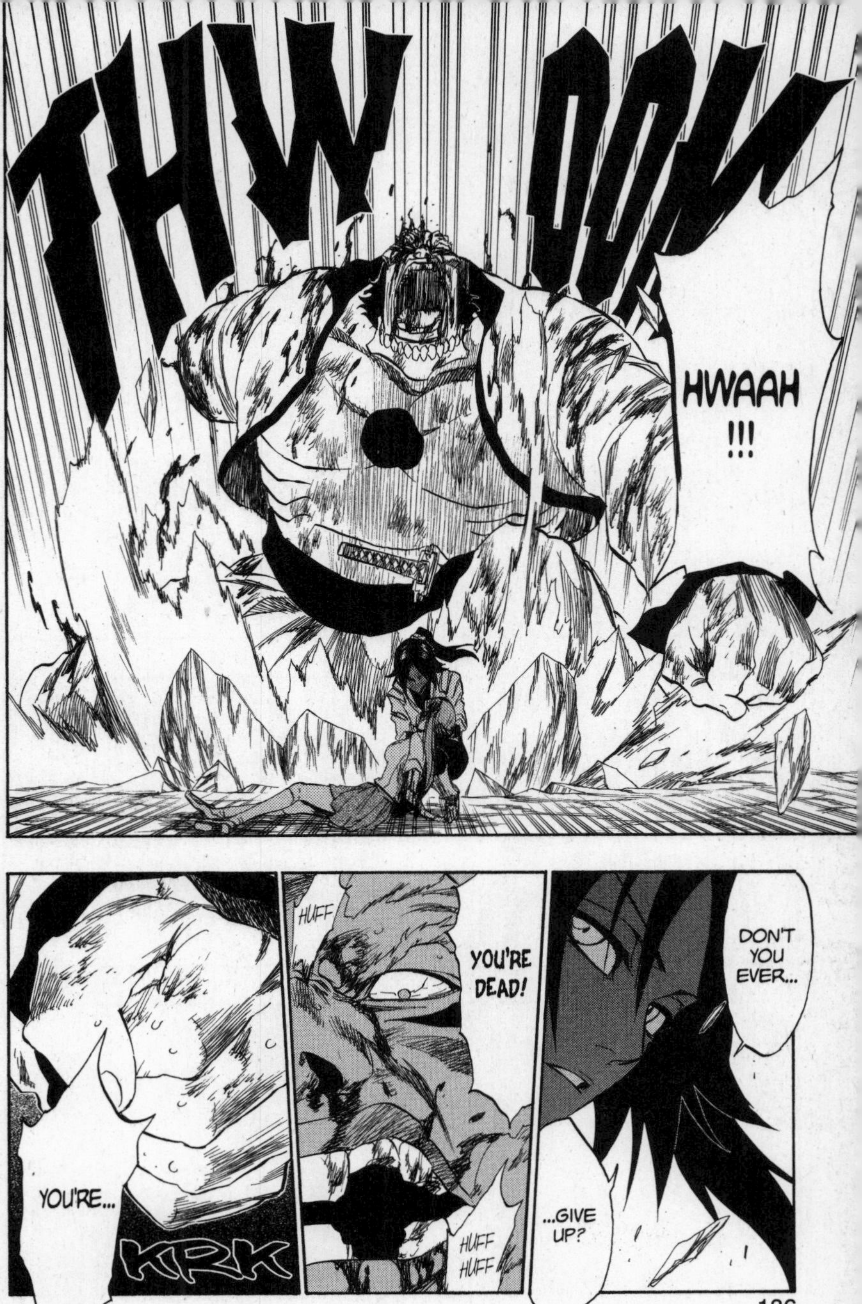
THWOOM
HWAAH !!!
DON'T YOU EVER...
...GIVE UP?
HUFF
YOU'RE DEAD!
HUFF HUFF
YOU'RE...
KRK

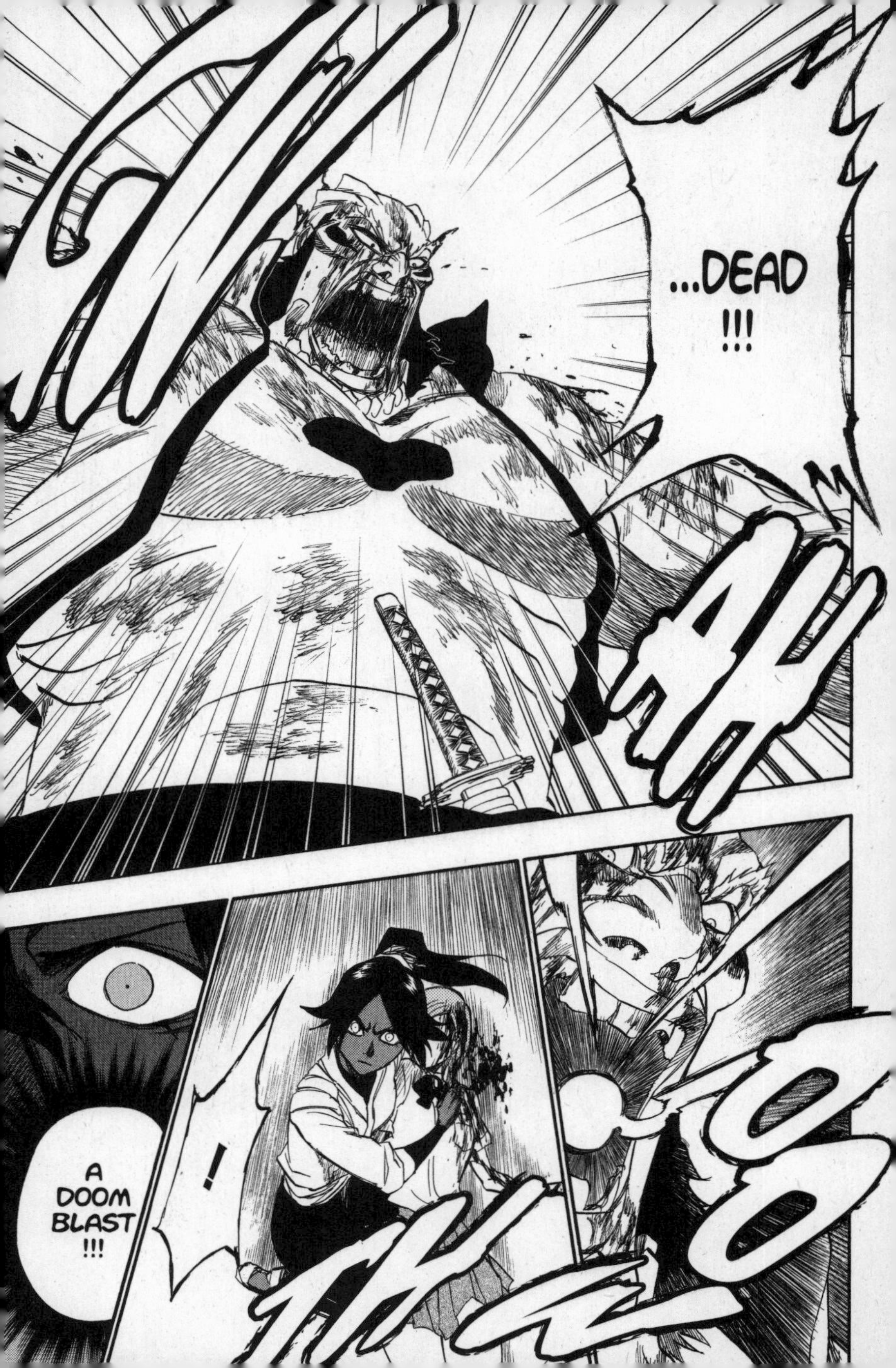
...DEAD !!!
!
A DOOM BLAST !!!

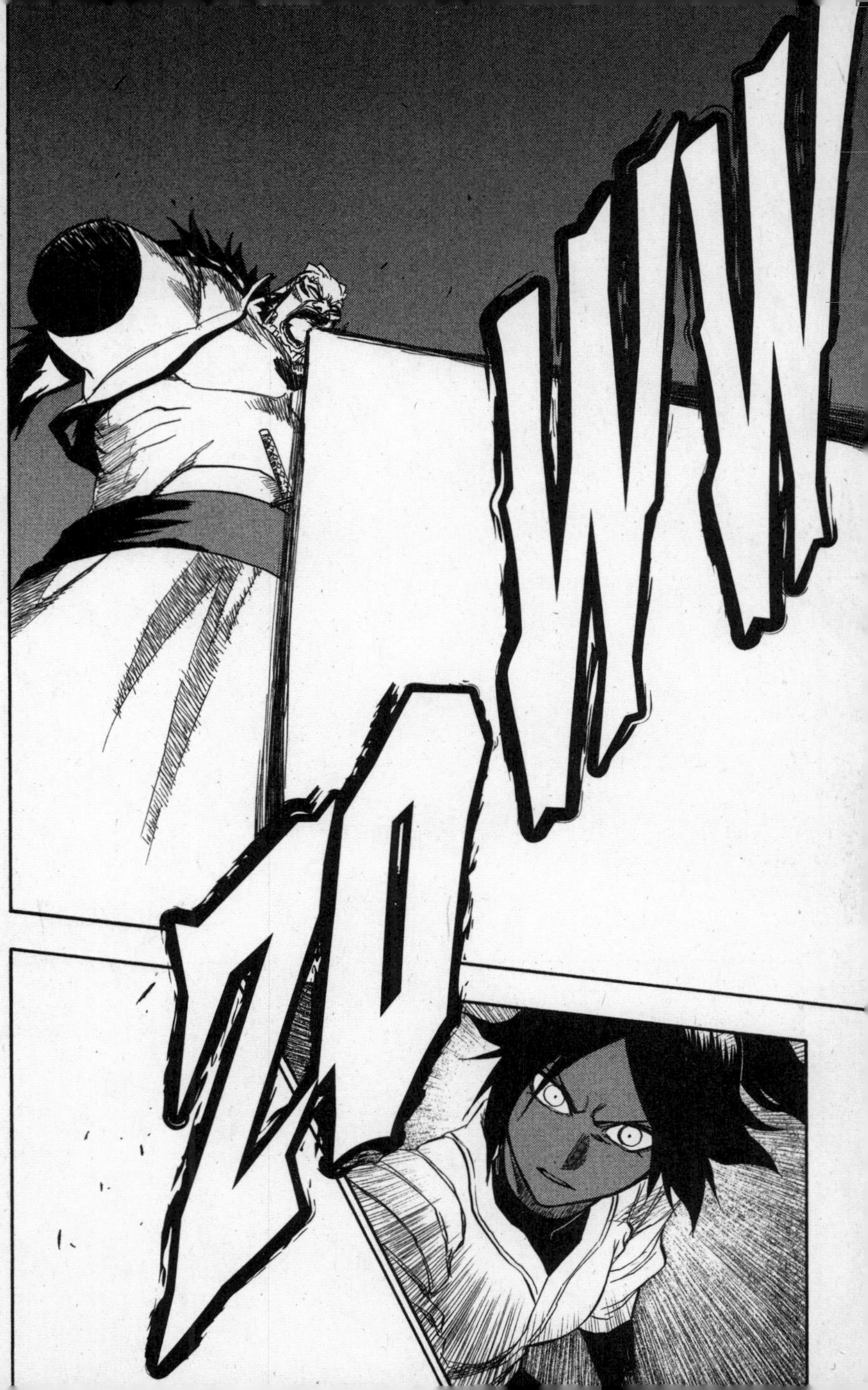

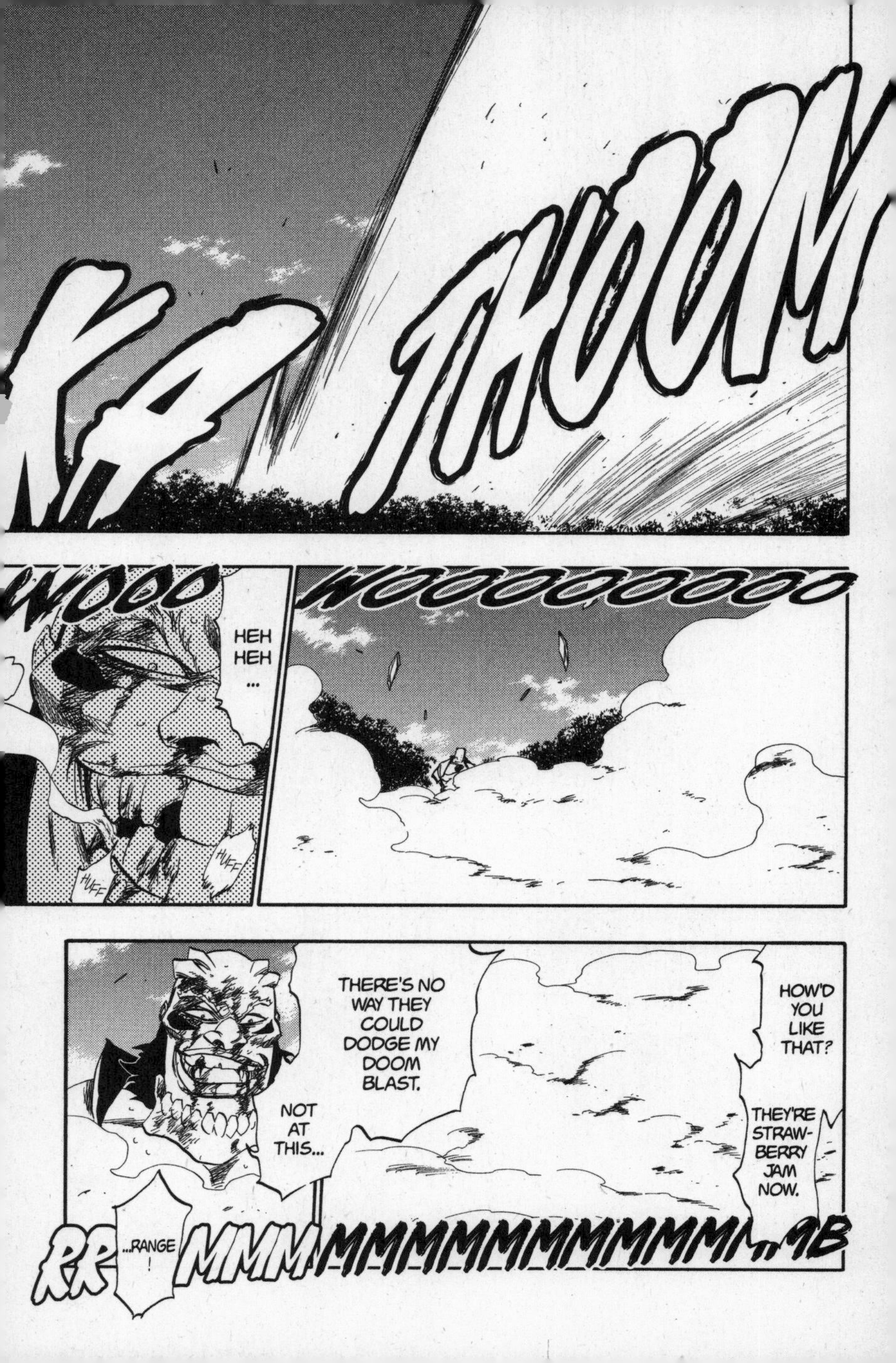
KA THOOM
WOOOOOOOOOOO
WOOO
HEH HEH ...
HUFF
HUFF
HOW'D YOU LIKE THAT?
THEY'RE STRAWBERRY JAM NOW.
THERE'S NO WAY THEY COULD DODGE MY DOOM BLAST.
NOT AT THIS...
...RANGE!
RRMMMMMMMMMMMMMMMMM...

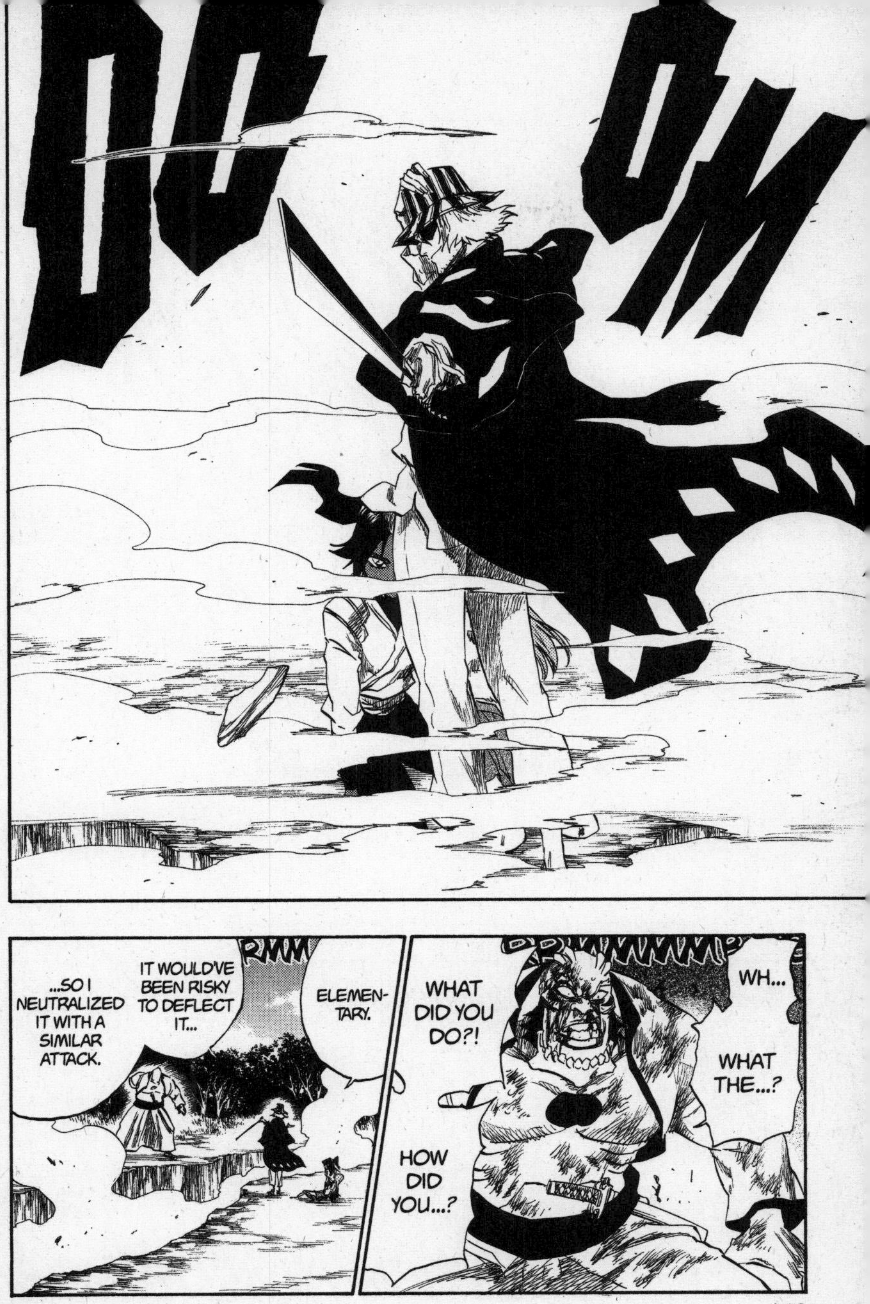
DOOM
WH...
WHAT THE...?
WHAT DID YOU DO?!
HOW DID YOU...?
RMM
ELEMENTARY.
IT WOULD'VE BEEN RISKY TO DEFLECT IT...
...SO I NEUTRALIZED IT WITH A SIMILAR ATTACK.

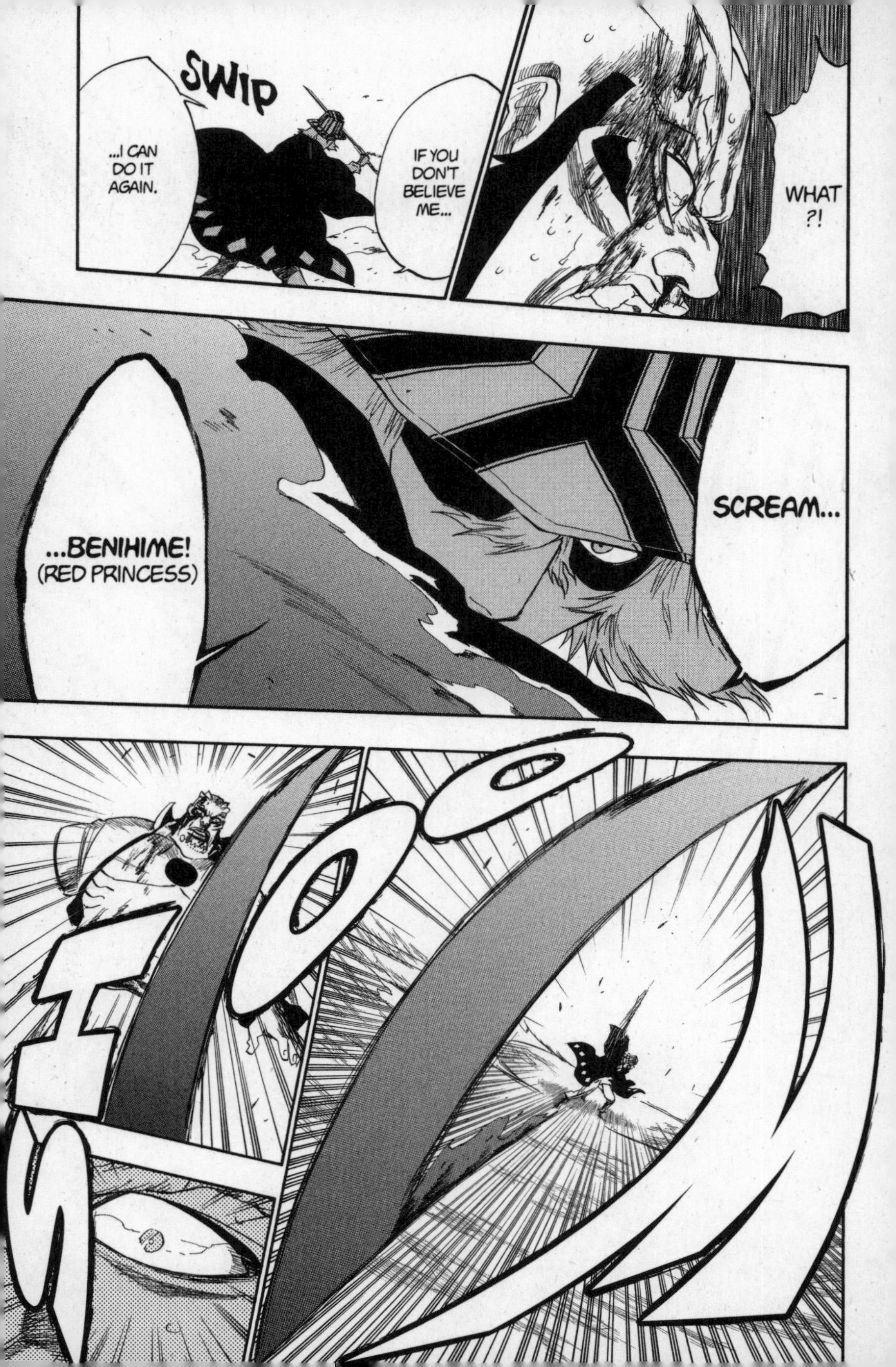
WHAT ?!
IF YOU DON'T BELIEVE ME...
SWIP
...I CAN DO IT AGAIN.
SCREAM...
...BENIHIME! (RED PRINCESS)

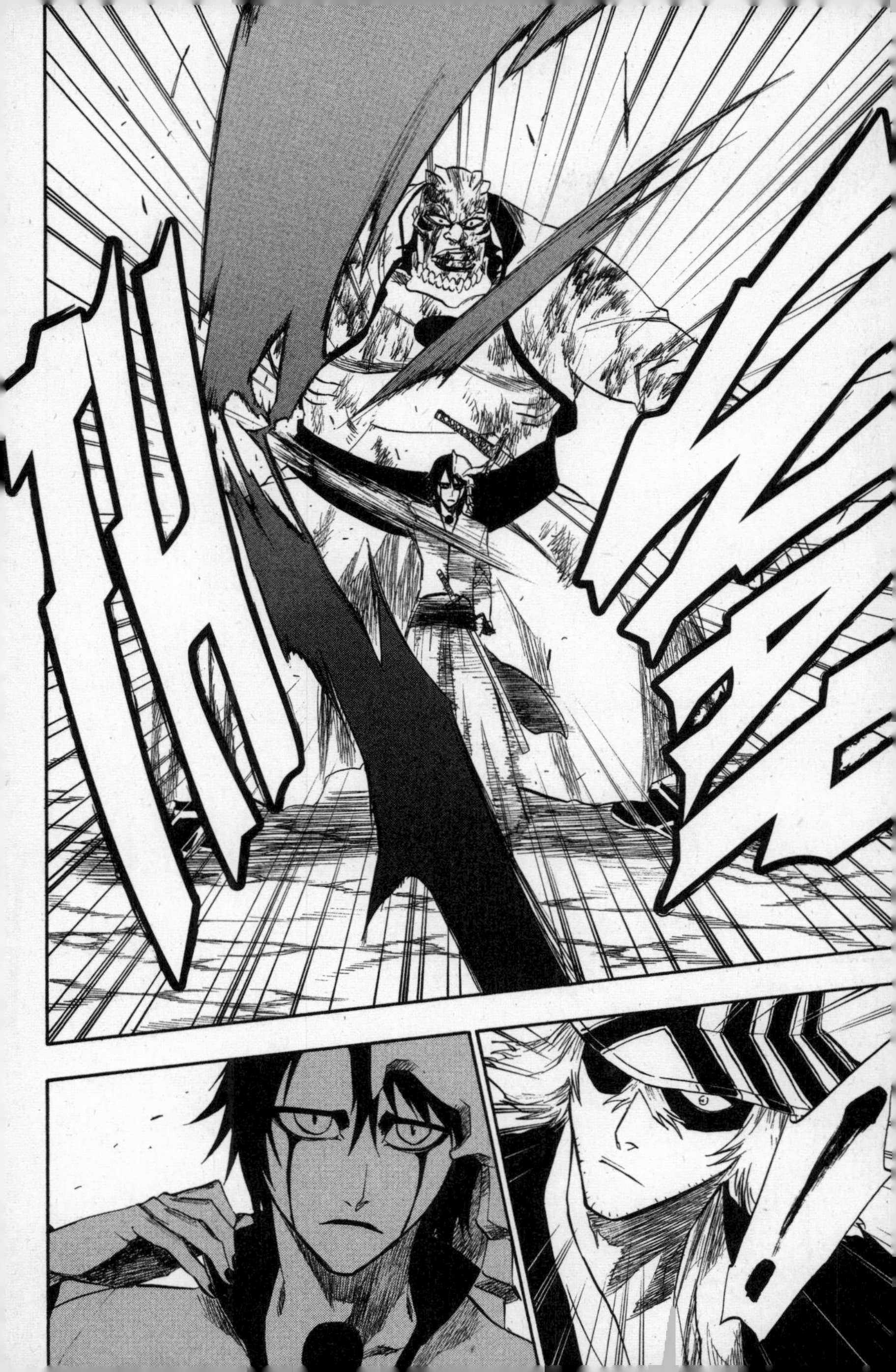

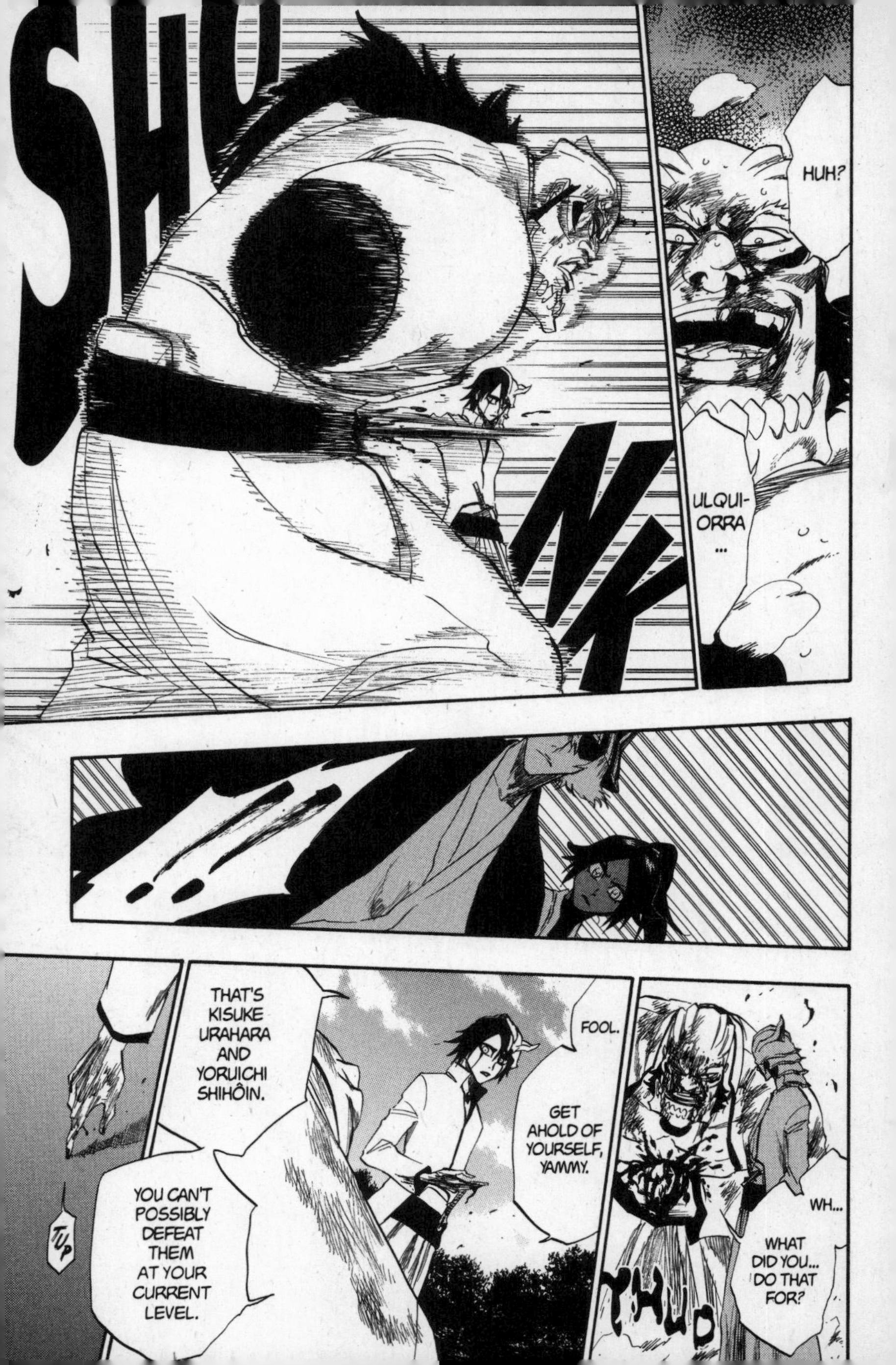
HUH?
ULQUI-ORRA...
SHU
NK
WH...
WHAT DID YOU... DO THAT FOR?
THUD
FOOL.
GET AHOLD OF YOURSELF, YAMMY.
THAT'S KISUKE URAHARA AND YORUICHI SHIHÔIN.
YOU CAN'T POSSIBLY DEFEAT THEM AT YOUR CURRENT LEVEL.
TUP

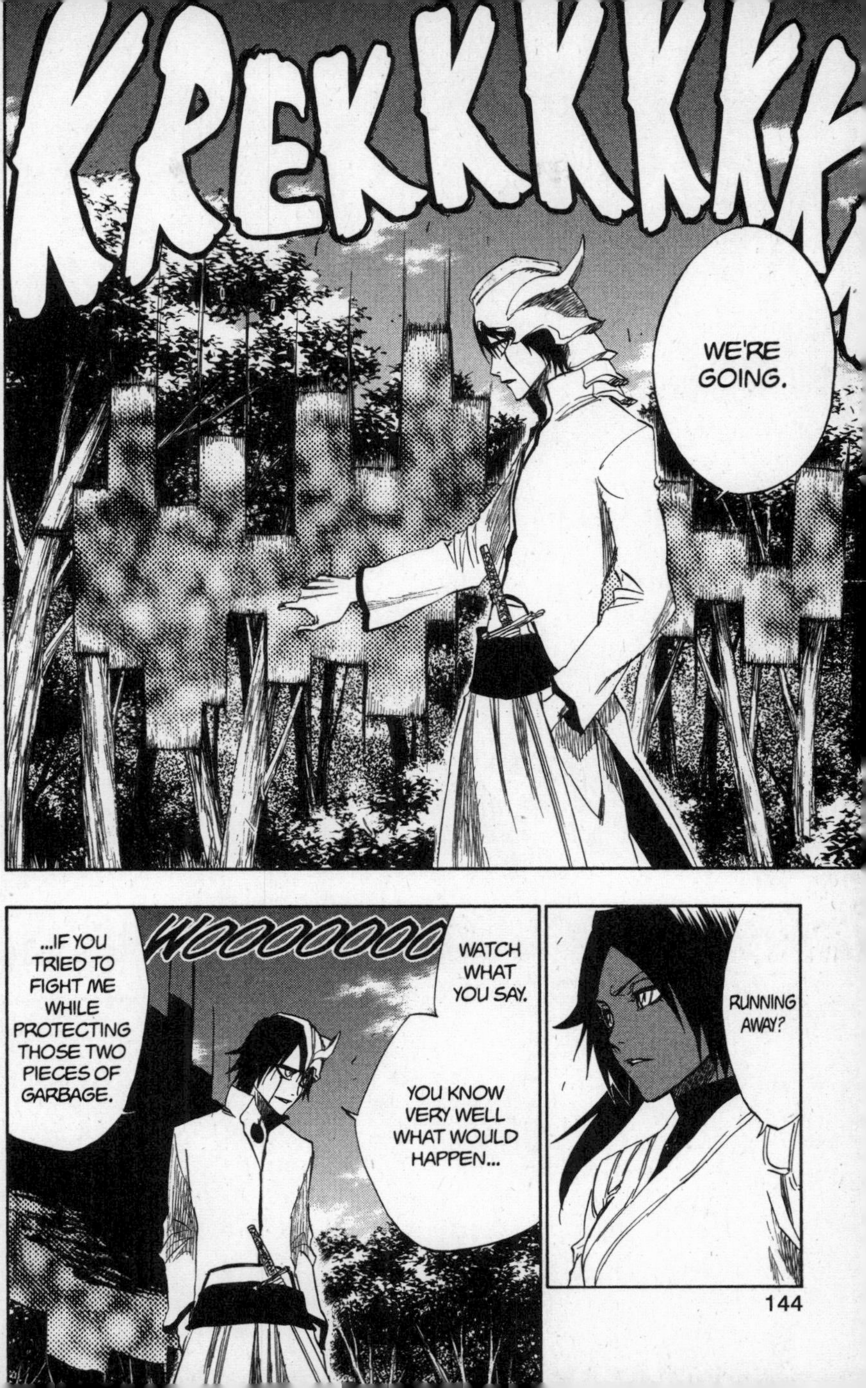
KREKKKKK
WE'RE GOING.
RUNNING AWAY?
WATCH WHAT YOU SAY.
WOOOOOOOO
YOU KNOW VERY WELL WHAT WOULD HAPPEN...
...IF YOU TRIED TO FIGHT ME WHILE PROTECTING THOSE TWO PIECES OF GARBAGE.

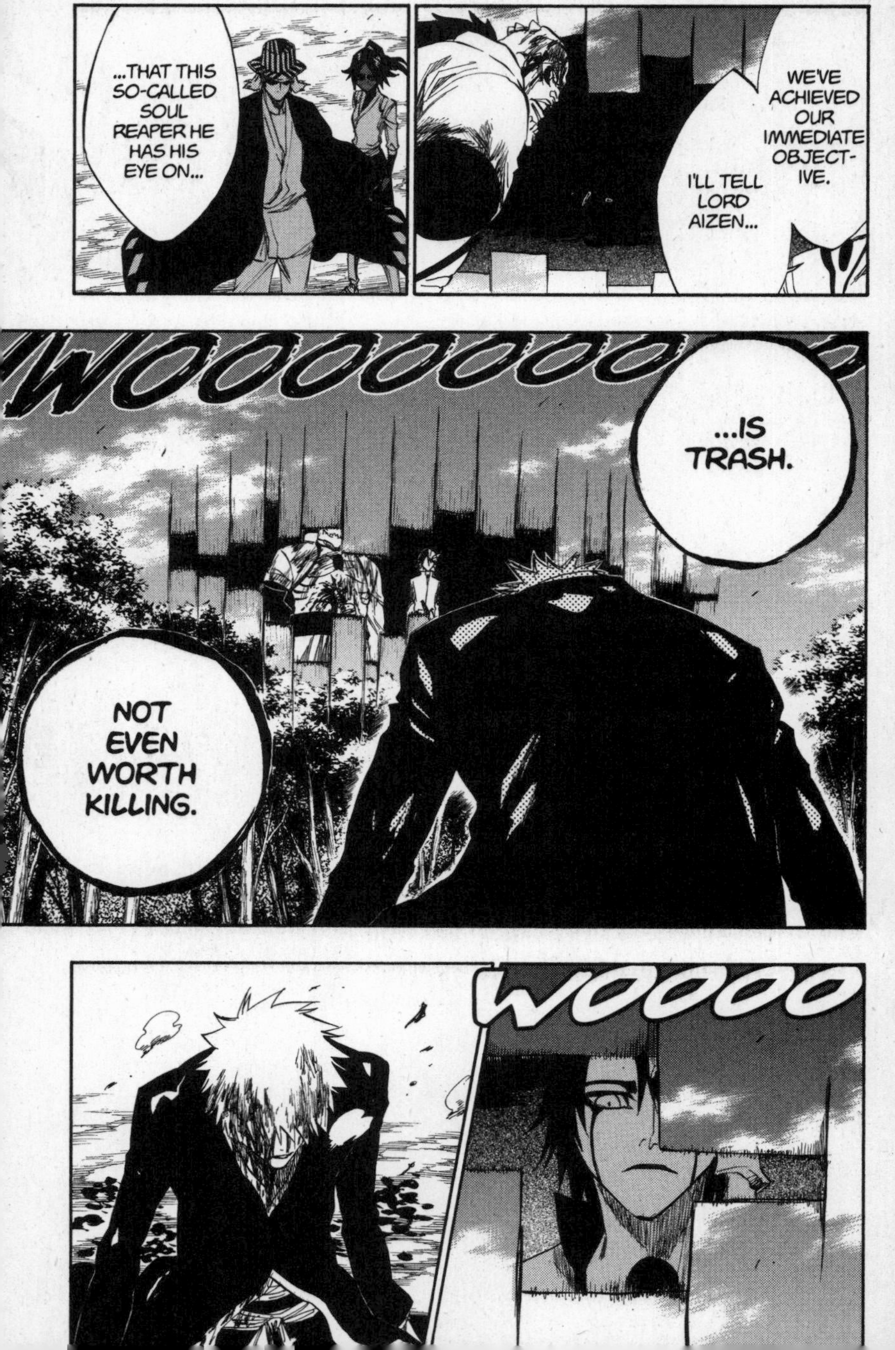
WE'VE ACHIEVED OUR IMMEDIATE OBJECTIVE.
I'LL TELL LORD AIZEN...
...THAT THIS SO-CALLED SOUL REAPER HE HAS HIS EYE ON...
WOOOOOOO
...IS TRASH.
NOT EVEN WORTH KILLING.
WOOOO

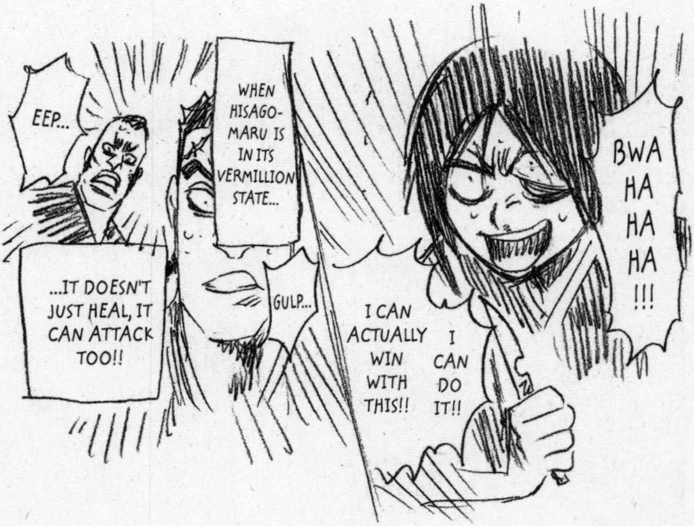
BWA HA HA HA!!!
WHEN HISAGO-MARU IS IN ITS VERMILLION STATE...
EEP...
I CAN DO IT!!
I CAN ACTUALLY WIN WITH THIS!!
GULP...
...IT DOESN'T JUST HEAL, IT CAN ATTACK TOO!!

195. Death & Strawberry (Reprise)

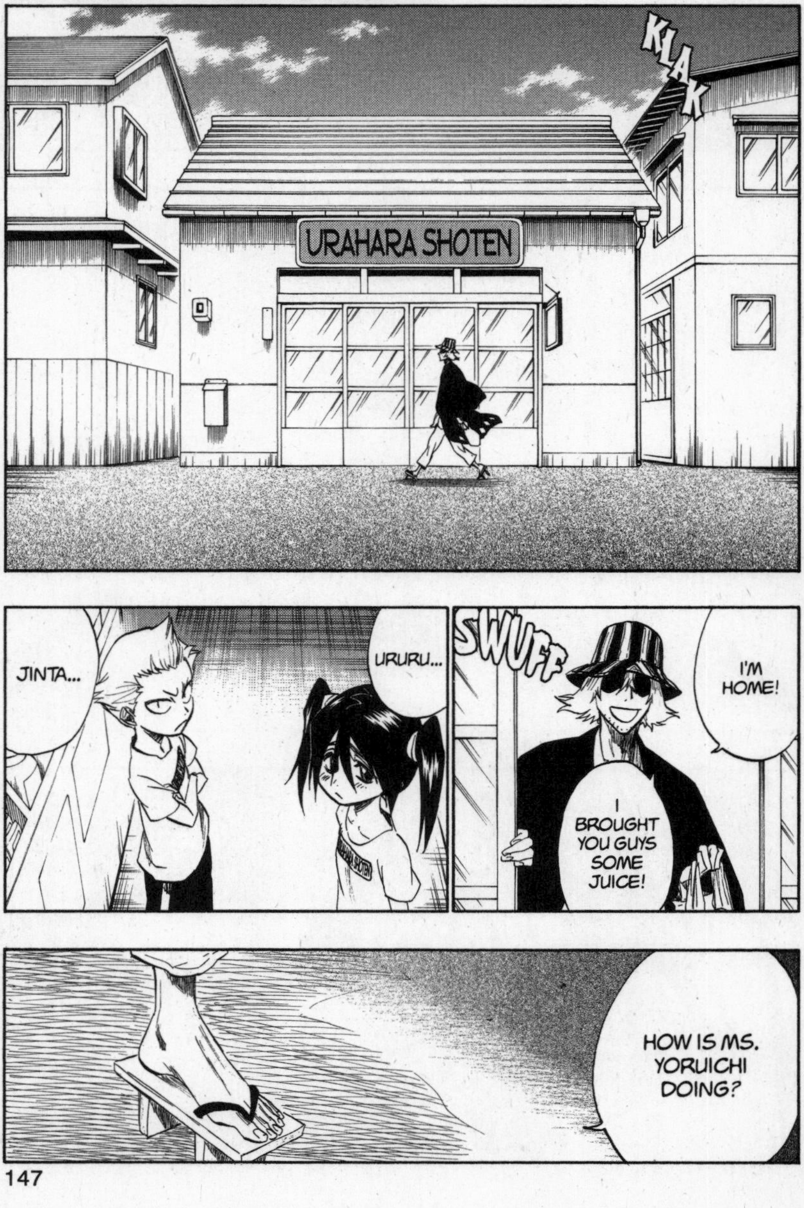
KLAK
URAHARA SHOTEN
SWUFF
I'M HOME!
I BROUGHT YOU GUYS SOME JUICE!
URURU...
JINTA...
HOW IS MS. YORUICHI DOING?

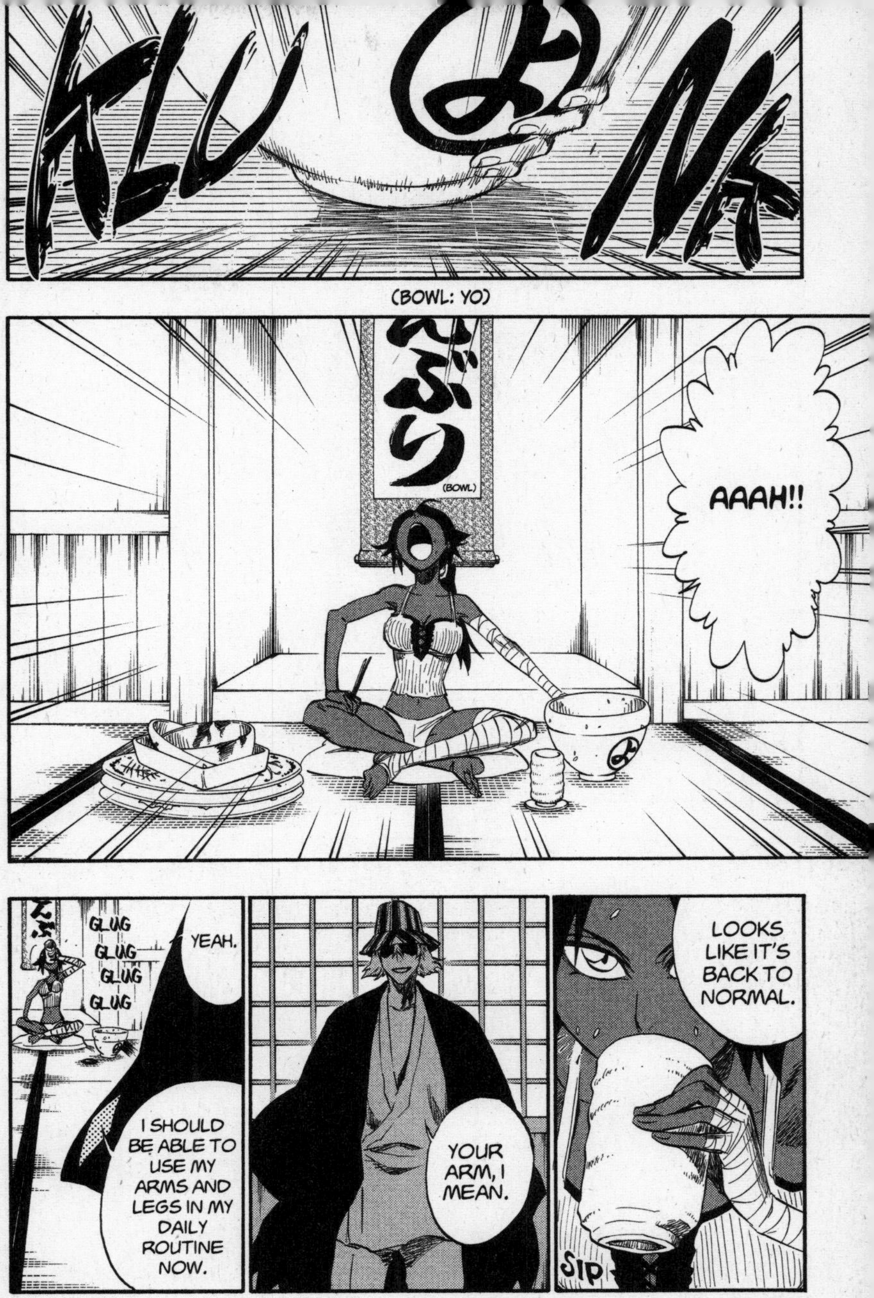
(BOWL: YO)
(BOWL)
AAAH!!
LOOKS LIKE IT'S BACK TO NORMAL.
SIP
YOUR ARM, I MEAN.
YEAH.
I SHOULD BE ABLE TO USE MY ARMS AND LEGS IN MY DAILY ROUTINE NOW.
GLUG GLUG GLUG GLUG

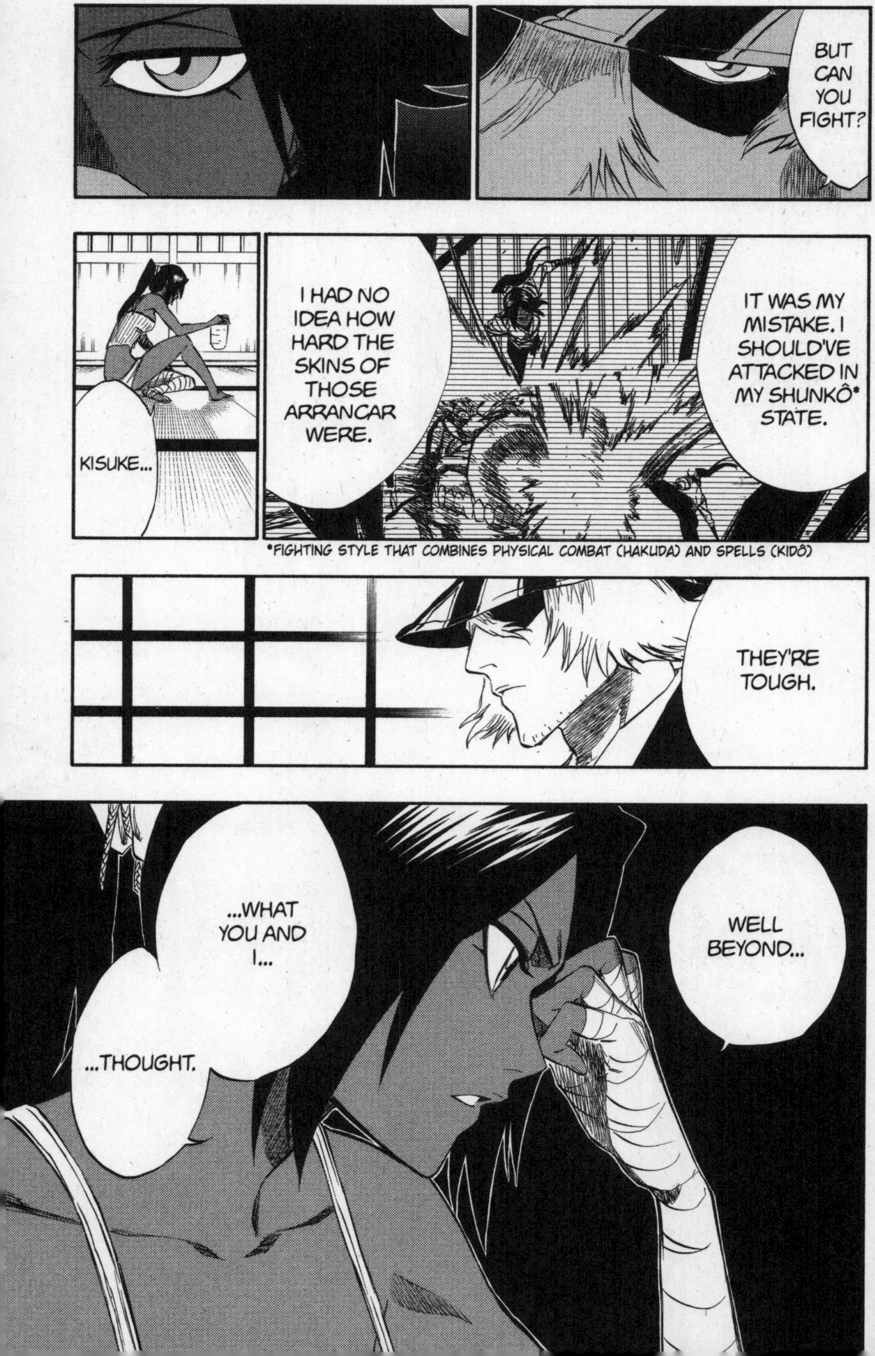
BUT CAN YOU FIGHT?
IT WAS MY MISTAKE. I SHOULD'VE ATTACKED IN MY SHUNKÔ* STATE.
I HAD NO IDEA HOW HARD THE SKINS OF THOSE ARRANCAR WERE.
KISUKE...
*FIGHTING STYLE THAT COMBINES PHYSICAL COMBAT (HAKUDA) AND SPELLS (KIDÔ)
THEY'RE TOUGH.
WELL BEYOND...
...WHAT YOU AND I...
...THOUGHT.

BLEACH

195. Death & Strawberry (Reprise)

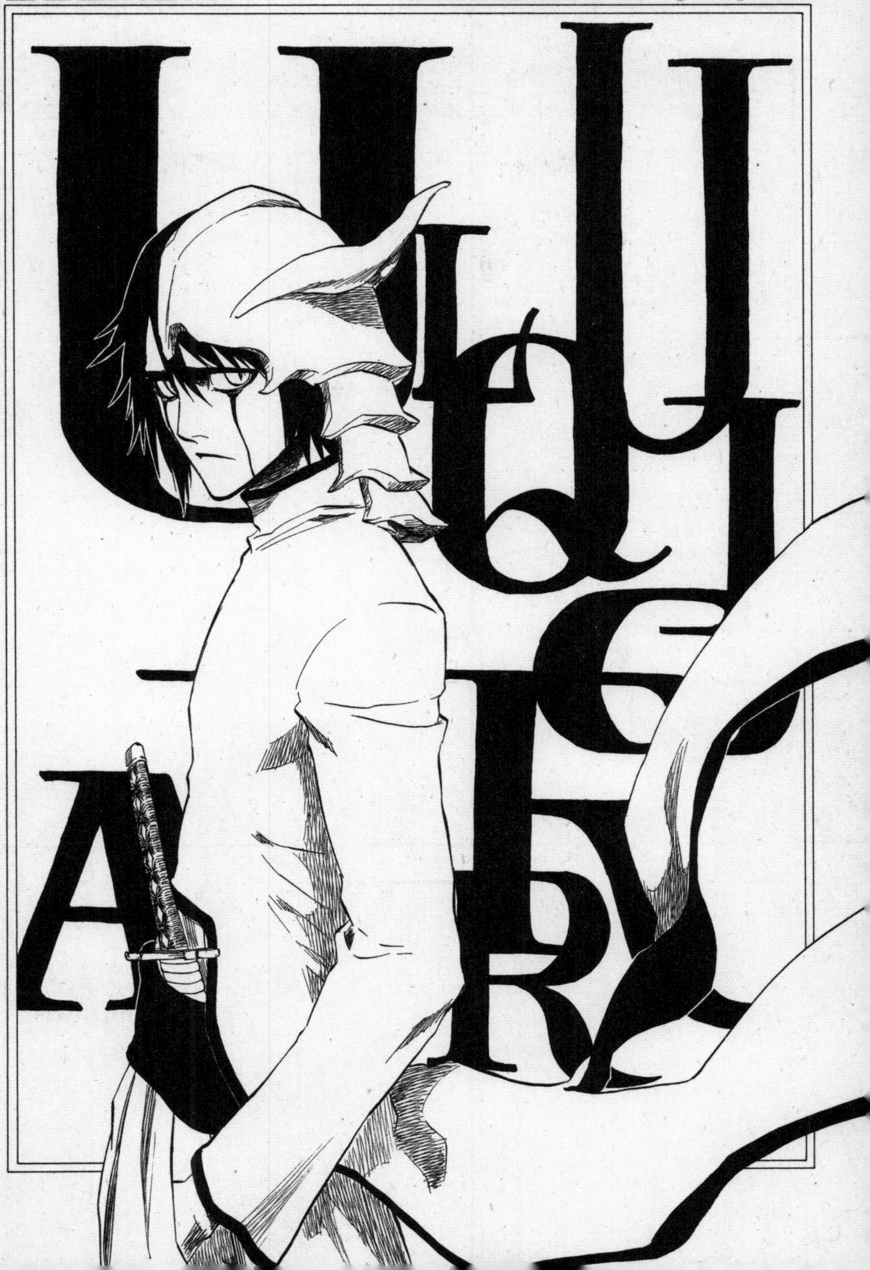

READ THIS WAY

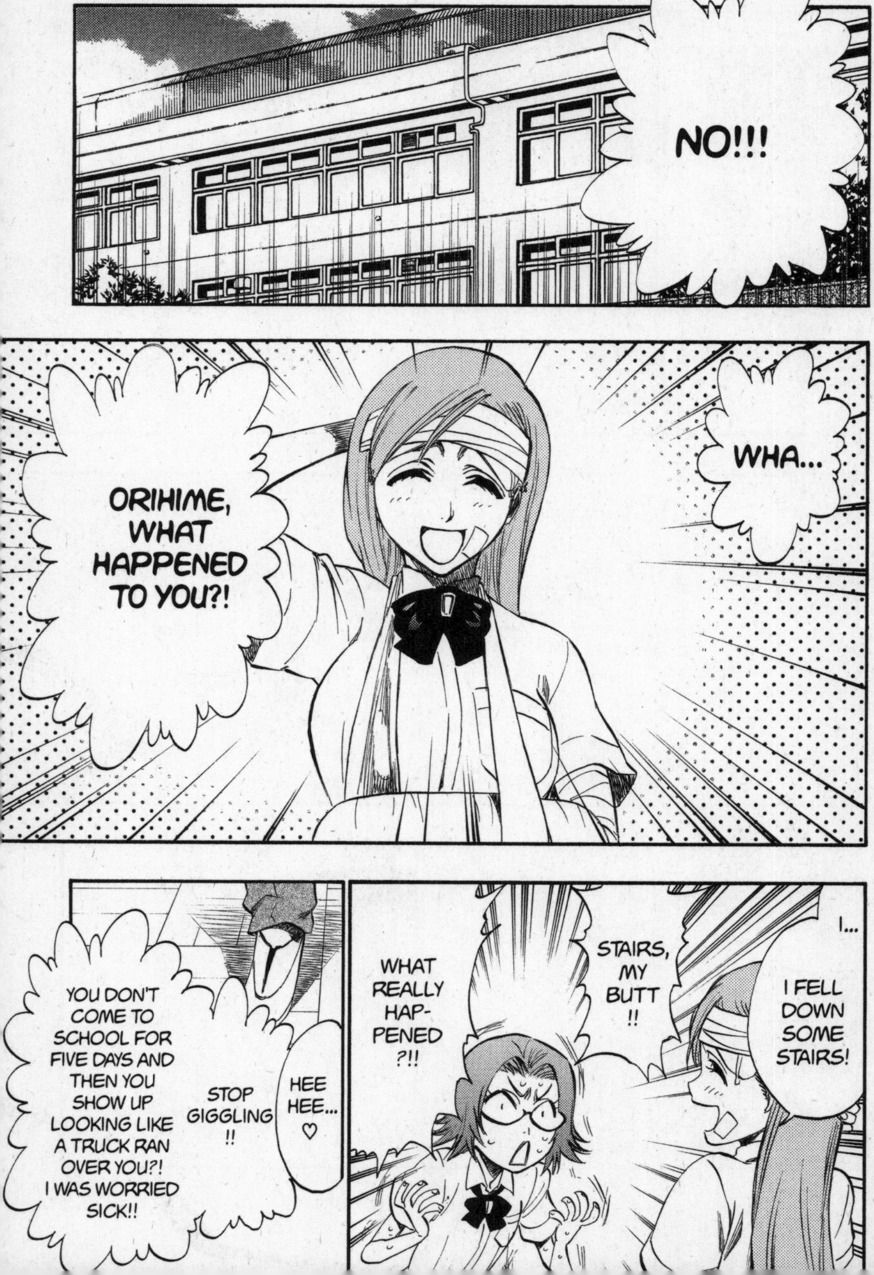
NO!!!
WHA...
ORIHIME, WHAT HAPPENED TO YOU?!
I...
I FELL DOWN SOME STAIRS!
STAIRS, MY BUTT!!
WHAT REALLY HAP-PENED?!!
HEE HEE... ♡
STOP GIGGLING!!
YOU DON'T COME TO SCHOOL FOR FIVE DAYS AND THEN YOU SHOW UP LOOKING LIKE A TRUCK RAN OVER YOU?! I WAS WORRIED SICK!!

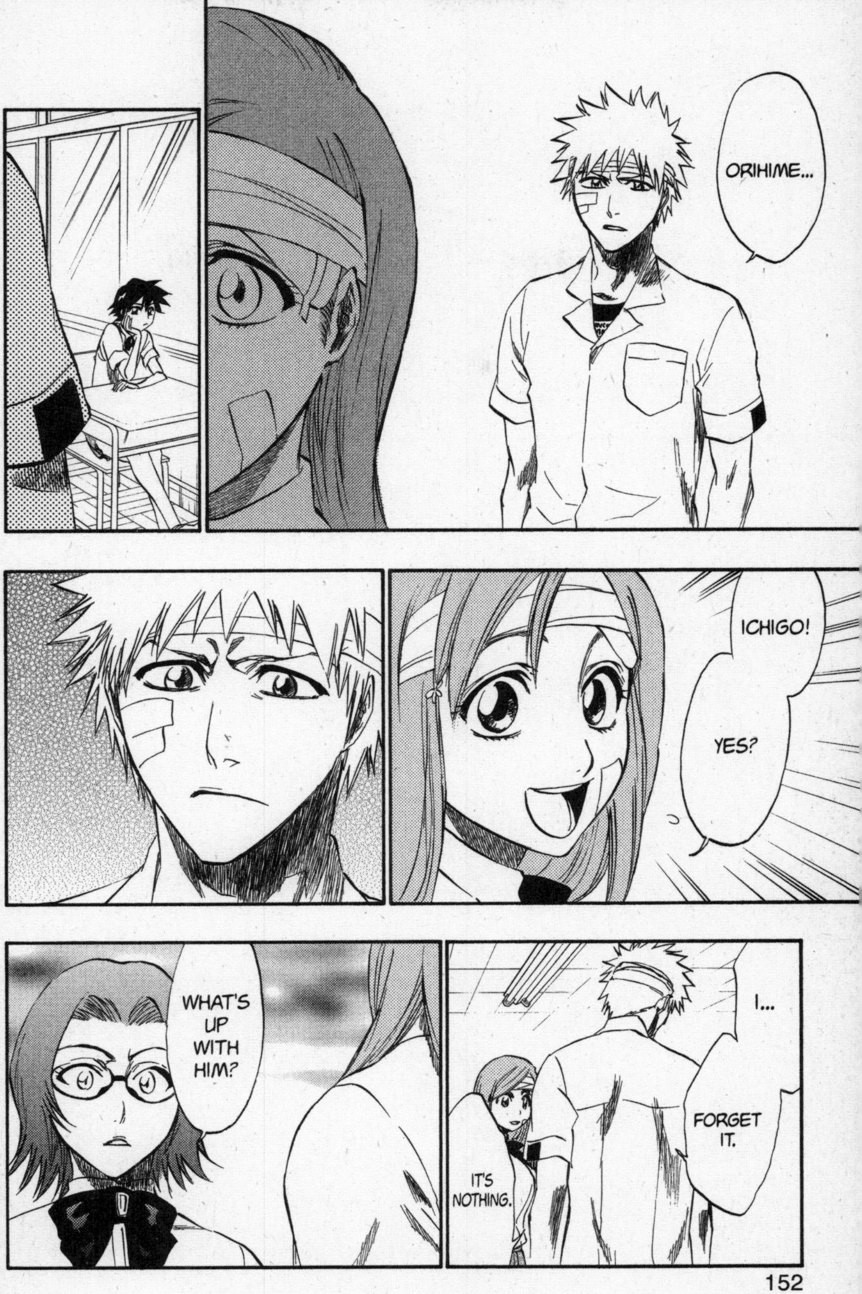
ORIHIME...
ICHIGO! YES?
I... FORGET IT.
IT'S NOTHING.
WHAT'S UP WITH HIM?

READ THIS WAY

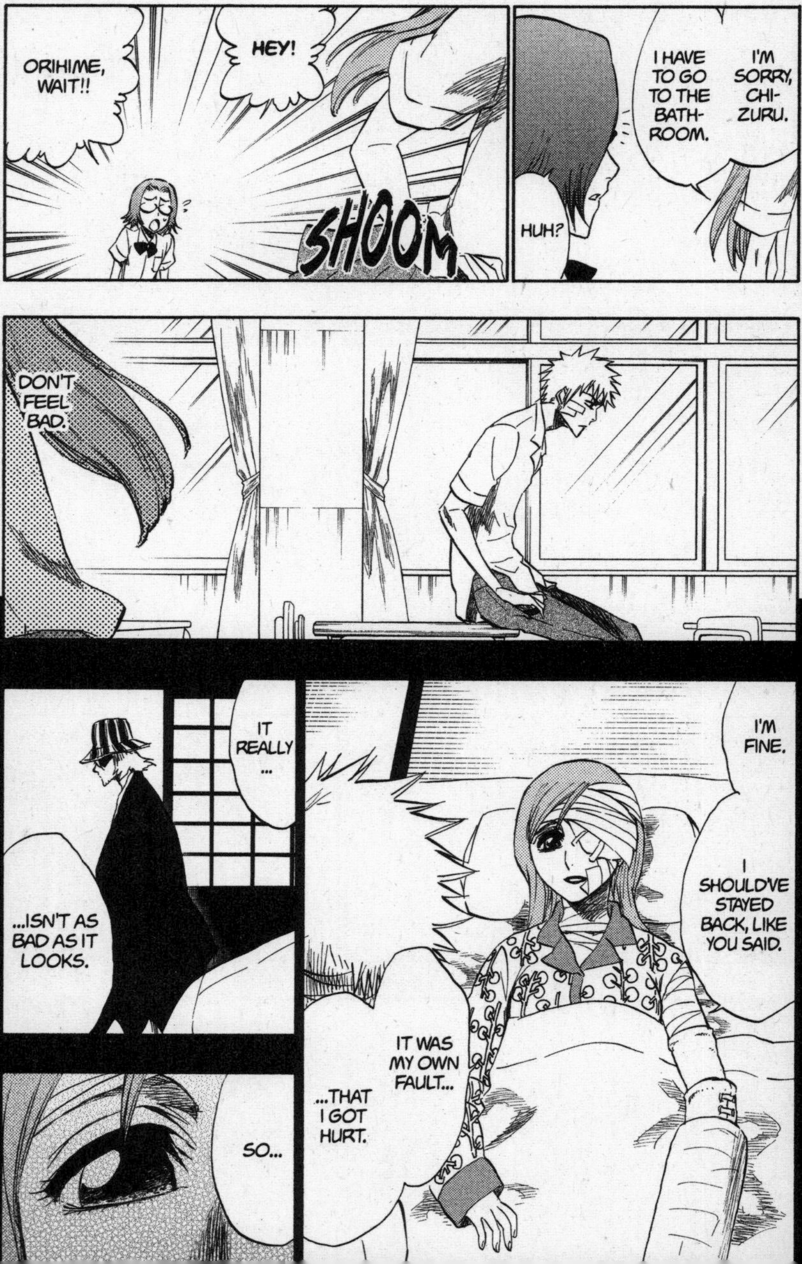
I'M SORRY, CHI-ZURU.
I HAVE TO GO TO THE BATH-ROOM.
HUH?
HEY!
ORIHIME, WAIT!!
SHOOM
DON'T FEEL BAD.
I'M FINE.
I SHOULD'VE STAYED BACK, LIKE YOU SAID.
IT WAS MY OWN FAULT...
...THAT I GOT HURT.
IT REALLY...
...ISN'T AS BAD AS IT LOOKS.
SO...

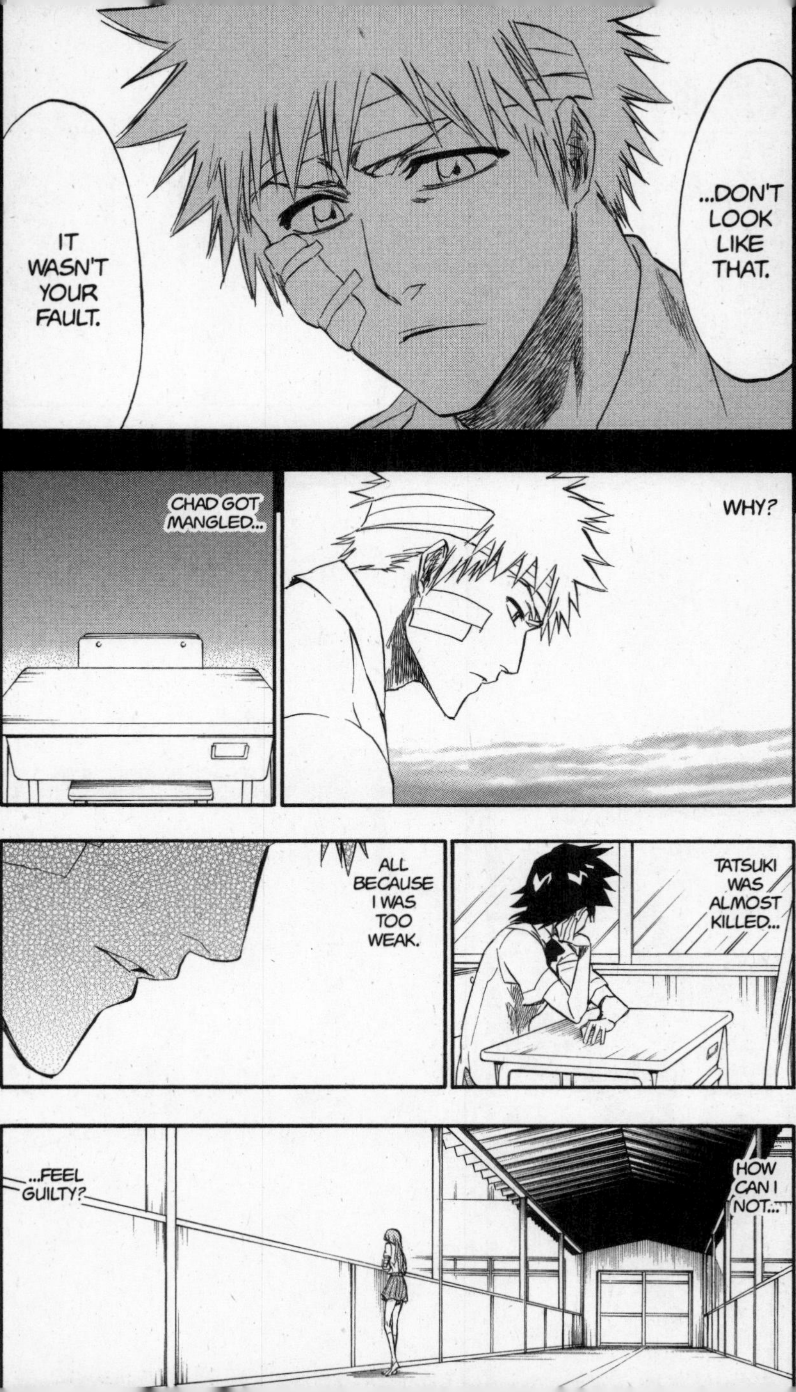
...DON'T LOOK LIKE THAT.
IT WASN'T YOUR FAULT.
WHY?
CHAD GOT MANGLED...
TATSUKI WAS ALMOST KILLED...
ALL BECAUSE I WAS TOO WEAK.
HOW CAN I NOT...
...FEEL GUILTY?

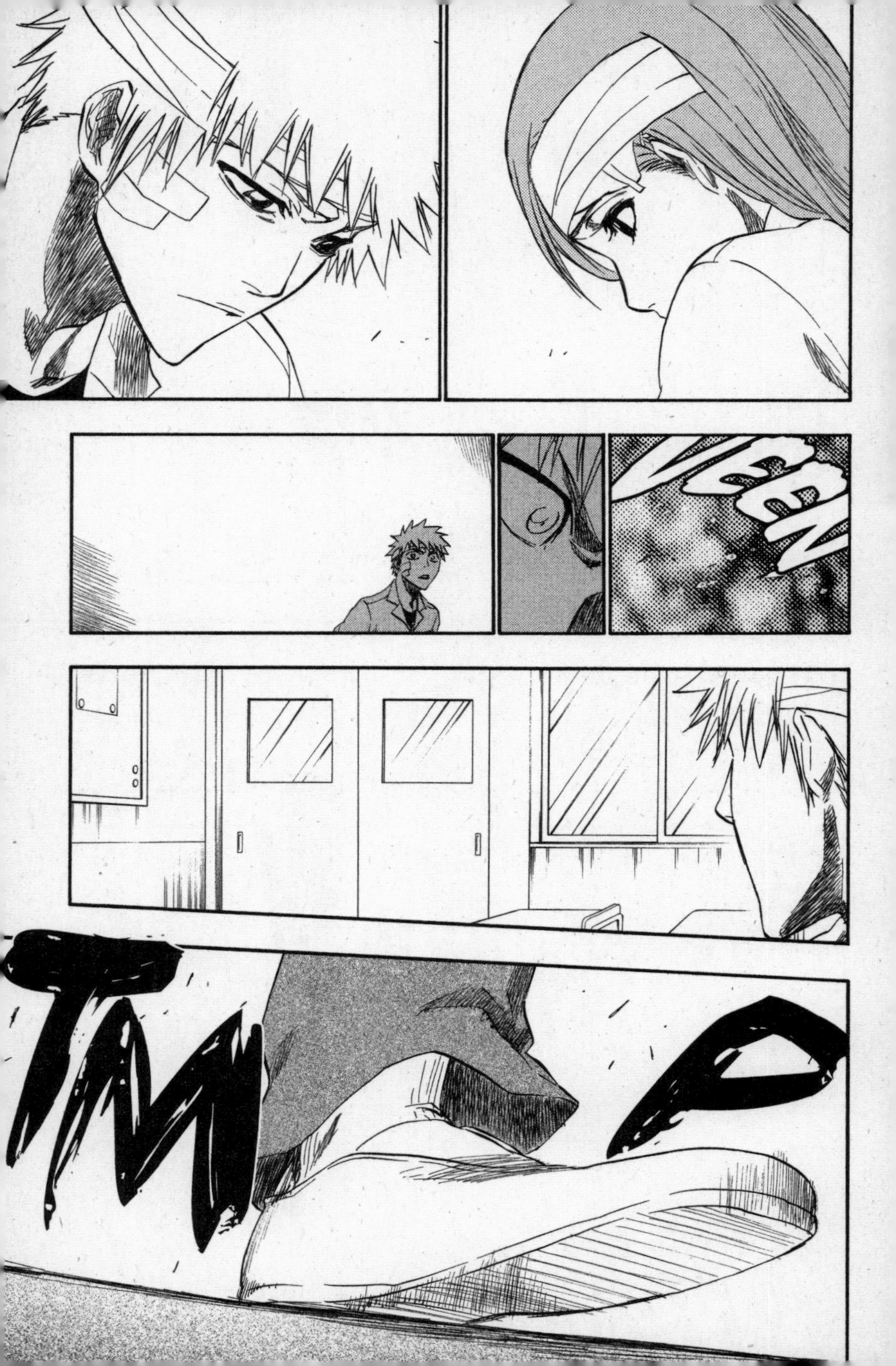
TMP

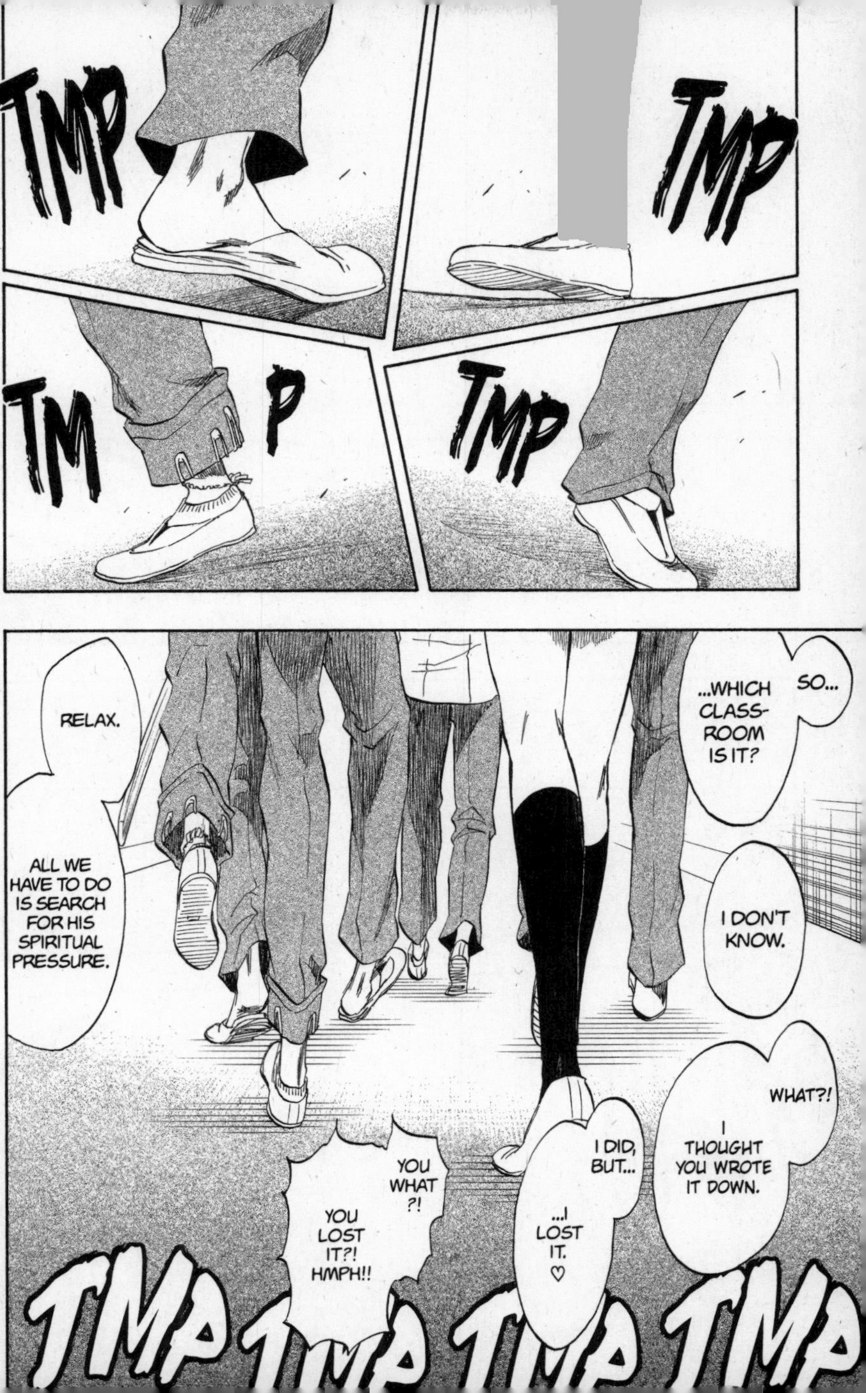
TMP
TMP
TMP
TM P
SO...
...WHICH CLASSROOM IS IT?
I DON'T KNOW.
RELAX.
ALL WE HAVE TO DO IS SEARCH FOR HIS SPIRITUAL PRESSURE.
WHAT?!
I THOUGHT YOU WROTE IT DOWN.
I DID, BUT...
...I LOST IT. ♡
YOU WHAT?!
YOU LOST IT?! HMPH!!
TMP TMP TMP TMP

READ THIS WAY

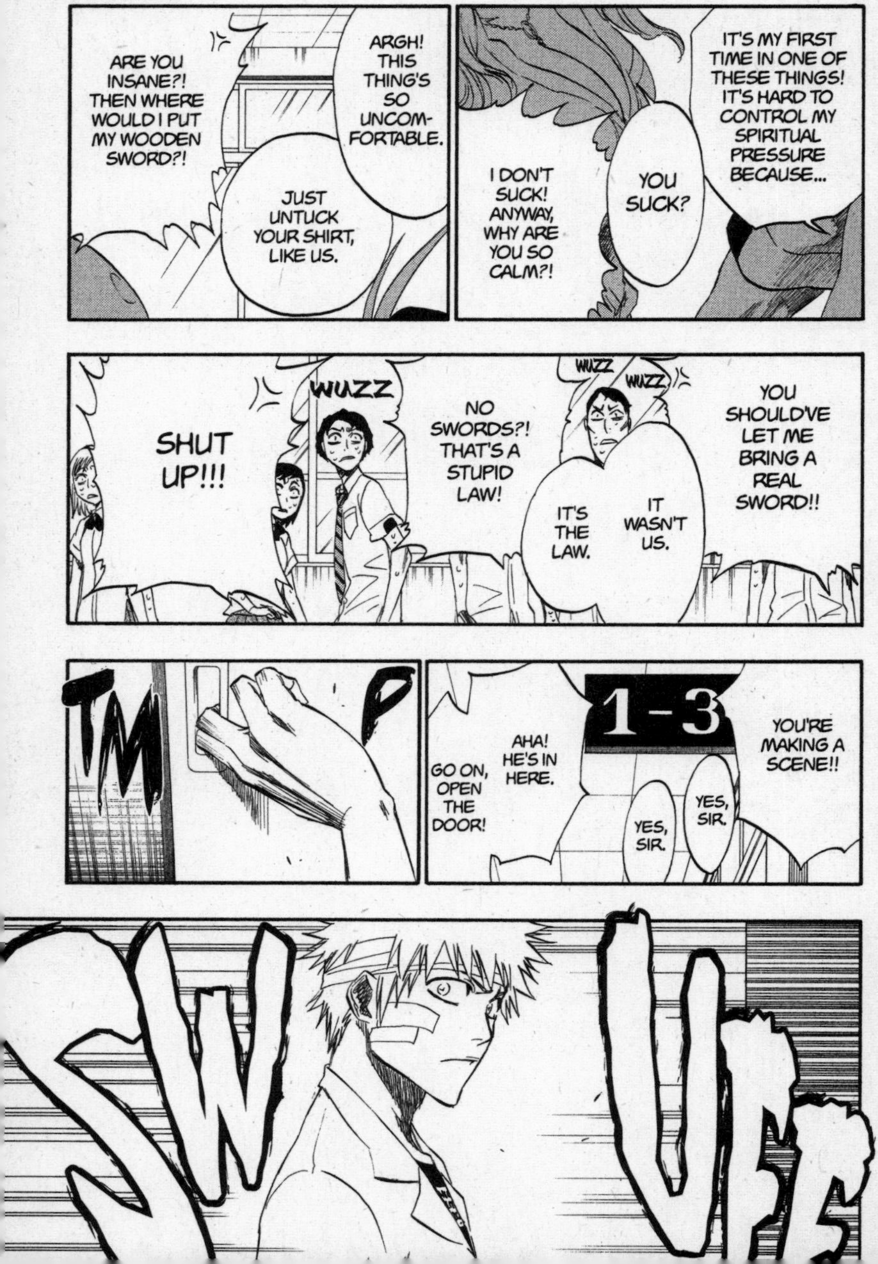
IT'S MY FIRST TIME IN ONE OF THESE THINGS! IT'S HARD TO CONTROL MY SPIRITUAL PRESSURE BECAUSE...
YOU SUCK?
I DON'T SUCK! ANYWAY, WHY ARE YOU SO CALM?!
ARGH! THIS THING'S SO UNCOM-FORTABLE.
JUST UNTUCK YOUR SHIRT, LIKE US.
ARE YOU INSANE?! THEN WHERE WOULD I PUT MY WOODEN SWORD?!
YOU SHOULD'VE LET ME BRING A REAL SWORD!!
WUZZ
WUZZ
IT WASN'T US.
IT'S THE LAW.
NO SWORDS?! THAT'S A STUPID LAW!
WUZZ
SHUT UP!!!
1-3
YOU'RE MAKING A SCENE!!
YES, SIR.
YES, SIR.
AHA! HE'S IN HERE.
GO ON, OPEN THE DOOR!
TMP

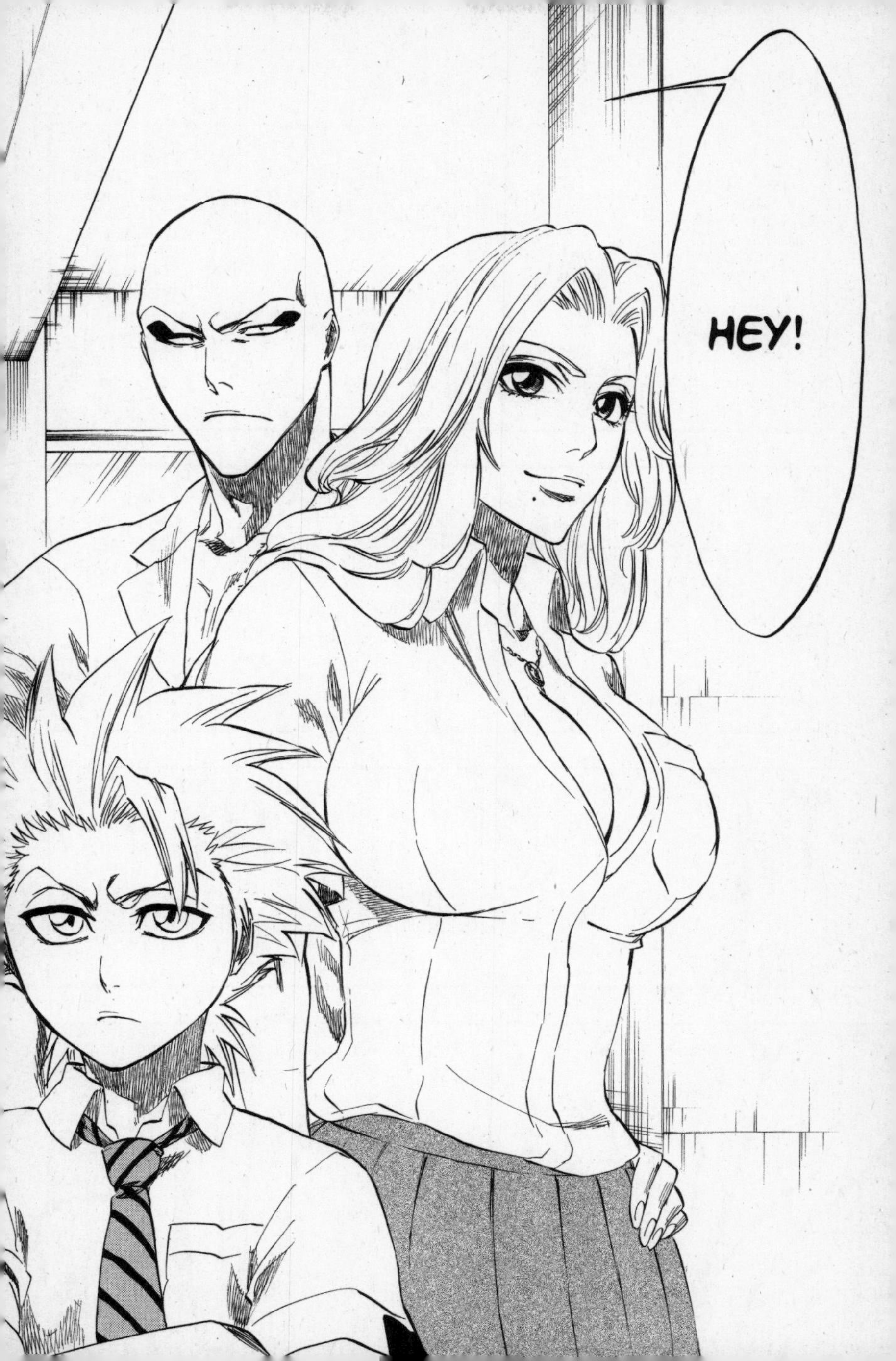
HEY!

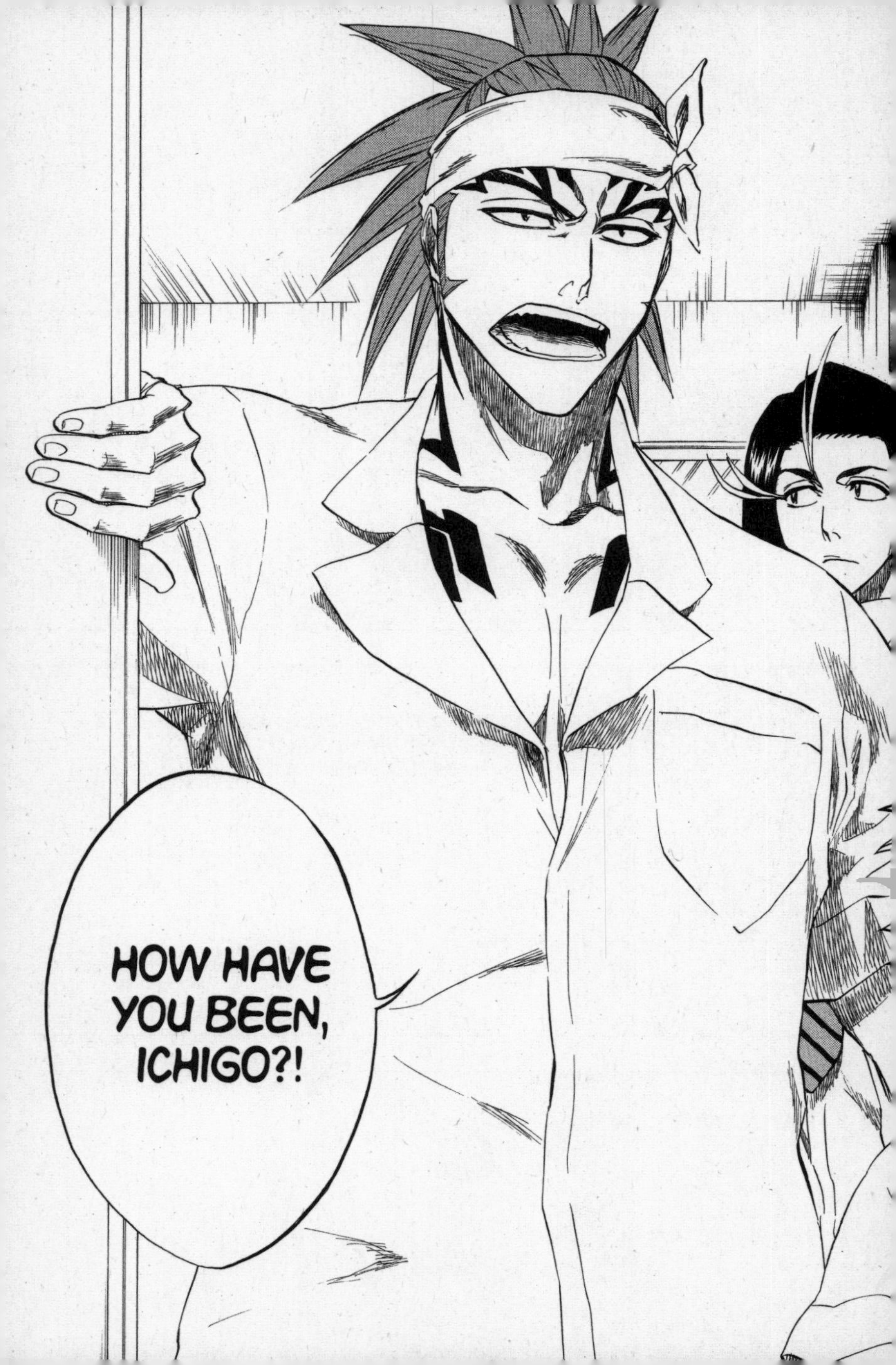
HOW HAVE YOU BEEN, ICHIGO?!

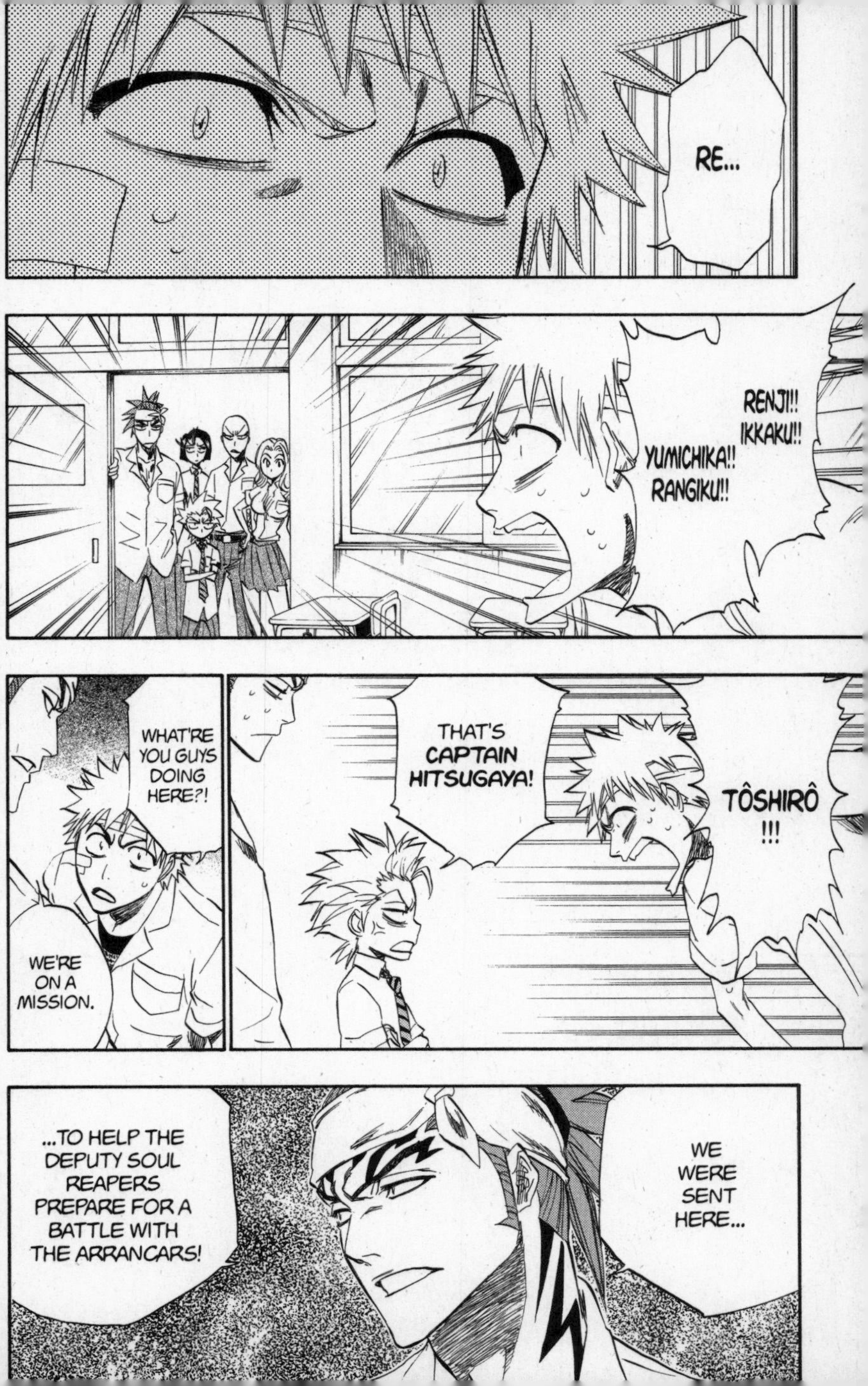
RE...
RENJI!! IKKAKU!!
YUMICHIKA!! RANGIKU!!
TÔSHIRÔ !!!
THAT'S CAPTAIN HITSUGAYA!
WHAT'RE YOU GUYS DOING HERE?!
WE'RE ON A MISSION.
WE WERE SENT HERE...
...TO HELP THE DEPUTY SOUL REAPERS PREPARE FOR A BATTLE WITH THE ARRANCARS!

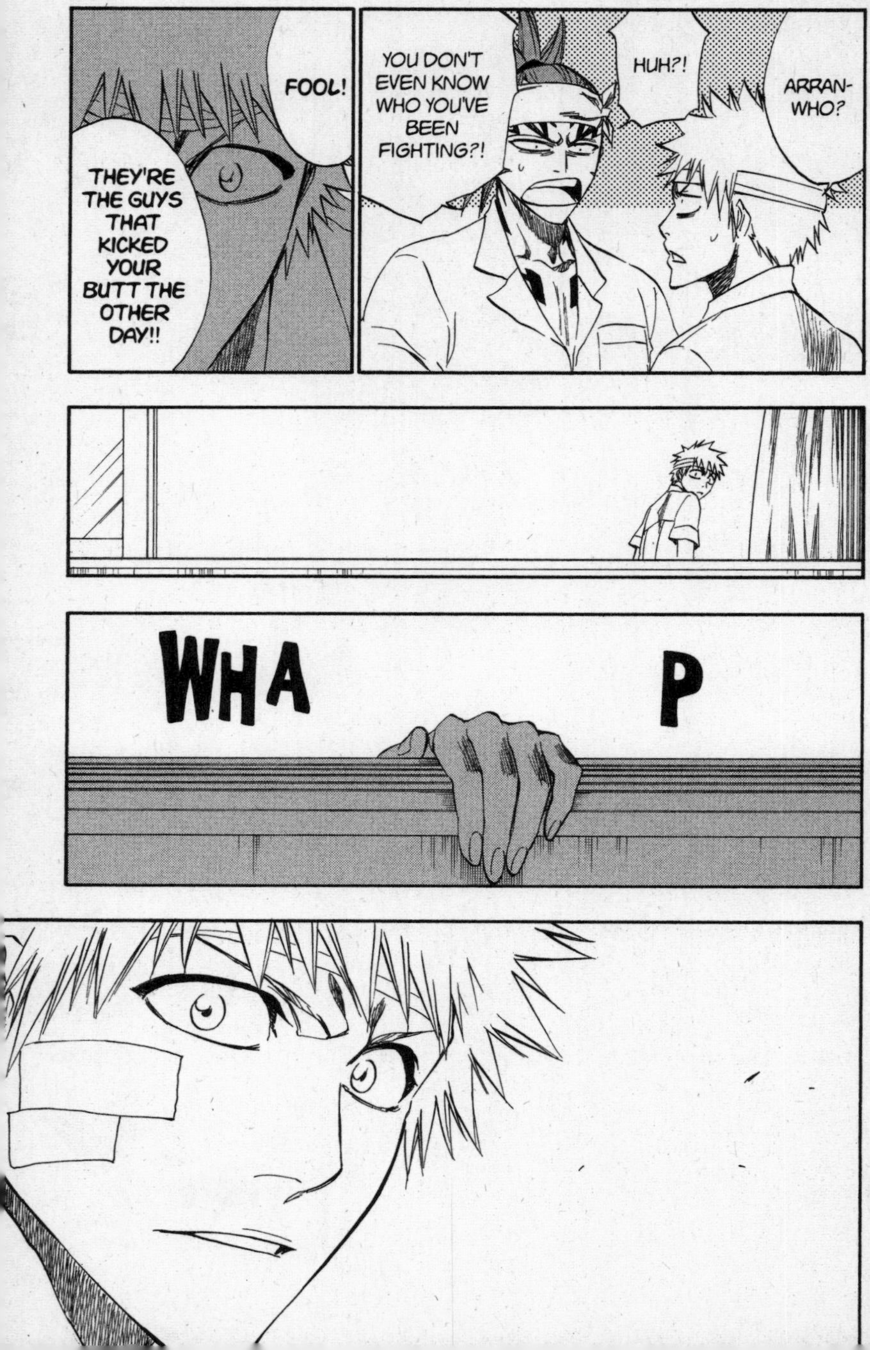
ARRAN-WHO?
HUH?!
YOU DON'T EVEN KNOW WHO YOU'VE BEEN FIGHTING?!
FOOL!
THEY'RE THE GUYS THAT KICKED YOUR BUTT THE OTHER DAY!!
WHAP

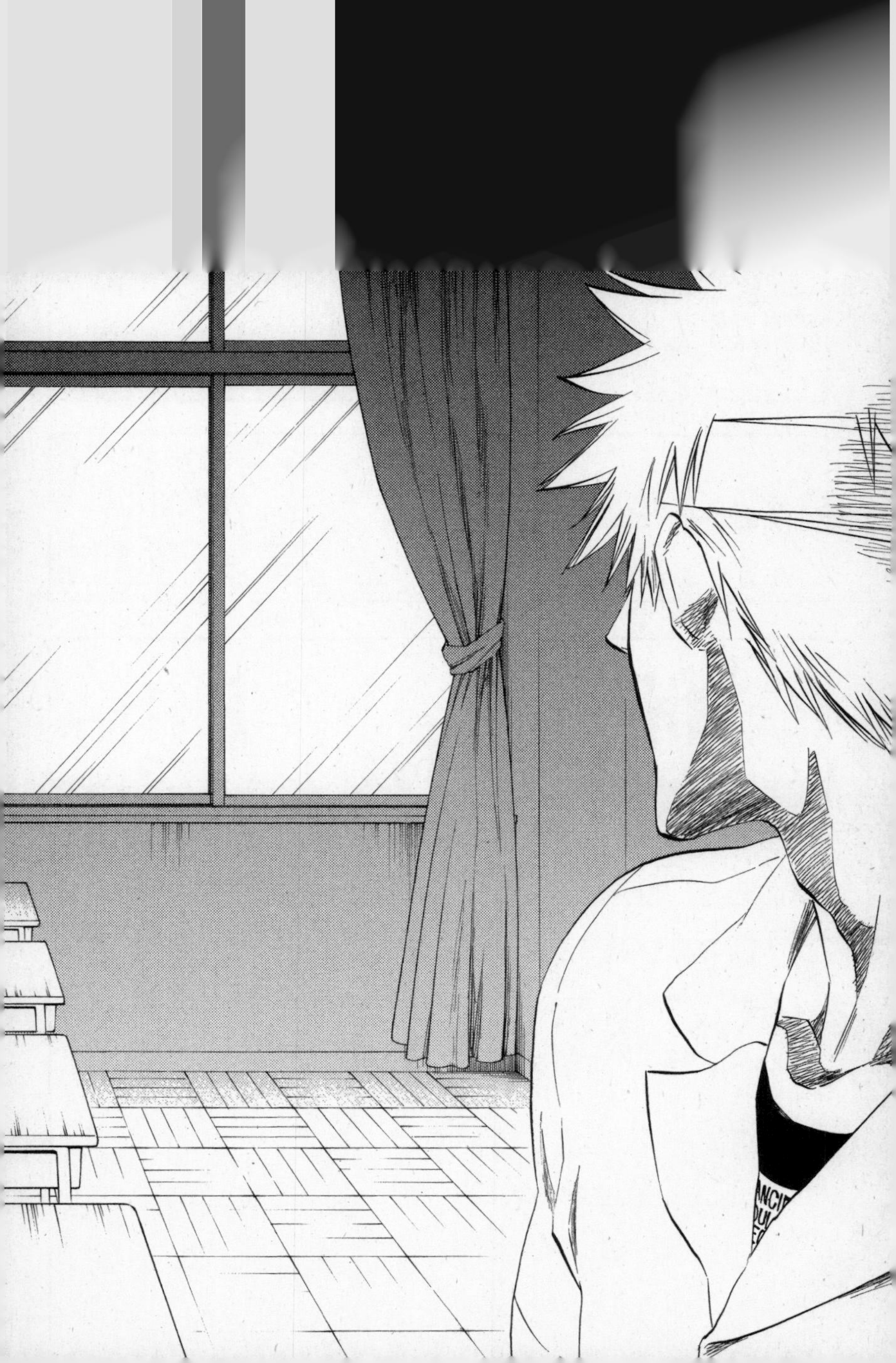

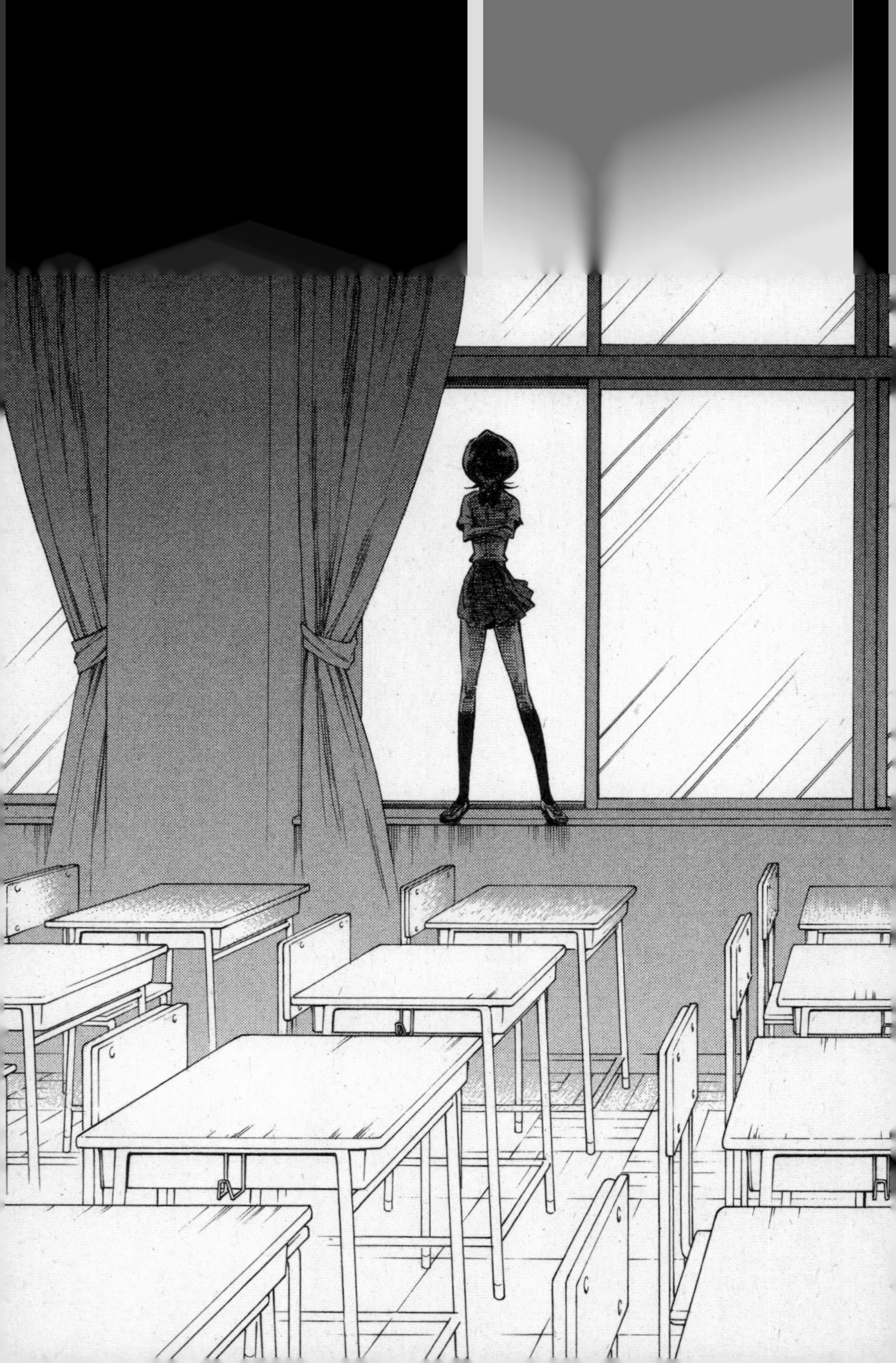

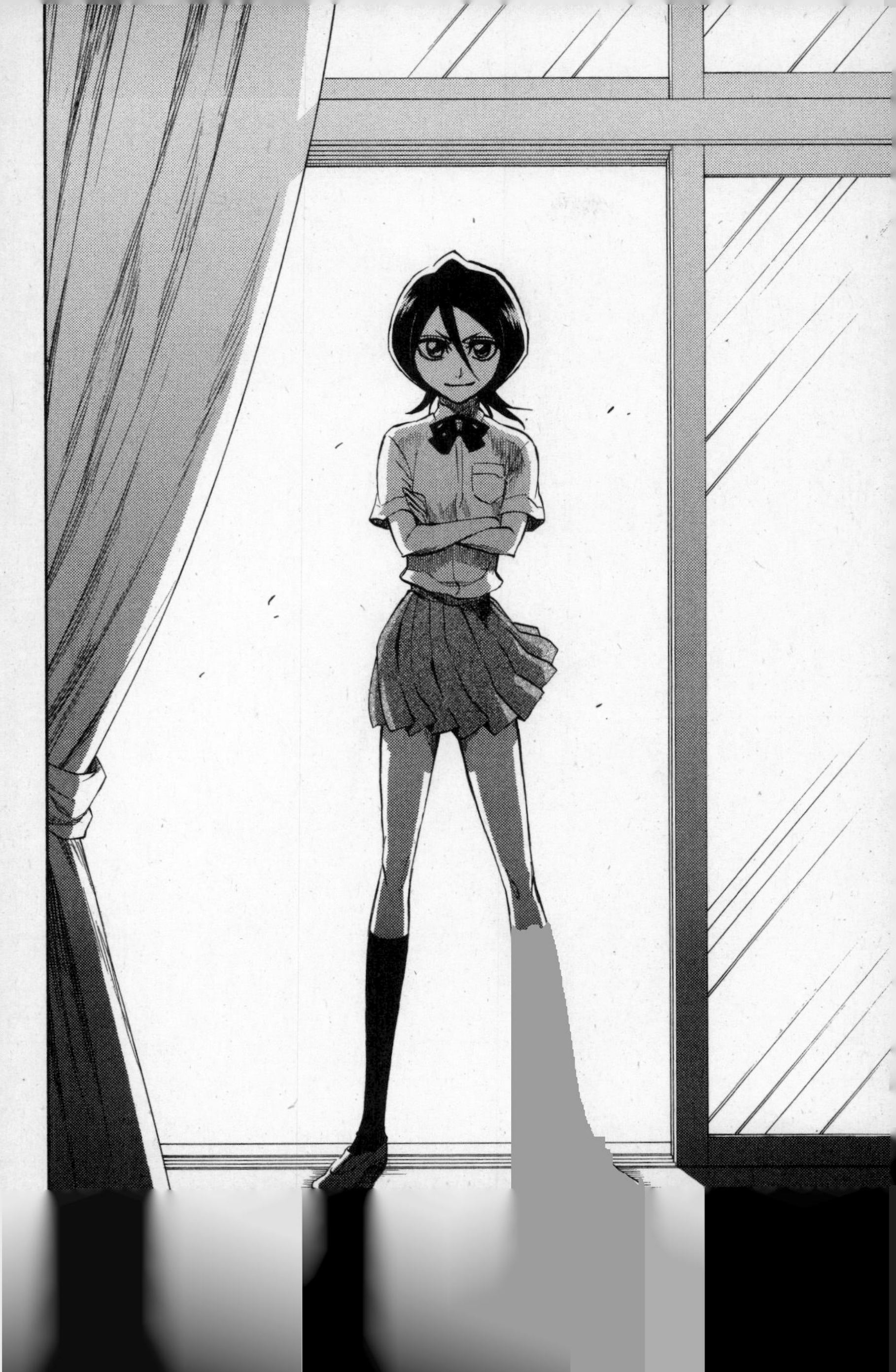

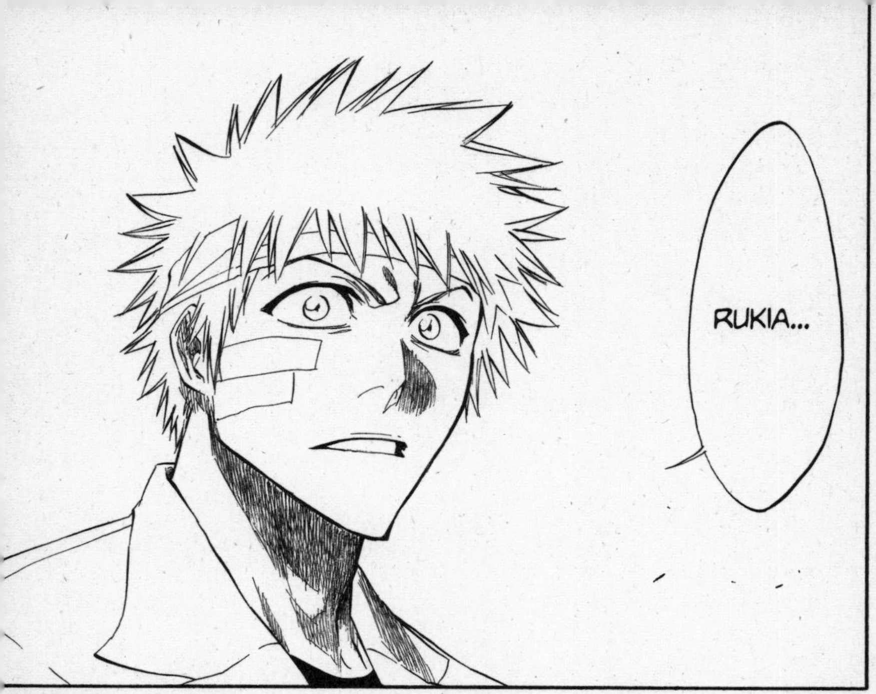
RUKIA...

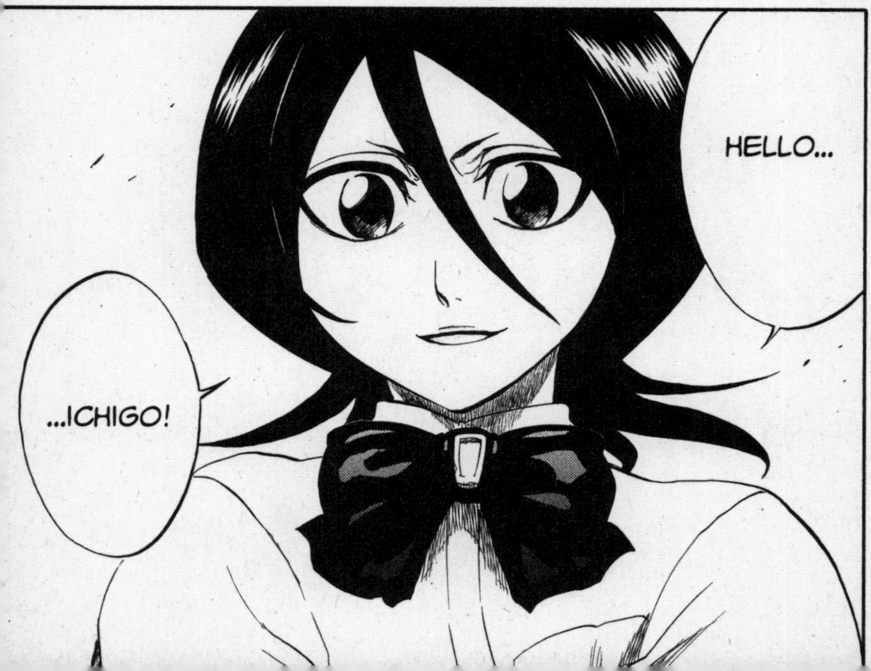
HELLO...
...ICHIGO!

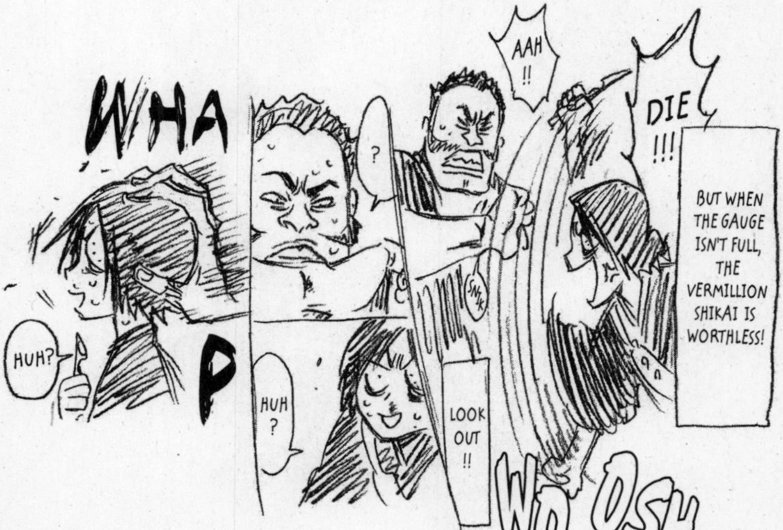

BUT WHEN THE GAUGE ISN'T FULL, THE VERMILLION SHIKAI IS WORTHLESS!
DIE !!!
WOOSH
AAH !!
SNIK
LOOK OUT !!
?
HUH ?
WHAP
HUH?

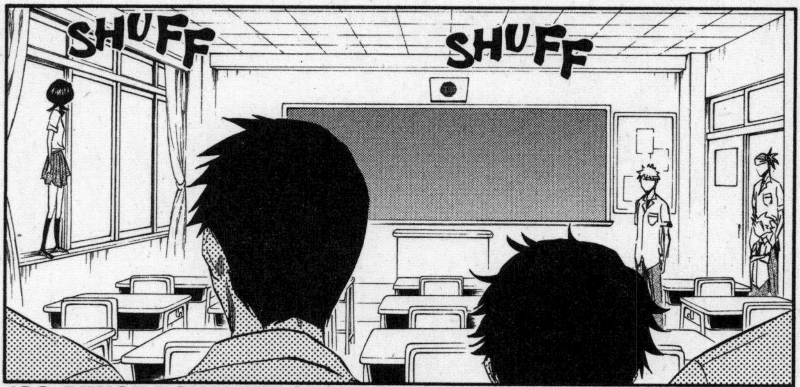
SHUFF
SHUFF

196. PUNCH DOWN THE STONE CIRCLE

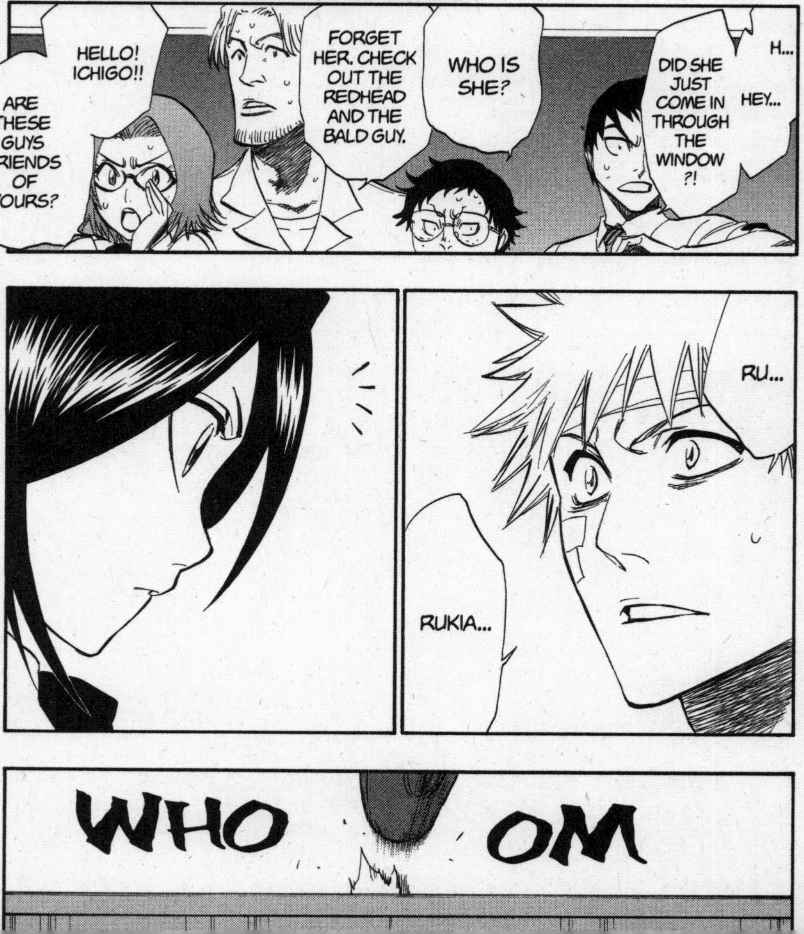
H... HEY...
DID SHE JUST COME IN THROUGH THE WINDOW?!
WHO IS SHE?
FORGET HER. CHECK OUT THE REDHEAD AND THE BALD GUY.
HELLO! ICHIGO!!
ARE THESE GUYS FRIENDS OF YOURS?
RU...
RUKIA...
WHO OM

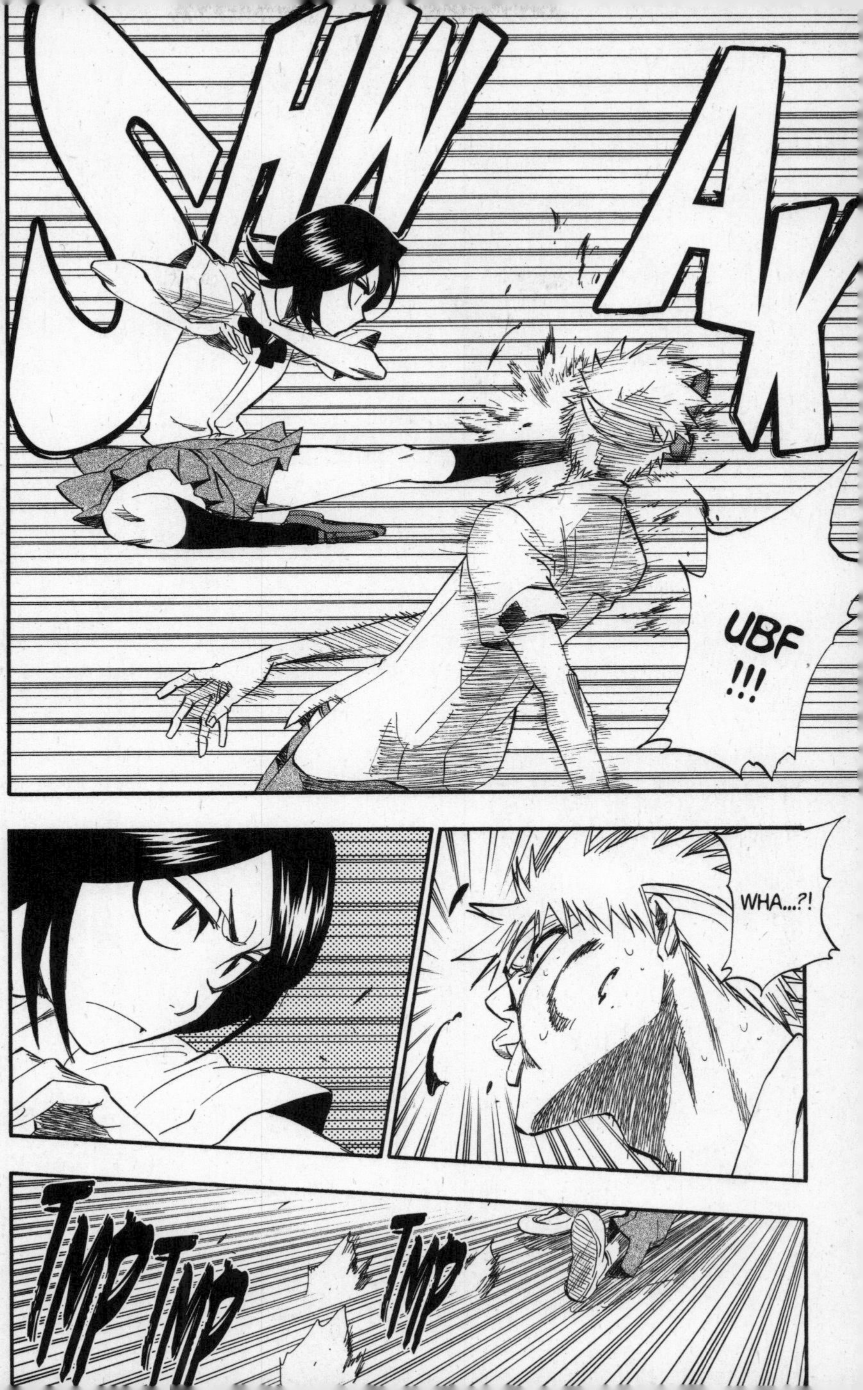
CHWAK
UBF!!!
WHA...?!
TMP TMP TMP

READ THIS WAY

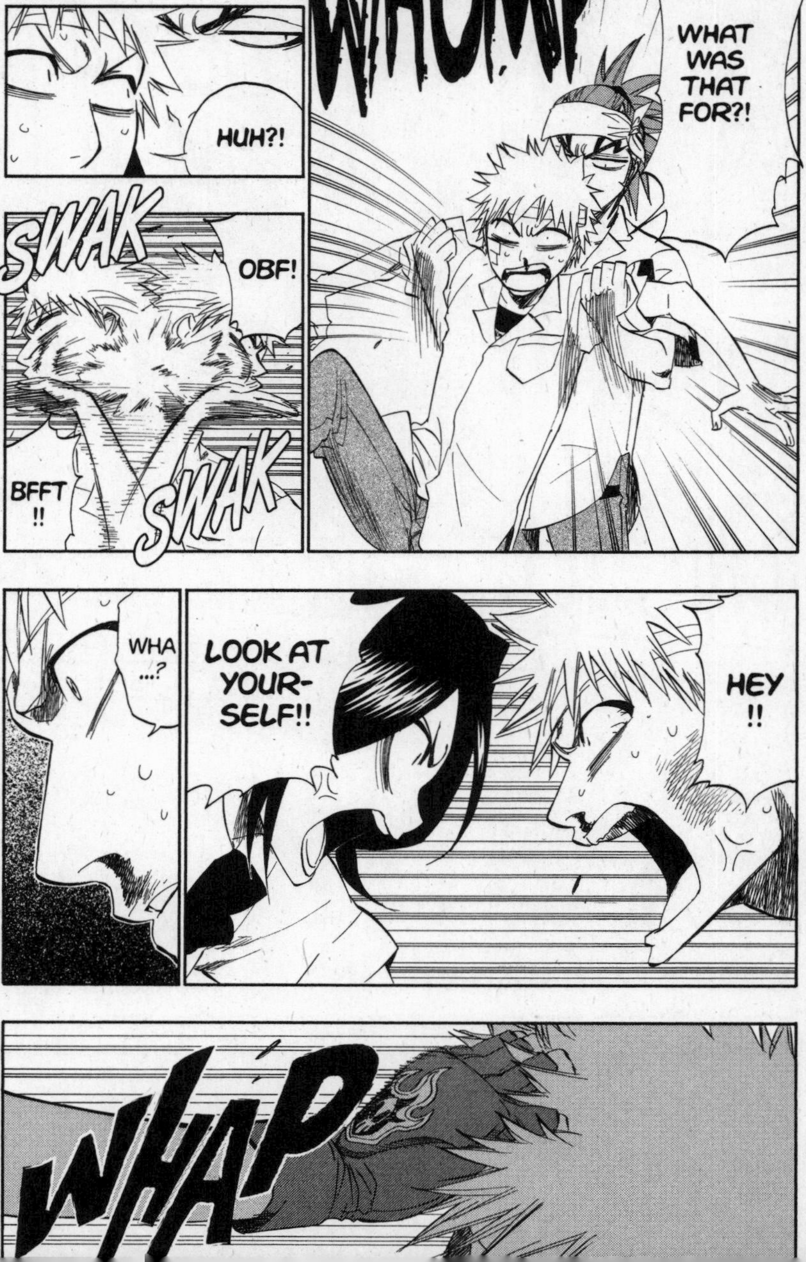
WHUMP
WHAT WAS THAT FOR?!
HUH?!
SWAK
OBF!
BFFT !!
SWAK
HEY !!
LOOK AT YOUR-SELF!!
WHA ...?
WHAP

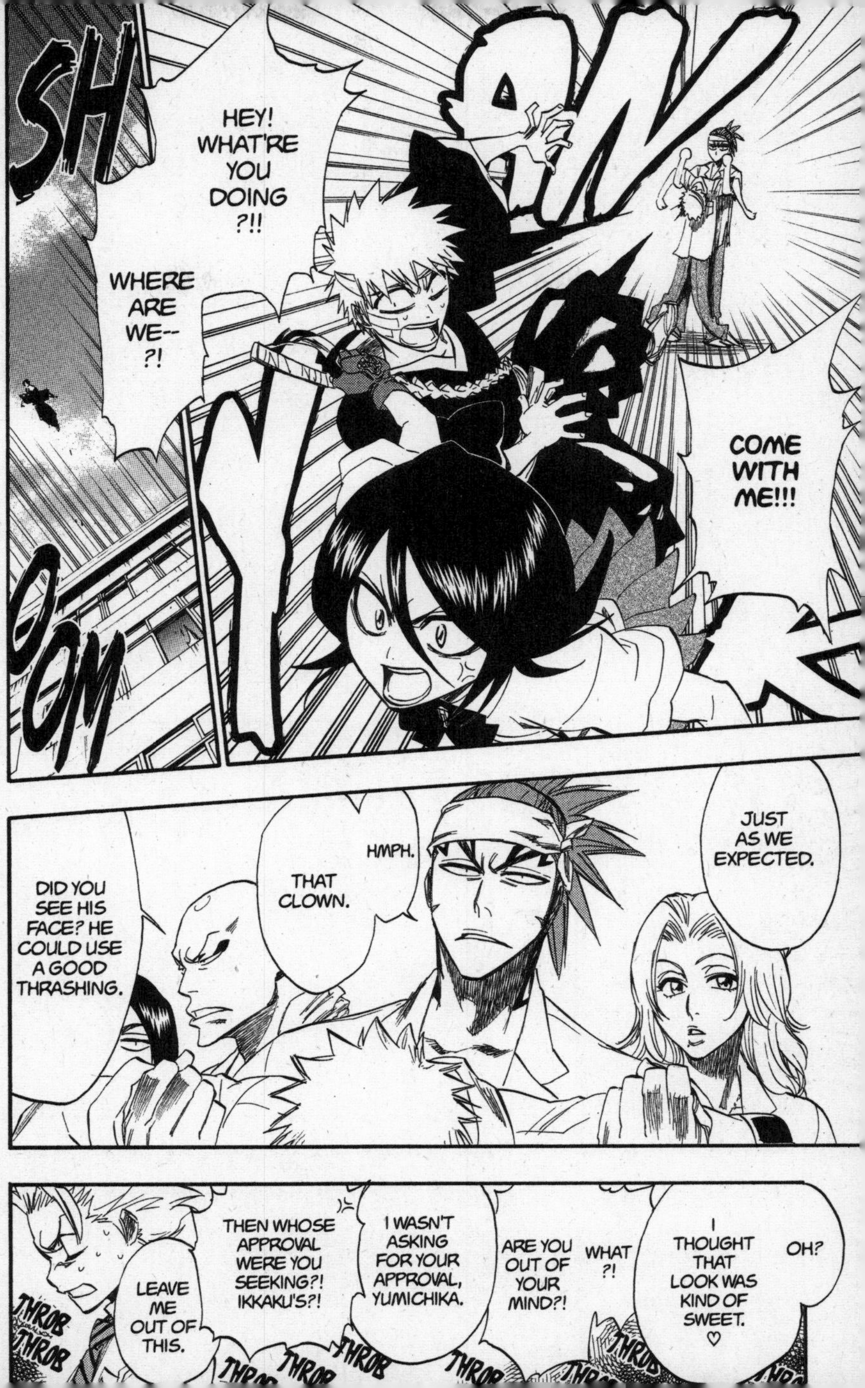
COME WITH ME!!!
HEY! WHAT'RE YOU DOING ?!!
WHERE ARE WE-- ?!
JUST AS WE EXPECTED.
HMPH.
THAT CLOWN.
DID YOU SEE HIS FACE? HE COULD USE A GOOD THRASHING.
OH?
I THOUGHT THAT LOOK WAS KIND OF SWEET. ♡
WHAT ?!
ARE YOU OUT OF YOUR MIND?!
I WASN'T ASKING FOR YOUR APPROVAL, YUMICHIKA.
THEN WHOSE APPROVAL WERE YOU SEEKING?! IKKAKU'S?!
LEAVE ME OUT OF THIS.
THROB THROB

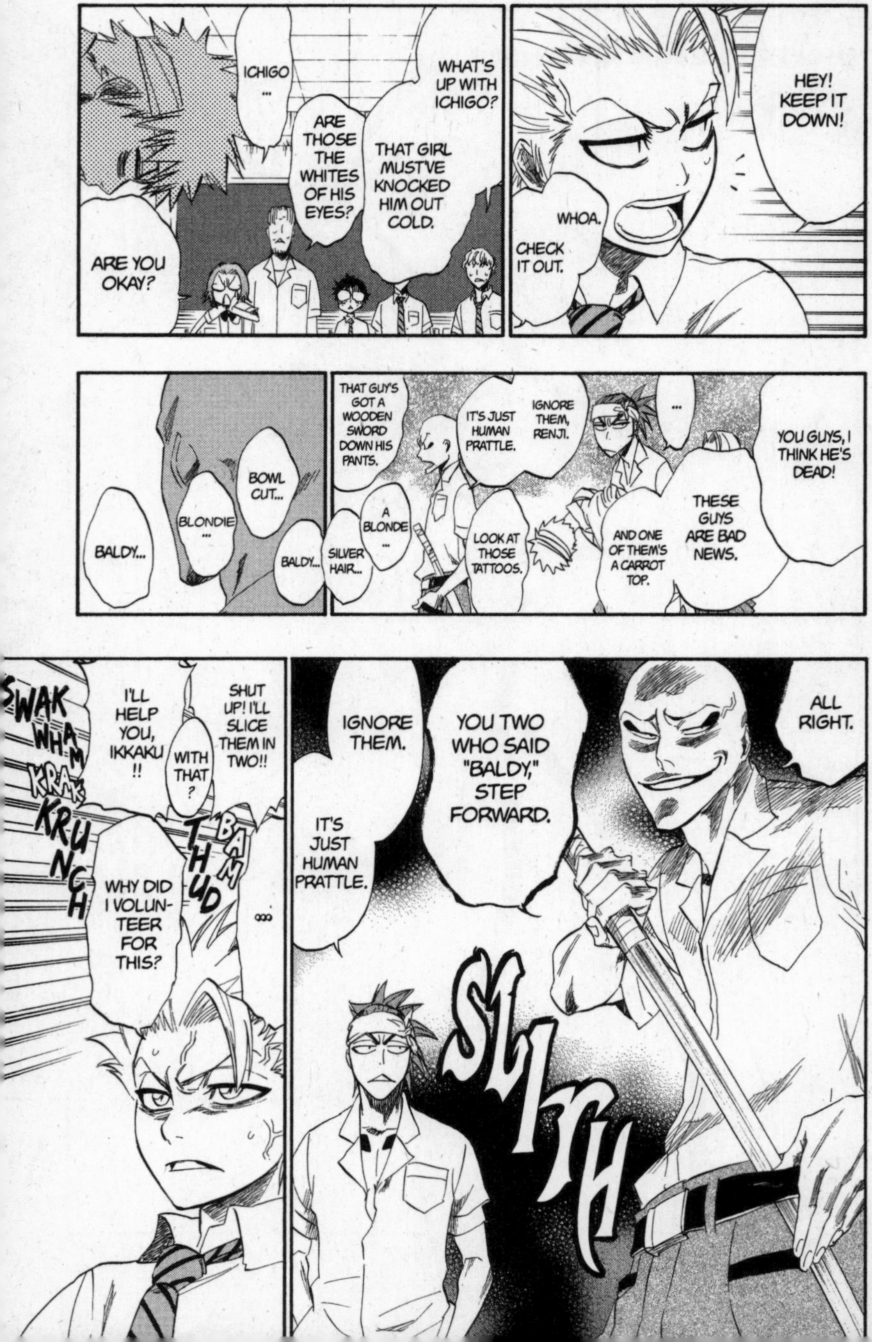
HEY! KEEP IT DOWN!
WHOA.
CHECK IT OUT.
WHAT'S UP WITH ICHIGO?
ICHIGO ...
THAT GIRL MUST'VE KNOCKED HIM OUT COLD.
ARE THOSE THE WHITES OF HIS EYES?
ARE YOU OKAY?
YOU GUYS, I THINK HE'S DEAD!
...
THESE GUYS ARE BAD NEWS.
IGNORE THEM, RENJI.
AND ONE OF THEM'S A CARROT TOP.
IT'S JUST HUMAN PRATTLE.
THAT GUY'S GOT A WOODEN SWORD DOWN HIS PANTS.
LOOK AT THOSE TATTOOS.
A BLONDE ...
SILVER HAIR...
BALDY...
BOWL CUT...
BLONDIE ...
BALDY...
ALL RIGHT.
YOU TWO WHO SAID "BALDY," STEP FORWARD.
IGNORE THEM.
IT'S JUST HUMAN PRATTLE.
SHUT UP! I'LL SLICE THEM IN TWO!!
I'LL HELP YOU, IKKAKU!!
WITH THAT?
BAM
THUD
...
SWAK
WHAM
KRAK
KRUNCH
WHY DID I VOLUNTEER FOR THIS?

Bleach 196. PUNCH DOWN THE STONE CIRCLE

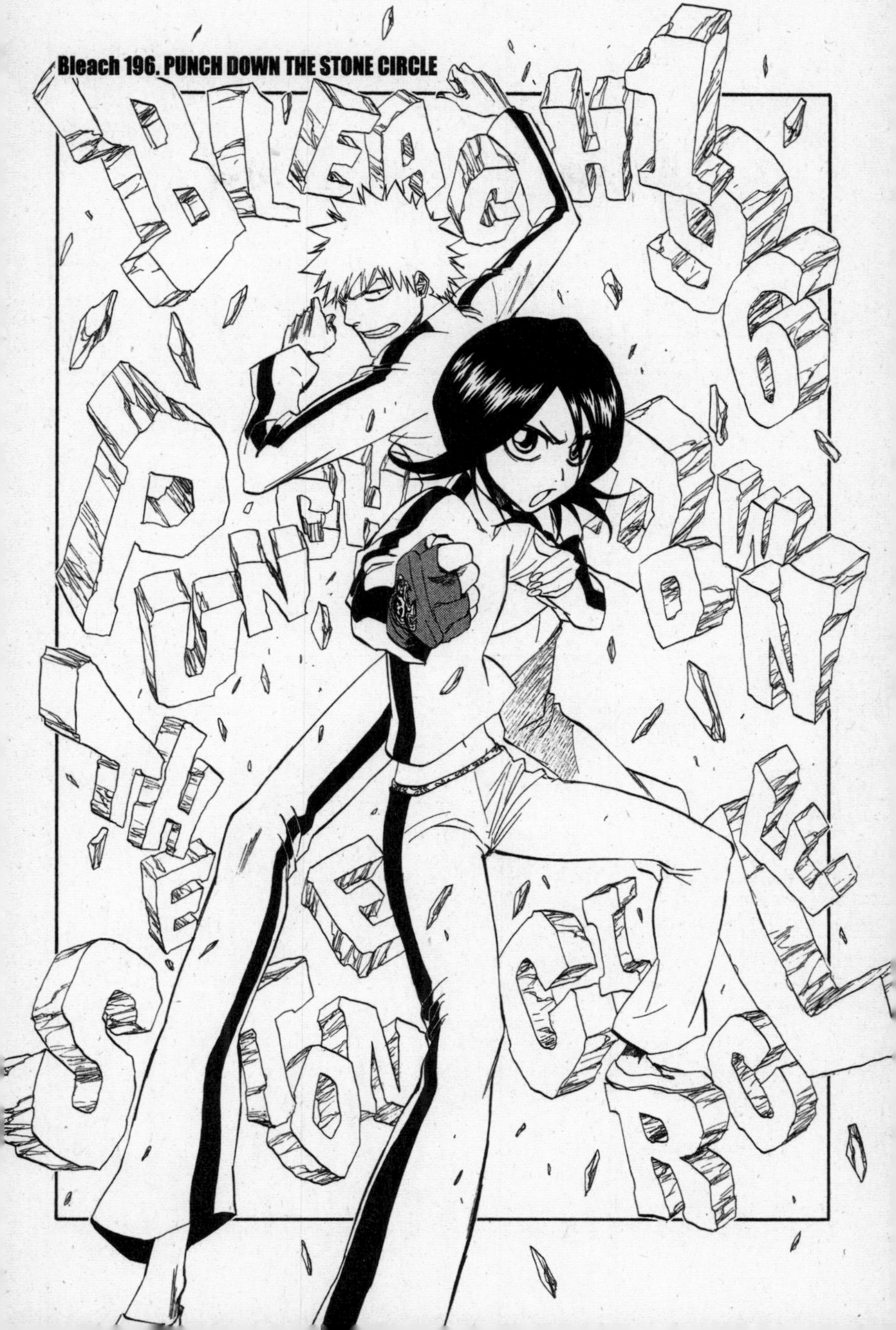
BLEACH 196
PUNCH DOWN THE STONE CIRCLE

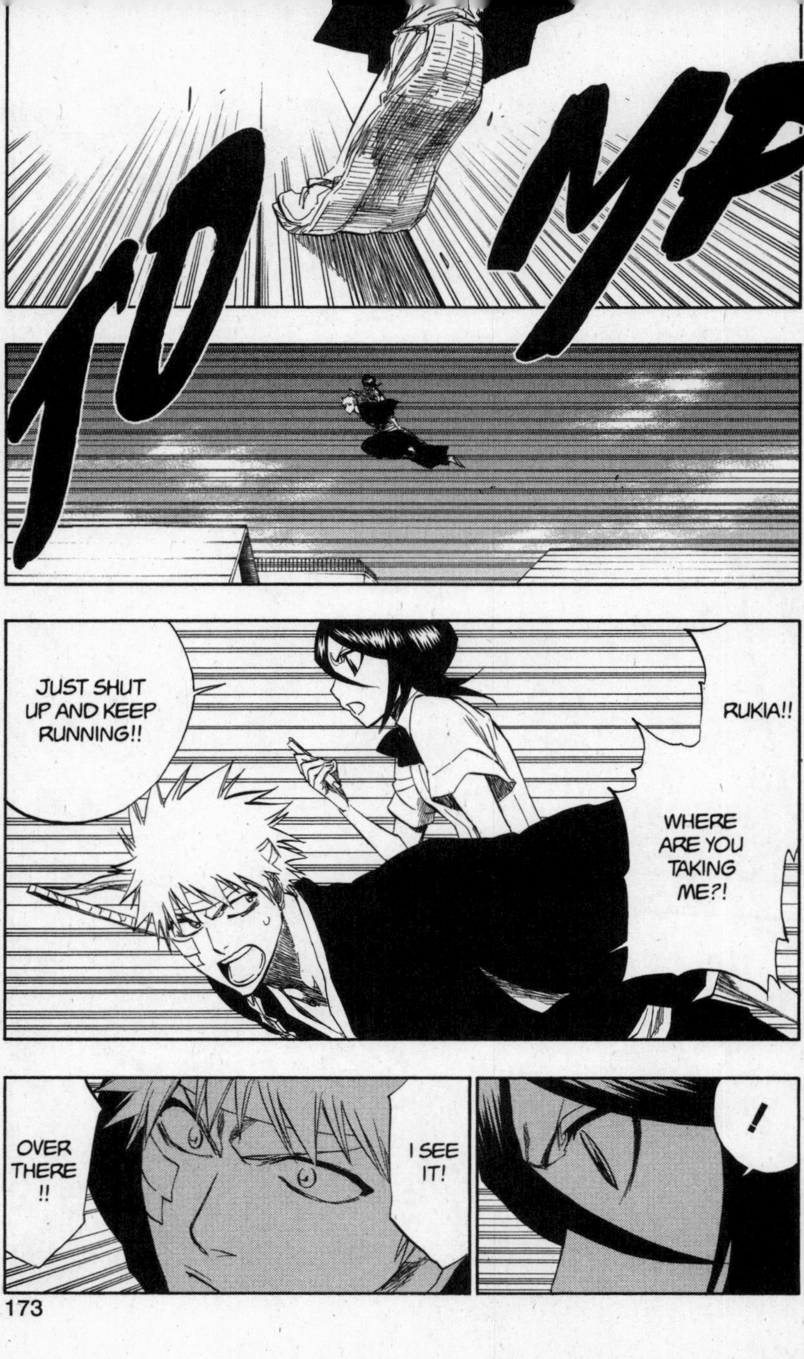
TOMP
RUKIA!!
WHERE ARE YOU TAKING ME?!
JUST SHUT UP AND KEEP RUNNING!!
!
I SEE IT!
OVER THERE!!

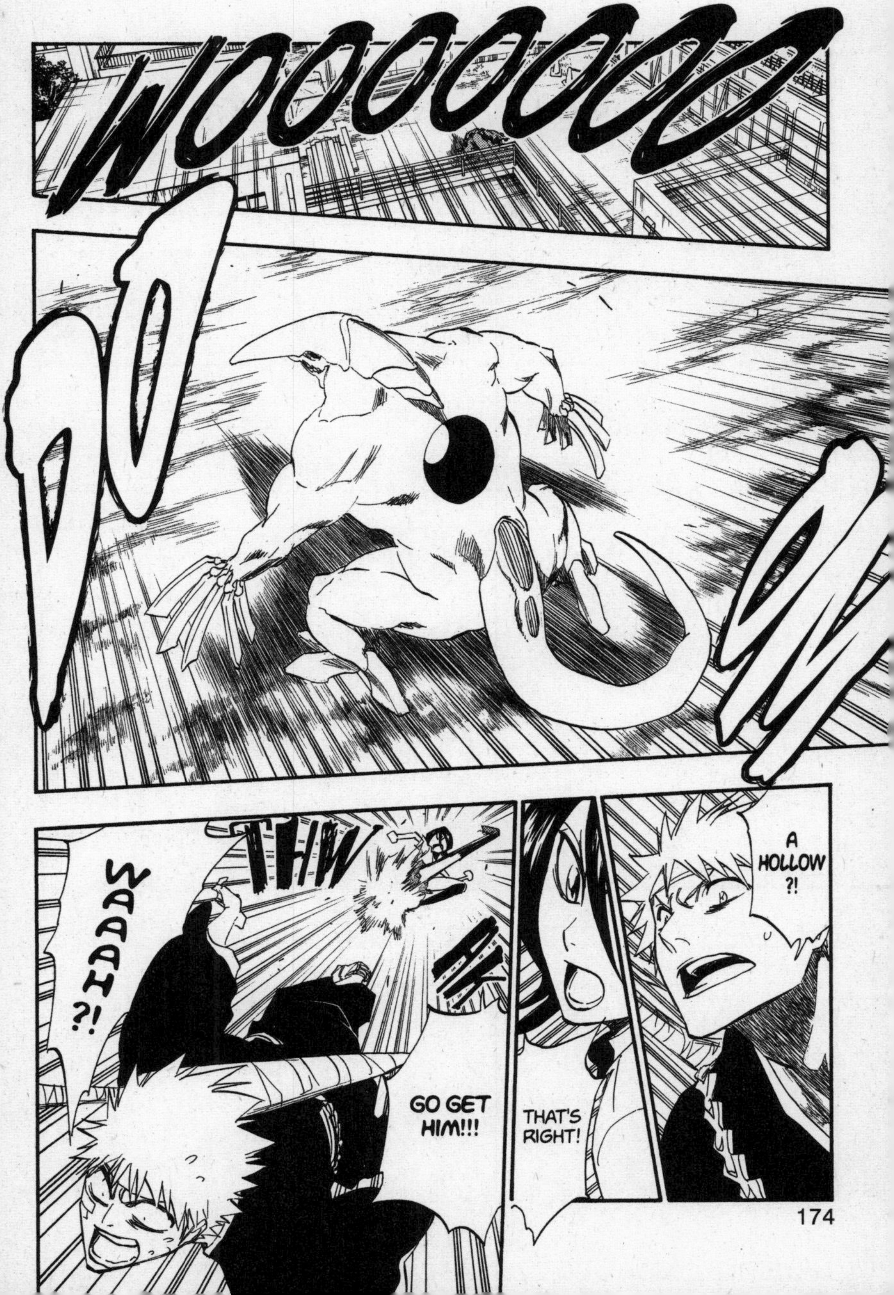
WOOOOOOO
DOOM
A HOLLOW ?!
THAT'S RIGHT!
GO GET HIM!!!
THWAK
WAAAAH ?!

READ THIS WAY

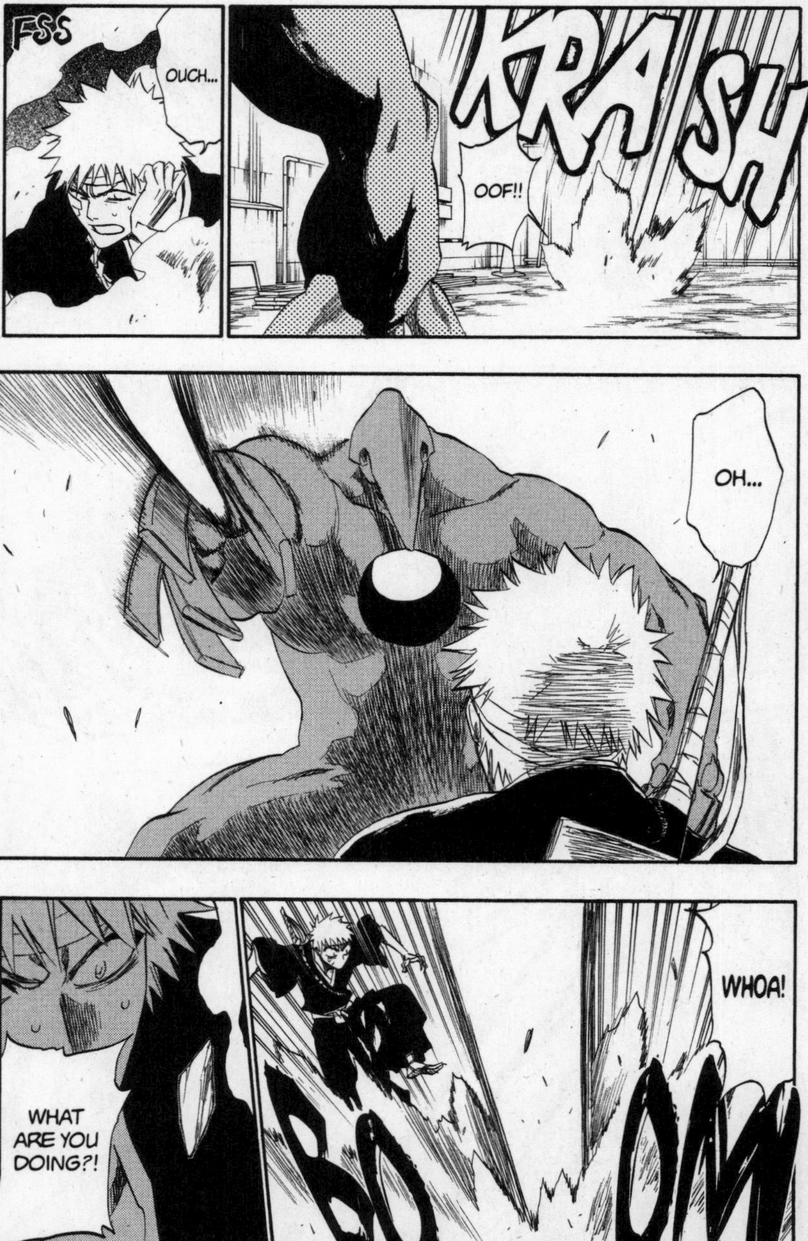
KRASH
OOF!!
FSS
OUCH...
OH...
WHOA!
BOOM
WHAT ARE YOU DOING?!

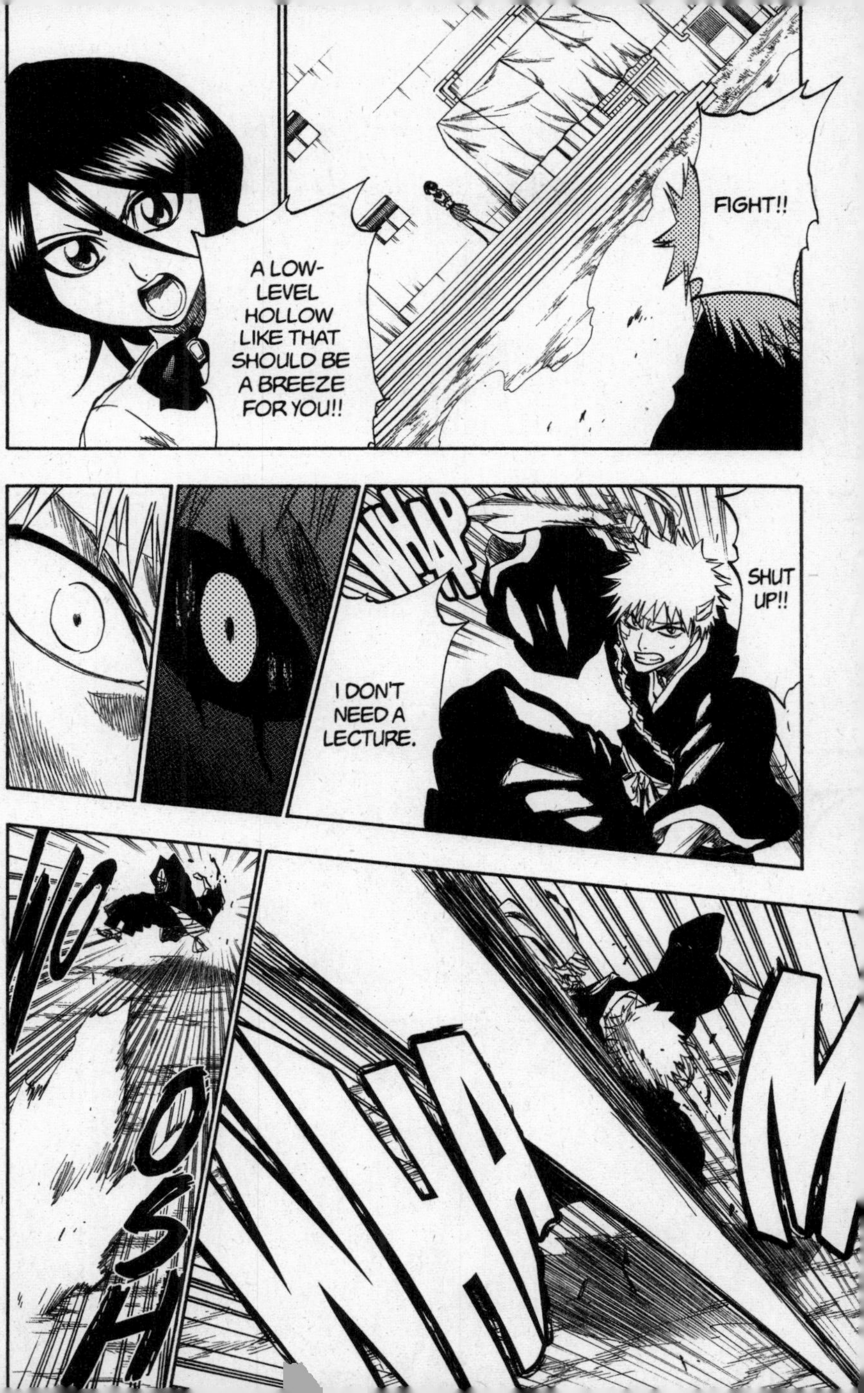
FIGHT!!
A LOW-LEVEL HOLLOW LIKE THAT SHOULD BE A BREEZE FOR YOU!!
SHUT UP!!
WHAP
I DON'T NEED A LECTURE.
WHAM
WHOOSH

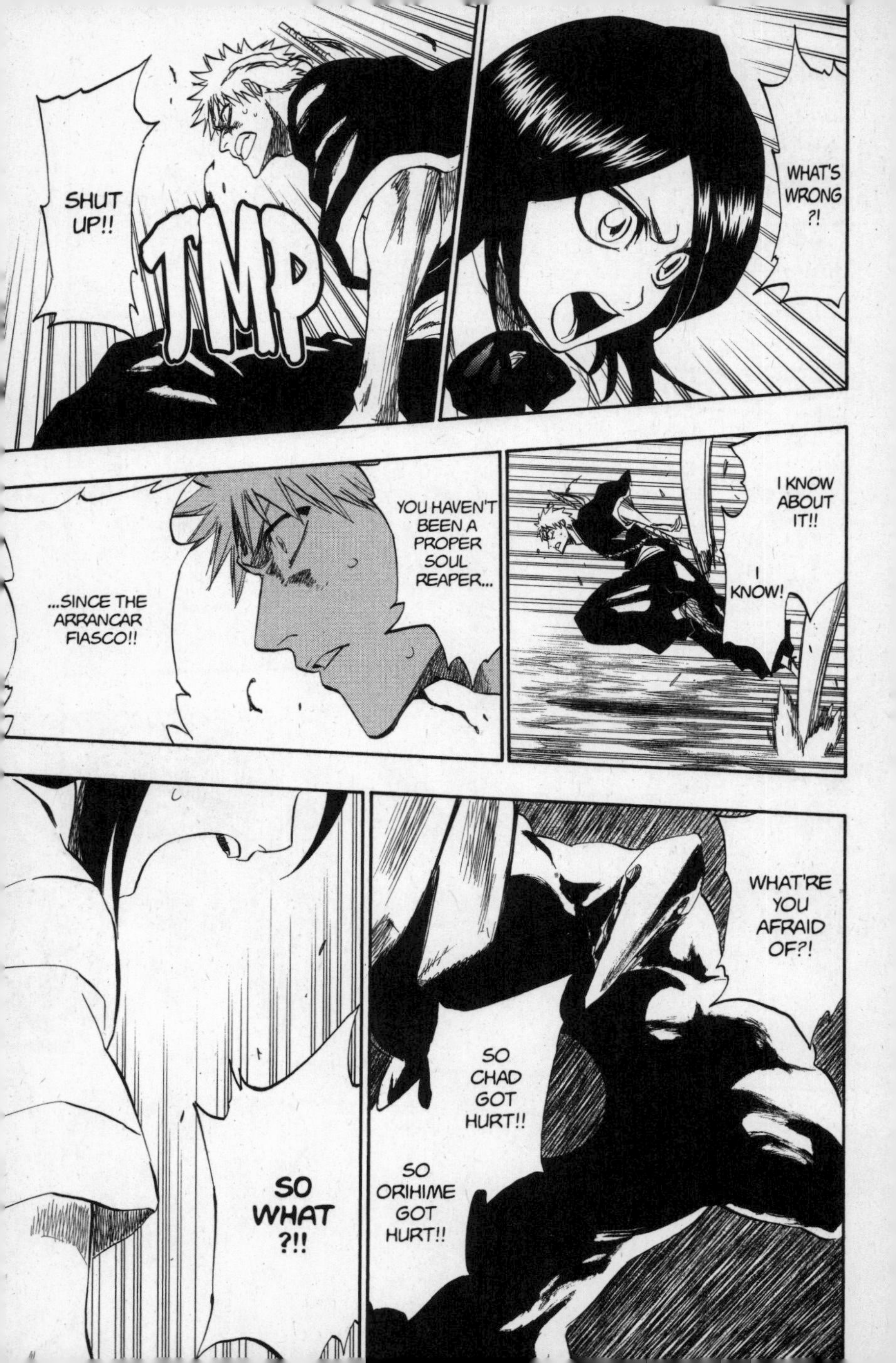
WHAT'S WRONG ?!
TMP
SHUT UP!!
I KNOW ABOUT IT!!
I KNOW!
YOU HAVEN'T BEEN A PROPER SOUL REAPER...
...SINCE THE ARRANCAR FIASCO!!
WHAT'RE YOU AFRAID OF?!
SO CHAD GOT HURT!!
SO ORIHIME GOT HURT!!
SO WHAT ?!!

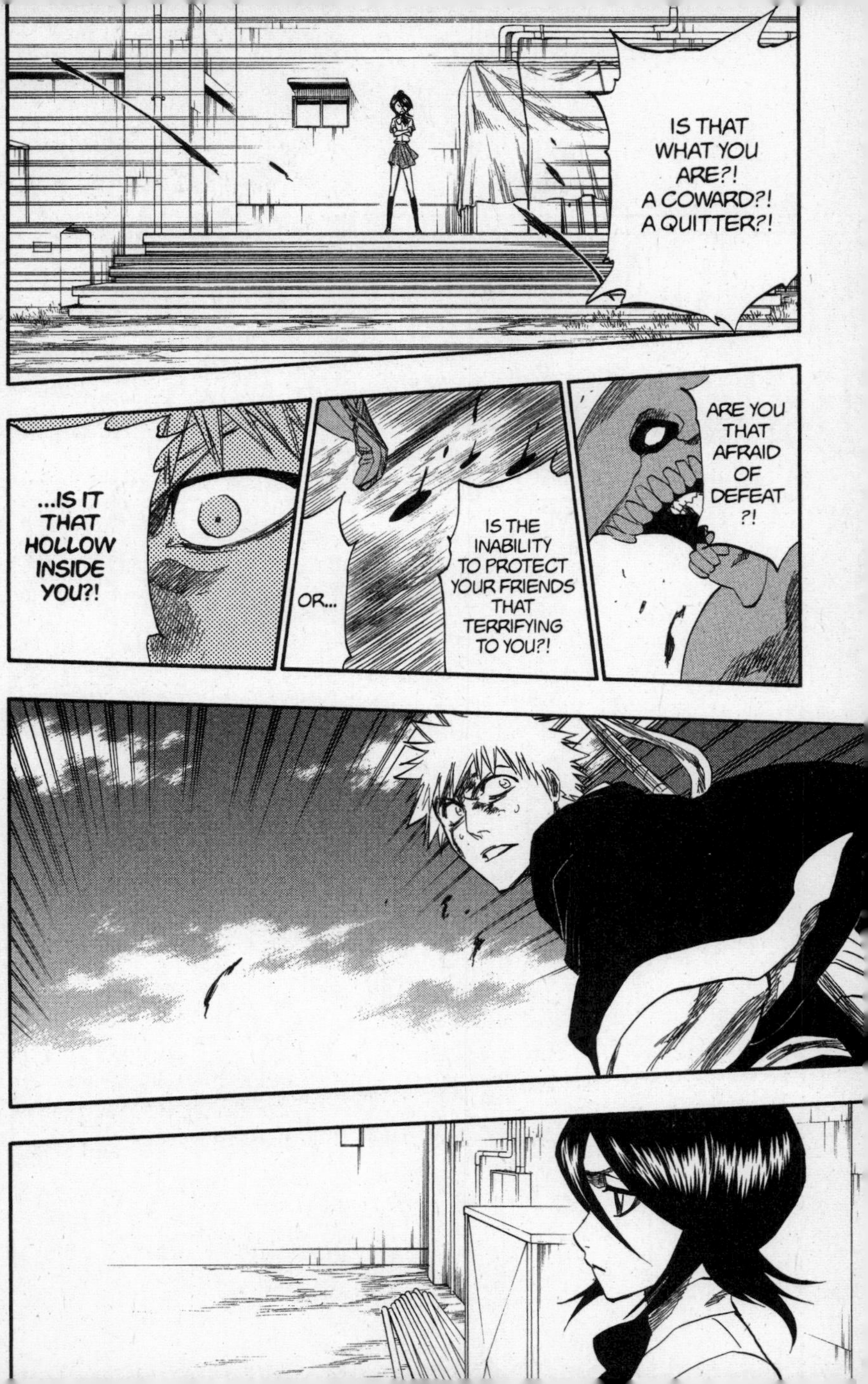
IS THAT WHAT YOU ARE?! A COWARD?! A QUITTER?!
ARE YOU THAT AFRAID OF DEFEAT ?!
IS THE INABILITY TO PROTECT YOUR FRIENDS THAT TERRIFYING TO YOU?!
OR...
...IS IT THAT HOLLOW INSIDE YOU?!

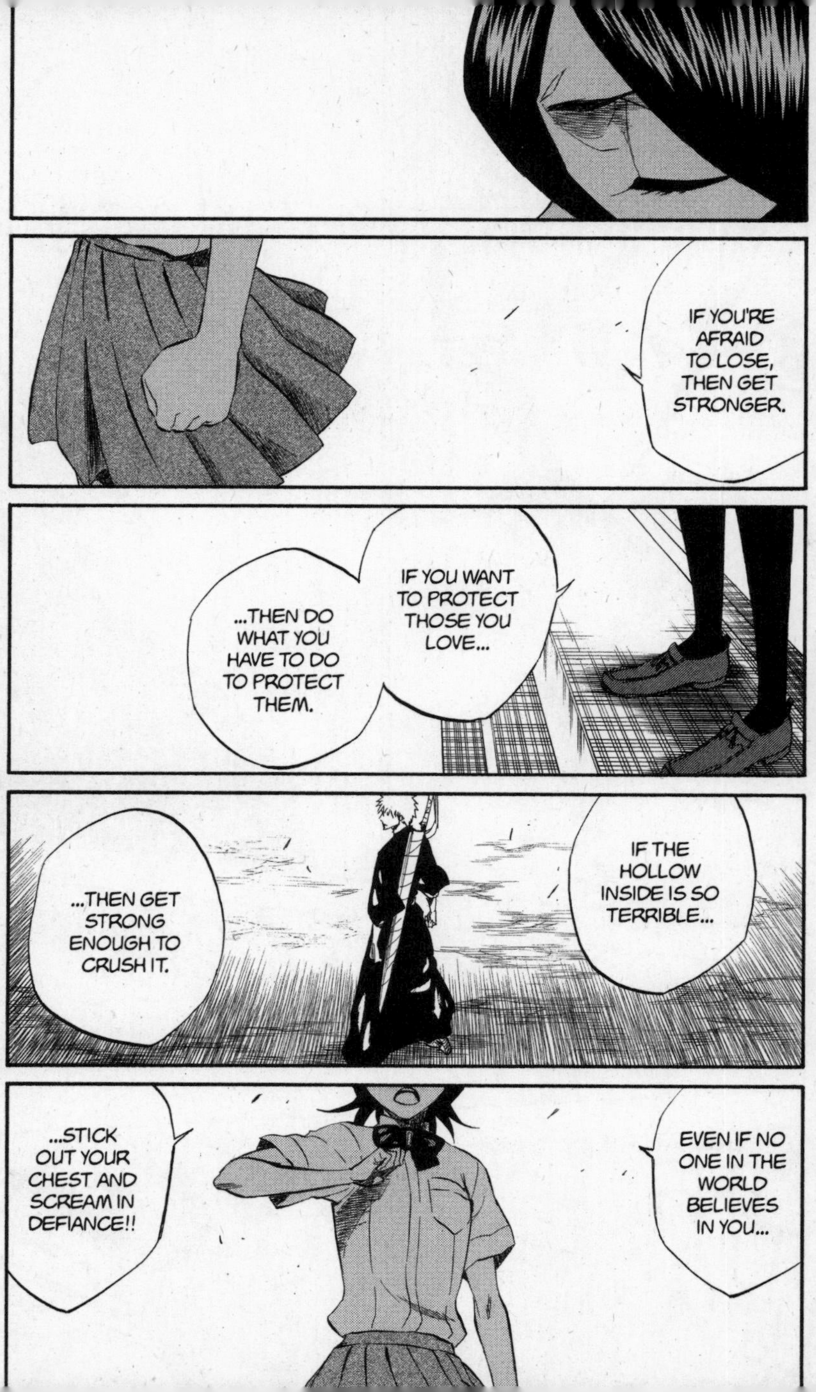
IF YOU'RE AFRAID TO LOSE, THEN GET STRONGER.
IF YOU WANT TO PROTECT THOSE YOU LOVE...
...THEN DO WHAT YOU HAVE TO DO TO PROTECT THEM.
IF THE HOLLOW INSIDE IS SO TERRIBLE...
...THEN GET STRONG ENOUGH TO CRUSH IT.
EVEN IF NO ONE IN THE WORLD BELIEVES IN YOU...
...STICK OUT YOUR CHEST AND SCREAM IN DEFIANCE!!

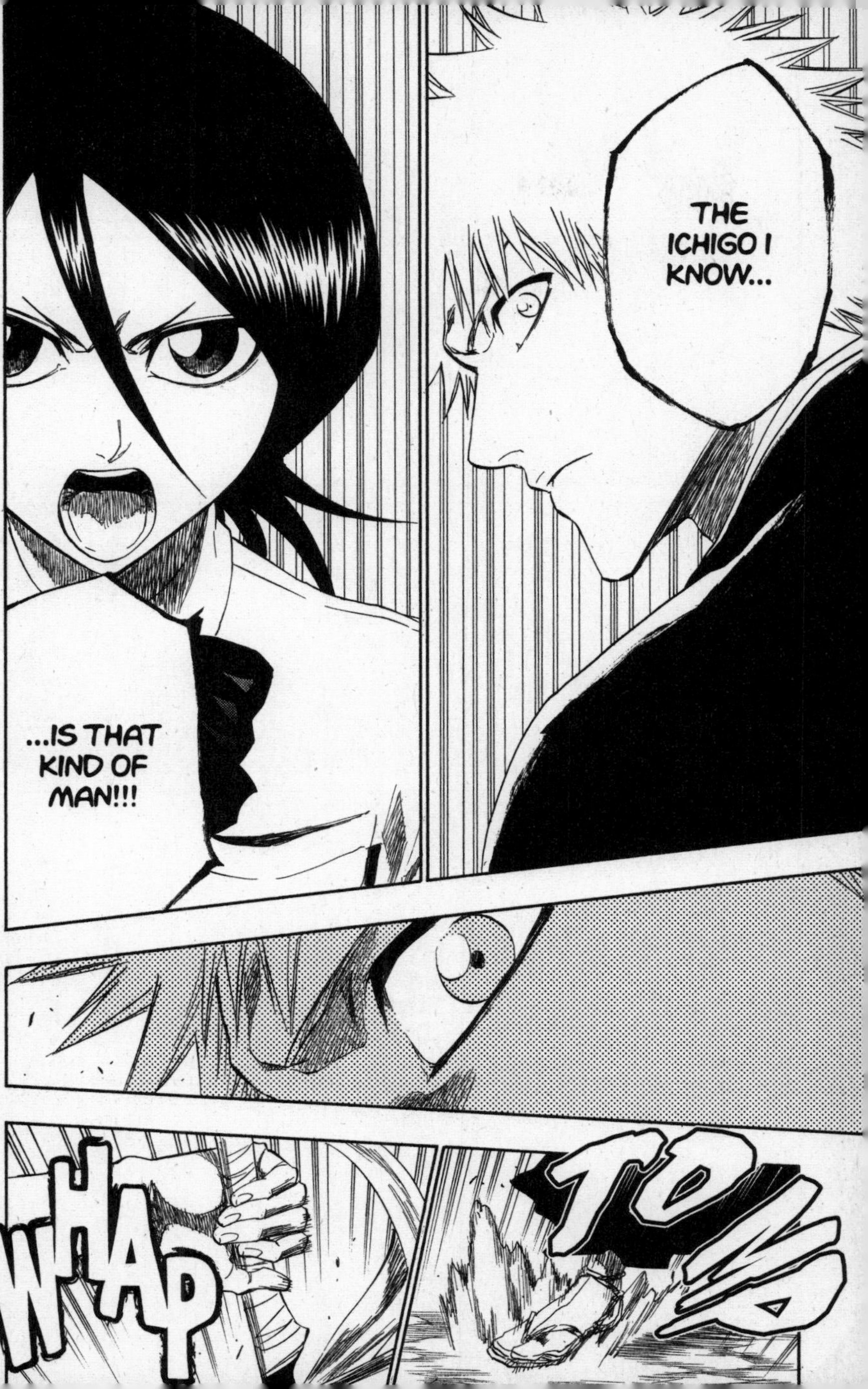
THE ICHIGO I KNOW...
...IS THAT KIND OF MAN!!!
TOMP
WHAP

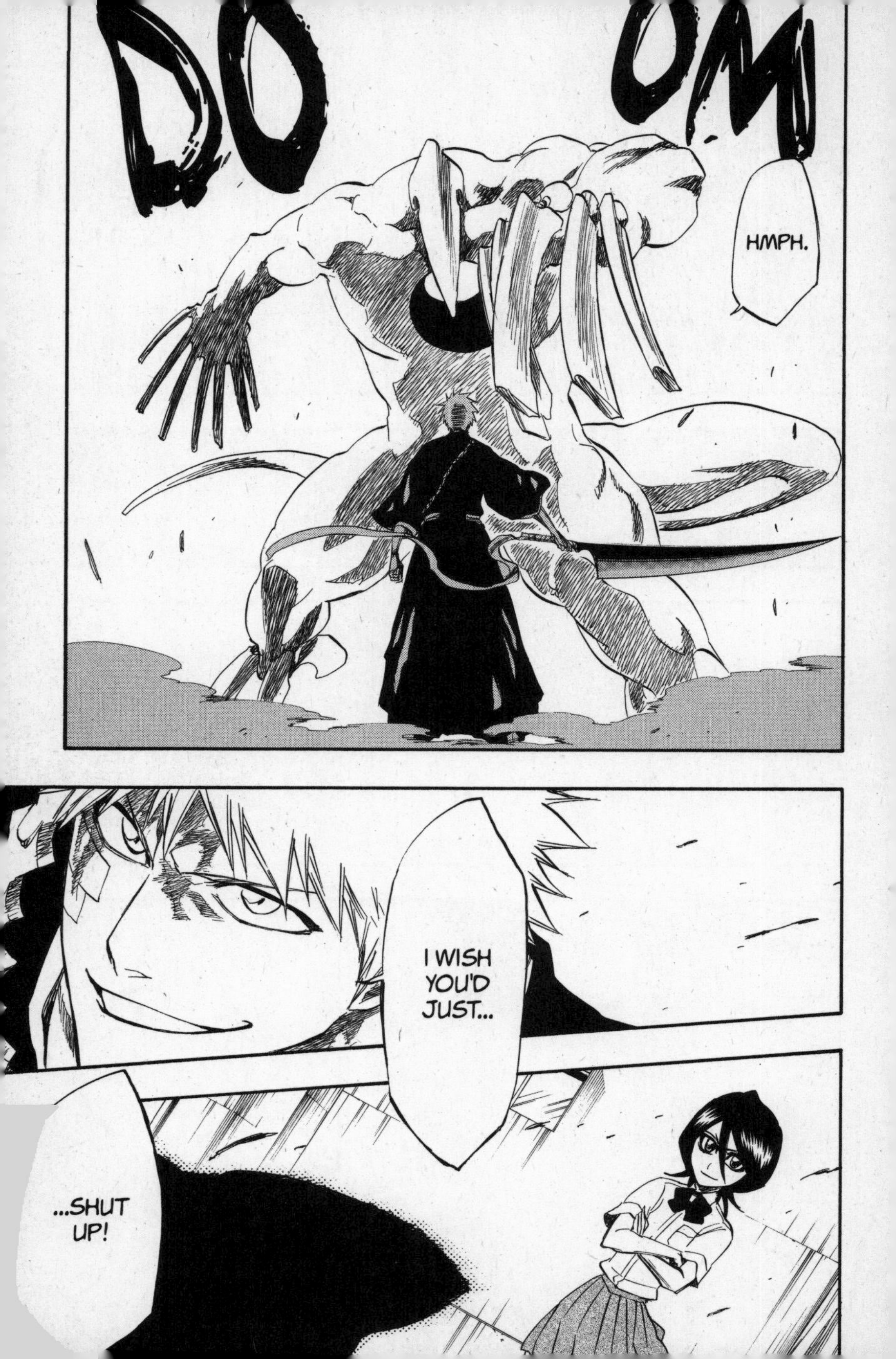
DOOM
HMPH.
I WISH YOU'D JUST...
...SHUT UP!

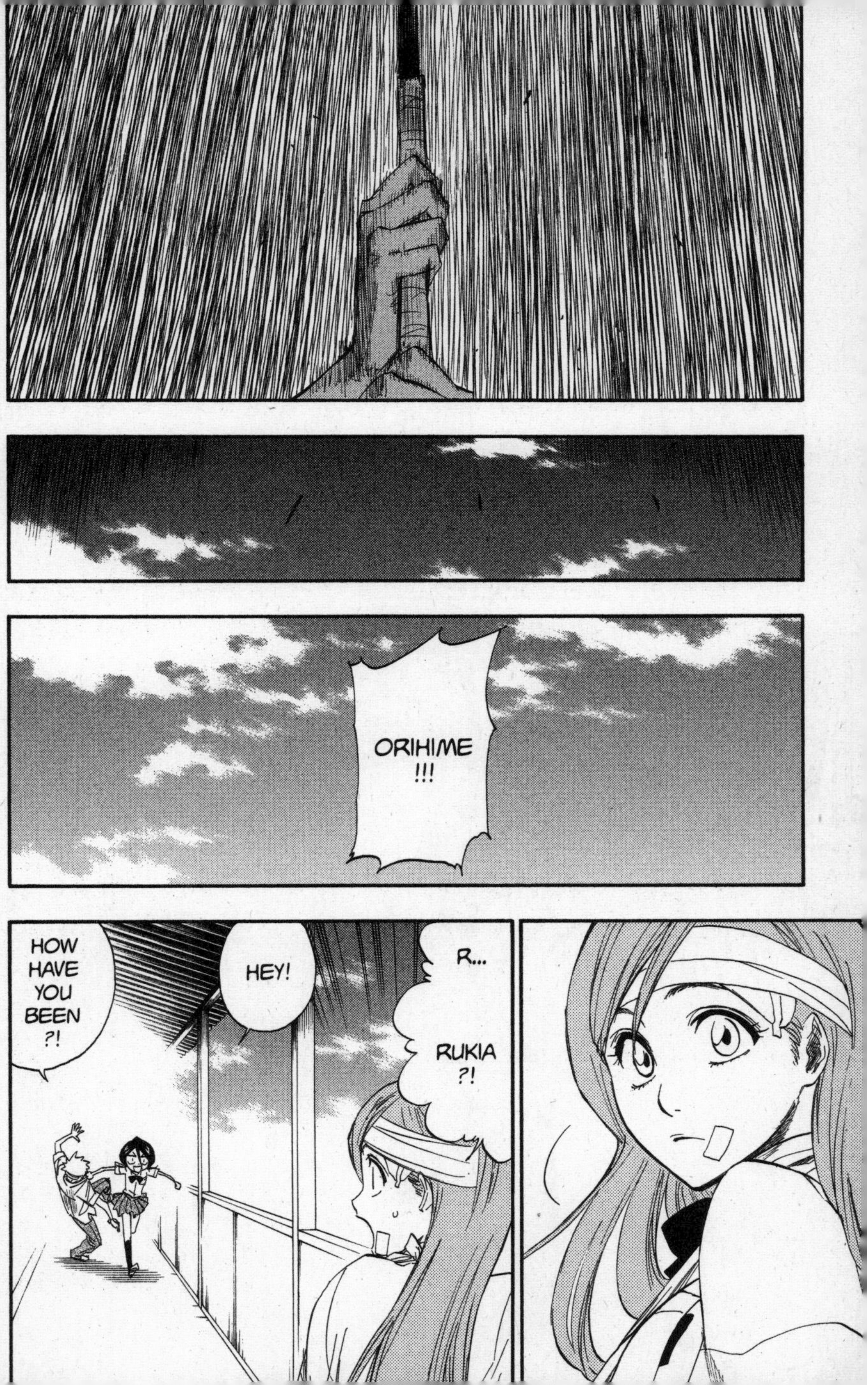
ORIHIME!!!
R...
RUKIA?!
HEY!
HOW HAVE YOU BEEN?!

READ THIS WAY

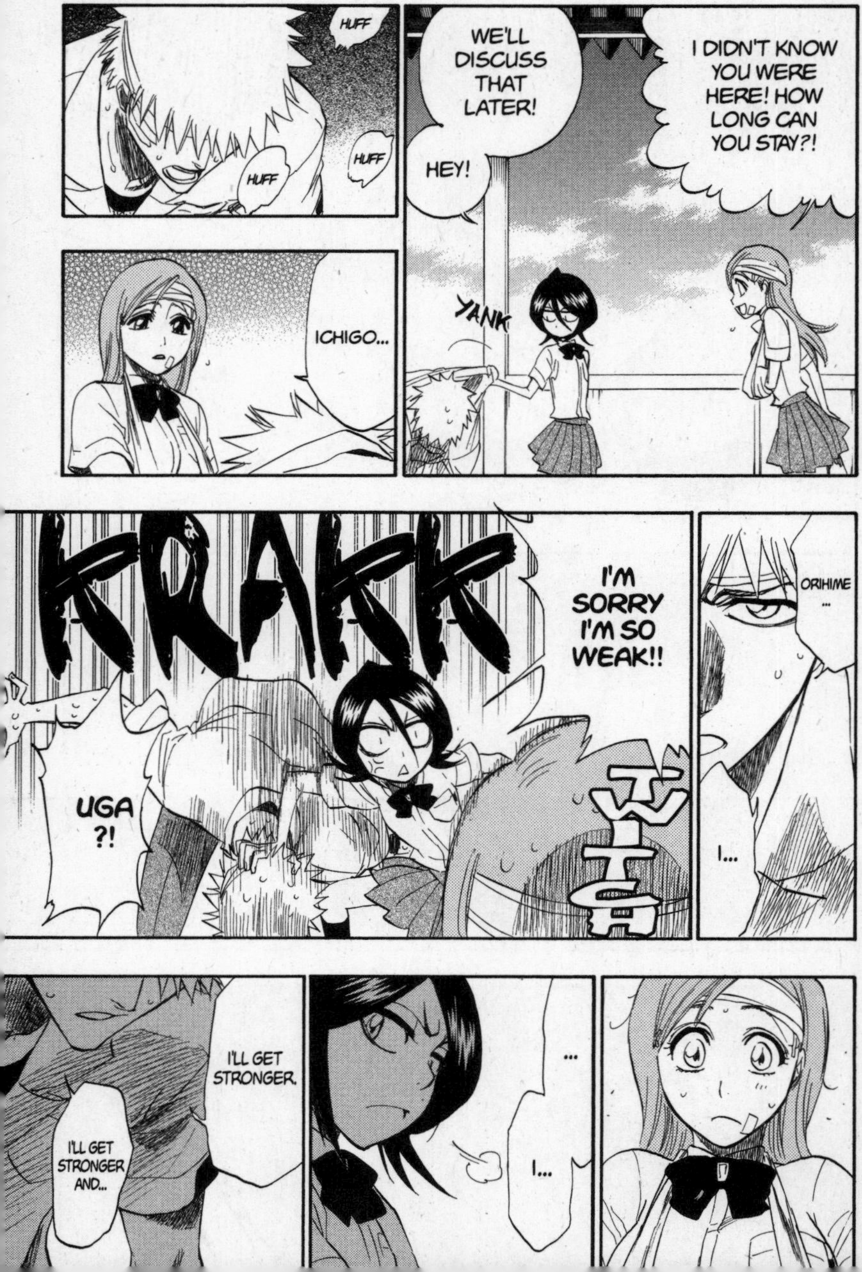
I DIDN'T KNOW YOU WERE HERE! HOW LONG CAN YOU STAY?!
WE'LL DISCUSS THAT LATER!
HEY!
YANK
HUFF
HUFF
HUFF
ICHIGO...
ORIHIME ...
I...
I'M SORRY I'M SO WEAK!!
KRAKK
TWITCH
UGA ?!
...
I...
I'LL GET STRONGER.
I'LL GET STRONGER AND...

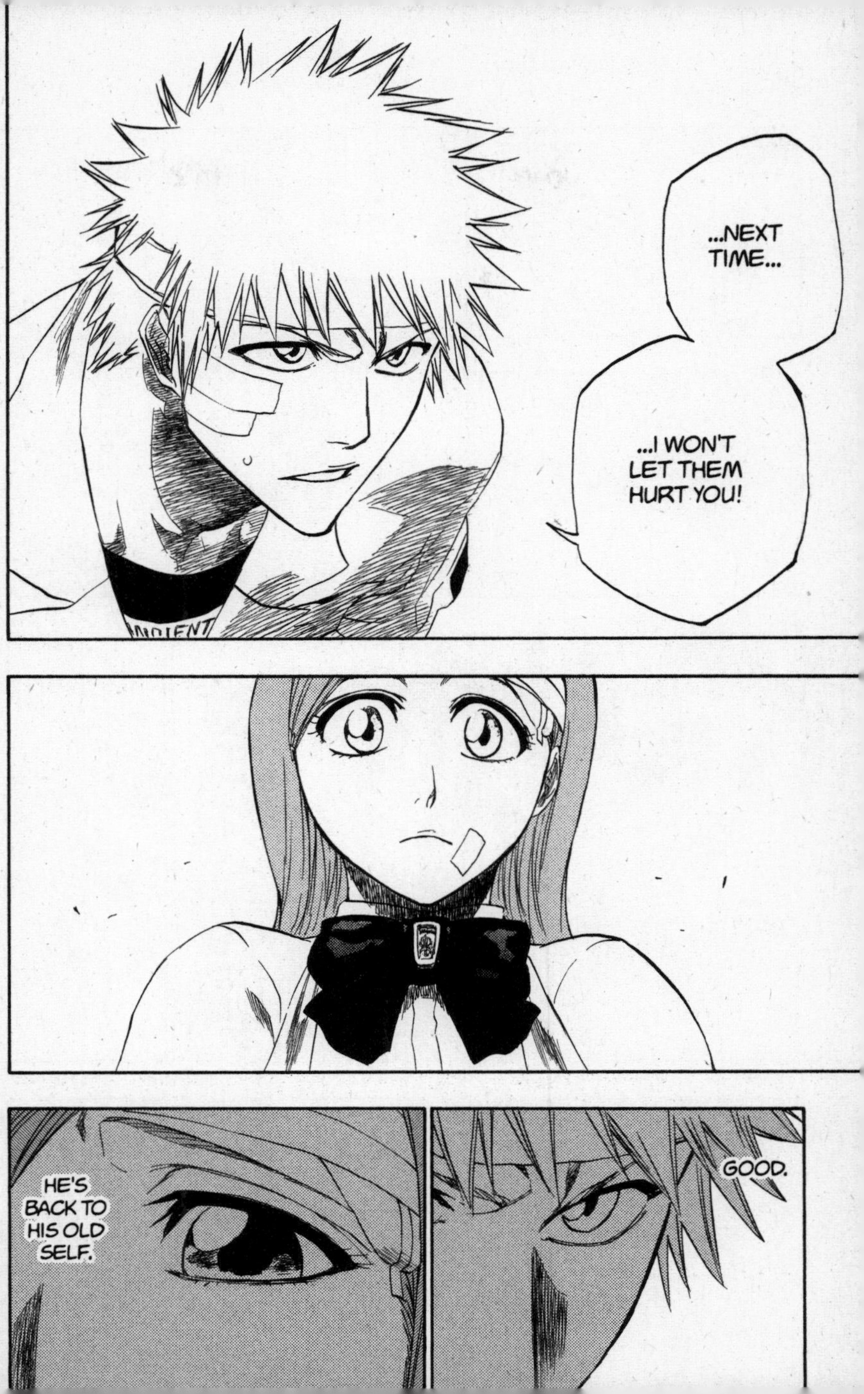
...NEXT TIME...
...I WON'T LET THEM HURT YOU!
GOOD.
HE'S BACK TO HIS OLD SELF.

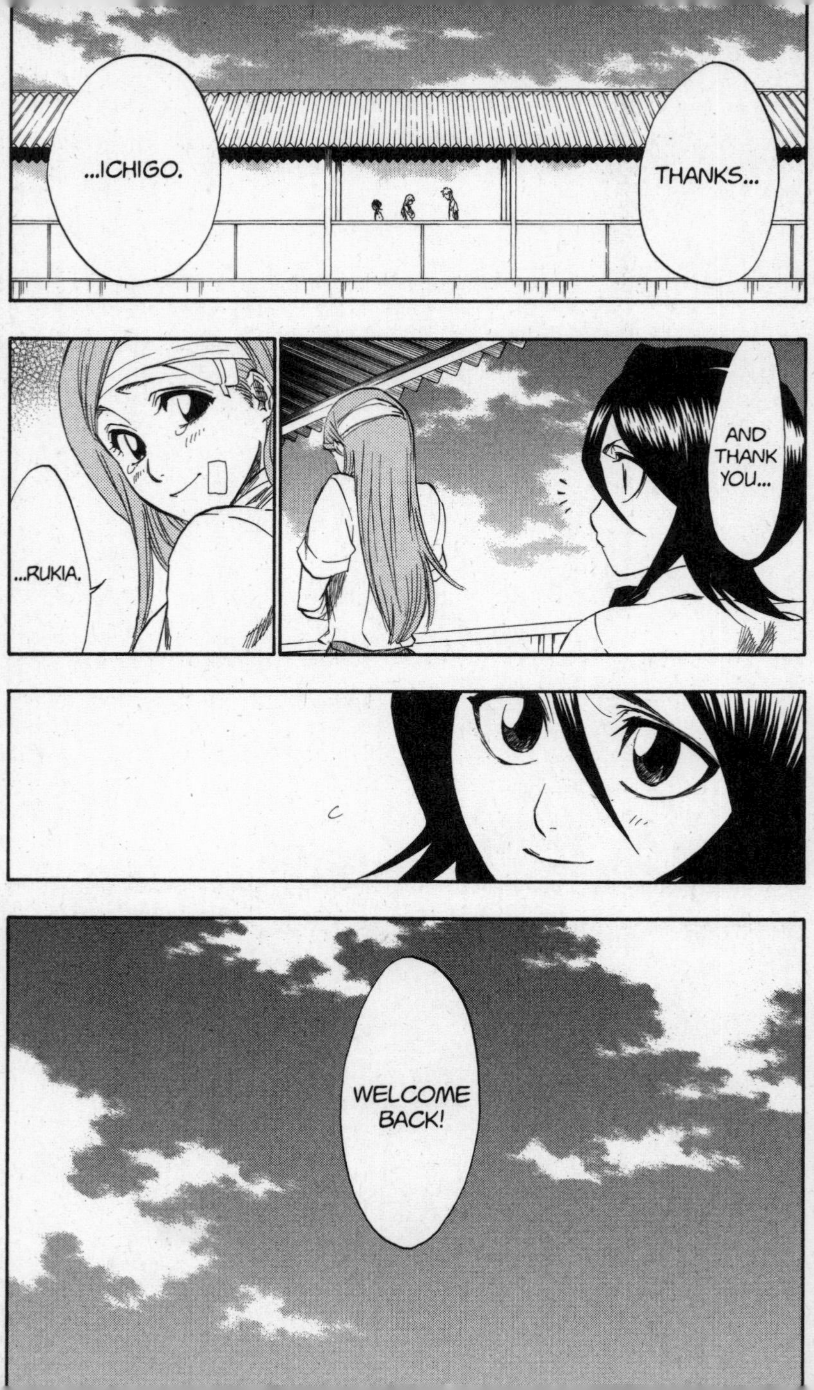
THANKS...
...ICHIGO.
AND THANK YOU...
...RUKIA.
WELCOME BACK!

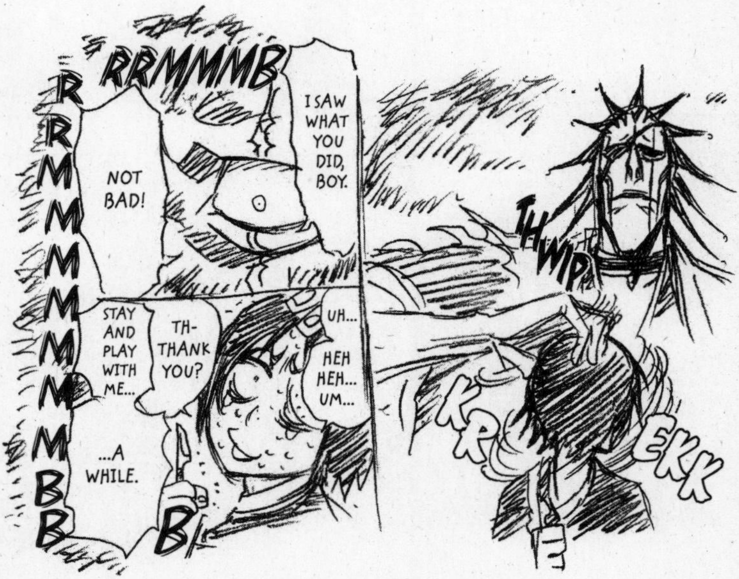
THWIP
KREKK
I SAW WHAT YOU DID, BOY.
RRMMMB
NOT BAD!
UH... HEH HEH... UM...
TH- THANK YOU?
STAY AND PLAY WITH ME...
...A WHILE.
RRMMMMMMMBB
B

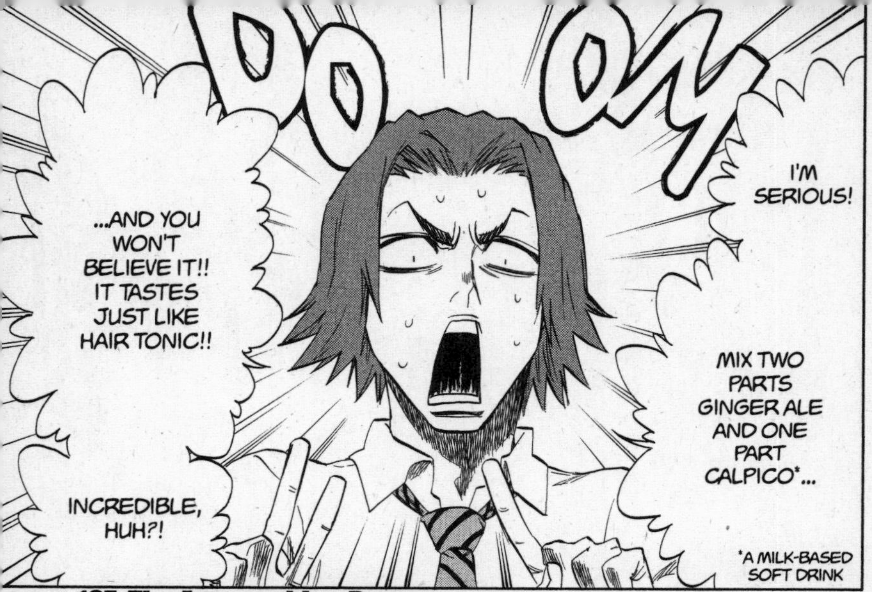
DOOY
I'M SERIOUS!
MIX TWO PARTS GINGER ALE AND ONE PART CALPICO*...
...AND YOU WON'T BELIEVE IT!! IT TASTES JUST LIKE HAIR TONIC!!
INCREDIBLE, HUH?!
*A MILK-BASED SOFT DRINK

197. The Approaching Danger

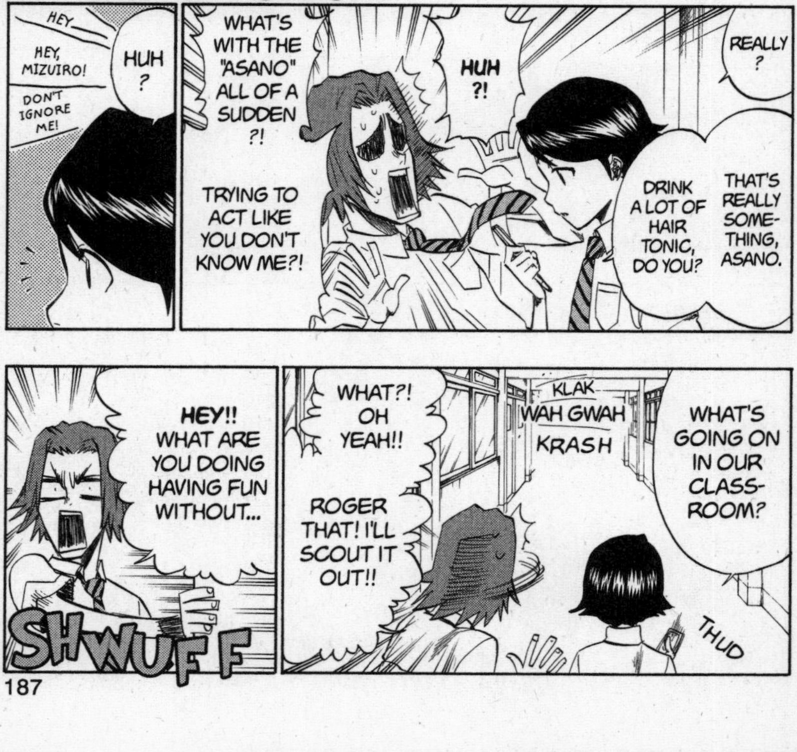
REALLY?
THAT'S REALLY SOME-THING, ASANO.
DRINK A LOT OF HAIR TONIC, DO YOU?
HUH?!
WHAT'S WITH THE "ASANO" ALL OF A SUDDEN?!
TRYING TO ACT LIKE YOU DON'T KNOW ME?!
HUH?
HEY
HEY, MIZUIRO!
DON'T IGNORE ME!
WHAT'S GOING ON IN OUR CLASS-ROOM?
KLAK
WAH GWAH
KRASH
WHAT?! OH YEAH!!
ROGER THAT! I'LL SCOUT IT OUT!!
THUD
HEY!! WHAT ARE YOU DOING HAVING FUN WITHOUT...
SHWUFF

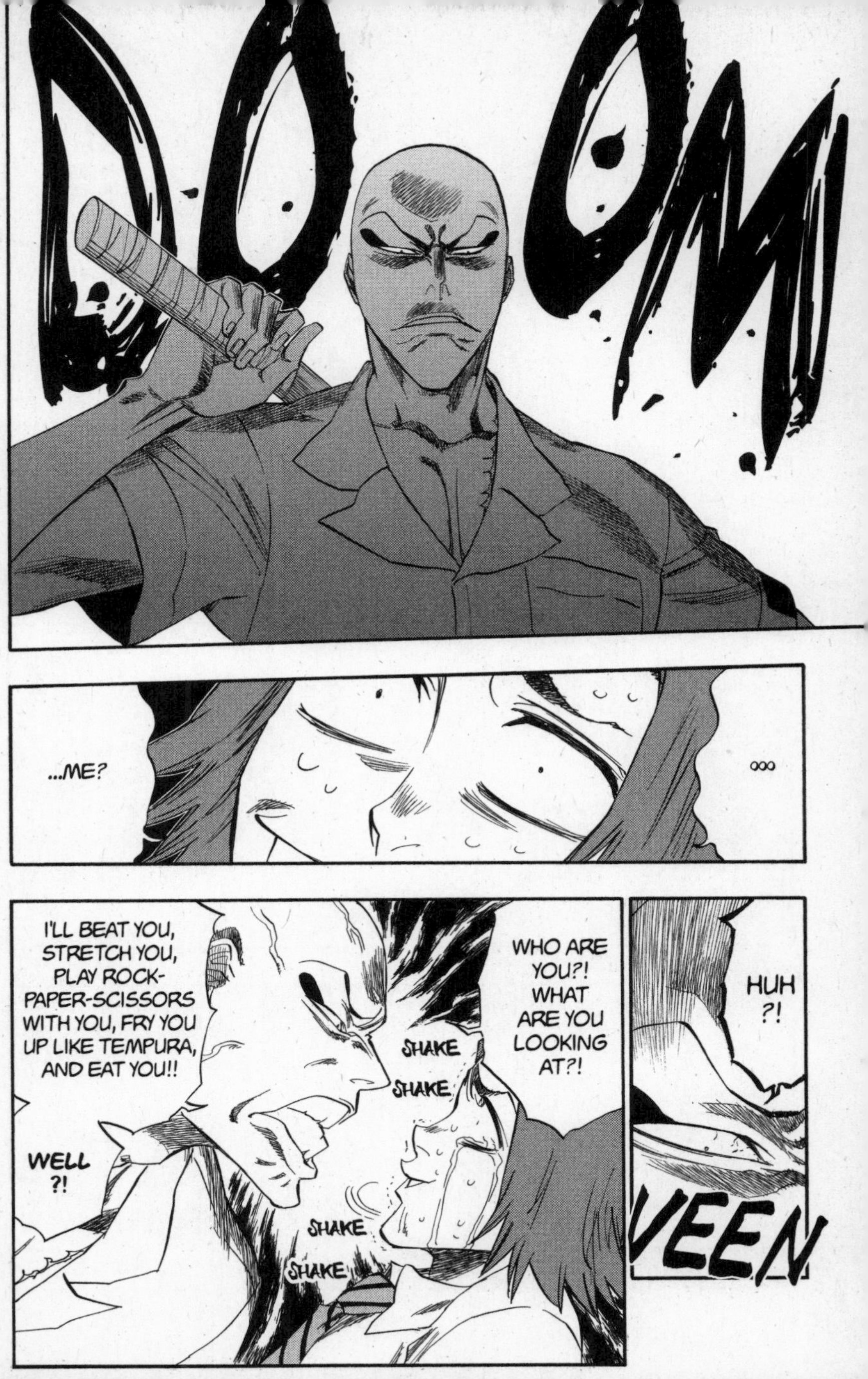
DOOM
...ME?
HUH?!
VEEN
WHO ARE YOU?! WHAT ARE YOU LOOKING AT?!
I'LL BEAT YOU, STRETCH YOU, PLAY ROCK-PAPER-SCISSORS WITH YOU, FRY YOU UP LIKE TEMPURA, AND EAT YOU!!
SHAKE
SHAKE
WELL?!
SHAKE
SHAKE

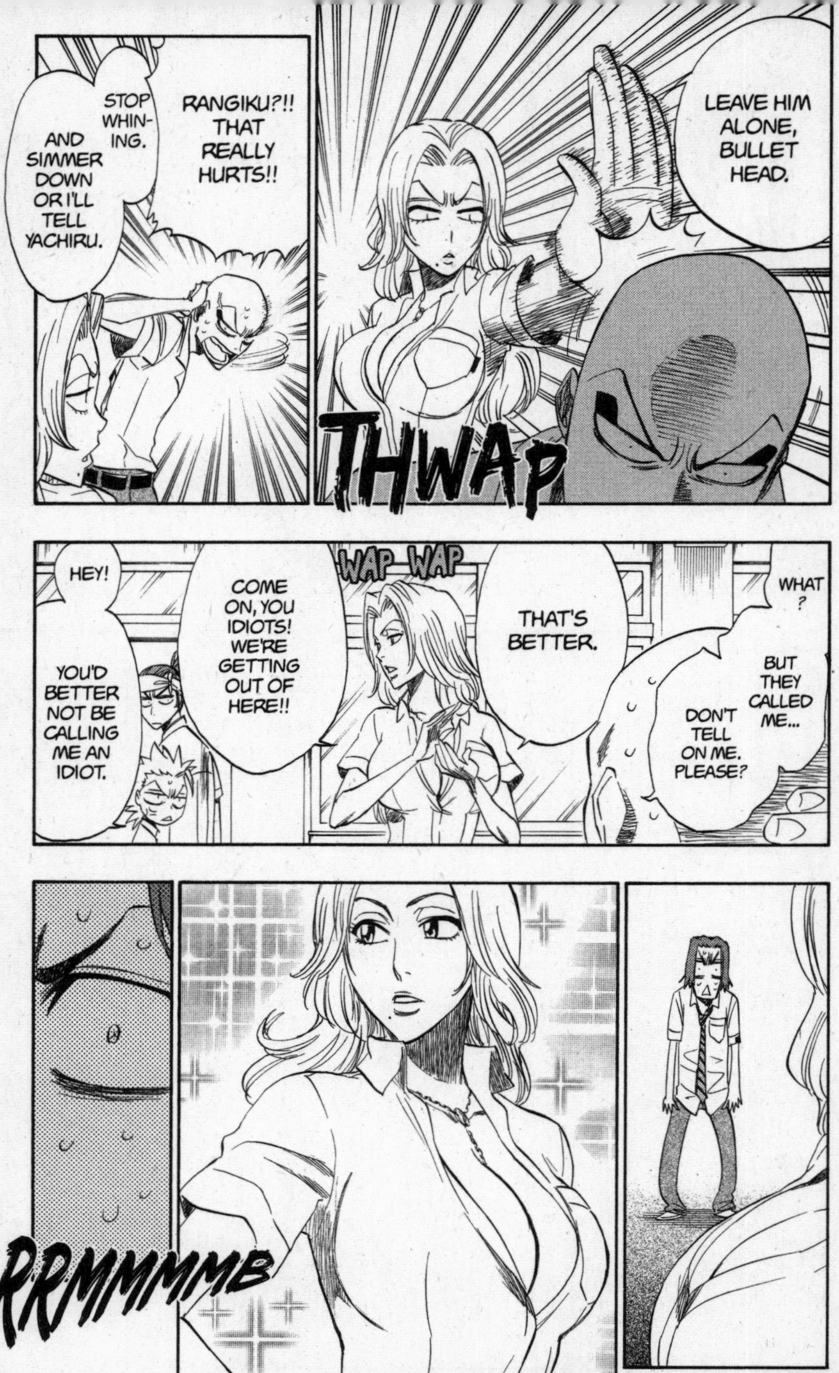
LEAVE HIM ALONE, BULLET HEAD.
THWAP
RANGIKU?!! THAT REALLY HURTS!!
STOP WHIN-ING.
AND SIMMER DOWN OR I'LL TELL YACHIRU.
WHAT?
BUT THEY CALLED ME...
DON'T TELL ON ME. PLEASE?
THAT'S BETTER.
WAP WAP
COME ON, YOU IDIOTS! WE'RE GETTING OUT OF HERE!!
HEY!
YOU'D BETTER NOT BE CALLING ME AN IDIOT.
RRMMMMMB

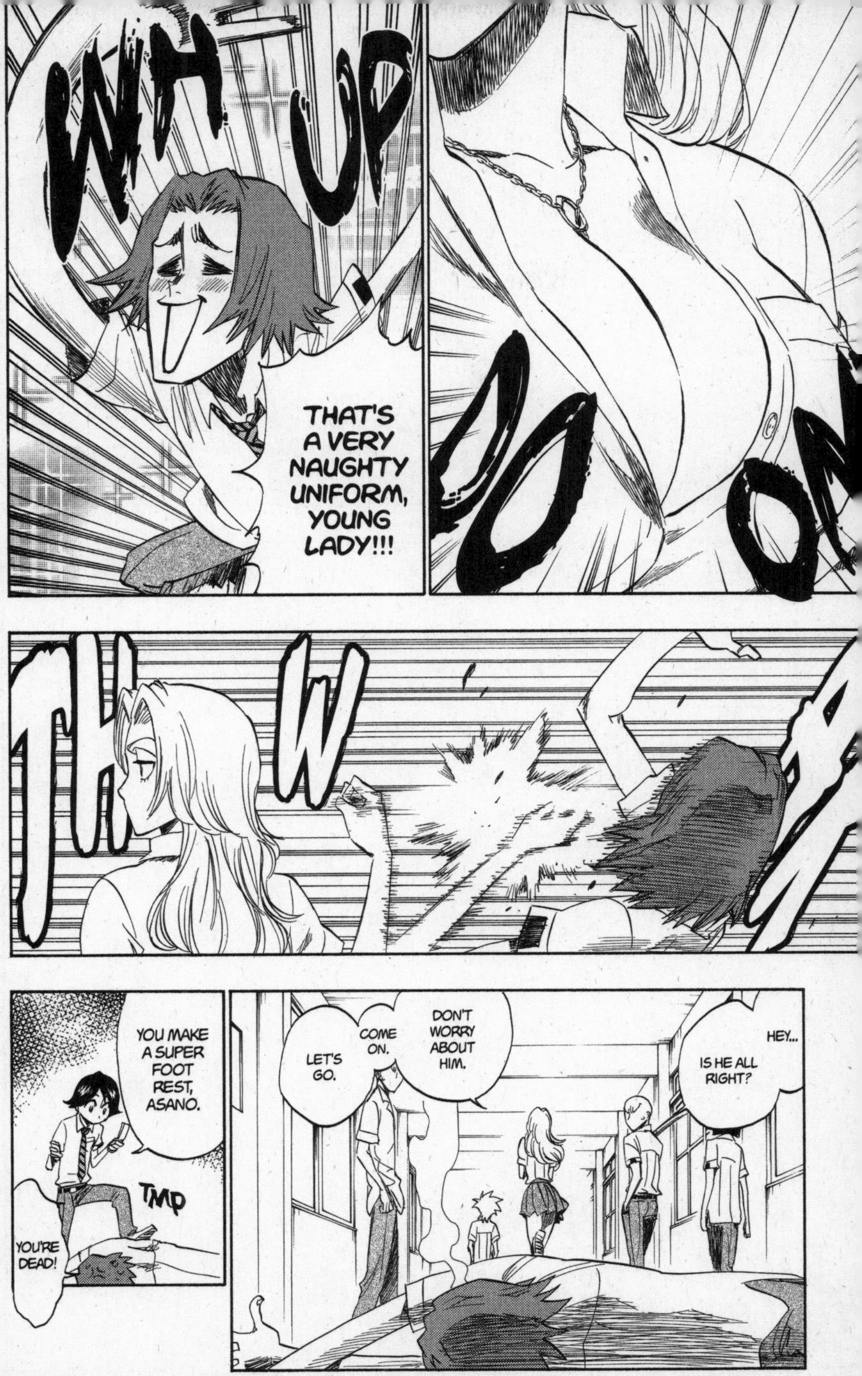
THAT'S A VERY NAUGHTY UNIFORM, YOUNG LADY!!!
HEY... IS HE ALL RIGHT?
DON'T WORRY ABOUT HIM.
COME ON.
LET'S GO.
YOU MAKE A SUPER FOOT REST, ASANO.
TMP
YOU'RE DEAD!

Bleach 197. The Approaching Danger

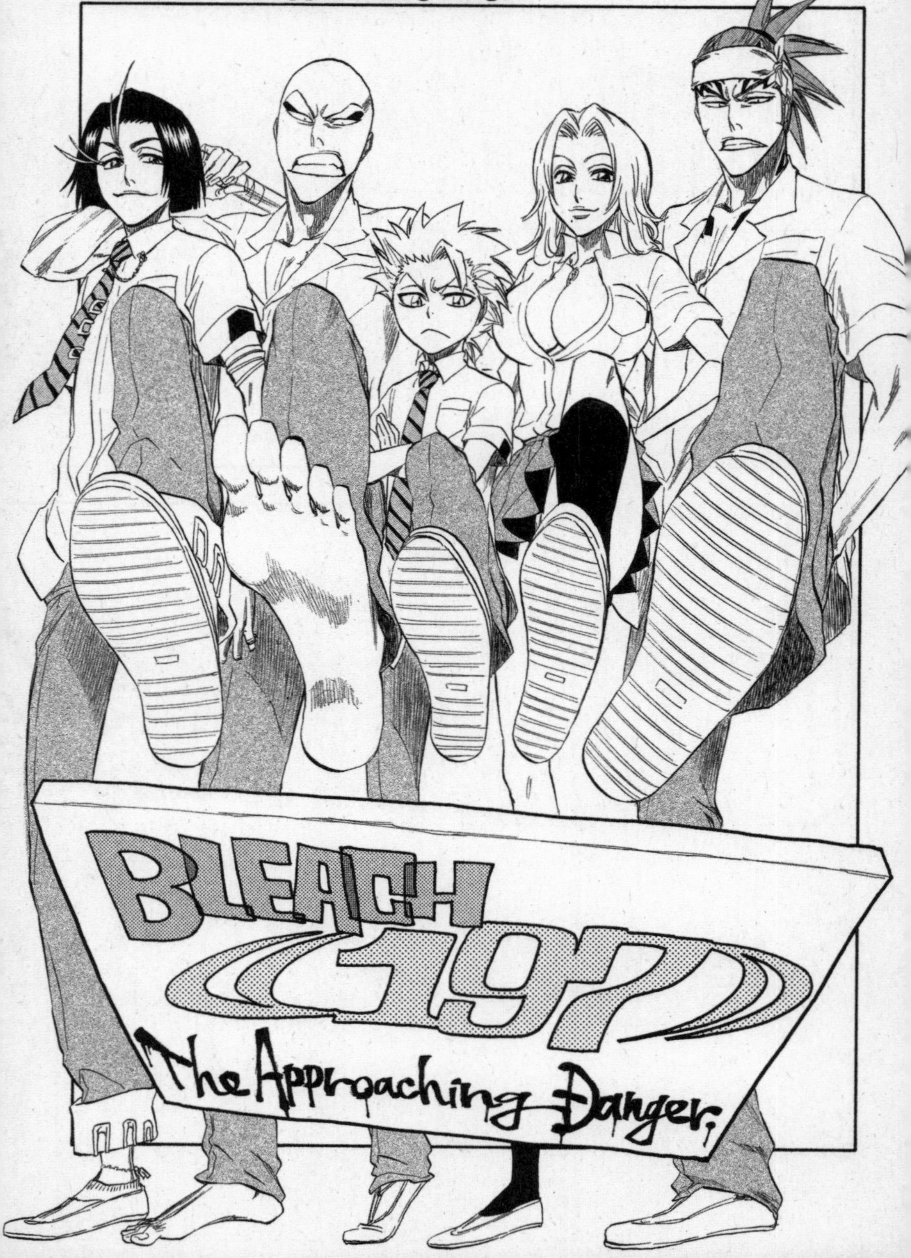
BLEACH
197
The Approaching Danger

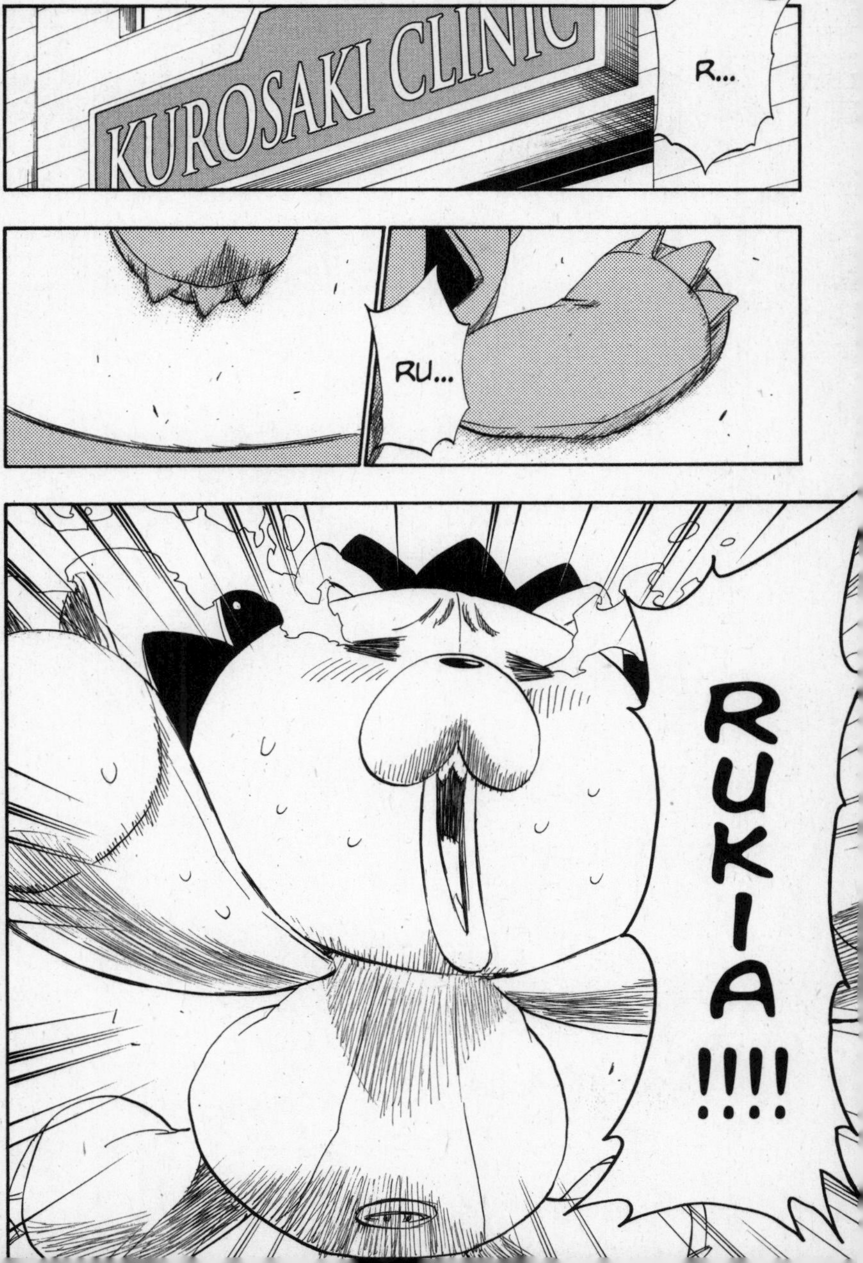
KUROSAKI CLINIC
R...
RU...
RUKIA!!!!

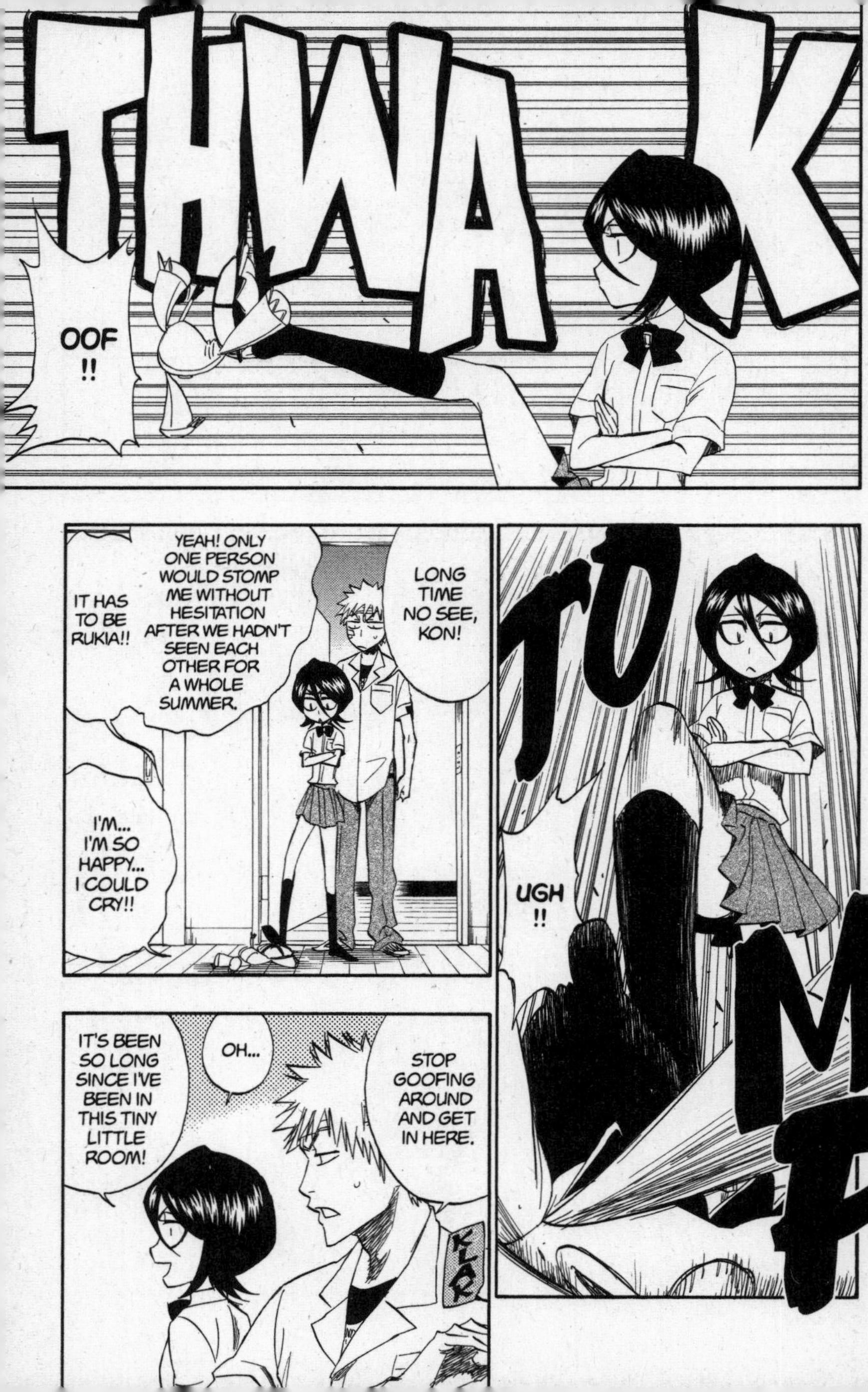
THWA K
OOF!!
TOMP
UGH!!
LONG TIME NO SEE, KON!
YEAH! ONLY ONE PERSON WOULD STOMP ME WITHOUT HESITATION AFTER WE HADN'T SEEN EACH OTHER FOR A WHOLE SUMMER.
IT HAS TO BE RUKIA!!
I'M... I'M SO HAPPY... I COULD CRY!!
STOP GOOFING AROUND AND GET IN HERE.
OH...
IT'S BEEN SO LONG SINCE I'VE BEEN IN THIS TINY LITTLE ROOM!
KLAK

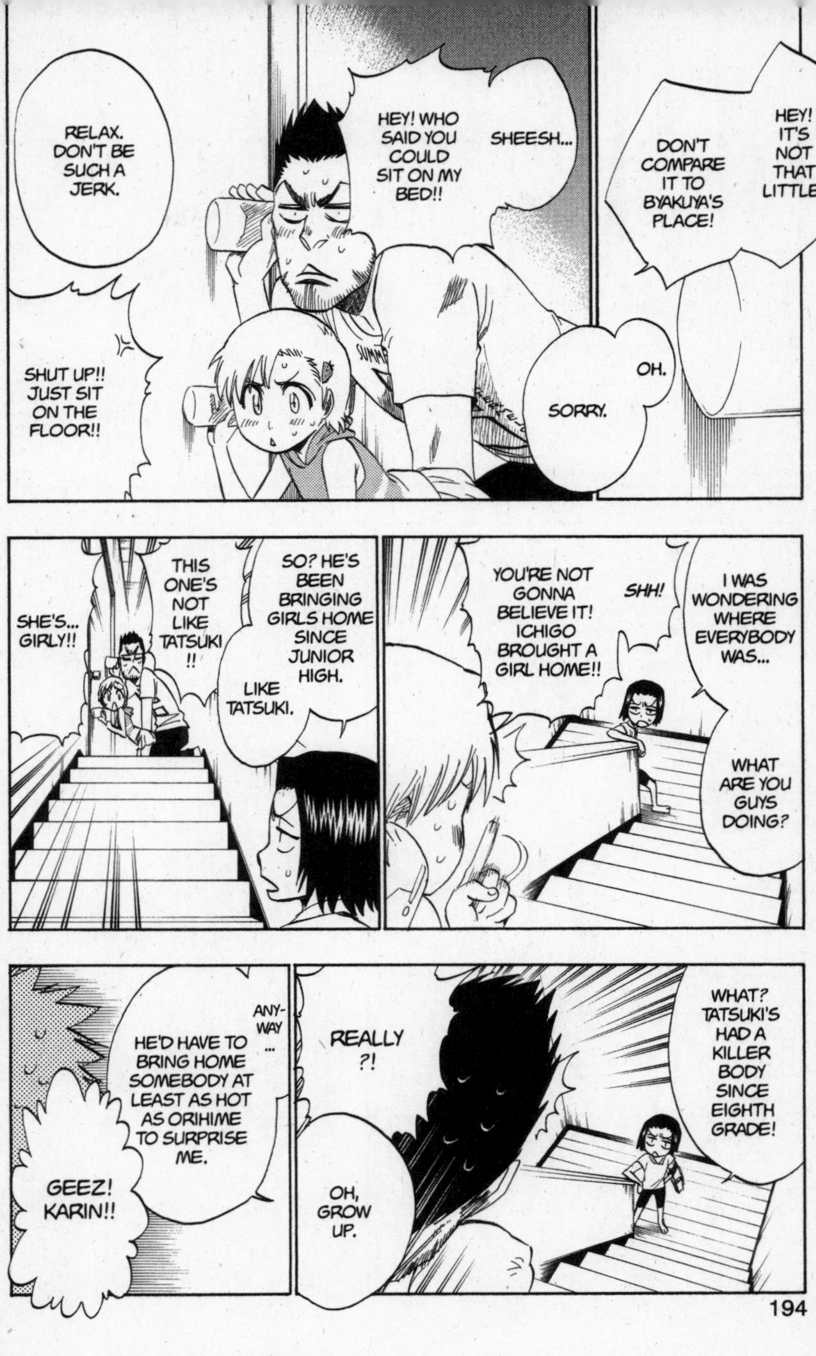
HEY! IT'S NOT THAT LITTLE!
DON'T COMPARE IT TO BYAKUYA'S PLACE!
OH.
SORRY.
SHEESH...
HEY! WHO SAID YOU COULD SIT ON MY BED!!
RELAX. DON'T BE SUCH A JERK.
SHUT UP!! JUST SIT ON THE FLOOR!!
I WAS WONDERING WHERE EVERYBODY WAS...
WHAT ARE YOU GUYS DOING?
SHH!
YOU'RE NOT GONNA BELIEVE IT! ICHIGO BROUGHT A GIRL HOME!!
SO? HE'S BEEN BRINGING GIRLS HOME SINCE JUNIOR HIGH.
LIKE TATSUKI.
THIS ONE'S NOT LIKE TATSUKI!!
SHE'S... GIRLY!!
WHAT? TATSUKI'S HAD A KILLER BODY SINCE EIGHTH GRADE!
REALLY?!
OH, GROW UP.
ANY-WAY...
HE'D HAVE TO BRING HOME SOMEBODY AT LEAST AS HOT AS ORIHIME TO SURPRISE ME.
GEEZ! KARIN!!

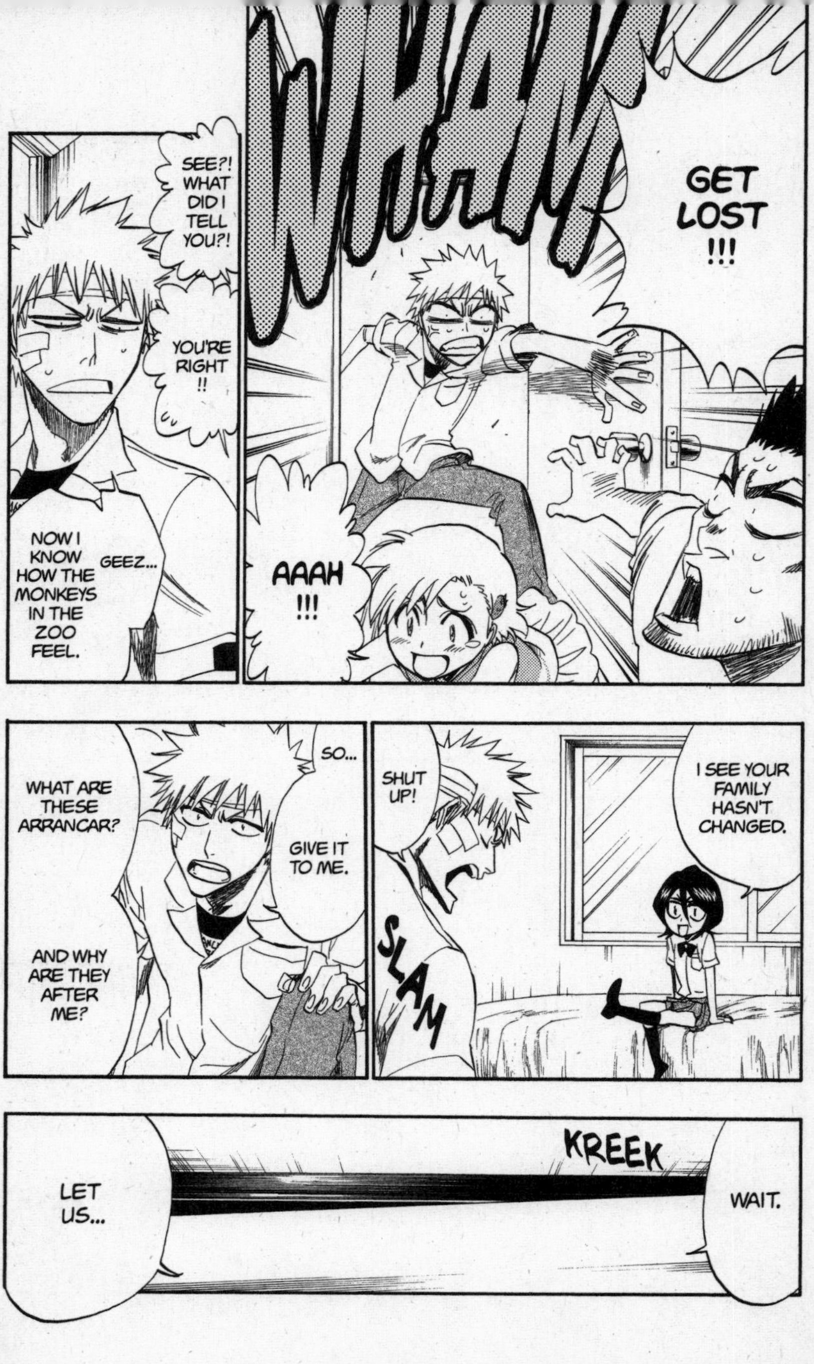
GET LOST !!!
WHAM
AAAH !!!
SEE?! WHAT DID I TELL YOU?!
YOU'RE RIGHT !!
GEEZ...
NOW I KNOW HOW THE MONKEYS IN THE ZOO FEEL.
I SEE YOUR FAMILY HASN'T CHANGED.
SHUT UP!
SLAM
SO...
GIVE IT TO ME.
WHAT ARE THESE ARRANCAR?
AND WHY ARE THEY AFTER ME?
WAIT.
KREEK
LET US...

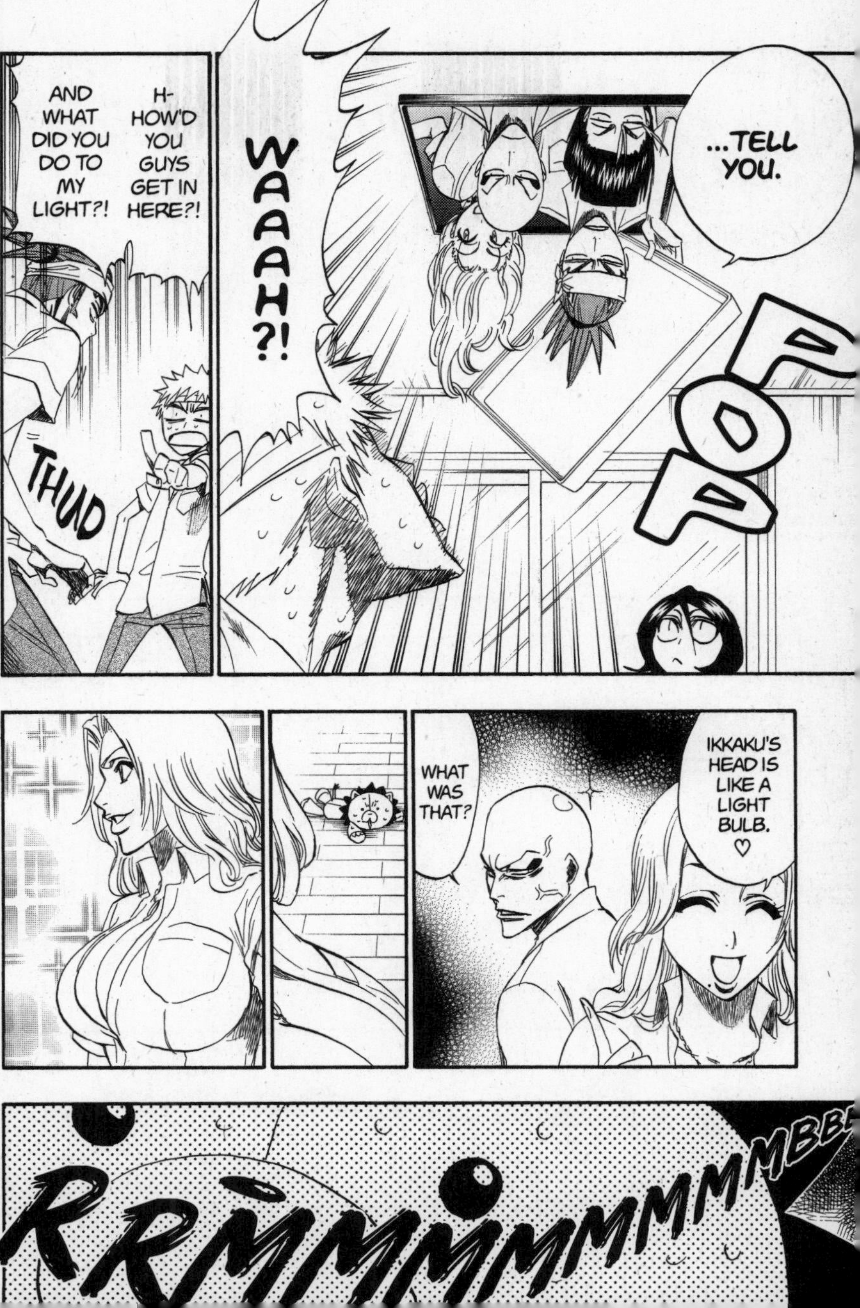
...TELL YOU.
POP
WAAAAH?!
H- HOW'D YOU GUYS GET IN HERE?!
AND WHAT DID YOU DO TO MY LIGHT?!
THUD
IKKAKU'S HEAD IS LIKE A LIGHT BULB. ♡
WHAT WAS THAT?
RRMMMMMMMMMMBB

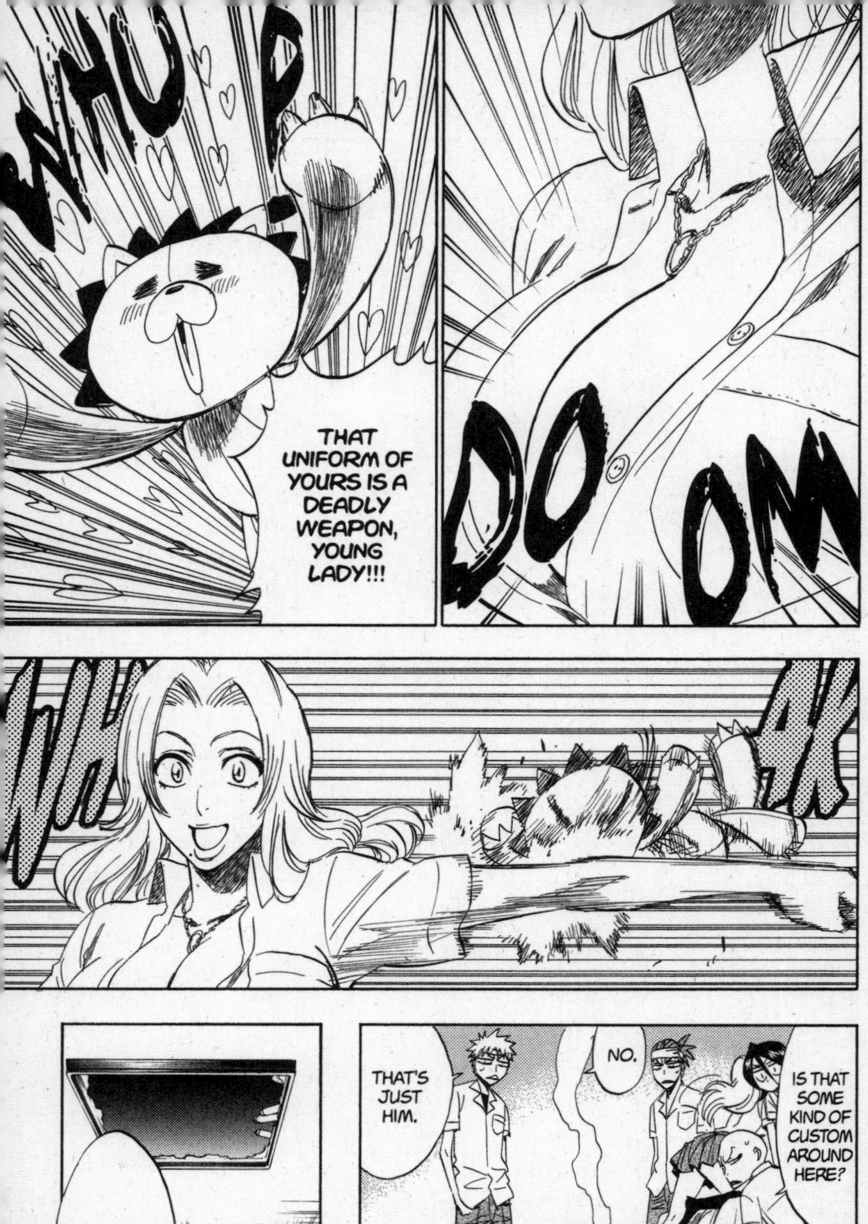
DOOM
WHUP
THAT UNIFORM OF YOURS IS A DEADLY WEAPON, YOUNG LADY!!!
IS THAT SOME KIND OF CUSTOM AROUND HERE?
NO.
THAT'S JUST HIM.
ARRANCARS ARE...

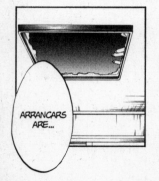

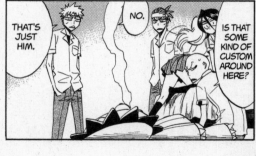

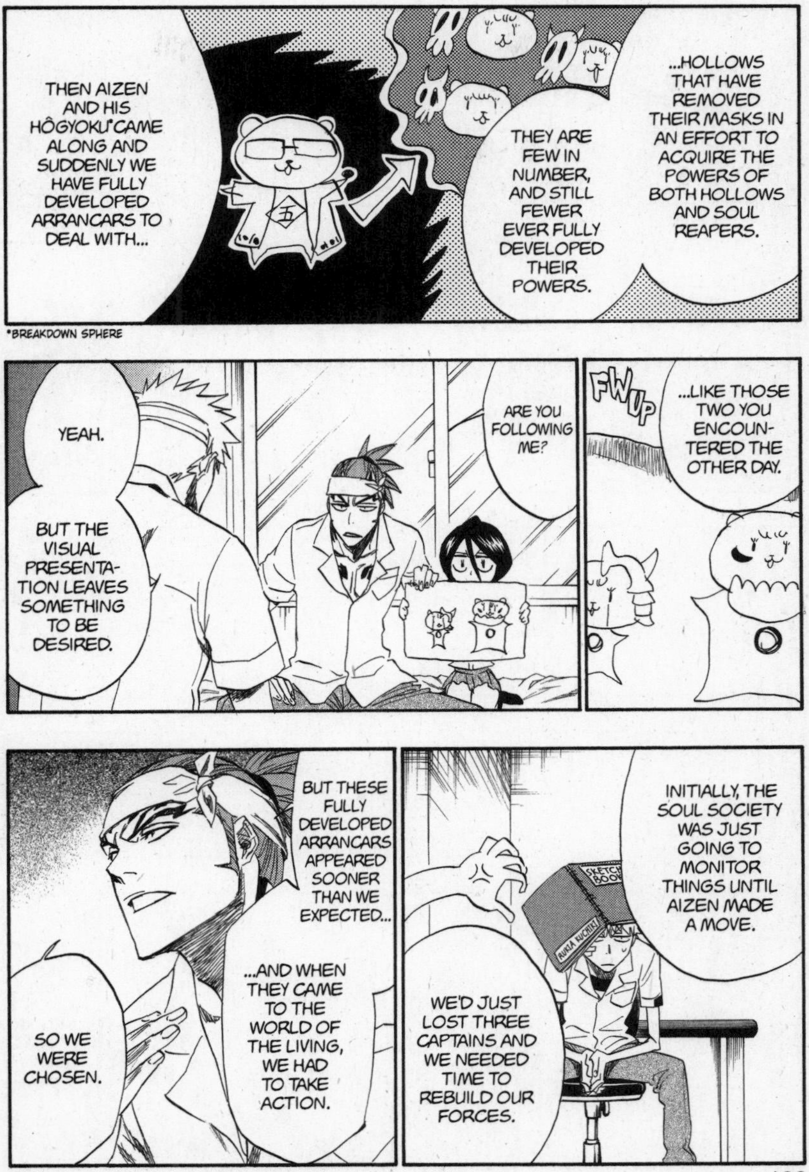
...HOLLOWS THAT HAVE REMOVED THEIR MASKS IN AN EFFORT TO ACQUIRE THE POWERS OF BOTH HOLLOWS AND SOUL REAPERS.
THEY ARE FEW IN NUMBER, AND STILL FEWER EVER FULLY DEVELOPED THEIR POWERS.
THEN AIZEN AND HIS HÔGYOKU* CAME ALONG AND SUDDENLY WE HAVE FULLY DEVELOPED ARRANCARS TO DEAL WITH...
*BREAKDOWN SPHERE
FWUP
...LIKE THOSE TWO YOU ENCOUNTERED THE OTHER DAY.
ARE YOU FOLLOWING ME?
YEAH.
BUT THE VISUAL PRESENTATION LEAVES SOMETHING TO BE DESIRED.
INITIALLY, THE SOUL SOCIETY WAS JUST GOING TO MONITOR THINGS UNTIL AIZEN MADE A MOVE.
SKETCH BOOK
RUKIA KUCHIKI
WE'D JUST LOST THREE CAPTAINS AND WE NEEDED TIME TO REBUILD OUR FORCES.
BUT THESE FULLY DEVELOPED ARRANCARS APPEARED SOONER THAN WE EXPECTED...
...AND WHEN THEY CAME TO THE WORLD OF THE LIVING, WE HAD TO TAKE ACTION.
SO WE WERE CHOSEN.

READ THIS WAY

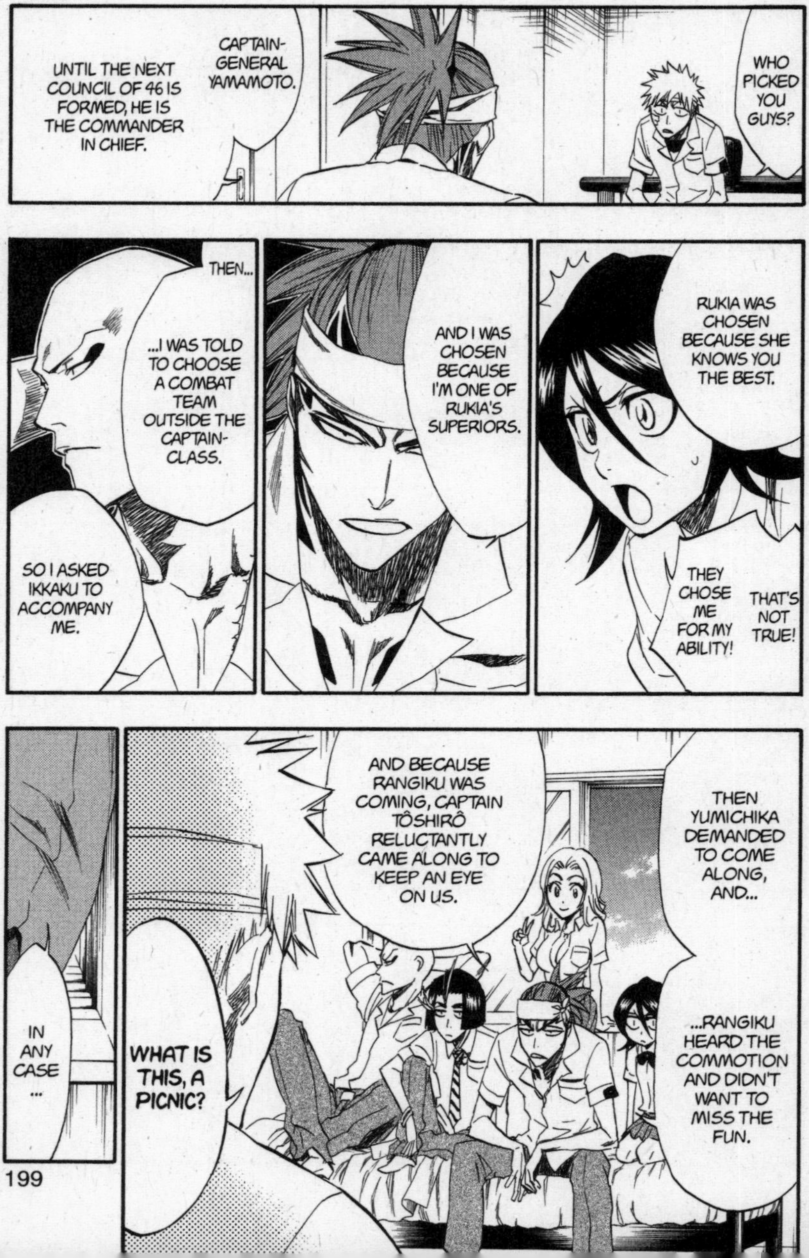
WHO PICKED YOU GUYS?
CAPTAIN-GENERAL YAMAMOTO.
UNTIL THE NEXT COUNCIL OF 46 IS FORMED, HE IS THE COMMANDER IN CHIEF.
RUKIA WAS CHOSEN BECAUSE SHE KNOWS YOU THE BEST.
THAT'S NOT TRUE!
THEY CHOSE ME FOR MY ABILITY!
AND I WAS CHOSEN BECAUSE I'M ONE OF RUKIA'S SUPERIORS.
THEN...
...I WAS TOLD TO CHOOSE A COMBAT TEAM OUTSIDE THE CAPTAIN-CLASS.
SO I ASKED IKKAKU TO ACCOMPANY ME.
THEN YUMICHIKA DEMANDED TO COME ALONG, AND...
...RANGIKU HEARD THE COMMOTION AND DIDN'T WANT TO MISS THE FUN.
AND BECAUSE RANGIKU WAS COMING, CAPTAIN TÔSHIRÔ RELUCTANTLY CAME ALONG TO KEEP AN EYE ON US.
WHAT IS THIS, A PICNIC?
IN ANY CASE ...

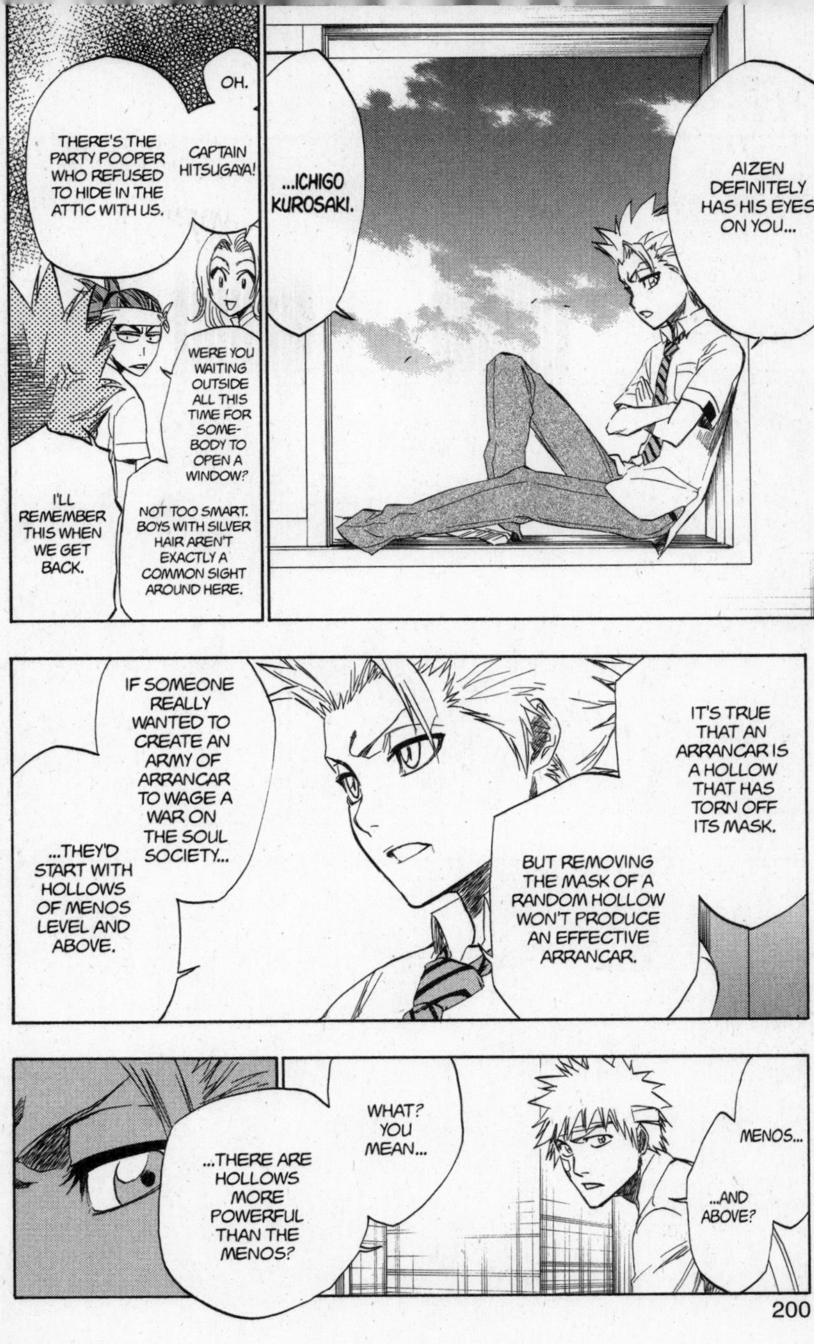
AIZEN DEFINITELY HAS HIS EYES ON YOU...
...ICHIGO KUROSAKI.
OH.
CAPTAIN HITSUGAYA!
THERE'S THE PARTY POOPER WHO REFUSED TO HIDE IN THE ATTIC WITH US.
WERE YOU WAITING OUTSIDE ALL THIS TIME FOR SOME-BODY TO OPEN A WINDOW?
NOT TOO SMART. BOYS WITH SILVER HAIR AREN'T EXACTLY A COMMON SIGHT AROUND HERE.
I'LL REMEMBER THIS WHEN WE GET BACK.
IT'S TRUE THAT AN ARRANCAR IS A HOLLOW THAT HAS TORN OFF ITS MASK.
BUT REMOVING THE MASK OF A RANDOM HOLLOW WON'T PRODUCE AN EFFECTIVE ARRANCAR.
IF SOMEONE REALLY WANTED TO CREATE AN ARMY OF ARRANCAR TO WAGE A WAR ON THE SOUL SOCIETY...
...THEY'D START WITH HOLLOWS OF MENOS LEVEL AND ABOVE.
MENOS...
...AND ABOVE?
WHAT? YOU MEAN...
...THERE ARE HOLLOWS MORE POWERFUL THAN THE MENOS?

READ THIS WAY

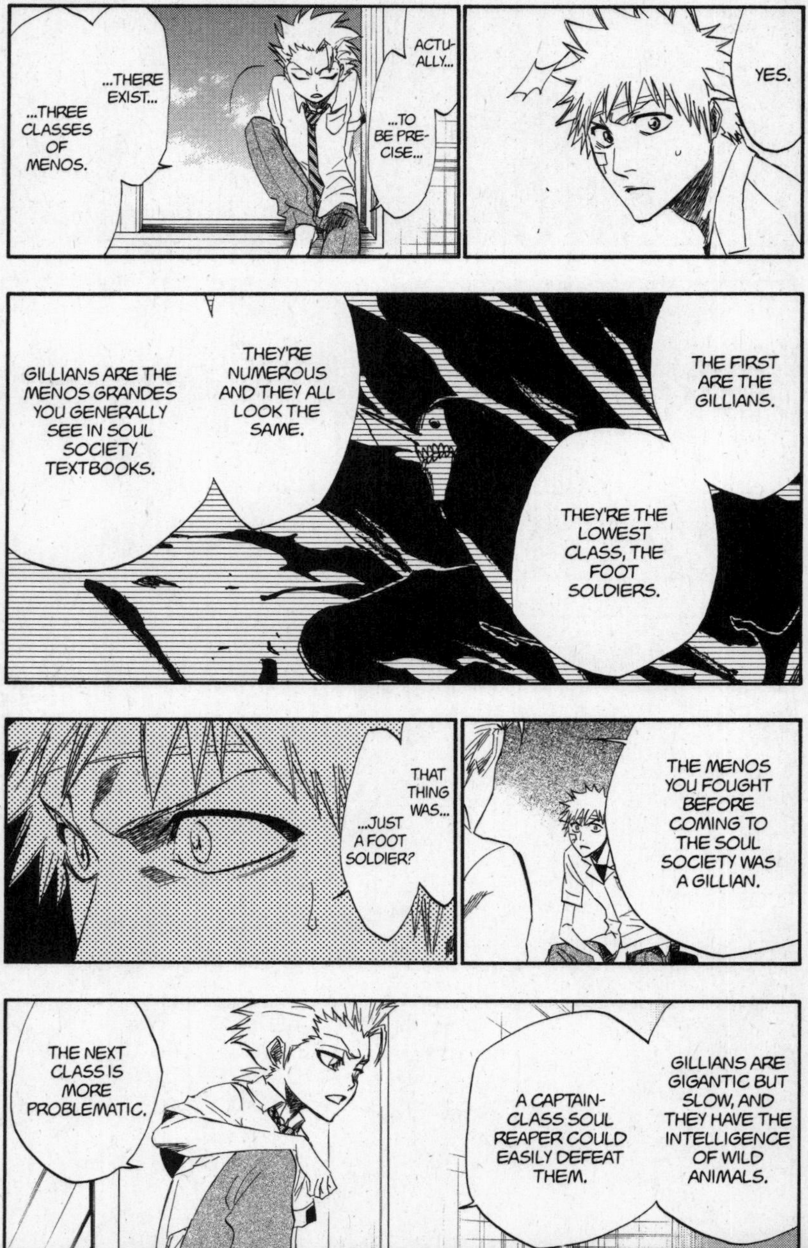
YES.
ACTUALLY...
...TO BE PRECISE...
...THERE EXIST...
...THREE CLASSES OF MENOS.
THE FIRST ARE THE GILLIANS.
THEY'RE THE LOWEST CLASS, THE FOOT SOLDIERS.
THEY'RE NUMEROUS AND THEY ALL LOOK THE SAME.
GILLIANS ARE THE MENOS GRANDES YOU GENERALLY SEE IN SOUL SOCIETY TEXTBOOKS.
THE MENOS YOU FOUGHT BEFORE COMING TO THE SOUL SOCIETY WAS A GILLIAN.
THAT THING WAS...
...JUST A FOOT SOLDIER?
GILLIANS ARE GIGANTIC BUT SLOW, AND THEY HAVE THE INTELLIGENCE OF WILD ANIMALS.
A CAPTAIN-CLASS SOUL REAPER COULD EASILY DEFEAT THEM.
THE NEXT CLASS IS MORE PROBLEMATIC.

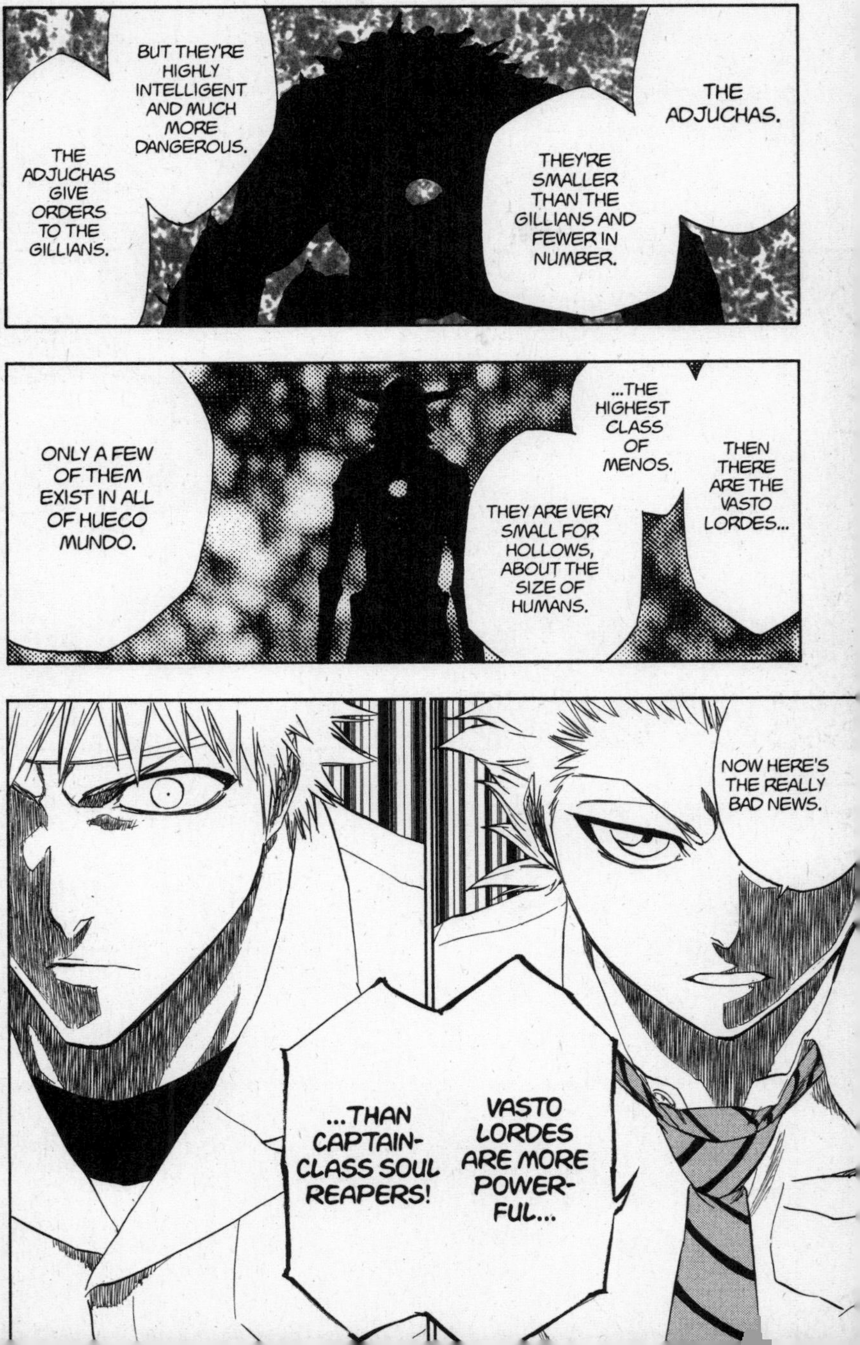
THE ADJUCHAS.
THEY'RE SMALLER THAN THE GILLIANS AND FEWER IN NUMBER.
BUT THEY'RE HIGHLY INTELLIGENT AND MUCH MORE DANGEROUS.
THE ADJUCHAS GIVE ORDERS TO THE GILLIANS.
THEN THERE ARE THE VASTO LORDES...
...THE HIGHEST CLASS OF MENOS.
THEY ARE VERY SMALL FOR HOLLOWS, ABOUT THE SIZE OF HUMANS.
ONLY A FEW OF THEM EXIST IN ALL OF HUECO MUNDO.
NOW HERE'S THE REALLY BAD NEWS.
VASTO LORDES ARE MORE POWER-FUL...
...THAN CAPTAIN-CLASS SOUL REAPERS!

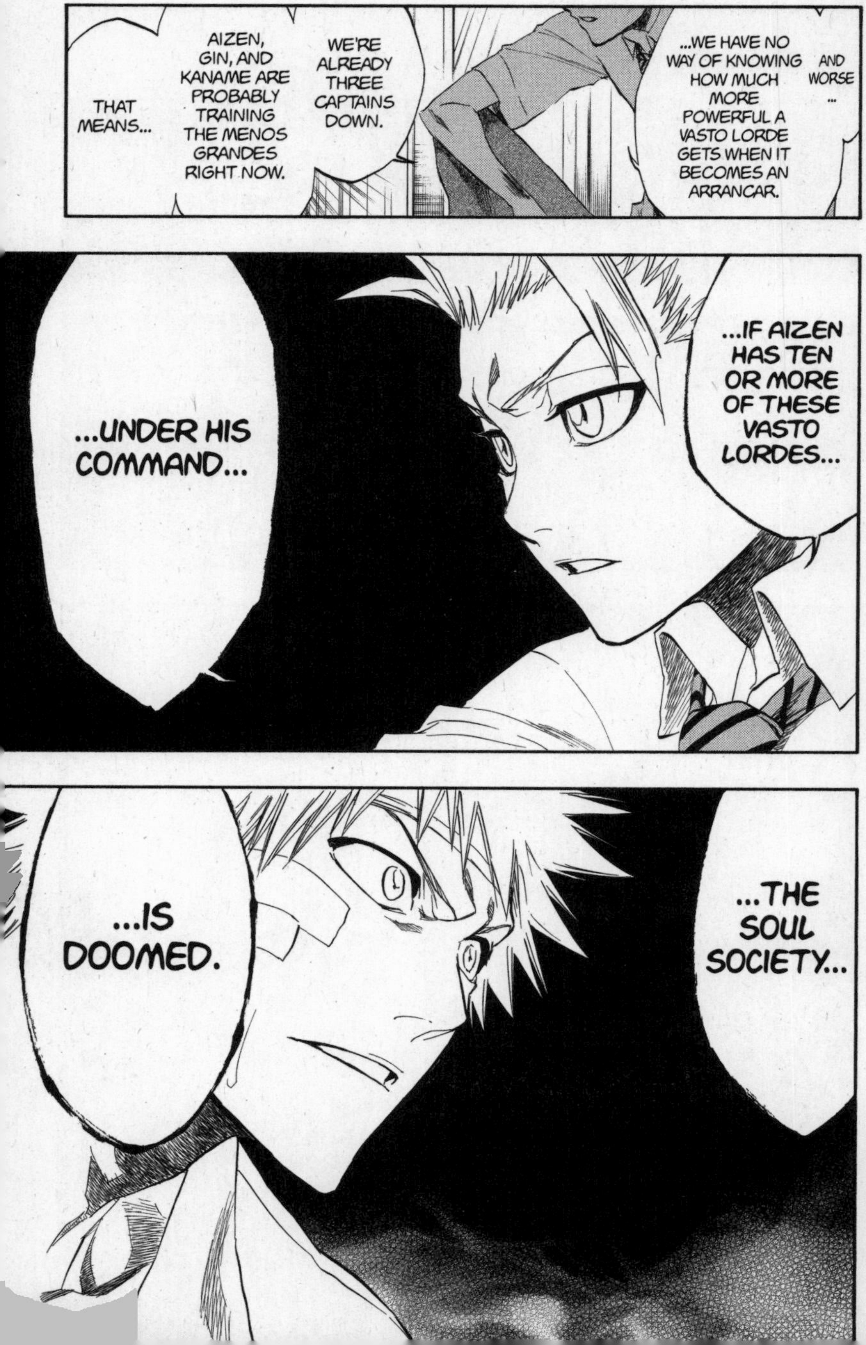
AND WORSE...
...WE HAVE NO WAY OF KNOWING HOW MUCH MORE POWERFUL A VASTO LORDE GETS WHEN IT BECOMES AN ARRANCAR.
WE'RE ALREADY THREE CAPTAINS DOWN.
AIZEN, GIN, AND KANAME ARE PROBABLY TRAINING THE MENOS GRANDES RIGHT NOW.
THAT MEANS...
...IF AIZEN HAS TEN OR MORE OF THESE VASTO LORDES...
...UNDER HIS COMMAND...
...THE SOUL SOCIETY...
...IS DOOMED.

KLAK.

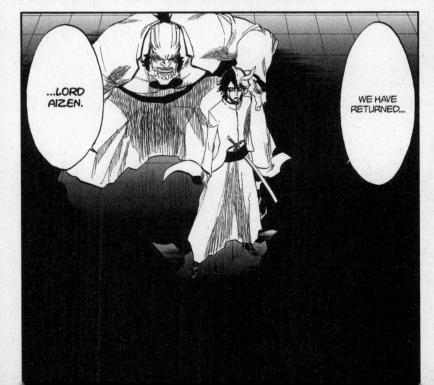

...LORD AIZEN.

WE HAVE RETURNED...

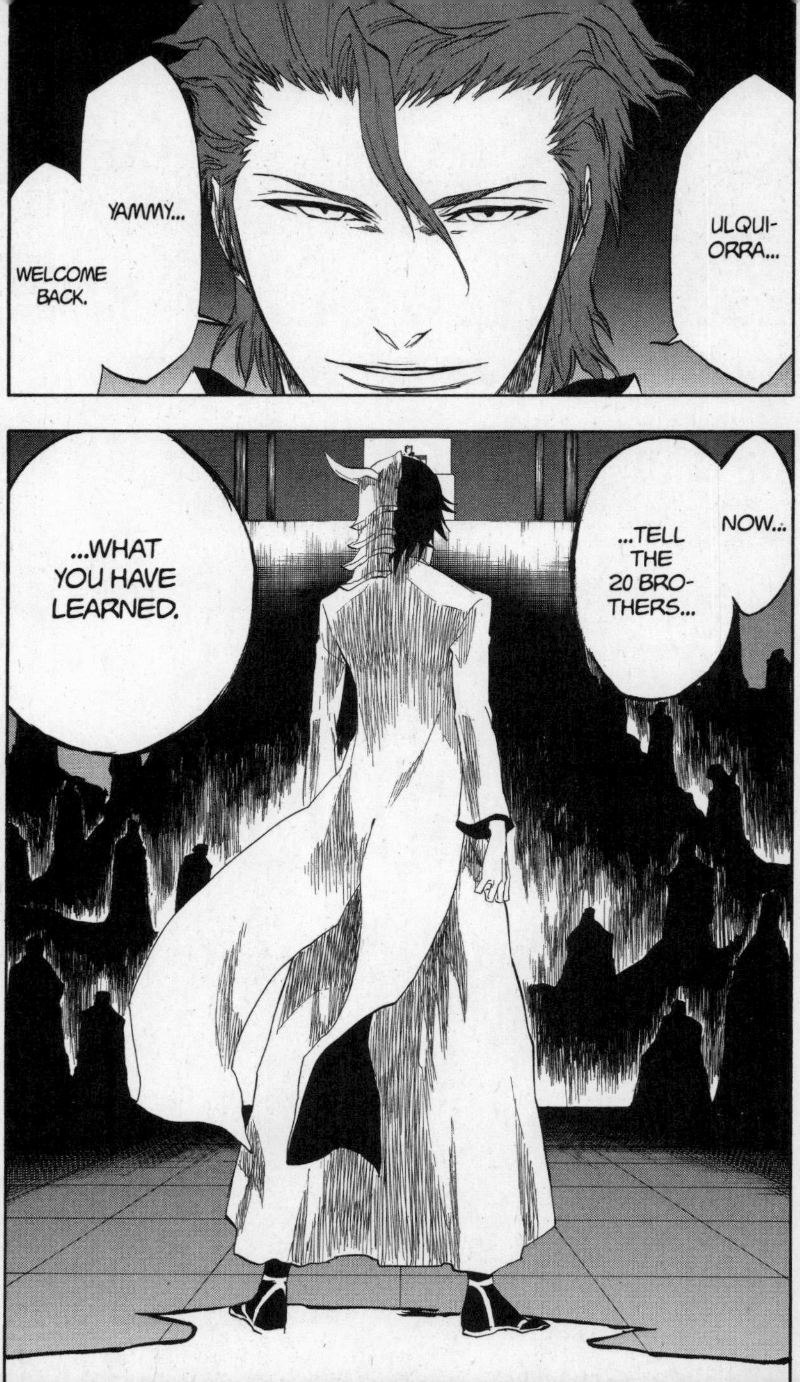
ULQUI-ORRA...
YAMMY...
WELCOME BACK.
NOW...
...TELL THE 20 BROTHERS...
...WHAT YOU HAVE LEARNED.

CONTI
NUED
IN
BLEACH
23

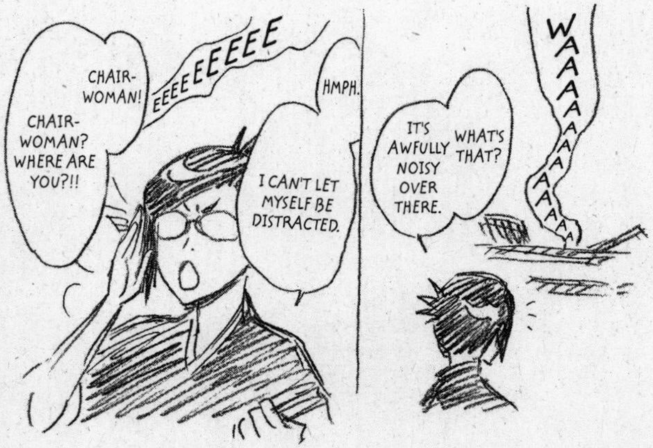
WAAAAAAAAAAAA
WHAT'S THAT?
IT'S AWFULLY NOISY OVER THERE.
HMPH.
EEEEEEEEE
I CAN'T LET MYSELF BE DISTRACTED.
CHAIR-WOMAN!
CHAIR-WOMAN? WHERE ARE YOU?!!

Next Volume Preview

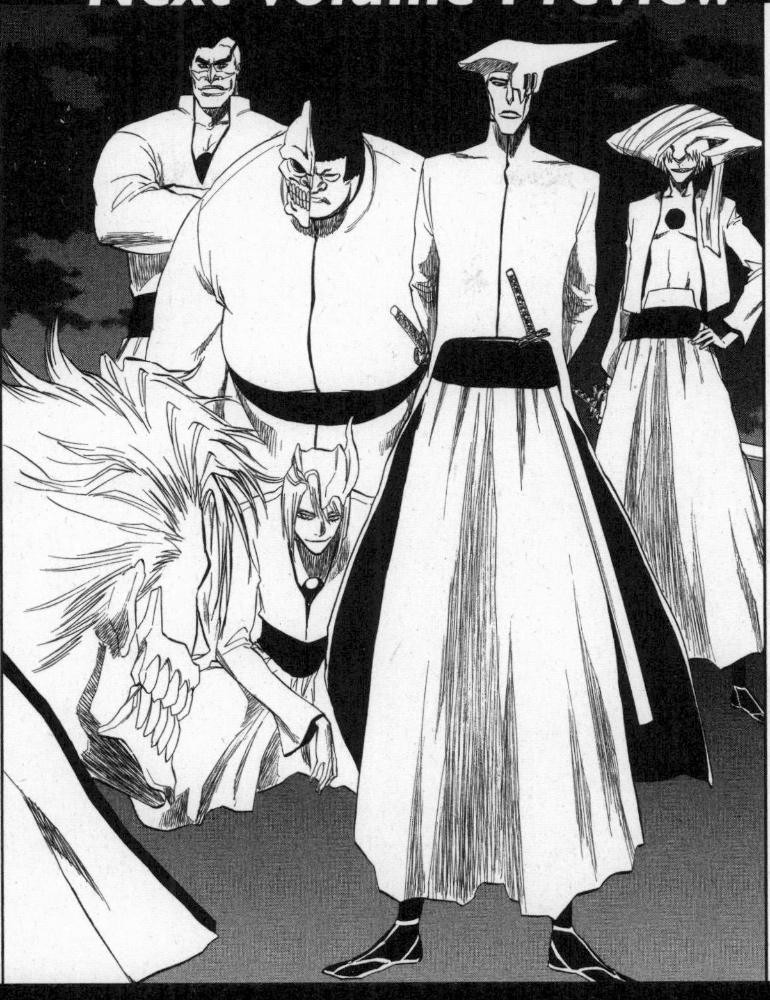

Grimmjow Jaegerjaques is leading a team of Arrancars to destroy Karakura Town! Even with the arrival of Soul Reaper reinforcements, can Ichigo and his friends withstand this dreadful new breed of Hollows?

Available Now!

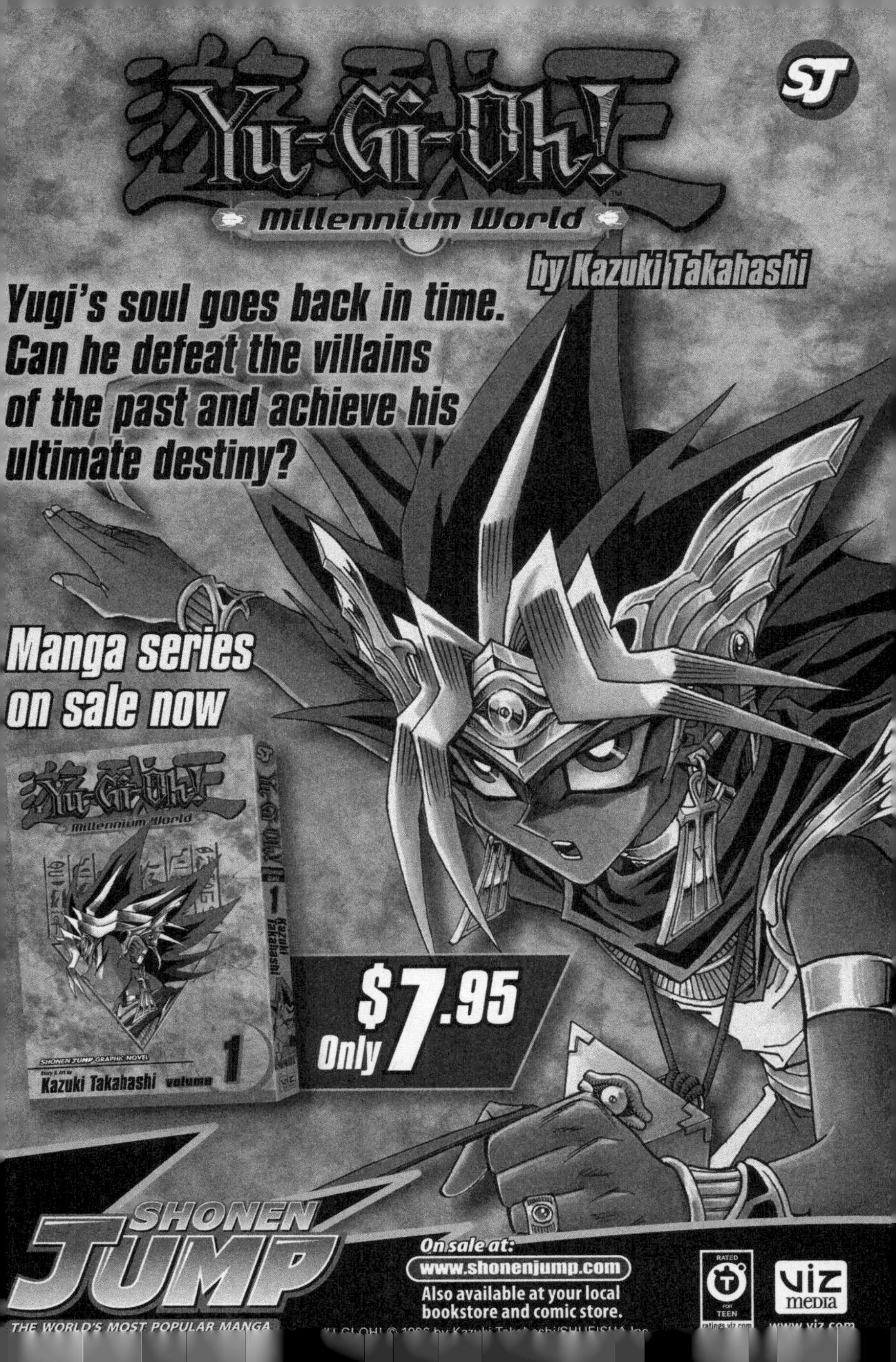
SJ
Yu-Gi-Oh!
Millennium World
by Kazuki Takahashi
Yugi's soul goes back in time. Can he defeat the villains of the past and achieve his ultimate destiny?
Manga series on sale now
Yu-Gi-Oh! Millennium World
SHONEN JUMP GRAPHIC NOVEL
Kazuki Takahashi volume 1
$7.95 Only
SHONEN JUMP
THE WORLD'S MOST POPULAR MANGA
On sale at:
www.shonenjump.com
Also available at your local bookstore and comic store.
RATED T FOR TEEN
viz media
www.viz.com

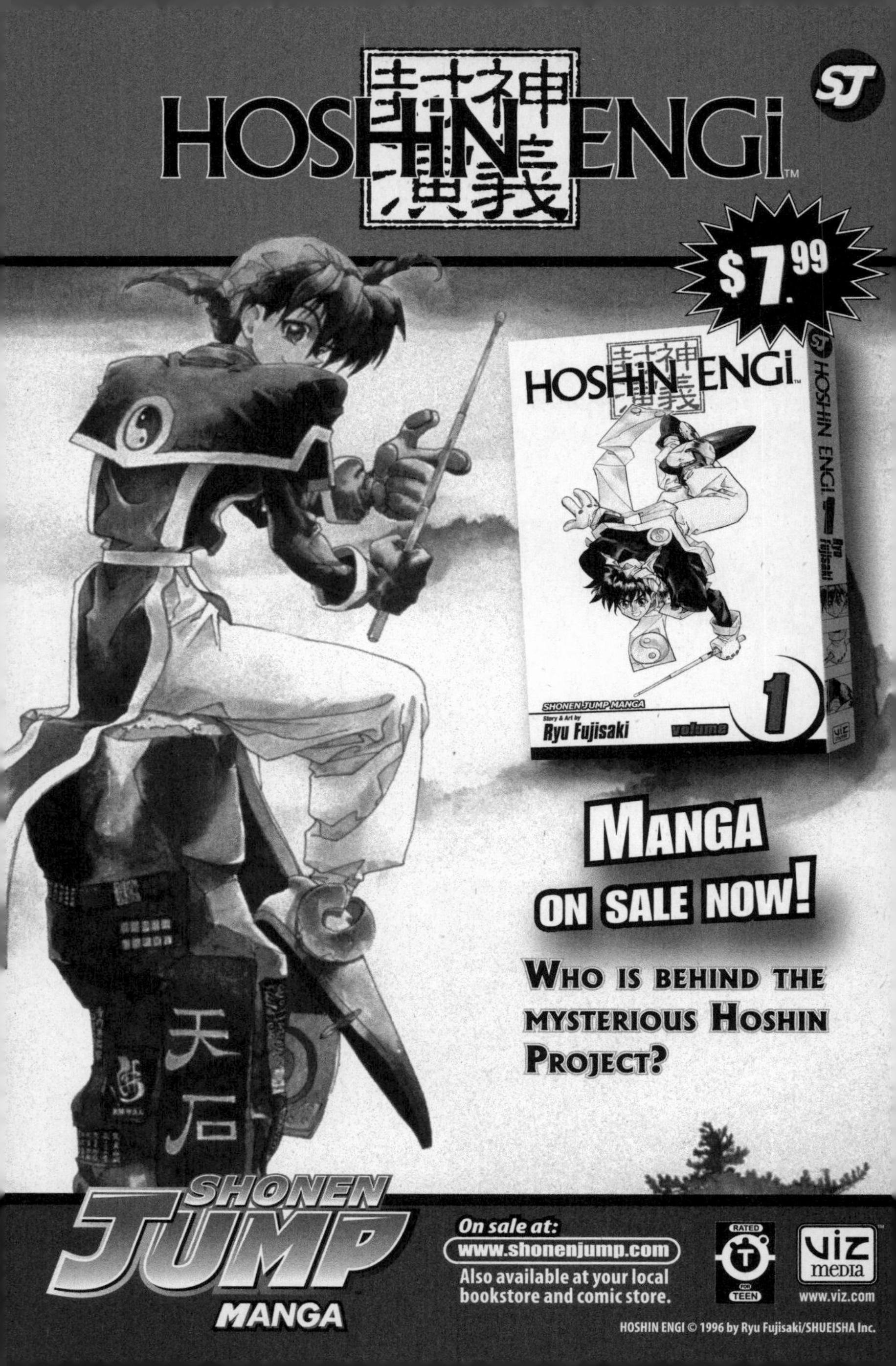
HOSHIN ENGI™
SJ
$7.99
HOSHIN ENGI
SHONEN JUMP MANGA
Story & Art by
Ryu Fujisaki
volume 1
MANGA
ON SALE NOW!
WHO IS BEHIND THE MYSTERIOUS HOSHIN PROJECT?
SHONEN JUMP MANGA
On sale at:
www.shonenjump.com
Also available at your local bookstore and comic store.
RATED T FOR TEEN
viz media
www.viz.com
HOSHIN ENGI © 1996 by Ryu Fujisaki/SHUEISHA Inc.

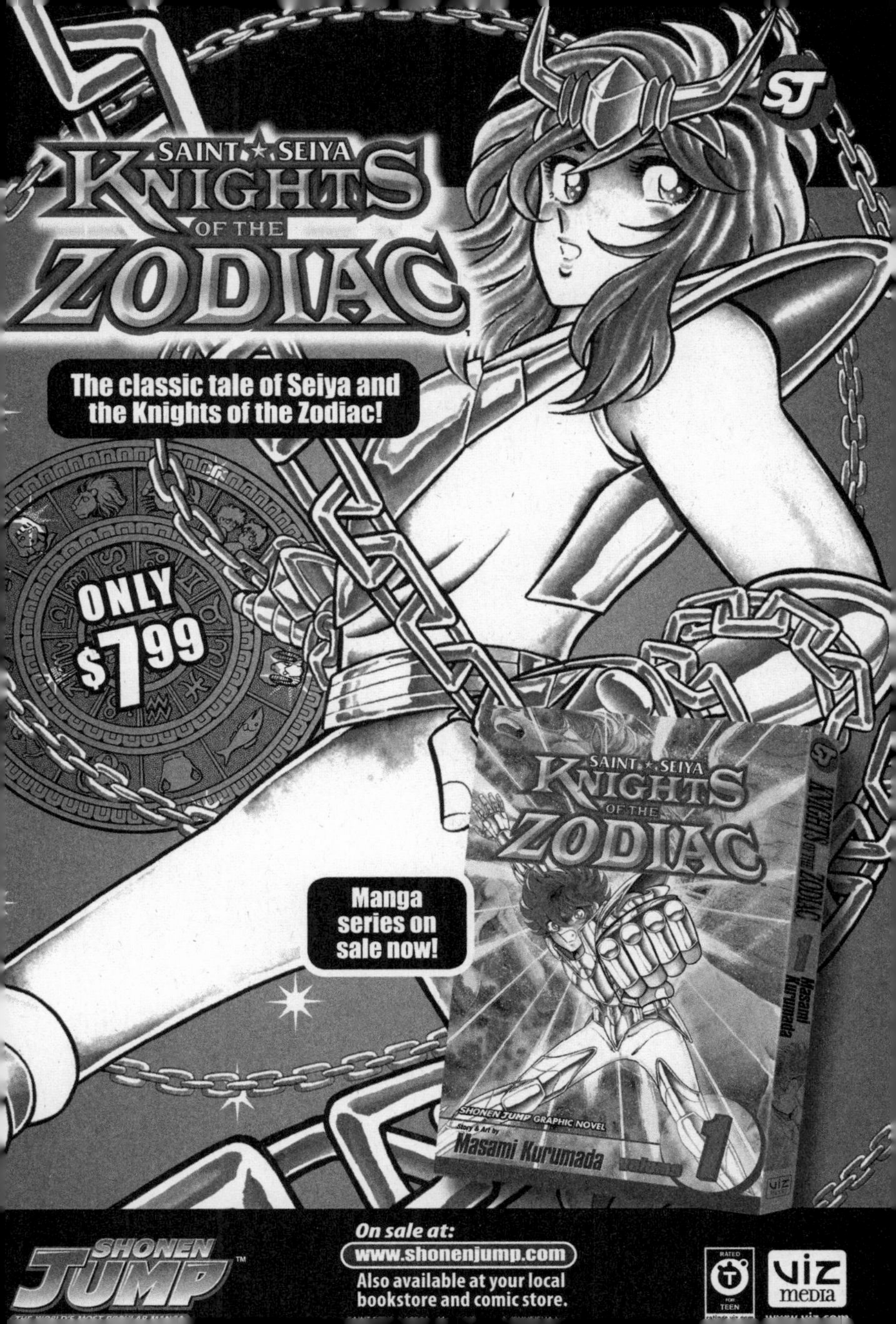
SJ
SAINT ★ SEIYA KNIGHTS OF THE ZODIAC
The classic tale of Seiya and the Knights of the Zodiac!
ONLY $7.99
Manga series on sale now!
SAINT ★ SEIYA KNIGHTS OF THE ZODIAC
SHONEN JUMP GRAPHIC NOVEL
Story & Art by
Masami Kurumada
1
SHONEN JUMP
On sale at:
www.shonenjump.com
Also available at your local bookstore and comic store.
RATED T FOR TEEN
VIZ media

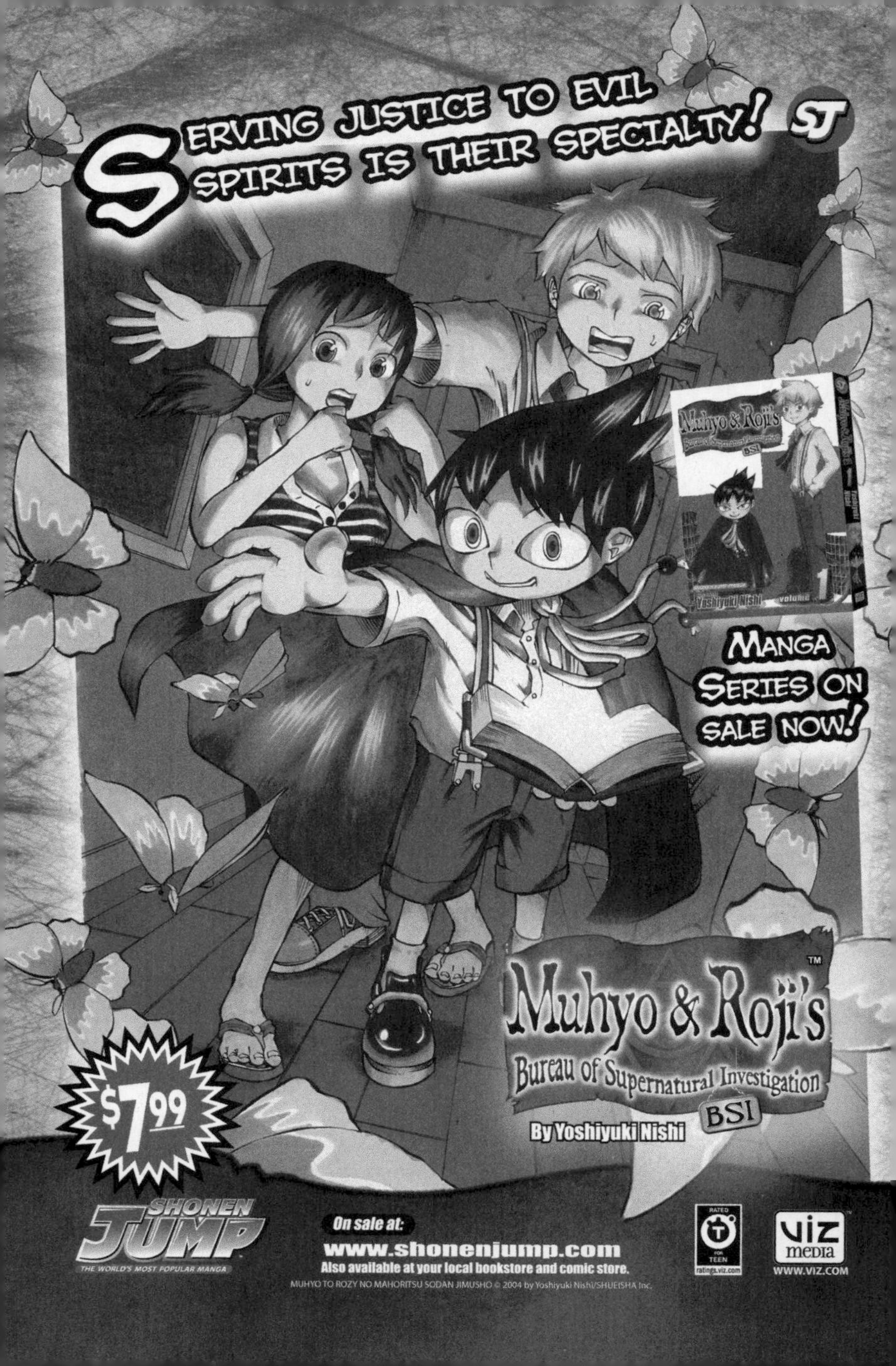
SERVING JUSTICE TO EVIL SPIRITS IS THEIR SPECIALTY!
SJ
MANGA SERIES ON SALE NOW!
Muhyo & Roji's
Bureau of Supernatural Investigation
BSI
By Yoshiyuki Nishi
$7.99
SHONEN JUMP
THE WORLD'S MOST POPULAR MANGA
On sale at:
www.shonenjump.com
Also available at your local bookstore and comic store.
MUHYO TO ROZY NO MAHORITSU SODAN JIMUSHO © 2004 by Yoshiyuki Nishi/SHUEISHA Inc.
RATED T FOR TEEN
ratings.viz.com
VIZ media
WWW.VIZ.COM

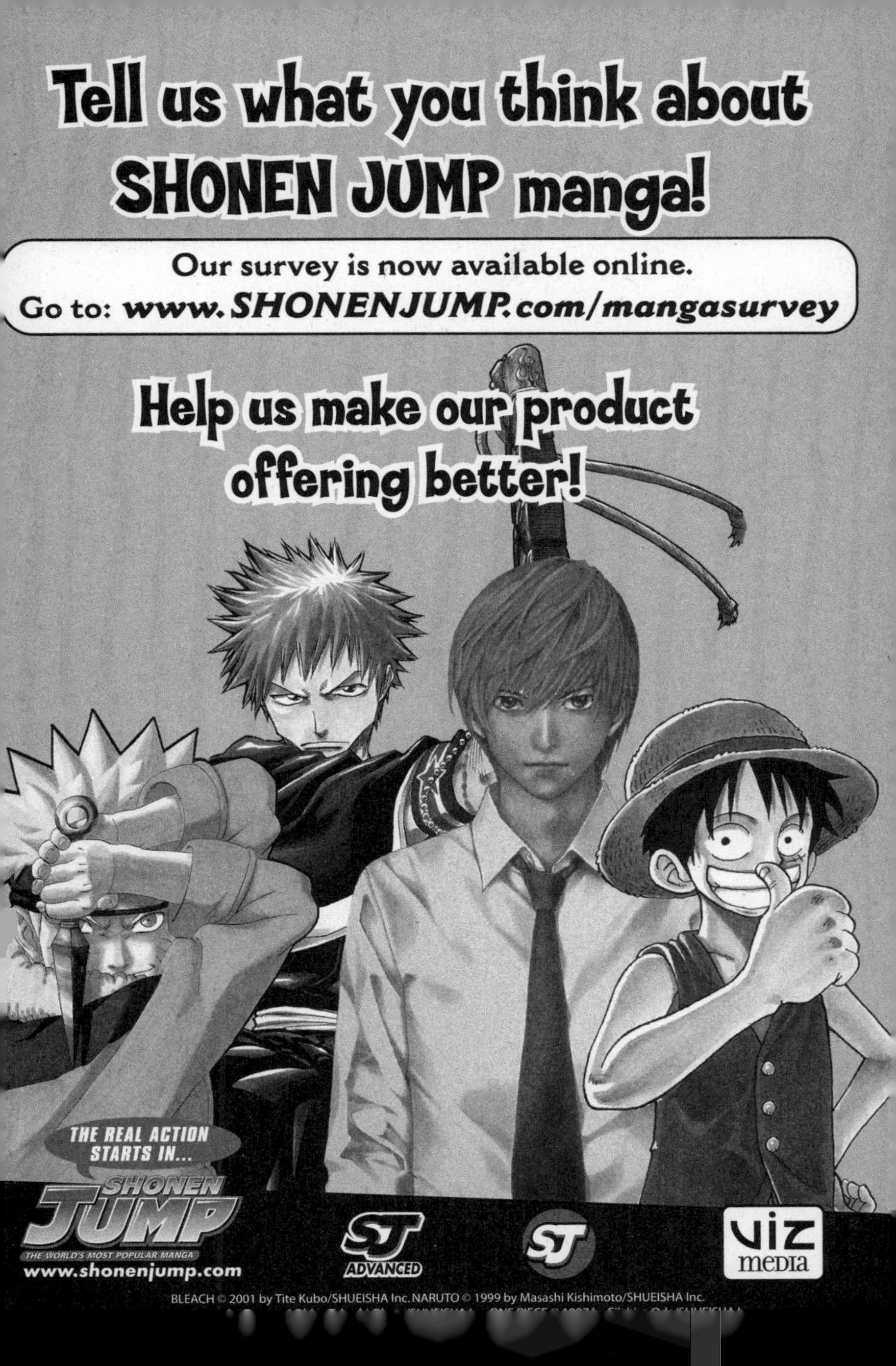
Tell us what you think about SHONEN JUMP manga!
Our survey is now available online.
Go to: www.SHONENJUMP.com/mangasurvey
Help us make our product offering better!
THE REAL ACTION STARTS IN...
SHONEN JUMP
THE WORLD'S MOST POPULAR MANGA
www.shonenjump.com
SJ ADVANCED
SJ
viz media
BLEACH © 2001 by Tite Kubo/SHUEISHA Inc. NARUTO © 1999 by Masashi Kishimoto/SHUEISHA Inc.

Save **50% OFF** the cover price!

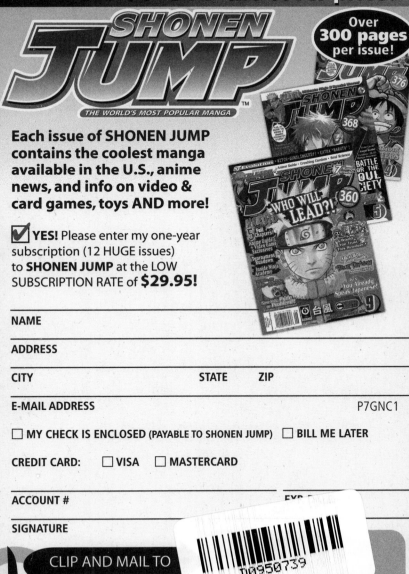

SHONEN JUMP
THE WORLD'S MOST POPULAR MANGA

Over 300 pages per issue!

Each issue of SHONEN JUMP contains the coolest manga available in the U.S., anime news, and info on video & card games, toys AND more!

☑ **YES!** Please enter my one-year subscription (12 HUGE issues) to **SHONEN JUMP** at the LOW SUBSCRIPTION RATE of **$29.95!**

NAME

ADDRESS

CITY   STATE   ZIP

E-MAIL ADDRESS   P7GNC1

☐ MY CHECK IS ENCLOSED (PAYABLE TO SHONEN JUMP)   ☐ BILL ME LATER

CREDIT CARD: ☐ VISA   ☐ MASTERCARD

ACCOUNT #   EXP.

SIGNATURE

CLIP AND MAIL TO

D0950739